MADE POSSIBLE BY . . .

MADE POSSIBLE BY ...

The Death of Public Broadcasting in the United States

JAMES LEDBETTER

VERSO

London • New York

First published by Verso 1997

© James Ledbetter 1997

All rights reserved

The right of James Ledbetter to be identified as the author of this work has been
asserted by him in accordance with the Copyright, Designs and Patents Act 1988

Verso

UK: 6 Meard Street, London W1V 3HR

USA: 180 Varick Street, New York, NY 10014-4606

Verso is the imprint of New Left Books

ISBN 1-85984-904-0

British Library Cataloguing in Publication Data

A Catalogue record for this book is available from the British Library.

Library of Congress Cataloging-in-Publication Data

A catalog record for this book is available from the Library of Congress.

CONTENTS

ACKNOWLEDGMENTS

What would a book about public broadcasting be without a list of grants? The Joan Shorenstein Center on Press, Politics, and Public Policy—part of Harvard University's Kennedy School of Government—aided this book through a Goldsmith Research Award. The Gerald R. Ford Foundation also provided a grant to cover expenses for the research I did at the Gerald Ford Library in Ann Arbor. I am grateful for both.

My agent, Kay McCauley of the Pimlico Agency, gave this book more attention and care than could possibly have been worth her time. Robert McChesney and Mike McCauley, both at the University of Wisconsin at Madison, gave encouragement and insightful comments on early versions of some chapters. My *Village Voice* colleague Thomas Goetz was especially generous with his time and work: chapters 6 and 10 reflect some of his original reporting, which he was kind enough to let me use.

This book is, in many ways, an expanded version of an article I published in the *Village Voice* in 1992. Joe Levy provided the original seed for that story, and Doug Simmons nursed it into print. In addition to that duo, the *Voice* has provided me with a series of talented editors who have encouraged and gently tweaked my weekly writing on media: Jonathan Larsen, Michael Caruso, Karen Durbin, Jeff Salamon, Matthew Yeomans, Don Forst, and Angela Ards. Connie Oehring gave the manuscript the strict proofread that it needed. Colin Robinson of Verso saw the import of the book immediately, and I greatly appreciate the support he has given me.

Shortly after the veteran radical journalist Andrew Kopkind died, I learned he had been keeping a hefty file on the political and cultural wars in public broadcasting, to which I was graciously given access. Too many archivists have assisted this book to be acknowledged by name, but I would like to thank the staffs of the Gerald Ford Library, the State Historical Society of Wisconsin, the Nixon Presidential Materials Project, the Carter Library, and the National Public Broadcasting Archive. Jeannie Bunton at the Corporation for Public Broadcasting provided stacks of material and was never too busy to answer questions. James Day could have treated me as a rival but instead treated me as a colleague, allowing me access to his impressive and well-organized records. Others who were generous with their time and memories include Gloria Anderson, Richard Brookhiser, Les Brown, Fred Friendly, Lawrence Grossman, Avram Westin, and the Coalition to Stop PBS Censorship.

Most of all, this book was made possible by Linda Marrow, whose keen editorial eye and boundless encouragement guided the project from before a word was written to after it was done. I could not have done it without her.

INTRODUCTION

ARE WE BEING SERVED?

It is a grand paradox of the Media Age that in the mid-1990s, as the United States stood on the edge of a telecommunications revolution, one of the highest Congressional priorities was cutting off federal funds for public broadcasting. In most Western nations, a publicly funded communications system would be the locus of research and experimentation; in the United States, it became the enemy. In 1994, a month before he officially took the title of Speaker of the House, Newt Gingrich chose to attack the Public Broadcasting Service (PBS) and National Public Radio (NPR) as symbols of a bloated, inefficient bureaucracy, the communications arm of lemon socialism. Speaking on a right-wing cable channel, Gingrich claimed that public broadcasting "has been eating taxpayers' money."[1] Gingrich and his Republican footsoldiers not only declared the public broadcasting system broken but implied that even when working properly, public broadcasting served no good purpose; Americans, according to Gingrich, were "paying taxes involuntarily to subsidize something which told them how to think."

These comments launched an excavation mission: for several weeks in early 1995, any criticism ever made of public television and radio was dug up and hailed as justification to kill them—or, in the budget lingo favored by Gingrich, to "zero them out." Public broadcasting, it was argued, is biased toward liberals: "You know, the liberals have NPR all day," Gingrich told an interviewer. "We have Rush [Limbaugh]. We pay for Rush through advertising. They pay for NPR through our taxes." Public broadcasting is biased against America; Dorothy Rabinowitz, television critic for *The Wall Street Journal,* proclaimed that public television portrays "the United States [as] the enemy of the world. . . . This is so intrinsic a part of the view of America that is portrayed out there. . . . It is what we see night after night."[2] (Rabinowitz made this remark, interestingly, on a public television program.)

Public broadcasting, declared the Family Research Council, undermines the family because instead of condemning gays and lesbians, it gives an "academic gloss to portrayals of homosexuality . . . that serves to validate it in a pseudosci-

1

entific sense." Public broadcasting, according to Senator Larry Pressler of South Dakota—who, as chair of the Commerce Committee, controlled PBS funding legislation—wastes taxpayer money while allowing a few tricksters to get rich off Barney dolls and lunchboxes. "There are many people who have made millions and millions of dollars on public TV who front as a nonprofit," sneered Pressler on *Nightline*, though he didn't name any.[3] Pressler also used open class warfare—usually the tactic of liberal Democrats—charging that public broadcasting was the exclusive purview of the ultra-rich. From the floor of the Senate, Pressler made an astounding claim about viewers of WETA, the PBS station serving Washington, D.C., railing that they "have an average household net worth of $627,000 plus an average investment portfolio of $249,000. One out of eight contributors," continued the senator, "is a millionaire, one out of seven has a wine cellar, and one out of three spent time in Europe in the past three years. This is the target audience for PBS' prime time programming."[4] *New York Post* TV critic John Podhoretz declared that public television "corrupts artists, who start tailoring their projects to the social and political fashions of the moment so they can get the most money for them."[5] Podhoretz—evidently unfazed by the tens of millions of dollars' worth of federal subsidies, tax breaks, and interest savings his employer, Rupert Murdoch, has received over the years—declared that the very existence of government-subsidized television "represents a potentially tyrannical assault on free speech."

A concerned observer could only conclude that the nation was in great peril so long as public broadcasting continued. In Gingrich's heady world of Alvin Toffler–inspired utopianism, the best way to get culture and information to the masses was to abandon public broadcasting and instead give the poor tax credits to buy laptop computers or "information vouchers," allowing them access to the information superhighway best developed by private enterprise. The very use of the term "public" was deemed suspect. "I don't understand why they call it public broadcasting," Gingrich told a group of Republican staffers. "As far as I'm concerned, there's nothing public about it; it's an elitist enterprise. Rush Limbaugh is public broadcasting."[6]

In the span of little more than a quarter-century, the nation's elected leaders had made a complete turnaround. Following the recommendations of the Carnegie Commission on Educational Television, Congress passed the Public Broadcasting Act of 1967 (see chapter 1) with the understanding that public television was needed precisely because commercial television was the "vast wasteland" once denounced by Newton Minow. In 1995, a different Newt proclaimed that the country's most successful commercial radio host was, by definition, a public broadcaster. Public broadcasting honchos protested the Limbaugh remark, claiming that Gingrich had deliberately misrepresented the role of public television and radio. Those voices, however, did not speak as loudly as that of KBDI, Denver's PBS affiliate, which a few months late, began carrying Limbaugh's television program five nights a week.[7]

Such capitulation to criticism helps explain the most perplexing aspects of the GOP's winter of withering attack on public broadcasting. Most of the liberal left—whom Gingrich and allies claimed were running the PBS/NPR show—not only declined to rally a defense for public broadcasting but actually seconded key points of the Republican critique. Liberals and leftists were not invited to submit their remarks at Congressional hearings, and they tended to see corporate underwriters (as opposed to, say, family-hostile homosexuals) as the villain. Nonetheless, several prominent left-wing writers concurred that the whole enterprise deserved to be abandoned. "I'm with Gingrich on this one," said Alexander Cockburn, writing in *The Nation*.[8] Tom Carson, television writer for *The Village Voice*, enthusiastically greeted the fate that awaited PBS's cutesy logo: "Off with those three little heads!" Lewis Lapham, the editor of *Harper's Magazine* who once hosted the PBS program *Bookmark*, had already written the service off in 1993, charging that "PBS insults its audience by speaking to them as children who must be ceaselessly amused and entertained" and that "as one of many instruments in what has become an entirely new media orchestra, PBS can no longer be heard to be making a distinctive sound."[9]

This is not to say that in the dark hour of early 1995, no one defended public television and radio. Executives of the Corporation for Public Broadcasting (CPB) produced polls which conveniently found that 86 percent of Americans agreed that PBS provided "an important alternative to network television," and that Americans rank public television and radio as the third, and fourth, best values for tax dollars spent, right behind military defense and law enforcement.[10] (Reporters who asked for the full text of poll questions were politely rebuffed and reminded that the CPB, as a private, nonprofit corporation, is not subject to the disclosure requirements of the Freedom of Information Act.) Public television viewers, accustomed to responding to on-screen requests for money, dutifully phoned Congress to complain as their local stations instructed. Several Members of Congress claimed to be faithful fans of one program or another, and Congresswoman Nita Lowey even donned *Sesame Street* hand puppets to prove that public broadcasting was essential to the nation. For all the burlesque theater, and contrary to Gingrich's pledge that he "would not recognize any proposal that will appropriate money for the CPB," the subsidy for public broadcasting survived. The Corporation for Public Broadcasting did, however, see its federal appropriation shrink from a planned $312 million in fiscal year 1996 to $250 million in fiscal year 1998[11]—the biggest cut in its 30-year history.

MONEY DOESN'T CHANGE EVERYTHING

Unfortunately, reducing the argument to a question of greater or lesser sums of money put off any examination of the wide-ranging, sometimes venomous criticisms raised by right and left. Such deferrals have been the norm since long before Gingrich and his lieutenants took over Congress: the most common defense public broadcasters and their advocates offer to nearly any critical charge is to plead poverty. Despite 30 years of debate and promises, a variety of experiments, and more commission reports than any mortal could digest, American public broadcasting lacks any systematic, long-term way to pay for itself. So much of public broadcasting's internal bickering and inefficiency grows out of the endless struggle for money; if funding were adequate and reliable, goes the argument, many—perhaps most—of the system's problems would evaporate.

To bolster this case, advocates point to the far greater levels of government support in other industrialized nations. According to the Corporation for Public Broadcasting, in 1993 the national government of Japan spent $32.02 per citizen on public television, Canada spent $31.05 per citizen, and Great Britain $38.99—and the U.S. federal government just $1.09.[12] Even taking into account *all* U.S. public broadcasting expenses (including those funded by membership dollars, corporate sponsors, state governments, et al.) the U.S. per capita figure comes out to $6.83—still dramatically below the other nations. The point is commonplace among non-American observers as well: after viewing several weeks of American television in 1973, the British literary and television critic Raymond Williams pronounced the American commitment to public broadcasting a "palliative," and declared: "The fatal flaw, in the whole structure, is the lack of money for production."[13] More recently, media historian Robert McChesney observed that "in international discussions of public broadcasting, the term 'PBS-style system' is invoked to refer to a public system that is marginal and ineffective. It is the fate that the BBC, CBC and others wish to avoid. The funding system is the primary culprit."[14]

Public broadcasting's money troubles should not be underestimated. As is shown throughout this book, the struggle for funds has hampered every incarnation of public television and radio on every level: producers, distributors, local stations. The hand-to-mouth-to-screen existence is made more tense by the strings that come attached to every funding source. The sobering reality, however, is that if the Corporation for Public Broadcasting and its nationwide affiliates were funded at three or four times current levels—a political pipe dream—the system would still be hobbled by a host of contradictions that public broadcasting's chieftains have refused for decades to resolve. That continuing refusal—more than any sense of wasted taxpayer money—accounts for the meager enthusiasm for public broadcasting among the American political intelligentsia (at least those not bought off by PBS and NPR).

Most of the difficulties revolve around the concept of "public" broadcasting, an adept, stirring term that was never precisely defined, and therefore attracted factions of supporters with conflicting interpretations. For example: in order to serve the population—which has invested trust, airwave resources, and taxpayer dollars—a public broadcasting system must try to reach as many viewers as it can. It may not be necessary to maximize audiences for every single program, but clearly public broadcasting must be viewed by a reasonable portion of the nation's audience. At the same time, public broadcasting must resist or surmount commercial and dumbing-down pressures that inevitably accompany efforts to attract large audiences. Willard Rowland, a onetime PBS researcher who is also one of the system's most incisive critics, has succinctly labeled this dilemma the "contradiction of popularity."[15]

Isolated offshoots of this contradiction spring up regularly on PBS: Why, for example, would PBS refuse to fund a sequel to *Tales of the City* when it garnered some of the highest ratings in the system's history? Why are some genres appropriate to copy from commercial television—such as nature programming, college football, and, at least briefly, a game show—while others—daytime soap operas—are not? More generally, the contradiction of popularity is hardwired into public broadcasting's method of viewer and listener support. On the surface, "membership" in public broadcasting reflects an admirable commitment and a politically palatable voluntary tax: those who want to support the medium may do so. Measured by membership support, public television looks quite healthy: the number of dues-paying members of PBS doubled between 1980 and 1993, and now stands at more than 5 million nationwide. During the same period, contributors to public radio more than tripled. Collectively, those members contribute nearly $400 million annually,[16] an essential source of funds in tough economic times.

There is ample evidence, however, that in seeking to serve these millions of viewers and listeners—and secure their donations—PBS and NPR programming is moving further and further from the goals laid out by its founders. This is not merely a complaint from outside critics; it is an idea widely held by people within public broadcasting. Having collected testimony from dozens of station and program managers before authorizing the 1988 public broadcasting bill, Congress voiced its concern about PBS's programming drift: "Some public television stations increasingly are turning away from traditional public, educational or informational programming and broadcasting [instead] such programs as *Disney*, *The Avengers*, *Lassie*, *Ozzie and Harriet*, and *Star Trek*." During the late '80s and early '90s, the fastest-growing program on public television was reruns of *The Lawrence Welk Show*, now shown on the majority of public television stations. Recognizing that such vital fare might be better suited to commercial cable channels, the Congressional committee said it was "concerned that public broadcasting, in an effort to secure alternative financing and to increase ratings and viewership, is sacrificing its identity and uniqueness."

A telling example of pledge-drive antics came from Michigan, where in 1994 public television stations aired a series of hunting specials called *Spirit of the Wild*, hosted by rock guitarist Ted Nugent. A "Night of Nugent" featured Nugent pitching for pledges, playing guitar licks, and offering bowhunting instructions.[17] Tempted by premiums such as a black sweatshirt with Nugent's "World Bowhunters" logo, donors flocked to the stations with more than $300,000 in pledges; the series was then extended to Nebraska, Ohio, and other states. Without taking anything away from Nugent, his bowhunting escapades seem to fall outside the purview of a medium the Carnegie Commission instructed to capture "the great debates in public life, the crucial hearings, the great performances, moments of national tragedy and triumph."[18]

The question of public participation is equally vexing. Is the "public" in public broadcasting mere rhetoric, meant simply to mark a distinction from commercial television—or should the public have an active role in public broadcasting, one that transcends paying taxes and writing checks? Over the years, this question has been answered in various ways. Early experiments—such as the Public Broadcasting Laboratory (PBL) described in chapter 2—interpreted "public" liberally. For some episodes, for example, *PBL* brought members of the public into studios for moderated debates over timely issues. The early '70s PBS hit *The Great American Dream Machine* modified that formula somewhat by placing Studs Terkel in a bar with a half-dozen elbow-bending Chicagoans, mixing it up over Vietnam and Spiro Agnew. In one sequence, *PBL* gave cameras and sound equipment to local community activists, whose work was then edited and shown on the air. And the 1973 PBS series *An American Family* pushed a form of public participation to an extreme, documenting months of the day-to-day travails of the Loud family of Santa Barbara.

The dramatic or political success of such projects is debatable, but it is indisputable that today—despite a public deemed to be far more media-sophisticated—PBS allows the general public no comparable was to influence content. The system's early effort at institutionalizing public participation—the Advisory Council of National Organizations (ACNO), an umbrella group of unions, advocacy, and civic groups—has been disbanded (see chapter 7). Stifled by internal inefficiency and never taken terribly seriously by the CPB board, ACNO at its height rarely moved beyond a window-dressing role and was largely relegated to "lobbying efforts on behalf of funding bills."[19] The decline of any mechanism for public involvement means that today "the public" appears rarely on public television; even the simple vox populi has little place on the national PBS schedule. The majority of public television news and public affairs programs—such as *Nightly Business Report* and *Washington Week in Review*—provide no meaningful opportunity for public input, lacking a gesture as minimal as reading viewer responses on the air. (PBS's science and cultural affairs programming do no better.) By that small but significant measure, the commercial broadcast *60 Minutes* exhibits a greater dedication to interacting with the public than does *The NewsHour with Jim Lehrer*.[20] Overall, the current model of PBS's relationship with its audience conforms to what media writer Robert Cirino calls the "paternalistic, elite model of management operation."[21]

A third question is whether and how public broadcasting should be accountable to the public. Even more than at commercial stations, what begin as broadcasting decisions for PBS and NPR immediately become political debates. How should a broadcast network deal with material that some people—even if only a tiny minority—find offensive? The Public Broadcasting Act of 1967 addressed this question by insisting that public television programming would observe a "strict adherence to objectivity and balance." As is always the case in American media, though, those noble words serve only to kick the political debate to a different plane. How, precisely, is balance to be achieved? Through brief, recorded editorial responses (as many commercial community stations do in "viewpoint" segments)? Through equal time in programming? Through a panel discussion? Some on the right, notably Reed Irvine, interpret PBS's legislated balance requirements to dictate that every airing of a controversial issue must reflect each prevailing public view in the same program. If implemented, such a standard would clearly stymie any broadcast; as one public television host said in 1972, "You don't balance out the astronauts with the Flat Earth Society."[22] Others have proposed that PBS create an ombudsman position—comparable to that used by many American newspapers—to sort through complaints of bias; PBS has never given the idea serious consideration.

Finally, public television has failed to develop a satisfying formula for balancing local and national programming needs.[23] As discussed in chapter 6, the structure of public radio—more stations, more varied programming, and national shows with portions designed for local breakaways—has allowed for a generally better balance of local and national needs. The Carnegie commissioners were insistent that public television should "deepen a sense of community in local life," and should be a forum "where people of the community express their hopes, their protests, their enthusiasms and their will."[24] This role grew naturally out of public television's educational roots. In the 1970s, however, the Nixon White House used "localism" as a strong-arm tactic to weaken central programmers it deemed politically incorrect, thereby strengthening the power of local station managers (see chapter 3). Public affairs shows, for example, were deemed to be less threatening if they tackled strictly community issues. One major result of this tinkering was the ascendance, in the 1970s, of the Community Service Grant (CSG), a means whereby the Corporation for Public Broadcasting funneled money directly to local stations who had relative autonomy regarding its use.

For a nation accustomed to all-powerful networks, such a decentralized system seems illogical and radically inefficient. In a 1993 scathing assessment, Lewis Lapham declared that if the public television "system were to be represented on a geopolitical map, it would resemble the Holy Roman Empire during the last years of its decaying hegemony—351 petty states and dukedoms, each with its own flag, court chamberlain, and trumpet fanfare."[25] Lapham's satirical flourish echoed complaints from dozens of critics and former officers of public television who have for some time insisted that the hodgepodge system hampers national programmers from producing more than a handful of programs that could capture the national imagination.

In the '80s and '90s, however, a number of powerful forces within the public television bureaucracy have leaned on stations to move toward a more uniform schedule. PBS has recently implemented a so-called common carriage feed, whereby stations agree to show the national schedule on the same night—which benefits big underwriters who crave effective nationwide promotion. Consequently, locally based programming stands little chance of being picked up for systemwide distribution, an increasingly important revenue source for many stations. The unacceptable but inevitable result is that some of the nation's largest cities have virtually no public television devoted to what goes on in their own backyards. As recently as 1990, New York's WNET-TV, the largest PBS station, aired two half-hour programs every weeknight—*Live Wire* and *The Eleventh Hour*—devoted to New York City public affairs. But as of 1996, it had reduced this commitment to a miserly half-hour a week—significantly less than most of the city's commercial stations. Far from supplementing commercial television's skimpy community news offerings, WNET actually trails far behind; rather than provide an outlet for New York's four million blacks and Latinos, WNET lazily rebroadcasts *Visiones* and *Positively Black*—programs picked up from New York City's NBC affiliate.[26] Critic Marvin Kitman, who has tracked decades of public television on WNET, told an interviewer in 1993: "This station has totally abdicated its role as a local television outlet."[27] Large stations such as Boston's WGBH-TV and Los Angeles's KCET-TV have been hit by similar local programming vacuums.

A POLITICAL FAVOR BANK

As the Gingrich attack revealed, another part of the discomfort with public broadcasting stems from American skepticism about government's role in producing media. American public broadcasting has never been powerful enough for anyone to plausibly argue that it represents an instrument of state mind control (if it were, it would be a pathetically weak one). Nonetheless, the influence of government on PBS and NPR programming is a recurring and constraining problem for producers, audiences, and government officials themselves. From its inception, every close observer of American public broadcasting—critical or supportive—has agreed that the system should have stable, and preferably permanent, economic support. They have generally also averred that the funding system should, as much as possible, be insulated from the vicissitudes of politics; otherwise, the prospect of political influence, even censorship, is raised.

But these principles have become like the hollow prayers of a lapsed churchman: they are honored only in the breach. Despite endless commissions and task forces recommending alternative financing, public broadcasting has, since 1967, been dependent on one-, two-, or three-year Congressional appropriations, thus guaranteeing that it is under constant political scrutiny, fair or not. Moreover, though many from the left and right decry the politics of PBS and NPR programming, few analysts focus on what is perhaps the primary political vise that squeezes public broadcasting: the presidential appointees to the Corporation for Public Broadcasting.

It would be naive to expect any White House to decide on its nominations without some regard for political control. It is also true that there have been excellent CPB appointments, as well as appointments who have run against type.[28] But those brighter moments cannot change the fact that the CPB has been used over the years as a dumping ground for the worst sort of political hacks. Many crucial public broadcasting appointments seem to have been made on the basis of *nothing but* politics. Before the CPB came into existence, Lyndon Johnson

secured a position on the Carnegie Commission for one of his most loyal political aides. A Nixon nominee, Thomas Curtis, all but planned his U.S. Senate campaign during his brief stay on the CPB board. Gerald Ford nominated a pollster
actively engaged in Republican fund-raising who was, even while assuming his
CPB seat, feeding Ford confidential public opinion results about the '76 presidential campaign. Jimmy Carter nominated candidates his own advisors recognized were inferior, but whose appointments were badly needed political
markers with important senators. Ronald Reagan nominated Sonia Landau, who
did not let her work for the CPB interfere with her role as national chair of
Women for Reagan-Bush.

As in some other areas of government-supported cultural programs, a common way of using public broadcasting as a political favor bank has been to appoint
the wife of an important ally. Jimmy Carter appointed Gillian Sorensen—married to Democratic warhorse Theodore Sorensen—to the CPB, while Ronald
Reagan appointed Honey Alexander, wife of former Tennessee governor and erst-
while presidential candidate Lamar Alexander. It is a telling symbol of how these
very important leadership positions are filled that the copy of Honey Alexander's
résumé on file in White House archives makes no mention of any experience or
even interest in broadcasting, public or commercial. The résumé is, however,
printed on press release stationery from the Tennessee governor's office, lest
some White House functionary lose track of its political significance.[29]

Having the management of PBS and NPR so closely tied to the muck of
electoral politics makes the system extraordinarily vulnerable to political
attack. Since the McCarthy era and the late-50s *Quiz Show* Senate hearings, few
subjects have been as easy and bountiful a political target as television and
radio. A television and radio system funded with Congressionally controlled
money provides the ultimate hot-button issue, a grandstander's dream. This
was as true in 1968—when a group of congressmen denounced a documentary
shown on public stations as "nothing more nor less than communist propaganda"—as it was in the opening months of 1995, when the new Republican-con-
trolled Congress held more hearings on the budget for PBS and NPR shows
than it did on the budgets for Medicaid and Medicare, programs with a federal
budget more than 100 times larger than that of the Corporation for Public
Broadcasting. Indeed, the combination of budget crises and the Republican
Party's seemingly boundless antifederal rhetoric has made public broadcasting
an even more inviting target in the '90s. In 1996, Bob Dole became the first
major-party presidential nominee to find federal public broadcasting funds
such an urgent American trauma that he pledged to remove them in the speech
launching his campaign.

This book focuses on the interplay between American politics and the public broadcasting world, in the belief that pressure from Congress, the White House, and a few special interest groups plays a much greater role in shaping and determining the public broadcasting schedule than is generally recognized. Thus, this book is also an indirect document of how political debate in American media is circumscribed. It is true that political pressure on public television and radio rarely takes the form of yanking material off the air, but that is because the habits of self-censorship are so ingrained that naked censorship is rarely necessary. Americans regularly and with good reason honor our commitment to the ideals of free speech and unfettered debate. But throughout the 30-year history of public broadcasting, its taxpayer subsidy has repeatedly been used as a club with which to clobber that very commitment. Like a dog that has learned to flinch at the mere pantomime of the master's lashing, public broadcasters know to avoid topics and methods of criticism that might bring down the hand of rebuke. In those few instances when explicit threats are made to remove funding based on unpopular content—such as Dole's 1994 Senate attack on NPR for commissioning commentaries from a journalist convicted of killing a police officer—public broadcasters generally back down.

Such timidity has not always been the norm: it is learned behavior, based on survival instincts. The first great wave of retrenchment followed Richard Nixon's public and private war on perceived enemies in PBS; the system responded by dramatically slashing the amount of airtime devoted to critical assessments of sitting presidents and Congresses. Hence, today the best way to get a full-length documentary about a presidential-related topic on PBS is to produce one on a president who has not been in office for 20 years. (In the late '80s, Bill Moyers did air a set of critical investigations about Ronald Reagan's presidency—but they were after Reagan's reelection, and required the near-Constitutional crisis of the Iran-contra scandal to bring them about.)[30] The commentators on *Washington Week in Review* (known as "brunch with the living dead") may be free to tweak a president or legislator for a particular policy, but those with more sweeping, damning criticisms—from any political perspective—will simply not be invited to appear. In this way, public broadcasting's government subsidy functions like hush money to protect powerful incumbents.

Another method of political influence—the specialty of Democrats such as Jimmy Carter and Bill Clinton—is to voice support for public broadcasting as a way of controlling and defining it for political gain. Like many of public broadcasters' corporate backers, Democratic presidents have hoped that the virtues and prestige of public broadcasting would rub off on them. Lately this imagery game has taken on a peculiarly moralistic hue. Public broadcasting's planners offer a

litany of rote prohibitions—violated whenever necessary—against programming
that panders or titillates or sensationalizes. They draw on a recurring theme in
American life: that the media are an entity that people, especially children, need
to be protected from. Although such discussions have been most consistently and
effectively manipulated by "family values" organizations and virtue-mongering
Republicans, Democrats, too, enjoy the easy route of converting moral outrage
over television content into political advantage. As he entered a reelection campaign in 1996, Clinton surrounded himself with network executives to announce
"a breakthrough voluntary agreement to help parents protect their children from
violence and adult content on television," which included, for the first time, a network ratings system and the "V-chip" to screen out unwanted programs.[31]

   This mildly censorious impulse to "protect" is, oddly, also part of the contemporary rationale for keeping a system of public broadcasting. Public broadcasting's mandarins have proudly boasted that their "civilized" programs contain
none of the gratuitous violence found on commercial networks and cable channels, an argument happily adopted by the Clinton administration to beef up its
own values agenda. In a 1995 speech defending public broadcasting, for example, Vice President Al Gore said: "[O]ne of the problems that families face is how
they can find for their children television programming that is high value, that
doesn't hurt them, that doesn't fill them with images of violence and premature
sexuality, and values that are very different from those they would like to transmit to their children.[32]

   As I discuss in later chapters, PBS's conservative critics have ridiculed these
claims, arguing that such PBS broadcasts as *Tongues Untied* and *Stop the Church* display "values that are very different" indeed from the ones they would like to see on
television. But regardless of how honest such appeals are on either side, it is a
thin, pusillanimous argument to say that the chief virtue of public broadcasting is
that you don't have to be afraid of it. The lack of sex and violence in public broadcasting programming may or may not be a virtue, but more importantly it is a by-
product. Public television doesn't scare its viewers because public television
avoids just about anything that might offend anyone. It cares far less about programming of "high value" than it does about programming that cannot be assailed.

   For example, PBS eschews original drama and comedy series, ostensibly because there is a surfeit of them on commercial television and because a situation
comedy lacks the educational value of *Nova*. The edification justification, however,
evaporates as soon as it is made. What could possibly make a decade-old episode
of the BBC's *Are You Being Served?*—a public televsion staple, particularly on
smaller stations—more educational than the average network sitcom? PBS
seems positively frightened of original comedy programming. As discussed in

chapter 3, the first of what have been only a handful of occasions in which PBS has actually pulled a scheduled program off the air was in 1972; the show was a Woody Allen feature with parodies of Richard Nixon and Henry Kissinger thought to be too scathing. This helps explain why comic pianist Mark Russell—whose show was once the only original comedy offered on PBS—kept his satire so light. It seems unlikely that the American public television audience would suffer an intellectual breakdown if it were subjected to an original satire of network television like HBO's *Larry Sanders Show*, or an animation delight like Fox's *The Simpsons*; after all, British audiences, the original legitimator of most PBS "high-end" programming, lap these shows up, and manage to survive.

At the same time that public broadcasters boast of their civility over and against what PBS president Ervin Duggan calls the "culture of gangster rap and violent kick-boxing superheroes" permeating commercial media, public broadcasters have spent the last decade rushing as hard as they can to merge their services with those offered by commercial networks. Covering the 1992 presidential campaign, for example, PBS for the first time joined the team from NBC. Effectively admitting that it could or would not create its own series with black characters, PBS spent $1.8 million to produce a sequel to NBC's castoff *I'll Fly Away*. And many NPR listeners have wondered why they should donate money to hear reporters Cokie Roberts and Nina Totenberg when they appear with increasing frequency—and for free—on ABC News.

Another significant area where public broadcasting looks increasingly like its commercial counterpart is business journalism. At one time, public television's national business programming—which includes the half-hour *Nightly Business Report*, and the weekly *Wall Street Week in Review* and *Adam Smith's Money World*—might have been justified by arguing that televised business news was a rare commodity. But the 1980s and '90s witnessed an unprecedented explosion in this category, catapulting televised business and financial news into what is surely its Golden Age. In 1980, there was no regular, nationally available television programming devoted to business, but as the decade progressed, CNN created the half-hour daily business program *Moneyline*, and by the '90s had added its own all-financial channel, CNNfn, with nonstop market updates, interviews with business magnates, and feature reporting. The latter was launched as a direct competitor to General Electric's Consumer News and Business Channel (CNBC), which provides essentially the same programming. By 1996, it was simply preposterous to argue that there could be a significant number of viewers who wanted stock and bond updates and reports on mergers and acquisitions who had not figured out a way to get them before the *Nightly Business Report* came on public television. Suggestions from labor and consumer advocates that PBS could produce distinctive business programming by focusing on the lives of working people rather than the portfolios of investors have been ignored.

The redundancy of PBS's business journalism is reproduced in almost every other realm. Instead of seeking to outpace and outsmart the cable boom of the '70s and '80s, PBS largely ignored the obvious, leaving itself vulnerable in the '90s to a hostile takeover by the largest cable providers. Nature programming in the style of *National Geographic*, often represented on several nights of PBS's weekly schedule, has been made largely redundant by the Discovery Channel. C-SPAN and CNN cover major events of the day before PBS can even think of turning on a camera. Movie channels, Arts & Entertainment, Television Food Network, the Learning Channel—all have taken a chunk out of the once-distinct programming offered by PBS. With cable due soon to reach nearly every American household and to expand, as most predict, to either hundreds of channels or an individually tailored CD-ROM or "push technology" format, it is nearly impossible to see what makes PBS's programming unique—or even necessary.

The televisionaries who conceived of the need and role for public broadcasting did not foresee how a multichannel cable environment would alter television content and the advertising base that supports it. In the Big Three network environment of the 1960s, it seemed eminently logical to assume that corporate television sponsors would never be satisfied by the thin audiences attracted to offbeat or highbrow fare. But by scattering audiences to dozens of channels, by offering low-cost saturation advertising—and, most importantly, by charging subscription rates that few in the '60s would have dreamed possible—cable television's "narrowcasting" has succeeded in forging a commercial foundation that supports a great deal of PBS-type programming, even where the number of viewers is too small for A. C. Nielsen to care to measure.

The revolutionary development of cable television and its adoption of many crucial public television priorities is neither accidental nor wholly positive. Cable providers have been deliberately cultivated by federal policymakers who saw their growth as a politically beneficial wedge of deregulation, and their triumph is part of a vast transformation toward an electronic culture where Americans pay for resources that were once distributed for free; these are topics for other books.[33] What matters to this study is that cable's growth has robbed public television of one of its most powerful rationales. It is one thing to argue that PBS programming provides a unique service to poorer or remote populations unserved by cable; it is quite another to say that PBS should be satisfied with simply duplicating, in content and in form, benign programming that most American television viewers already watch elsewhere.

GAME SHOWS, BUT NO HUMAN RIGHTS

The melding of commercial and public broadcasting priorities is not schizophre-nia, or some random breakdown of public broadcasting's identity. It is a logical result of the increasing, now dominant use of public broadcasting as a marketing and promotional outlet. As public television relies more and more on corporate underwriting and an array of commercial gimmicks for its funding, its program-ming approach—even its on-screen talent—will look more and more like those of commercial networks. (Public radio, as I argue in chapter 6, while subject to precisely the same forces, behaves somewhat differently.) Today, corporate underwriting represents more than 16 percent of PBS's overall budget—up from 10 percent a decade ago—and 27 percent of its national programming costs. Though that may appear to be far from a controlling interest, there are vir-tually no programs on the PBS dial that are not in some way beholden to private, commercial firms.

Public broadcasters, quite naturally, perceive underwriting as an essential form of support. It is also, however, an inevitable censor. There are perspectives on certain topics—including gays and lesbians, American foreign policy, abortion, and the environment—that cannot be aired on national television without provoking a peculiarly American firestorm of criticism. The commercial networks, whose adver-tising lifeline almost automatically seeks in advance to avoid such controversy, learned back in the 1950s that the best way to prevent such flak was to sharply curtail the programming that makes it to the nation's living room. Networks enforce genres—soap operas, situation comedies, game shows, half-hour news-casts—because both advertiser and audience have signed an implied consent decree to not be offended by 99 and $^{44}/_{100}$ths of what is broadcast within those boundaries. Periodic debates about the immorality of "trash TV" talk shows prove the rule by highlighting its exception; they are by definition controversial because they are among the few programs to break the formulae of safe sterility.

Commercial television's self-imposed straitjacket is the primary reason why public television was founded. Few would have predicted that public television would, a quarter-century into its existence, have tailored a distinctive, but equal-ly bland, straitjacket of its own. Thirty years into the experiment of public televi-sion finds a typical evening that draws from depressingly few genres: largely duplicative news and business programming, aging imported British drama or mystery, nature and science programming often indistinguishable from that shown elsewhere, and arts programming that usually deviates little from the tastes of the local elite.

There are many observations to be made about such programs, but they share either the avoidance or the defanging of contemporary political controversy, the kind that would bring trouble for powerful patrons. Where, as Raymond Williams asked of American public television back in the '70s, are the documentaries? With the genre essentially extinct on commercial television, documentaries are clearly an area where public broadcasting could distinguish itself. And if the medium is to provide a sustained, intelligent, critical look at American society—as its founders certainly intended—it must examine the actions and faults of America's most powerful institutions: government, finance, insurance and real estate industries, oil companies, media, tobacco and agriculture, lobbyists, federal bureaucracies, pharmaceutical companies, auto makers, and the military. Yet public broadcasting treads cautiously around the nation's and the world's most pressing social problems. (The series *Frontline* is a valuable exception, although some PBS stations don't carry it, and not all topics are suited to its format.)

Originally intended, in E. B. White's oft-cited phrase, to "clarify the social dilemma and the political pickle," public broadcasting instead prefers to leave political pickles in the jar, to the great frustration of thoughtful advocates all along the political spectrum. For example, both feminist advocates on the left and family-values supporters on the right could presumably benefit from the debate over domestic violence that would surely ensue if public television were to air the Academy Award–winning documentary *Defending Our Lives*. PBS has repeatedly refused, citing rules against programs produced by "advocates."[34] The rationale is transparently ludicrous; as demonstrated in chapter 7, PBS programming has been underwritten by advocates for decades.

Similarly, American foreign policy debates in the 1980s and 90s have been dominated by human rights concerns: the left, for example, successfully used human rights as a lever to pry corporate and government investments out of South Africa's apartheid government, and tried more recently to force similar oil and arms embargoes on Nigeria because of gross human rights violations. The right has made the same arguments for its own purposes, sometimes successfully (as with the enhanced embargo of Cuba, Congress passed in 1996) and sometimes unsuccessfully (as with trade policy to China). Common sense and the search for common ground would suggest that public television is the ideal place for a regular series exploring human rights. Yet PBS executives refused financial support for *Rights & Wrongs*—a weekly program produced in New York that did precisely that—ostensibly because, as former PBS programming czar Jennifer Lawson said, human rights is an "insufficient organizing principle" for a television program.[35] This is a sad, disingenuous argument from a television operation content to run endless reruns of decades-old British situation comedies, and to spend more than a million dollars to produce *Think Twice*, the game show that enjoyed a mercifully brief PBS run in 1994–95.

Perhaps PBS should be rewarded for a degree of honesty about the culprit behind the homogenization and narrow political debate; it's implicit in the three little words that public broadcasting has introduced into our language: "Made Possible By . . ." Commercial announcements, euphemistically dubbed "enhanced underwriting credits," are now commonly seen at the beginning of, or between, most PBS broadcasts. The viewer of *The NewsHour with Jim Lehrer* sits through about a minute's worth of advertising from program underwriters—Fortune 500 giants such as Archer Daniels Midland, AT&T, and Pepsico—before the news begins. What was purposefully planned as a commercial-free environment ironically now sells itself as a preferred media buy because of desirable demographics and an "uncluttered" atmosphere. Ken Burns, creator of PBS's *The Civil War*, one of the most praised television events in recent years, said of the ad agency and corporate sponsor who produced his series: "Ayer and G.M. understood that public television is a tremendously good and effective buy."[36]

Out of hundreds of examples of corporate co-optation of PBS, one, for sheer brazenness, best symbolizes the problem. It is page 12 of the 1991 annual report of New York/New Jersey's WNET, the nation's largest public television station.[37] The page consists entirely of a photograph of a woman with two small children in a supermarket, pulling a box of cookies down from a shelf. The station used this photo to illustrate a series called *Childhood*—a curious choice, given that a still from the program itself would have been more revealing. The caption reads: "As part of the outreach effort to raise awareness of *Childhood*, series underwriter Nabisco Foods Group funded supermarket displays to encourage shoppers to tune into the program." It's worth asking who's promoting whom, as the small flyer touting the series is nearly drowned by a sea of familiar brand names: Oreos, Nilla Wafers, Fig Newtons. Following the infamous late-'80s leveraged buyout of RJR/Nabisco, the tobacco and food conglomerate came under the financial control of the investment bank Kohlberg Kravis & Roberts.[38] A glance at another page in the annual report shows that the chairman of the board of WNET is none other than investment banker Henry Kravis. Thus has the flagship station of a system conceived as an advertising-free beacon of enlightenment been transformed into a fancy place to hawk cookies.

In 1996, Kravis's connection to WNET was abused even further. The station began showing a program called *1 Zone*, a version of Channel One, the commercial in-school news program initially founded by Chris Whittle and later purchased by K-III, in which Kravis is a majority shareholder. Longtime children's television advocate Peggy Charren called the move a violation of public television's commercial guidelines, and said: "The idea that WNET thinks it can get away with this violation of the public trust is mind-boggling."[39]

It is such promotional service provided to corporate masters that makes public broadcasting's leadership seem complacent, oddly satisfied with its obsolescence. During the battles of 1995, PBS and NPR executives trotted out their best new clothes to argue that they were on the cutting edge: Web sites! Educational material for prekindergartners! Teleconferencing! These innovations may be praiseworthy, but they served to mask the larger corporate agenda, one on which public broadcasting executives and Gingrich Republicans actually agree—the assets that public broadcasting has accumulated over 30 years should be leased, borrowed, or outright taken over by private, for-profit businesses. Promoting the businesses of a local station's board of directors, leasing out the PBS logo to retailers, renting out studios to commercial programs—the '90s have seen a tidal wave of commercialism overtake public broadcasting. As I argue in chapter 10, this malling—hailed as entrepreneurism necessary for survival—is in fact the greatest threat to the original mission of public broadcasting. Unless that trend is reversed, public broadcasting, in any genuine sense, will not survive the century, making this book a lengthy obituary.

It would be, of course, an overstatement to say that public broadcasting has been a total failure. Over the last three decades, public television and radio have given birth to countless moments of excellence. Two generations of Americans have learned to read, count, and think with *Sesame Street*, which is still a model for educational television that is innovative, multicultural, and fun. PBS remains unique in its commitment to carry regular live broadcasts of opera, orchestra music, and ballet. Although perhaps not with every broadcast, Bill Moyers provides commentary and reporting on great questions of policy and intellect surpassing anything that commercial television could imagine.

To date, most of the books published about public television have discussed the topic almost exclusively from a structural or policy approach.[40] That perspective is vital. Yet the books are often flavorless because they so rarely deal with public television's programming—which, after all, is the portion of the public broadcasting system with which the public has its primary, and usually sole, identification. It is rather like writing a history of General Motors without ever sitting behind the wheel of a car. *Made Possible By . . .* tries to provide historical perspective on what has appeared on the public television screen as well as how it got there and what impact it had. This book strives to be thorough but makes no claim to be comprehensive. It gives relatively little attention, for example, to the vast history of educational broadcasting prior to 1967; there are already excellent histories of that era.[41] Although it was essential to include in this book a chapter on public radio, that clearly cannot begin to do justice to the rich and troubled history of that medium.[42]

To an extent, the decision to write about public broadcasting is an outgrowth of personal, and generational, experience. My generation—born in the mid-'60s—is the first American group to be raised from the cradle watching institutional, government-funded public broadcasting. I fondly recall my Oscar the Grouch finger puppet, for whom I constructed a live-in garbage can from a used frozen orange juice canister; since that time, tens of millions of Americans, and equal numbers across the globe, have soaked up hundreds of millions of hours of *Sesame Street* (whether or not they actually learned anything during those hours is the subject of some debate,[43] though I certainly remember being entertained). I recall my parents watching *Last of the Mohicans* on *Masterpiece Theatre*, and having to explain what made Channel 24 (WEDH, the Hartford, Connecticut, PBS station of my youth) different from other channels, and why it ran those interminable auctions. Discussing the research for this book, I discovered a surprising number of my peers who can, almost as if under posthypnotic suggestion, recall a Boston-area zip code because it was chanted in sing-song on every episode of *Zoom!* "Oh two-one three-four." (That, it must be agreed, is a form of learning, albeit one with limited practical application.) As an adult, I confess to an addiction to NPR's news programming, and I have appeared occasionally as a guest on public radio and television, primarily on programs since canceled; readers can decide if these experiences sway my analysis in any way. It is the critic's sometimes unpleasant task to emphasize what is wrong, but this volume is written with the belief that public broadcasting has provided many moments of unique brilliance, and in the hope—admittedly dim—that it will continue to do so.

1

IN THE SHADOW OF VIETNAM

Excepting the broadsides launched by a few professional ideologues, American public television is rarely considered part of a political philosophy; most fans of *Barney* or *This Old House* would be hard pressed to discern an ideology behind their favorite shows. Still, an archaeological dig to PBS's roots unearths the 1967 report of the Carnegie Commission, *Public Television: A Program for Action*. This blueprint for American's public broadcasting networks is a classic document of the Great Society. The report was not officially issued by the Johnson administration, and was not specifically designed to improve the lives of the poor or elderly. But barely hidden in its bureaucratic plan is the seemingly indestructible optimism that marked the American public sector of the 1960s. It is a quiet manifesto, expressing the belief that government action and technology can and should be catalysts for perfecting the human spirit.

"Public Television," the Commission report declared simply in its introduction, "includes all that is of human interest and importance which is not at the moment appropriate or available for support by advertising."[1] In a more expansive section entitled "Fulfilling the Promise," the Commission laid bare its grand belief that public television could transform the airwaves from what FCC commissioner Newton Minow had, just a few years earlier, dubbed "a vast wasteland" into a tool for enlightenment. "Public Television programming can deepen a sense of community in local life. . . . It should bring into the home meetings, now generally untelevised, where major public decisions are hammered out, and occasions where people of the community express their hopes, their protests, their enthusiasms, their will. It should provide a voice for groups in the community that may otherwise be unheard."[2]

As if the community mission were not broad enough, the Commission believed, along with Marshall McLuhan and the trendier communications theorists of the 1960s, that the technology of television could transform the planet into a global village[3] (provided that the technology was guided by the proper, government-funded hands). The Commission's international rhetoric was sweeping: "Through Public Television programs, and through advances in the technology of communication, Americans should have rapidly increasing opportunities for greater insight into the nature of other nations and cultures, for a clearer understanding of struggles and settlements between nations, for a view far beyond our own borders into the ways of the rest of the world."[4]

For a nation immersed in an Asian war that would eventually destroy hundreds of thousands of lives on both sides, those seemed eminently worthy pursuits—all the more worthy because commercial television was shunning them. The existence of a government regulatory agency is an acknowledgment—sometimes implicit, sometimes explicit—that the free market alone is incapable of achieving certain social goods (such as a clean environment or safety in the workplace). The Carnegie Commission report, and the initial federal funding for public broadcasting, constituted a much rarer American observation; namely, that the media market alone is incapable of achieving certain cultural goods.

The Carnegie commissioners were candid on this point. Dr. Hyman Goldin, a 20 year FCC veteran and the Commission's executive secretary, concluded that commercial broadcasting's cutthroat competition for viewers was the culprit that limited what could be put on the air. "A public affairs program or a news analysis sometimes will deteriorate as it passes through the various stages of production," wrote Goldin, "because the producer is seeking desperately for some device to increase its rating. . . . In the end, commercial television remains true to its own purposes. It permits itself to be distracted as little as possible from its prime goal of maximizing audience."[5]

The Commission was echoing a sentiment widely held among the country's opinion-makers: Americans were poorly informed, in measurable part because commercial television made them that way. In an influential March 1967 *New York Times Magazine* article, "A Program for Public Television," veteran *Times* editor Lester Markel—who himself hosted a weekly educational television program—complained that "the state of the Union, informationally and culturally, is not what it should be and . . . television is not contributing what it could toward the advancement of that state." Of the 34 new programs introduced in the 1966–67 TV season, Markel noted, "not one was related even remotely to public affairs." Here again, ratings-driven decisions were to blame: "The fact is that news operations are not rated as *Bonanzas* and so are relegated to the off-hours."[6]

Thus, one tenet of the Carnegie report was that public broadcasting had to be insulated from commercial forces in order to achieve its ideals. This implied at least some government funding—an unsurprising conclusion, since most industrialized nations already had taxpayer-funded broadcasting agencies. In the debt-conscious America of the 1990s, when federal money for virtually every purpose —not least public broadcasting—has undergone tremendous scrutiny, it seems strange that in 1967 so few opposed federal funding of television and radio. What little grumbling existed over the Public Broadcasting Act (which was written by Johnson's White House and passed the House of Representatives by a nearly 3-to-1 vote) focused on fears that it might create a government propaganda channel.[7] Senator Strom Thurmond grumbled that a government-funded radio and television network "violates both the spirit and the letter of the 1st Amendment," and in the House, Thurmond's fellow South Carolinian Albert Watson dubbed the proposed technological creation a "Frankenstein."[8] (One member of Congress who voted against the bill was Kansas Republican Bob Dole, who would go on to attack public television and radio programming and boast about his longstanding opposition to its public funding.) Such cranky sentiments, however, were little match for the broad array of voices supporting Johnson's bill. During eight days of hearings on Capitol Hill, Congress heard near-uniform support for public broadcasting from network executives, university presidents, union leaders, religious groups, educational broadcasters, officials of AT&T and Western Union, and the above-mentioned Lester Markel.

The leading communications authorities of the day told Congress they were standing on the edge of a historical era. Rosel Hyde, chairman of the FCC, called the Public Broadcasting Act the "most significant [communications legislation] to come before Congress in many years. It holds great promise of a real breakthrough in making noncommercial broadcasting a truly vital force benefiting millions of Americans."[9] Newton Minow, whose "vast wasteland" comment made him perhaps the most famous regulator in American history, predicted that the creation of federallyfunded public broadcasting "will go down as one of the really enduring things of this administration in the long run of history."[10] Although some quibbled with individual aspects of the bill, every single witness called before the Senate committee supported its passage.

Taxpayer-funded public broadcasting represented a pinnacle of what historian Godfrey Hodgson has called the reigning "liberal consensus" of postwar America. The position conservatives developed in later years—namely, that regardless of public broadcasting's content, government has no business subsidizing an industry best developed by the private sector—was little in evidence, even among conservatives. (One of American television's best-known conservatives, John McLaughlin, testified before the Senate in support of the act.)

The consensus supporting government funding can be attributed in part to prevailing Great Society generosity, and in part to the deference given to the prestigious Carnegie Commission, chaired by MIT president James Killian. Largely, though, public television was envisioned as an educational, rather than an entertainment, medium. With educational programming still little known, no one was casting a vote in favor of or against *The French Chef*; they were deciding, as one Congressional witness framed it, whether America's taxpayers would support "the full realization of our country's educational ambitions."

Not even the networks, the anticipated competitors of public broadcasting, could afford to be seen as opposing that patriotic mission. CBS pledged $1 million for public broadcasting's first season, with its president Frank Stanton declaring: "There seems to me nothing more likely than public television to effectively rally national resources for the public good"[11]—a remarkable statement, particularly considering that it was delivered in the midst of the Vietnam War and the War on Poverty. But then public television, as envisioned in the Senate hearings, was almost a social program unto itself. Raymond Hurlbert, the head of the already existing Alabama Educational Television Commission, pledged that on his state's stations, federal funding would be used to expand such televised services as nurses' training, driver training, adult literacy, family hygiene, farming programs, and forestry.

Another reason why there was comparatively little opposition to using federal funds for public broadcasting is that government seed money has long been used to nurture new American communications systems. As Johnson noted in the signing ceremony for the Public Broadcasting Act, Congress in 1844 authorized $30,000 for the first telegraph line between Washington and Baltimore, enabling Samuel Morse to send his famous first message. In addition, by 1967, the federal government had spent tens of millions of dollars on what amounts to a Cold War Broadcasting System: the radio networks Radio Free Europe and Voice of America, and the United States Information Agency (USIA), a cultural propaganda bureau that has been a fertile source for public broadcasting personnel. Furthermore, while direct and sustained federal funding of communications medium is unusual, the U.S. government indirectly supports every type of major media in the country, in amounts easily totaling more than a billion dollars every year. Commercial television licenses, for example, are "purchased" from the FCC for a tiny fraction of their actual worth in the marketplace, and are almost always renewed by their previous owners (as opposed, say, to auctioning them off every few years or, as economist Milton Friedman has suggested, selling them to the highest bidder and letting market forces dictate their future). Newspapers and magazines have, for more than a century, enjoyed discounted postage, a subsidy that, if removed, would surely cause many casualties in the print world. And few media organs in the United States would be profitable without one massive subsidy: the tax deductibility of advertising expenses.

The volume and vacuity of television advertising was, in fact, often used in the late 1960s as evidence of the desperate need for an enlightened noncommercial television network. In 1968, veteran CBS broadcaster Fred Friendly complained: "Three soap companies—Procter & Gamble, which spends $161,000,000 per year on television advertising, Colgate-Palmolive, which spends $71,000,000 per year, and Lever Brothers, $58,000,000—account for about 15 percent of the nation's total television sales. This is one reason why Americans know more about detergents and bleaches than they do about Vietnam or Watts."[12] Friendly caustically concluded: "[A] visitor from another planet could only infer that we are bent on producing a generation of semiliterate consumers." That scenario was too much for a nuclear superpower to bear; as a *Harper's Magazine* editor scolded in the mid-'60s, "The best brains in television, its best hours, and its best dollars are dedicated to making the American people fat, dumb, and happy—at a moment when the Soviets are straining all their resources to make *their* people lean, smart, and tough."[13]

THE POLITICS OF PUBLIC BROADCASTING

It's worth asking why the Johnson administration was willing to embrace such an experiment at a time when the financial and political toll of the Vietnam War was already becoming clear. Johnson was quite bold for launching an independent public broadcasting system, and for his grand pledges that it would be "carefully guarded from Government or party control."[14]

But Johnson, a consummate political realist, never intended the system to be completely independent from his own personal and political goals. One reason for Johnson's approval is that he was the first president with substantial personal holdings in broadcasting. As far back as 1943, Lyndon and Lady Bird Johnson had been in the radio business, and for as long as that Johnson had juggled that business with political favors.[15] Although all the Johnson media holdings, beginning with radio station KTBC, were held in Lady Bird's name, Johnson's executive interventions—such as fast-tracking a request before the FCC or securing an affiliation with CBS—speak to his active political interests in the media. When the Carnegie Commission was setting up shop, Johnson ensured a hidden presence by turning to the very man who had run his Texas stations: the administration got J. C. Kellam appointed as one of the Carnegie commissioners. Kellam was a longtime Johnson pal whom Johnson lured away from a job as a high school football coach in 1933. After World War II, Kellam was made general manager of

Johnson's Texas station KTBC. In his Johnson biography, Robert Caro cites a friend of both men who said: "Lyndon had Jesse absolutely in his power. And Jesse knew it."[16]

By 1966, Kellam was a trustee for all of the Johnson family's broadcasting interests. It was supremely useful, then, for the Johnson administration to have a man on the Carnegie Commission acting as its eyes and ears. According to Douglass Cater, who was Johnson's point man on the public broadcasting legislation, Kellam regularly kept the White House informed of the Commission's proceedings.[17] John Hayes, a Johnson friend and partisan who had been appointed as U.S. ambassador to Switzerland, was also on the Carnegie team; Oveta Culp Hobby, chairman of the board of the *Houston Post* Company, was also a close ally of Johnson's.

This is not to suggest that Johnson established public broadcasting to enrich himself or his family. But he had an inside expert's understanding of the political power inherent in broadcasting, and was not about to let that power develop in a federal agency without retaining his own influence. In another classically Johnsonian example of the political horse-trading behind the establishment of federal funding of the Carnegie plan for public television, the administration tried to entice John Gardner—author, humanist, and Carnegie commissioner—to accept the post of Secretary of Health, Education, and Welfare (HEW).[18] In the recollection of Hartford Gunn—a friend of Killian's who headed Boston's WGBH and later PBS—the administration said it was willing to get behind public television if Gardner would come on board[19]; both sides kept their half of the bargain. This made Gardner, as HEW secretary, responsible for public broadcasting's initial federal monies, which were appropriated through what was then called the Office of Education (OE).

A second tactic helping Johnson control what would become the nation's public broadcasting system was altering the Carnegie Commission's recommendations about the appointment process. The Carnegie report called for Congress to create a "Corporation for Public Television," a freestanding nonprofit corporation that could receive and disperse government and private funds. It envisioned a board of directors made up of "twelve distinguished and public-spirited citizens"; six would be appointed by the President, and those six would choose another six. Some would serve six-year terms and others just two years. The administration's public broadcasting bill, however, created a 15 member board—all of whom would be presidentially appointed.

But as with all federal legislation, Johnson's control was limited by Congress's. Members of the House, for example, added the amendment that no more than eight directors of the Corporation board could be from the same political party; House Republicans also inserted a provision that "no noncommercial educational broadcasting station may engage in editorializing or may support or oppose any candidate for political office." John Burke, whose 1971 doctoral thesis examined in detail the political maneuvers in getting this bill through, declared this amendment "the only poorly conceived and improperly justified section" in the Act;[20] he also noted that there was essentially no opposition to its inclusion.

The administration displayed far more creativity in harnessing for its own purposes the national desire to inaugurate public broadcasting than it did in finding a method of paying for it. Surely one of the great intellectual gaps in the history of public broadcasting is that so few of its progenitors spent any time meditating on the influence and consequences of government financing. Although the Carnegie Commission's report noted that "freedom from political control will be all the greater if [the Corporation for Public Television] . . . is not dependent upon the government,"[21] it nonetheless felt that government money was essential. The backdrop of Great Society thinking perhaps made it inevitable that federal funds would be considered a catchall solution (and, as examined below, the Commission also urged private and foundation support for the fledgling system). But it is difficult to think of an example in American history where the federal government has funded a project over which it did not try to exert control.

The Carnegie Commission had a legitimate, if politically naive, belief that excise taxes on television could provide a healthy chunk of the $56 million it saw as necessary for the Corporation for Public Television's first year. It dismissed using "the ordinary budgeting and appropriations procedure followed by the government" because that system was "not consonant with the degree of independence essential to Public Television."[22] Instead, it urged the government to collect a tax of 2 percent (which would rise to 5 percent) on television sets and place that money in a trust fund. The Commission had several reasons. First, taxes on television and radios are the most common methods by which governments outside the U.S. finance their television programming. Second, the U.S. had used excise taxes before, as the Commission's executive secretary explained: "[E]xcise taxes were part of the financing of the Korean War, for example. They'd been on sets, and only recently had been taken off sets. So we had that precedent."[23] Finally, excise taxes would avoid making commercial networks pay for public television, and thus theoretically help bring broadcasters into the camp of public television supporters. That particular strategy did not work; ABC president Leonard Goldenson strongly opposed the TV excise tax proposal, as did almost all powerful Americans whose opinions were solicited. As a result, the excise tax idea never made it into the Public Broadcasting Act, and has never been seriously considered since.

THE MILITARY-COMMUNICATIONS COMPLEX

Johnson's influence over the early development of public broadcasting also tapped the ultimate power source: the American military. While the Carnegie Commission laid out a public television blueprint that emphasized programming, the legislation tackled the more basic question of logistics and technology. In 1960s America, a broadcasting network required stations, and the lions share of resources under the Public Broadcasting Act was earmarked not for program development or national administration but for the construction of stations and the ever-vital "interconnection." The technological leap needed to create public broadcasting could not simply spring up divorced from its surroundings. As Herbert Marcuse asserted, technology "is always a historical-social project: in it is projected what a society and its ruling interests intend to do with men and things,"[24] and there can be little doubt that in 1967 a primary directive of American society was fighting and winning the war in Vietnam.

Vietnam not only dramatically raised the levels of U.S. military spending but, in the views of many contemporary experts, transformed the entire relationship between government, private industry, and the economy. In December 1967, just a few weeks after Johnson signed the Public Broadcasting Act, onetime Boeing economist Murray Weidenbaum gave a speech before the American Economics Association. Weidenbaum, who had since become a professor, soberly argued that the routinization of Pentagon spending had created a whole new economic animal. "The close, continuing relationship between the military establishment and the major companies serving the military establishment," argued Weidenbaum, "is changing the nature of both the public sector of the American economy and a large branch of American industry. . . . In a sense, the close, continuing relationship between the Department of Defense (DOD) and its major suppliers is resulting in convergence between the two, and reducing much of the distinction between public and private activities in an important branch of the American economy."[25]

Indeed, to hear Pentagon officials tell it, they were obligated to reach out from strictly military duties and embrace educational and social services. In 1968, then Defense Secretary Clark Clifford declared that the DOD was "one of the world's largest educators, and should be one of the world's best," and underscored the department's "deep obligation to contribute far more than it has ever contributed before to the social needs of our country." Toward that end, the DOD made alliances with the Office of Education, the same division that doled out funds for public broadcasting. The education journal *Phi Delta Kappan*, in a special issue on "The Military and Education," noted "the growing power of the Pentagon and the willingness of Defense Department leaders to exercise that power outside of its traditional functions," and said that problems arising from "the increasing intimacy of the military and civilian educational efforts . . . range from baffling to frightening."[26]

Nowhere had the line between private industry and military need blurred more than in the information and communications industry. Throughout the twentieth century, the development of cutting-edge communications systems in America has not occurred without substantial input from—if not outright control by—the American military. If this seems odd, recall that the rapid growth of radio as a means of communication in America took place during World War I, and that in 1918, Navy Secretary Josephus Daniels tried unsuccessfully to have the radio communications industry nationalized under military control. The Internet, touted in the 1990s as the freest of possible communications networks, was originally developed by the U.S. Department of Defense as a means of linking computers so that they might withstand a nuclear attack.

As America's massive military and nuclear arsenal grew in the 1950s and 1960s—along with the bureaucracy necessary to run them—they created unprecedented demand for communications systems. By the late 1960s, the U.S. government had invested some $50 billion in telecommunications, and was spending approximately $4 billion annually for communications equipment. The majority of that money was consumed by the Department of Defense, for run-of-the mill telephone and telegraph use but also for such military-specific needs as surveillance satellites and electronic communications required for ballistic missiles. The government became completely dependent on private companies such as Western Union (which operated the government's voice network, the Federal Telecommunications System) and AT&T (which operated the Defense Communications System, the network connecting all U.S. military bases worldwide).[27] In fiscal year 1968, for example, AT&T was the Pentagon's sixth largest contractor, putting the "communications" company ahead of more directly "military" companies, including Sperry Rand, Martin Marietta, Hughes Aircraft, and Grumman Aircraft.

As one commentator noted in the early 1970s, the relationship became symbiotic: "The government's dependence upon the communications industry as a supplier of hardware and services is matched by the industry's reliance upon government as financier of telecommunications advances."[28] Vietnam had helped create a subset of the military-industrial complex against which Dwight Eisenhower had warned: the military-communications complex.

The track record of military involvement in communications made it impossible that a valuable communications asset like public broadcasting could be born without some connection to the U.S. military. The U.S. government's first involvement in taxpayer-subsidized educational broadcasting began as part of a Cold War reflex. Along with other Soviet technological achievements, the Sputnik satellite launch in 1957 convinced American policymakers that American children needed more training in the sciences. One major response was the National Defense Education Act (NDEA) of 1958, a massive commitment of nearly $300 million to develop technical skills among American youth. An Eisenhower aide called the NDEA "our most important and most controversial initiative," and recalls that he asked a top aide to leave government to establish an "Emergency Committee" to support the act.[29] This emergency atmosphere was reflected in the legislation, which justified itself with the catchall Cold War rationale: "[T]he security of the Nation requires the fullest development of the mental resources and technical skills of its young men and women."[30]

And if national security required cultivating the competence of American youth, then there was no price too high and no technology too obscure for the government to invest in. A section of the NDEA was earmarked for "research and experimentation in the new media," and included a total appropriation of $18 million. In real dollars, this amount was significantly greater than Congress was willing to spend on the first "public broadcasting" bill a decade later. During the law's first two years, the federal government made 31 grants toward the use of television in education.[31] It is also noteworthy that although National Educational Television (NET)—the Ford Foundation–sponsored precursor to PBS—is generally considered to have been one of the most "liberal" public broadcasting entities, it included among its board members the chairman of the U.S. Atomic Energy Commission, and officers from such militarily dependent companies as General Electric and IBM.[32]

The various military-tied legacies help explain the otherwise puzzling fact that so many men involved in the planning and control of public broadcasting's first stage came from one or another sector within the U.S. military-industrial complex. Often these men might more plausibly have been sending planes and bombs to Vietnam; sometimes they were the same men. This is not to say that public broadcasting was designed as an extension of military communications networks. Such networks, however, did and do exist, and they were in part a technological model for the Office of Education's financing of public broadcasting; by 1968, the United States Army owned a vast library of videotaped instructional films, which some 4.8 million viewers watched annually through a centralized network, making Army Command "the operator of the largest and most sophisticated closed-circuit television system in the world."[33] It is simply a

natural reflection of how technology was developed and controlled during the
1960s that the only Americans sufficiently versed in the logistics of creating a
new network were part of the military-communications complex.

Consensus opinion within the broadcasting community was that Dr. James
Killian would take the post as the first president of the Corporation for Public
Broadcasting. He was a logical candidate, as the president of the Massachusetts
Institute of Technology and the head of the Carnegie Commission; he had also
served on the boards of AT&T and General Motors, and had been a White House
technical advisor to both Eisenhower and Kennedy on matters that included military intelligence. But Killian turned the position down, and Johnson—to the
surprise of many—appointed Frank Pace, Jr. The choice could hardly have made
less sense. Pace had no broadcasting or media experience, but he had been
Secretary of the Army from 1950 to 1953 during the Korean War, and had also
served as the chief executive officer of General Dynamics, a major manufacturer
of military fighter planes and bombers. (Pace also sat on the boards of Continental Oil and Time, Inc.) Television historian Erik Barnouw has immortalized
how awkwardly this pillar of the military-industrial complex approached the
new world of public broadcasting: Pace announced shortly after his appointment
that "he had already commissioned research on an important idea—how public
television might be used for riot control."[34]

But Pace was by no means the only architect of public broadcasting with substantial ties to the military. At the same time that the Carnegie Commission was
drawing its blueprint for public television, a parallel effort was taking place at
the Ford Foundation. Ford stood as the unequaled champion of supporting educational broadcasting: in the quarter-century between 1951 and 1976, Ford
spent nearly $300 million on noncommercial radio and television.[35] To put that
support in perspective, in 1967, the year the Public Broadcasting Act was signed,
the Ford Foundation spent more than $23 million on educational broadcasting—
about five times as much as the federal taxpayer contribution Johnson recommended. (A more detailed account of Ford's support is presented in chapter 2.)

The Ford effort took a new twist in 1966, when the Foundation began plot-
ting a system that would unite satellite communication with educational broadcasting. Johnson would eventually make satellite communications an explicit
part of the Corporation for Public Television's agenda, but that followed more
than a year of intense Ford Foundation work on the subject. McGeorge Bundy,
the former national security advisor who had personally ordered American
bombing raids on North Vietnam in early 1965, left the government and moved
to the Ford Foundation to oversee this plan. (Bundy's departure was another
example of the revolving door between Ford and the Johnson administration's

war team; Defense Secretary Robert McNamara recruited his famous Pentagon "whiz kids" from his former perch as president of Ford Motor Company.)

Bundy obtained his position without being knowledgeable about, or even comfortable with, the medium of television. "I used to call him a Guttenberg man," recalls Fred Friendly, the man Bundy hired to help him. "He would ask me to get him a copy of a program, and I would get him a tape, and then he would ask if I could get him a transcript."[36] Friendly in 1966 had recently lost his job at CBS because he wanted to broadcast the Senate hearings on Vietnam (the "Fulbright hearings") during the daytime slot when the network insisted on showing its regularly scheduled reruns of *I Love Lucy*. Friendly was anxious not only to develop genuine public broadcasting but to bring educational broadcasting out of its technological dark age. Only in 1967, for example, did it become possible for the first time—with help from the Ford Foundation—for a program to be shown regularly at the same time on all the nation's educational television stations, via the expensive long-distance lines owned by AT&T. Until that time, tapes had to be shuttled from one station to another, where they would be broadcast, usually copied, and shipped off again. (This primitive procedure, in an apt metaphor, was called "bicycling.")

Satellite television transmission was little understood and still experimental, but Friendly made it his personal passion. In Friendly's account, he quickly became an expert on satellite technology by working with a battery of national security and military men.[37] This included Harold Rosen and Paul Visher—both from Hughes Aircraft—former Deputy Defense Secretary Eugene Fubini, and Leonard Marks, formerly of the State Department. Marks was also a personal attorney for Johnson and his wife, handling the legal interests of their Texas broadcast properties; for a time he had been the director of the government's international propaganda arm, the United States Information Agency, handled its satellite communications. Thus even the "liberal" wing of public television advocates during this period carried a military/intelligence background.

The plan these men assembled for public television was impressive—and immediately controversial. One of Friendly's important insights was that a financial solution would be needed for public television's "interconnection," the exorbitant cost of long-distance lines. Friendly's estimate in 1967 was that the three networks were paying approximately $50,000,000 a year to a division of AT&T for the necessary lines. While the networks offset such an expense through advertising revenue, public television couldn't.

The solution, Friendly argued, was a satellite system. In 1964, a synchronous satellite orbit had been achieved for the first time: a satellite that reaches a particular distance from the earth will orbit at precisely the same speed as the planet, and thus functions as if it were stationary. (This distance, which is 22,300 miles from the earth's equator, is called the Arthur C. Clarke ring, named for the author of *2001: A Space Odyssey*.) The possibility for regularly beaming television signals to and from a satellite suddenly seemed viable. The Friendly-Ford plan proposed that the networks would continue to pay the same $50–$80 million a year for long-distance broadcasting, which with satellite beaming would cost only $25–$30 million a year, and public TV would get a large portion of the savings.

In April 1967, the Ford Foundation formally petitioned the Federal Communications Commission to construct a satellite system for public television's interconnection. The Foundation's plan may have been a rather dry one about little-understood science, but it was imbued with the rhetoric of public service, and—like its Carnegie counterpart—presented public broadcasting almost as a moral imperative. Noncommercial television, insisted the Foundation, "has unlimited potential, for human welfare and for the quality of American life." Indeed, said Friendly and Bundy and their allies, "nothing is more needed—for television itself as well as for the country—than a first-rate national non-commercial service." The system could be easily funded through the satellite scheme, which was "not magic, or sleight-of-hand. It is a peoples' dividend, earned by the American nation from its enormous investment in space."[38]

The Ford plan's idealism quickly crashed against a mundane but powerful reality: the U.S. government in the late '60s had no thorough policy governing the use of communication satellites. Instead of helping to speed the Ford plan along, nearly all the forces needed to make it work erected speed bumps. The networks, predictably, were less than enthusiastic about the Ford plan, in part because it would cost them money. "[T]he commercial networks and AT&T were absolutely scared out of their minds with Fred Friendly's scheme," recalled Hartford Gunn.[39] "So when Jim Killian came in with *his* suggestion—that there be a corporation and da-de-da and the federal government—oh, *great idea!* And everybody patted Jim on the back." The networks also wanted to run the satellites themselves. ABC, with the help of Hughes Aircraft, had submitted its own plan for satellite television as early as 1965; Western Union was adamantly opposed to the Ford plan for the same reason.

Dwarfing all these obstacles, however, was the ultimate legislative barrier: the 1962 Communications Satellite Act. Attempting to grapple with the birth of space-age communications, the federal government had given a monopoly privilege to a semiprivate corporation called COMSAT. The company's board included six directors elected by communications giants such as Western Union and AT&T, who also held half the corporation's stock, and three directors who were presidentially appointed. Two years later, a comparable international consortium, INTELSAT, was created, with COMSAT playing the leading role. Formally speaking, the satellites that the Ford Foundation was planning to use for domestic television were managed by COMSAT but owned by INTELSAT. As such, their use was governed not by the FCC, but by the State Department.

The advocates of a "people's dividend" might have been able to tap the expertise of satellite technology's military overseers—the only group in America at this time with sufficient expertise to create a new communications network—but they would not be able to wrest control from them, especially not with a war on. COMSAT took a rather proprietary attitude toward use of the heavens. During a May 1967 Senate hearing on the Public Broadcasting Act, COMSAT chairman General James McCormack, in full military dress, protested that the Ford proposal encroached on COMSAT's "statutory mission." Invoking the power of the President and the Secretary of State, the general noted that "the Satellite Act imposes on COMSAT many exacting controls to safeguard the public interest," and said he assumed Congress would not want "to open up domestic satellite service to additional entities which would not be bound by the safeguards to the public interest."[40] The Ford Foundation could simply not be trusted with the "public interest"; instead, COMSAT proposed a more sweeping system for satellite television, which, unsurprisingly, was to be financed, owned, and operated by COMSAT.

As a consequence of the stalling, the Johnson administration, preoccupied with simply getting a bill through, "never took [the Ford satellite proposal] seriously," according to Douglass Cater.[41] "We didn't get it signed and in business until late in 1967. By that time the president was going through his own problems about whether to run for a second term. He didn't sit down with me and discuss it; by that time, the momentum was lost." Lost with the momentum was the best hope to date for a practical yet innovative scheme to insure long-term funding for American public broadcasting; 30 years later it would remain unfound.

SATELLITE POLITICS

Although the Public Broadcasting Act ultimately did not incorporate the recommendations of Bundy and the Ford group, most forward-thinking experts in the federal government believed that satellites represented the future of American telecommunications. By the summer of 1967, as the Public Broadcasting Act was being fine-tuned on Capitol Hill, the Johnson administration's public broadcasting brain trust had turned its energies to a commission with a broader, but related, mandate. On August 14, 1967, Johnson announced the formation of the Task Force on Communications Policy.

Johnson's speech reflected some of the same boundless optimism that infused his promises about public broadcasting. Johnson stressed that satellite technology was inherently international: "The communications satellite knows no geographic boundary, is dependent on no cable, owes allegiance to no single language or political philosophy."[42] Johnson invited the Soviet Union to join him in developing INTELSAT, and even touted satellites' potential to "contribute to world peace and understanding."

At the same time, however, satellite transmissions had highly sensitive military and surveillance applications that the White House knew it needed to protect.[43] Thus, it should hardly be startling that the man Johnson appointed to head this delicate communications group was Eugene V. Rostow, who was Under Secretary of State for Political Affairs. (Rostow was also the brother of Walt W. Rostow, Johnson's national security advisor and a fervent hawk on Vietnam.) The Task Force also contained representatives from the Defense Department, and virtually every Cabinet department. The White House placed its public broadcasting experts—Cater and Marks—on board too.

The Task Force's report broke down the American communications system into several components: domestic and international satellite transmission, television, and telecommunications. It noted that although these made up the best communications system in the world, the U.S., unlike most developed countries, had no overarching communications policy. The Task Force did not suffer from that lack; it offered sweeping suggestions for every facet of communications. It urged the newly formed Corporation for Public Broadcasting to create low-frequency broadcast facilities in Los Angeles's impoverished South Central neighborhood, and on an Arizona Indian reservation. The Task Force was convinced it had struck just the right balance between monopoly and free market forces that would help the fledgling cable television industry grow without hindering broadcasters. The Task Force even engaged in detailed speculation about where best to place earthstations in Latin America in order to blanket that continent in satellite transmissions.

Also needed—of course—was a new executive branch agency dedicated to communications research and funding. And while the Rostow group stopped short of endorsing the Bundy-Friendly satellite scheme—there was no guarantee that it could generate the predicted savings—it did recommend the creation of a "modest operational pilot domestic satellite program."[44] A "completely neutral and disinterested entity"—possibly NASA—would dole out the satellite use to broadcasters and other users, and charge them appropriately.

The Rostow report marks the last, greatest executive branch attempt to centralize control over American communications. It was also one of the last thorough attempts to establish a sustainable, independent, and cheap delivery system for public broadcasting. Yet the Rostow report's recommendations essentially evaporated, illustrating how sensitive communications issues were at the time. When Johnson announced the creation of the Task Force in August 1967, he said he would ask it "to make its final report within one year."[45] The Task Force missed that deadline by approximately four months, a crucial gap since, by December 1968, not only had Johnson decided to remove himself from office but Democrats had already lost the White House to Richard Nixon. On December 9, 1968, a front-page *New York Times* story reported that the Rostow commission was preparing to recommend a "drastic reorganization" of the U.S. communications industry. Surprisingly, the angry, lame-duck Johnson—who had so expansively celebrated the Rostow group's mission—refused to release the text of the report. Two months after his inauguration, Nixon agreed to make the document public; after another two months, the administration made it available, confident that its own communications policies would render the report obsolete.[46]

Although there is no official account of what stalled the report's release, Rostow hinted in 1969 that the FCC's excessive interest in cable regulation had caused a delay.[47] But Task Force members disagreed among themselves over weightier matters. The vice chairman, General James D. O'Connell, wrote a detailed, almost passionate dissent, arguing that the report did not give sufficient weight to the role of communications in protecting national security. O'Connell emphasized the vital role that America's communications networks would play in the case of national emergency, and cautioned against policy that might undermine that role. While consumers, for example, presumably benefit from communications efficiency, O'Connell's concern with communications "survivability" meant that redundancy in the communications network was actually important. "[T]he larger, the more redundant and more flexible the network under unified central control, the better off we would be in case of natural disaster or military attack."[48] The implication was that any government-developed satellite system that might present a competitive threat to companies such as Western Union or AT&T might run counter to the nation's national security needs. (And indeed, the report specifically recommended lenient FCC policy toward Western Union so that it could cope with the loss of telegraph business created by the growth in long-distance telephone calls.)

O'Connell claimed that the Cuban missile crisis "proved beyond doubt that separate communication systems, tailored to individual [government] agency needs, could not be relied upon in a crisis to meet vital national requirements," and thus President Johnson had declared in 1964 that "the objective of the communication program is to create a communication system capable of surviving attack and adequate to conduct and coordinate Federal, State and local civil defense activities." He therefore strongly cautioned against federal policy that might unduly alter the nation's communications landscape: "Over-emphasis on the objectives of rapid innovation and competition in the domestic networks could have serious implications for the national defense and national security functions of the domestic carrier services."[49]

Had such words been written during peacetime, they might have been considered the overzealous enforcement of Cold War imperatives. But with the U.S. deeply mired in Southeast Asia, arguments that tampering with telecommunications might threaten national security could not be ignored. During wartime, a heightened scrutiny envelops all forms of communication. (Just before the Normandy invasion, for instance, military officials interrogated the crossword puzzle editor of the London *Daily Telegraph* because five answers over a month's time had coincidentally been codewords related to the planned Allied landing spots in France.)[50] Satellite technology might be, as Johnson had proclaimed, intrinsically international, but the U.S. government was not about to sacrifice its "national defense and national security" needs so that someone in Rangoon could phone Jakarta directly.

O'Connell's argument is of particular interest because he occupied a position—the office of White House Director of Telecommunications Management—that had substantial bureaucratic overlap with public broadcasting. Not long after the Rostow report was released, that office evolved into the Office of Telecommunications Policy (OTP), which during the Nixon administration was the agency that oversaw public broadcasting. As is related in chapter 3, OTP would try almost any means to remove criticism of the executive branch and the Vietnam war effort from public television's airwaves—a pattern that has repeated itself many times since.

Public broadcasting was born during the awkward adolescence of American telecommunications, a time when rapid growth spurts and a desire to change the rules met with stern paternal reprimands. While the visionaries behind public broadcasting believed that changing the medium of television would change the country, they never fully grasped that the medium itself could not change against the wishes of the society's most powerful elements—the federal government, the military, and large corporations. Those forces were not opposed to the laudatory social goals of public broadcasting; after all, instructional television was seen as a way of improving the skills of American children so that they could compete economically with the Soviets. At the same time, however, those forces were unwilling to pay for a communications system they could not influence. And when interconnecting public television and radio stations meant bumping up against the imperatives of military intelligence and security planning, they were starkly opposed; there was little mystery as to which side would prevail. As the 1960s waned and public broadcasting became a media player that regularly sought to make a national impact, military scrutiny merged with federal budgetary control to define the limits of what could be discussed and debated over the public airwaves.

2

THE GENTLEMAN'S LIVING ROOM

"The chances are quite small that the federal government of the United States
will ever establish and finance a non-commercial television network. Our
traditions, our native philosophies, our inbred attitudes—powerful forces
all—would work to resist such a move. . . . Picture the furor in the House of
Representatives—or the Senate, for that matter—the morning after this
independent network, supported by the people, had presented a candid
documentary on segregation, or socialized medicine, or birth control, or our
policy toward Spain or Red China. In one area, at least, the non-commercial
broadcaster would become more bullied, more ineffectual, more timid than
his commercial colleague."
—From *A True Fourth Network: Why and How,* NET PAMPHLET, MID-1960S

There are few phrases in the English language more boring than "educational
television." It conjures an image of endless hours of earnest teachers scribbling
formulae on blackboards, their chalk dust settling on the shoulders of dazed students and even more dazed cameramen. The Carnegie Commission thus made a
great rhetorical leap forward by coining and popularizing the grander concept of
"public broadcasting."[1]

But in truth, educational broadcasting in the United States—while certainly
producing its share of low-budget, pedestrian programming—has a proud history.
And the system that we understand today as "public broadcasting" incorporates
many of the facilities, ideas, and programs that had been in place long before the
Carnegie team assembled. While contemporary critics often blame public broadcasting's ills on its taxpayer subsidy, in reality much of the content and structure
of public broadcasting is owed to its educational roots.

The idea of a nationwide system of educational broadcasters can be traced to
the 1920s, and was written into the landmark 1934 federal Communications
Act, which ensured that a portion of the radio spectrum would be reserved for
educational stations. In 1951—when television was far from a fixture in every
American household—the Federal Communications Commission made a similar

provision for television, setting aside 80 VHF stations and 162 UHF stations for educational television use.[2] (Reserving spectrum space does not guarantee that it will be used. The nation's first educational television station, KUHT in Houston, went on the air in 1953, and by 1960, there were still only 44 such stations in operation, less than a fifth of the number that the FCC had made space for a decade earlier.)[3]

In the same period, the early '50s, another event took place that would have a profound effect on public radio and television: the estates of Edsel Ford and Henry Ford were settled. On the surface, the connection between Henry Ford and public broadcasting seems highly improbable, even laughable. While alive, Ford was known and hailed for industrial innovations such as the assembly line and the $5 work day. But his experiences as a shaper of public opinion were often unsuccessful, to the point of disaster. Like his counterpart Walt Disney, Ford had visions of grafting his idiosyncratic, boosterish vision of America onto the public mind. Hoping to remedy his well-known judgment that history—as taught in America—was bunk, Ford attempted to project an idyllic, theme-park past onto the Longfellow Inn in South Sudbury, Massachusetts. Here, in 1923, Ford bought a few hundred acres and created a reproduction of a flour mill that had never actually existed, and a little red schoolhouse that Ford claimed, with scant evidence, was the actual school mentioned in Sarah Hale's poem "Mary Had a Little Lamb."[4] Despite Ford's ploy of leading a lamb around the grounds, the press remained unconvinced.

Far more embarrassing was the *Dearborn Independent*, the weekly newspaper Ford published from 1919 to 1927. Whatever its journalistic accomplishments, it is remembered today solely for the 91-week campaign of hate it launched against Jews. Ford was responsible for the worldwide dissemination of the classic anti-Semitic tract *The Protocols of the Elders of Zion*, and has the noxious distinction of being the only American named in Adolf Hitler's *Mein Kampf*.

To be fair, Ford practiced what was, in his time, a benign hiring policy toward blacks, and he espoused a proto-environmentalism; thus, the eventual association of his Foundation with innovative and progressive causes is not wholly surprising. It would be stretching the case, however, to say that liberalism was the Foundation's plan. As with most large legacy foundations, the Ford Foundation was launched as a way of preserving family wealth from inheritance (and other) taxes, and was for a time the method by which the Ford family maintained control of the company's voting stock. This explicit capitalist motivation did not save the Foundation from repeated attacks from the McCarthy right, typified by a 1952 column written by journalist Westbrook Pegler headlined "FORD FOUNDATION IS FRONT FOR DANGEROUS COMMUNISTS."[5]

As noted in the previous chapter, the Ford Foundation's underwriting of non-commercial broadcasting between the 1950s and the 1970s is unparalleled in American broadcasting history. "For many years the Ford Foundation was practically the sole supporter of the [educational television] system," wrote broadcasting scholar Marilyn Lashner, noting that "Ford alone kept the system viable until other sources were forthcoming."[6]

Discerning specific motivations behind corporate philanthropy is a difficult task. Some—including those within the Ford Foundation itself— have portrayed the multimillion-dollar effort as an attempt to establish a fourth network (albeit a nonprofit one). While that may have become a prime goal of the organization, the Foundation's official history portrays its involvement in broadcasting as an outgrowth of its broader efforts to support adult education, to improve the American psyche. Like many predecessors and successors among the ruling class, the Foundation was concerned about the decaying American character. A 1948 Ford study, which laid out the areas where the Foundation was to become active, struck a Thoreauian pose in its consideration of education and mass media. It noted the "high degree of public apathy prevailing in this country and the lack in the lives of many persons of a realistic and meaningful set of values."[7] Known informally as the Gaither Report, this seminal document committed the Foundation to "support activities for more effective use of mass media (such as the press, the radio, and the moving picture) and of community facilities for non-academic education and for better utilization of leisure time for all age groups."

Poised for this edifying battle was the Foundation's Prince Valiant, the Fund for Adult Education, a multimillion-dollar bankroll designed to bring sweetness and light to the American masses. In a nearly forgotten assessment of the Ford Foundation's activities, the American social critic Dwight MacDonald declared the Fund "an enterprise of almost indescribable ambition, complexity, and vagueness."[8] MacDonald skewered the "philanthropoids" who created and ran such outfits, doubting that American adults had much appetite for prefabricated chats about Asian agriculture, or similar conversational stimulants that the Fund thrust into their hands.

Nonetheless, the Fund, formally launched in 1951, was the birthplace of regular financing of what would eventually become public broadcasting. The Fund's first chief was Alexander Fraser, the president of the Shell Oil Company. It was Fraser who authorized the first Ford commitment to television and radio, thus inaugurating a lifelong connection between the petroleum industry and public broadcasting. Yet even within the Foundation, the Fund's mission and expenditures were hotly contested. In one instance, Henry Ford II browbeat the head of the Fund, claiming to be flabbergasted by the sum that had been approved for educational broadcasting (even though he had been present at the meeting where it was approved.) In mid-1955, not long after the Ford Foundation's first president, Paul Hoffman, left to run Dwight Eisenhower's reelection campaign, the Ford trustees voted to eliminate the Fund. But the Fund returned, in large part because the Sputnik launch reasserted the importance of American education.[9]

The Fund's flagship broadcasting project was a tape facility in Ann Arbor, Michigan. Here banks of videotape recorders whizzed away 24 hours a day to churn out thousands of copies of broadcasts to be shipped out to the several dozen educational television affiliates. Through the mid-'60s, this tape factory cost $1 million a year to operate—one-sixth the entire budget of the Ford-sponsored National Educational Television and Radio Center (NETRC).[10] Counter to any perception that foundation money channeled to such nonprofits simply disappears into the ether, the NETRC was, by the '60s, the largest videotape duplication plant in the world, and one of the largest buyers of tape for television.[11]

The NETRC also produced burgeoning "public" programs, notably the award-winning *Omnibus*. In an era when network executives believed that Sunday was too much of a family day for viewers to be absorbed in the National Football League, this 90-minute program aired on CBS on Sunday afternoons from 1952 to 1956 (in its final season, *Omnibus* moved to ABC on Sunday evening). The beneficiary of a huge $3 million grant from the Ford coffers, *Omnibus* was seen regularly by as many as 17 million viewers, and provided the American mass audience with its first introduction to Alistair Cooke, the later master of ceremonies for PBS's highly successful *Masterpiece Theatre*.

Omnibus was an adventurous mixture of high- and middlebrow, offering everything from figure skating to a Gertrude Stein play, from a profile of Harpo Marx to *Antigone*. A typical episode from early 1955 featured violinist Yehudi Menuhin, who played the first movement of a Bach violin concerto with a small orchestra, then walked over to an armchair, where he discussed various musical styles and techniques; after his monologue he strolled back over to the orchestra to perform a piece by a different composer. Next was a film of an ocean spear fisherman, introduced by the cameraman, who explained the technical wizardry that allowed him to shoot underwater. Finally, a history professor and troupe of actors—including Jessica Tandy and Hume Cronyn—reenacted the life of John Quincy Adams, dressed in historical costume on a stage consisting of chairs and slide projections to suggest various locales.[12]

Omnibus, seen today, certainly tugs at the attention span of an MTV-conditioned mind. But in it can be glimpsed many of the seeds of public and niche-cable television: *National Geographic*, the Discovery Channel, Arts & Entertainment, *Forsyte Saga*. Over time, however, *Omnibus* developed something of a

reputation for sleaze, even by the shaky standards of 1950s television. A prominent TV critic lamented that the once-grand *Omnibus* had "grown notorious for
its pliant susceptibility to commercial promotional gimmicks." One such scheme
involved a housing expert named Charles Abrams, invited by *Omnibus* to discuss
worldwide housing problems. A script called for him to be asked if he didn't
think that prefabricated aluminum houses were part of the solution, to which he
would reply affirmatively, while being led to a model of just such a house; the
structure was manufactured by a Canadian aluminum company that was an
Omnibus sponsor. Unfortunately for the program, Abrams had just returned from
the Ivory Coast, where the government's use of imported aluminum housing
instead of cheaper native labor and materials had provoked a political crisis—and
he declined to follow the script.[13]

BIRTH OF A NET-WORK

Ford's commitment to noncommercial television deepened in 1963, with the
birth of National Educational Television (NET). Although on the surface the
establishment of NET was a simple consolidation and expansion of earlier groups
(including the Fund for Adult Education), NET became by the mid-'60s a vital
new force in American television. Part of that change was geographical: in 1959,
the Ford Foundation moved the nerve center of its educational television operations from Ann Arbor to New York City. Equally important was an increase in
funds: in 1963, the Ford Foundation upped its spending on educational television
to $6 million a year. But probably most crucial was the shift away from its 15-
hour-per-week, in-school schedule toward five hours a week of programs "of
substantially higher quality."[14]

During the period from 1963 to 1966, NET produced a number of programs
that became clear prototypes for PBS shows—in format, in topics covered, even
in personnel. NET's first regular public affairs program, the weekly *At Issue*, was
produced by Alvin Perlmutter, who would go on to produce *The Great American
Dream Machine* and *Adam Smith's Money World*. In 1966, the incipient network
launched the ambitious *NET Playhouse*, which presented original dramatic productions for five seasons, including Arthur Miller's adaptation of Ibsen's *Enemy of
the People*, plays by Tennessee Williams, and experimental theater from New
York's La Mama theatre, *NET Playhouse* was clearly an inspiration for PBS's
American Playhouse.[15] By the late '60s, *NET Journal* brought to educational stations
tough and usually independently produced documentaries on a weekly basis,
paving the way for *Frontline*. This continuity between NET and PBS programming

is especially remarkable given that most observers agree that the Carnegie Commission report and subsequent federal legislation were designed in part to strengthen local stations and reduce the national influence of NET.[16]

NET was able to draw upon a few strong local educational stations who had been producing dynamic programming since the '50s. Pittsburgh's WQED, for example, established in 1954, was one of the early educational TV innovators; its general manager John White became the president of NET in 1958. WQED combined some programs picked up from commercial television with specialized local programming, which included a Pittsburgh Pirates baseball clinic, live broadcasts from the Pittsburgh Symphony Orchestra, and live rodeo action from the Allegheny County Free Fair. In 1958, WQED produced one of the most memorable programs in the history of educational programming, when Jonas Salk and Robert Frost had a two-hour-long unscripted conversation, broadcast without interruption.[17] WQED also produced a children's puppet program initially known as *Children's Corner*, which transformed in 1968 into *Mister Rogers' Neighborhood* and became a NET staple.

NET also made strides in fulfilling one of the great potential strengths of American noncommercial television: the ability to serve the nation's substantial minority communities.[18] Blacks, Latinos, Asians, Native Americans, and gays and lesbians may have much or little in common, but as television became the dominant mass medium in the 1950s and 1960s, all these groups were confronted with an irreal world that not only looked nothing like them but frequently demeaned them with bigoted or otherwise offensive depictions. This media deficiency and its ripple effects on race relations were noted by the riot-inspired Kerner Commission: "Most television programming ignores the fact that an appreciable part of their audience is black. The world that television and newspapers offer to their black audience is almost totally white, in both appearance and attitude. . . . [O]ur evidence shows that the so-called 'white press' is at best, mistrusted, and at worst, held in contempt by black Americans." A broadcast history is not the place to judge stereotyping committed by decades-old programs. But it is self-evident that too many local commercial television stations have historically fulfilled their statutory obligation to serve the public interest by offering a weekly half-hour talk show to a black host at 6 a.m. on Saturday, while the networks have rarely accomplished anything more than placing a black or Latin mask on standard sitcom formulae.

NET (and, later, public television), freed from the dictate of maximizing audience, had the ability to air some programming—even in prime time—that would be of immediate interest to only a few. In 1964, NET contracted with San Francisco's KQED to produce three documentaries exploring black life and issues in America: *Take This Hammer*, featuring James Baldwin touring San Francisco; *The Messenger from Violet Drive*, a profile of Black Muslim leader Elijah Muhammad; and *Louisiana Diary*, an account of the strains behind registering black voters.[19] Discounting instructional programs (which serve their own minority audiences), NET's regular commitment to such minority programming began in 1968, with the debut of the weekly *Black Journal*.[20] In 1969, after the formation of the Corporation for Public Broadcasting, NET's *Black Journal* became the first program to receive a CPB grant. In modified form, this program continues today as PBS's *Tony Brown's Journal*; Brown took over as the program's host in its third season. NET's commitment to minority programming continued a year later, with a $475,000 grant to WNDT for two 20-week seasons of a black-oriented interview and variety program called *Soul!*, hosted by the late Ellis Haizlip.

In the early '70s there were other black-oriented public broadcasting programs: a short-lived series called *Black Perspectives on the News* (which filled in for *Black Journal* when it was canceled for the 1973 season, along with other public affairs programs) and on Boston's WGBH a program called *Say Brother*. *Say Brother* has been a remarkable survivor of public television's internecine warfare. In 1970, when a Polaroid vicepresident named Stanford Calderwood became WGBH's station manager, he immediately picked a fight with *Say Brother*'s producer, Ray Richardson, who insisted that he was not bound by "white regulators," such as the FCC's Fairness Doctrine and the prohibition against on-air profanity.[21] The black-produced program is credited with being the first television show to use the word "fuck" on the air. Even though Richardson was fired and the program temporarily canceled, it re-emerged under a new producer and, as of 1996, may have been the longest continually running public television show in America.

While these programs had their share of shortcomings, at no other time in American history has national television programming so strongly reflected the presence and diversity of black Americans. The television lens went into aspects of black life that most white Americans had thought little about (such as the dilemma faced by black infantrymen ostensibly fighting in Vietnam to protect freedoms they did not have at home), and the programs included interviews with figures far outside the mainstream, such as cultural critic Amiri Baraka (formerly LeRoi Jones), Kathleen Cleaver (at a time when her husband was a fugitive from American law enforcement), and Louis Farrakhan. It is virtually impossible to imagine a commercial television talk show, then or now, granting—as *Soul!* did in 1972—an hour-long interview to Farrakhan, who spoke unopposed, except by a host's friendly questions, before an audience filled entirely with applauding followers.[22]

The fledgling educational "network" functioned, at least occasionally, as a kind of repository for material the commercial networks deemed too controversial.

For example, CBS commissioned a film in 1967 by the British documentary film-maker Felix Greene; the result was an 85-minute documentary called *Inside North Vietnam*. It was the first American look into enemy territory, and thus was politically explosive. The film showed that the U.S. military had used antipersonnel bombs, which belied Pentagon claims that it struck only military targets. Author Cleveland Amory gave the film a positive review in the mainstream magazine *Saturday Review*, but CBS declined to air it, and the film became available to NET.

With the possibility that NET would air the film, a chorus of freelance military censors sprang into action, in effect labeling the film treasonous. Former U.S. Rep. Walter Judd, who had not seen the film, sent the following letter to every Member of Congress:

> Dear Friend,
>   I hope you will read and sign the accompanying letter protesting the proposed showing on the Educational TV network of Felix Greene's film on North Vietnam. . . . When American youth are giving their lives in a war against a ruthless enemy, surely we have an obligation to protect their families and the public against anything that strengthens that enemy.[23]

Eventually 33 Members of Congress signed the letter. Their protest, sent to NET president John White, called Greene "a propagandist for Communist China and Communist North Vietnam," and dubbed the film—which none of them had seen—"nothing more nor less than communist propaganda."[24] The documentary was eventually shown, but with a NET compromise that was to become a model for many controversial public broadcasts to come: air the documentary, followed by a panel discussion. In case viewers were incapable of digesting *Inside North Vietnam* by themselves, TV newsman David Schoenbrun and political scientist Robert Scalapino helped them sort things out. Such mitigating measures were rarely employed by the more aggressively independent commercial networks— but then, by this time they had already decided not to air such inflammatory material. Additionally, more than 10 percent of the educational stations decided not to broadcast *Inside North Vietnam*, even with the balancing panel discussion.

To Robert Lewis Shayon, critic for the *Saturday Review of Literature*, the Congressional furor over *Inside North Vietnam* underscored "the importance of funding public TV in such a way that it is not subject to annual Congressional appropriations."[25] In a prescient thought experiment, Shayon suggested: "Suppose that John White, when he faced his decision, had been scheduled to appear before a Congressional Committee to ask for next year's program money—or, for that matter, that any affiliate had to weigh its decision whether to carry the NET program before requesting Congressional appropriations. Under such conditions, postponement could easily become the order of the day for public TV."

That scenario came true, even without Congressional appropriation. NET president White was called before a closed session of a House committee because an episode of *NET Journal* called "Fidel" was considered to be sympathetic to Castro's Cuba. White managed to convince the committee that the documentary was acceptable, and reminded the congressmen that since NET received no federal funds, he and his colleagues were under no obligation to appear before Congress.[26]

"THE SINGLE MOST REVOLUTIONARY CONCEPT"

The NET programming could rarely be properly labeled radical, and certainly stopped short of endorsing any of the Maoist, African nationalist, or Marxist-Leninist revolutionary rhetoric that floated through sectors of American society in the late '60s and early '70s. After all, NET remained under the reasonably strict control of the Ford Foundation; in a famous 1965 article, former NET employee Richard Elman lashed out at Ford for enforcing Establishment standards on NET producers.[27] In one instance, Ford Foundation officials criticized a NET reporter, working on the *Pathfinders* series, for asking excessively probing questions about nuclear arms outside an Atomic Energy Commission (AEC) facility. Insiders could not help but see a connection to the NET board of directors, which included AEC chairman Glenn Seaborg.

NET did display, however, a tolerance for listening to marginalized radical voices that was unknown on the commercial networks, and no doubt startled a few viewers who flipped over to what they had come to think of as a highbrow educational station. In 1966, the Ford Foundation, under the influence of McGeorge Bundy and Fred Friendly, decided to fund a two-year, $10 million public broadcasting experiment, eventually dubbed the Public Broadcast Laboratory (PBL), which served as the name of both the entity and the program itself. In Friendly's view, one of the chief hurdles between educational television and network status was educational stations' inability to "interconnect"; that is, they did not have the ability to transmit the same broadcast at the same time. In a postnetwork, cable environment, most Americans take interconnection for granted, but it was a major problem for educational television at the time. As one broadcasting executive explains the problem: "It was impossible for any program to have any national impact, because you didn't know where it was going to be. If you lived in New York, it might be on Tuesday at 9, and if you lived in Philadelphia, [just] that far south, it could be on Wednesday."[28]

PBL was inspired in part by a Canadian public affairs program called *This Hour*

Has Seven Days, but developed its own unique identity. The program that *PBL's* forefathers envisioned has no counterpart on American television, before or since—it was TV utopia, and interconnection was to be its cornerstone. In the jet-fueled rhetoric of its proposal, PBL said it hoped "to build broadcasts with cutaway time so that each station, if it so desires, can relate the national question to the local community. . . . The Mayor of the affiliate city or traffic commissioner or hospital administrator or anyone who is intimately concerned may appear on the affiliate station during a cutaway, to relate local views to the PBL's overall report."[29] Interconnection, PBL feverishly pledged, "has the power to fuse issues and explode them simultaneously in living rooms across the country."

While the preliminary document gave few specific hints about the program's content, PBL declared that "everything that is of interest to people—or that should be of interest to people—is fair game" for its broadcasts. Jettisoning network's stopwatch rigidity, PBL insisted that "reports will run for as long or as short a period as they need to run." Capturing the immodest spirit of '60s thought, PBL declared its experiment "the single most revolutionary concept in the history of American broadcast communications."

Of course, you can't make a revolution without breaking a few heads, and even before its debut, PBL created trouble. Initial plans were for the program to have its headquarters at Columbia University, where it would be called the "Columbia University Experimental Broadcasting Laboratory," chaired by Edward Barrett, the longtime head of Columbia's prestigious journalism school. But according to PBL president and executive producer Avram Westin, the university's trustees "realized that what Fred [Friendly] was talking about, what I was talking about, was a kind of information program which . . . could take political positions, economic positions that the trustees of Columbia didn't necessarily want to endorse. So that took care of that. We were out of there."[30]

In retrospect, Columbia's withdrawal was probably a prudent move. *PBL's* first episode aired on November 5, 1967, and was, quite simply, a shock. *PBL* sought to capitalize on the timing of its debut, basing its first segment on the Election Day to follow in two days, which featured several candidates attempting to become the first black mayors in the history of their cities. On that same Election Day, Johnson signed the Public Broadcasting Act into law. (White House support for the legislation was too far along to be thwarted by *PBL's* success or failure; the outraged reactions to *PBL's* maiden broadcast, according to LBJ's public broadcasting expert, went completely unnoticed in the administration.)[31]

While most white American television viewers had some passing knowledge of the civil rights movement—this was still several months before the assassination of Martin Luther King, Jr.—*PBL* tried to take them deep inside the debate. The program's only anchor was broadcast veteran Edward P. Morgan, who had for more than a decade produced regular commentaries on the ABC radio network (which were, intriguingly, sponsored by the AFL-CIO). Morgan sought less to pander to *PBL*'s audience than to preach to them. "Black and white Americans are shouting at each other," he pronounced. "In the vicious babble, too few are listening."[32]

The program cut to reports from three cities—Boston; Cleveland; and Gary, Indiana—each the site of a closely contested campaign featuring a Democrat poised to become his city's first black mayor. The report from Cleveland, by correspondent Greg Shuker, accused the city's white incumbent, Ralph Loker, of using Rev. King as part of an "outright racist appeal" against the black challenger Carl Stokes. A film clip showed Loker asking an audience; "Will Dr. Martin Luther King be mayor of Cleveland if Carl Stokes is elected in primary?" and predicting that a Stokes victory "would give the noted racist King control of his first city in the United States."

PBL's choice to cover Stokes (who won two days after the program's debut) was a fortuitous bit of self-promotion that today might be called "synergy." The Ford Foundation had also made a $175,000 contribution for voter registration to the city's chapter of the Congress for Racial Equality, an organization locally perceived as a virtual arm of Stokes's campaign. This grant was quite controversial, cited by Stokes's opponents at the time as improper outside interference and as evidence of the Foundation's political bias. (Eighteen months later, Nixon black-bagger Tom Huston would recall the Cleveland grant as a reason for the IRS to investigate the Foundation's tax-exempt status.)[33] By contrast, the debut *PBL* episode, which mentioned in passing the Foundation grant, had no effect on the election's outcome because Cleveland's educational television station made an advance decision not to carry it.[34]

The next segment of *PBL*'s debut began with a short film made by a self-described revolutionary poet named Russell Meeks. PBL producers, taking their "public" charge literally, had given Meeks a movie camera and told him to film what it was like to live on what he called the "stinkin' west side of Chicago." His minidocumentary bombarded viewers with one disturbing image after another: children eating out of dumpsters, bombed-out buildings, a convulsing dog dying in the street in front of an abandoned lot where children played baseball. Echoing the rhetoric of Black Power militants such as H. Rap Brown, Meeks called King's nonviolence strategy "the philosophy of the fool," and declared himself part of a new breed of activists who would "rather die on our feet than live on our knees." In his film, white merchants were "exploiters of our people"; the police were "gestapo." His conclusion called for complete racial segregation: "No more to you, white America. You shall pay for the past."[35]

A 100-member panel discussion—with 50 white participants and 50 black participants—followed, filmed in the studio of Chicago's educational station WTTW. Here Meeks and many militant supporters fleshed out his racial criticisms. When a white participant questioned Meeks's refusal to endorse the philosophy of nonviolence, Meeks, in a typical verbal assault, pointed his finger and said: "Ask the U.S. government about violence. They live on it. This is the most violent society in the world that you run, baby." One black teenager must have frightened a good portion of white viewers when he stood in front of a microphone and said simply: "I am for violence."

After a half-hour of racially raw discussion, the stage was given over to a production of an Off-Broadway play called *Days of Absence*. This provocative, didactic play, written by Douglas Turner Ward, explored what would happen if, on one day in a small Southern town, all the black people disappeared. In the *PBL* production, the entire cast was black but acted in whiteface, a technique called "reverse minstrel."

As if *PBL*'s assault on the country's segregation were not sufficiently outrageous, the show ended with a jab at the Johnson administration. In his closing statement, Morgan referred to "all the little Vietnams floating through American cities," and questioned why America was fighting for justice and democracy in Vietnam when it had "yet to fulfill basic goals at home."

The social cinema verité of *PBL*'s debut and subsequent broadcasts certainly got notice. The enormously influential *New York Times* critic Jack Gould, who until that point had been an enthusiastic supporter of public broadcasting in general and the Ford Foundation's work in particular, said that the debut "had flashes of provocative heat but far more moments of journalistic and theatrical ineptitude."[36] Ironically, because the boards of many educational television stations were comparatively conservative, *PBL*'s provocative debut actually undermined its mission to create a truly interconnected national network: fully one-quarter of the 119 stations to which *PBL* was available did not air it. Some of these stations cited financial pressure, while others declared the program too controversial, but there was no mistaking that the televising of outspoken racial politics created a regional blackout. No one in South Carolina, Alabama, or Georgia saw *PBL*'s first installment because none of the stations in those states broadcast it.[37]

Criticism of *PBL* was not limited to the outside. Weeks before the program ever debuted, the board members tried to micromanage the first episode's content. The board's official minutes show that race—not surprisingly—was an explosive issue even for the PBL board, which was almost entirely white. Peter Mennin, the president of the Juilliard School of Music "and others were troubled by the fact that the Black Nationalist spokesman [in the program] was highly articulative and the others inarticulate. Several observed that the program should somehow have provided alternatives to the extremist 'solution.' "[38] The language of board minutes is by definition neutral; in actuality, PBL board meetings were far less polite. The weekly meetings of the board of directors became, according to *PBL* executive producer Avram Westin, veritable wrestling matches (as violent as they could get within the confines of Manhattan's posh Century Club).

The second *PBL* episode featured a segment poking holes in the official government account of the Gulf of Tonkin incident. In July and August of 1965, the U.S. destroyer *Maddox* was on a surveillance mission that brought it into the territorial waters of North Vietnam; the claim that the ship had been fired upon provided the Johnson administration the political leeway needed to escalate the Vietnam War. *PBL*'s skepticism was on target: thirty years after the incident, McNamara, in a visit to Vietnam, acknowledged that the crucial North Vietnamese attack on the destroyer had not occurred as it was related to the U.S. Congress and public. But at the time, to air such questions on national television was considered offensive, even treasonous. PBL's weekly board meeting after this story had aired began in typically genteel fashion, with generous glasses of Scotch and a roast beef dinner. But Westin recalls that it turned ugly: "I was called a Communist. I was called an enemy sympathizer. It was practically, 'Where's the Vietcong flag in your office?' "[39]

Other segments on vital '60s topics—hippie communes, Berkeley's Free Speech Movement, draft dodgers and deserters—raised similar hackles among the board. In a frustrated—and ultimately futile—attempt to preempt what he saw as *PBL*'s countercultural excesses, Columbia's journalism school dean Barrett declared: "Nothing shall appear on this program that does not belong in a gentleman's living room."[40]

It is not entirely clear what PBL's board thought the show should look like. In a scathing review of the first season, the board declared that "*PBL* has rarely departed from either the topics or the intellectual levels of conventional television."[41] They did not care for Morgan's frank on-air editorials: "*PBL*'s chief commentator," the board said, "does not lead us forward toward some new form of comment or interpretation; he heads us back toward a very old rhetorical form called 'the harangue.' " Some of the board's criticisms point toward a revival of an *Omnibus*-style format, where classical music and academic art criticism could have a venue. In its more idealistic moments, the board suggested that *PBL* should "adapt for television the technical and artistic innovations that have appeared on film in the last ten years." There were also more down-to-earth concerns; one PBL staffer noted in a memo that "friends of board members who run 'Outward Bound' have pushed hard for a segment on this program."[42]

The PBL board—which included weighty critics of American politics such as Richard Hofstadter—eventually plotted a coup, arguing after the first season that the program should be canceled unless a new executive producer could be found. But Westin and his crew had considerable clout with Friendly and thus with the Foundation. While that relationship made many in the NET and educational worlds jealous,[43] it also inoculated them against outright removal. For *PBL*'s second season, however, a former Johnson administration aide named Frederick Bohen was installed as *PBL*'s executive editor—a compromise that proved satisfactory to neither side.

AN INFLUENTIAL FAILURE

By early 1969, the explosions that PBL had hoped to create in American living rooms were occurring mostly in its own offices. One segment exposed one of the government's most delicate missions: military spending. The *PBL* episode that aired on January 5, 1969, had initially contained a segment about the military budget that maintained that the Johnson White House had looked favorably upon, among others, a Texas-based construction firm called Brown & Root. This Houston-based firm was part of a consortium (with Morrison-Knudsen and J. A. Jones) that had built virtually all the U.S. military's support bases in Vietnam. The approximately $1.6 billion in contracts the consortium received in the war years made it the country's 35th largest military contractor.

These contracts also earned Brown & Root a Senate inquiry. In May 1968, Senator Abraham Ribicoff, a Democrat from Connecticut, issued a report accusing the company of trying to use sloppy bookkeeping to steal more than $100 million from the government. Ribicoff said the construction firm did not "take proper steps to insure receipt, storage, theft protection, and accountability for shipments." The company's defenses in response to an accounting inquiry were, Ribicoff thundered, "incredible. . . . It is hard to believe that the Navy would acquiesce in what appears to be some form of coverup or subterfuge. In my view, the information given to us was completely unconvincing."[44]

Picking up on Ribicoff's accusations, the *PBL* broadcast hinted that the Johnson White House favored Brown & Root because the firm had been generous to Johnson's political campaigns. (While a quid pro quo is always difficult to prove, biographer Robert Caro has amply documented that Brown & Root provided tens of thousands of dollars to LBJ's 1948 Senate campaign—sometimes delivered in cash in brown paper bags.) Although the portion of the program dealing with political donations took up a mere 40 seconds of broadcast time, it was yanked by Bohen, who had worked in that very White House just a few months earlier. This provoked a fight with William Anderson, the executive producer in charge of that segment. Upon hearing that Anderson was trying to publicize the dispute by crying that he had been censored, Bohen fired him, and proclaimed that the political payback charges had been made "without documentation and by innuendo."[45] Even with Johnson on his way out of the White House, the fledgling public television system he had created was not going to be used to bash him.

The few postmortems for *PBL* that have been published maintain that it fell victim to its own hype, and that—like much of NET's public affairs program-ming—it was out of step with its audience and its affiliates.[46] In their more opti-mistic moments, critics have argued persuasively that as a challenging news program airing on Sunday evening, *PBL* was the unspoken archetype for *60 Minutes*, the vastly successful newsmagazine that debuted on CBS—Westin and Friendly's network alma mater—in 1968, a year after *PBL*'s debut.[47] Former NBC newsman Elie Abel told a Senate subcommittee in 1972 that "if *PBL* has to be accounted a failure, it must be one of the more influential failures of recent times. I say we need more of them."[48]

PBL makes a superb case study for the strengths and limits of public broadcast-ing of its day. Although it dropped its formal Columbia connection and strove to speak to Everyman, *PBL* could barely cloak its elitism: a heavy portion of its on-screen experts had some connection to an Ivy League university. In its first sea-son, it actually broadcast portions of an economics seminar from Princeton's bureaucrat-mill, the Woodrow Wilson School. Two weeks later, *PBL* might have been able to claim that it was tapping into the West Coast–leaning conservative American future, because it featured a lengthy interview with Ronald Reagan—but it filmed him as he toured the Yale campus. And cultural programming was often forbidding to a mass audience, focusing on avant-garde dance groups and plays staged in foreign tongues without subtitles.

There was both a bias and a balance to *PBL*'s public affairs programming. A reasonably sophisticated viewer would have little difficulty discerning the sym-pathies of *PBL* producers, especially on race matters, where the sympathies were generally overtly integrationist and intolerant of those who were not. At the same time, however, *PBL* made a formal commitment to tell the "other," i.e., conservative, side of issues where its liberalism was showing (it was rarely con-sidered necessary to give a left or radical position by way of "balance"). Thus, *PBL* viewers were introduced to conservative figures, many of whom, in 1967–8, had little nationwide reputation: Reagan, Herman Kahn, Henry Kissinger, George Wallace, and Catholic editor Brent Bozell.

True to its name, and despite the board's denunciations, *PBL* was also genuinely experimental. Discussing issues simultaneously with guests from across the country, which is today a standard feature on *Nightline* and *MacNeil/Lehrer NewsHour*, was pioneered on *PBL*.

PBL is perhaps best thought of as the first demonstration of the limits of public broadcasting. Although not directly funded by federal taxpayer dollars, *PBL* came of age in the era when Americans were urged to consider educational TV as public TV, and—as seen with the Brown & Root incident—the federal government had ways to make its opinions heard. Unlike commercial broadcasts, in which producers, sponsors, and on-air talent are generally in agreement with the goal of maximizing audience, *PBL* had to serve many masters, with visions that were sometimes directly in conflict: its elite board of directors, the more parochial needs of educational stations (who were jealous of the huge sums *PBL* had available), the Ford Foundation—and of course the program's viewers, about whom little was genuinely known.

NONCOMMERCIAL, YES—BUT ANTICOMMERCIAL?

NET's lack of reliance on commercials had a liberating effect on its content, allowing it to broadcast loosely categorized public affairs programming with an explicit, almost angr, anticommercial focus. The debut episode of *PBL* had several advertising parodies, making, for example, a stinging commentary on wasteful aspirin manufacturers who spent hundreds of millions of dollars to create demand for relatively expensive products that are chemically identical to cheaper generic products. When PBS was created (distributing programs for the first time in the fall of 1970), its programs inherited the anticommercial animus. *The Great American Dream Machine*'s debut program, on Wednesday, January 6, 1971, featured a funny, scathing commentary from Nicholas von Hoffman about advertising techniques used in popular medical journals. Von Hoffman could scarcely cloak his contempt that the classic seductions of American advertising—"family values," power, success, and especially love and sex—were also used to peddle prescription drugs, which most consumers believe are dispensed strictly on the basis of medical need. This was no idle observation: von Hoffman cited Senate estimates that claimed that 10 percent of the nation's hospital admissions were attributable to wrongly prescribed drugs. This, he argued, was an inevitable consequence of the half-billion-dollar annual barrage that doctors faced from the manufacturers of prescription drugs. In von Hoffman's view, this was "an industry out of control."[49]

While TV shows from Alfred Hitchcock to *Saturday Night Live* have poked gentle fun at advertising's methods, the *Dream Machine*'s frank, barbed attacks on the influence of advertising dollars have almost no place in the history of ad-driven American television. Yet the newly launched NET adopted this stance as a natural, humorous extension of its noncommercial mandate: *Laugh-In* meets Ralph Nader. The "anticommercial" had enough currency at the time that in the early 1970s, the Federal Trade Commission (FTC), which regulates false advertising, seriously considered establishing equal-time provisions for such spots. FTC chairman Miles Kirkpatrick questioned why an advertiser "should have the right to monopolize the consumer's attention by trumpeting the virtues of his products when a consumer who learned of an aspect undesirable to him might not buy it if the attention monopoly were ended?"[50] The networks and the Nixon White House shot this notion down.

Given sponsors' proprietary feelings about the format and content of TV commercials, it is unsurprising that NET's targeted satire and other dissection of advertising caused trouble. In the years just preceding the passage of the Public Broadcasting Act, NET's public affairs programming had started rattling a number of industry groups. After much internal debate and caution, NET allied itself with the Consumers Union to produce a regular program called *Your Dollars Worth*, which consistently picked apart rigged marketing schemes and the deceptive pitches of television ads. A *New York Post* critic said of the series: "It's the only endeavor on the homescreen which is studiously dedicated to helping the viewer save, rather than spend money."[51] On more than a few occasions, that proved to be a dangerous task. An exposé of over-the-counter drugs greatly upset the pharmaceutical industry; another on unscrupulous television repair shops caused vociferous blasts from trade associations. A December 1966 episode called "Gasoline: What Price Combustion?" argued that there were no essential differences between major brands of gasoline, and that indeed, gas distributors often swapped shipments of thousands of gallons to keep down their shipping costs. The program specifically disputed claims, made in television ads, that a special ingredient called "platformate" in Shell gasoline helped car engines run better for longer. The NET film explained that platformate was simply a concocted brand name for a chemical contained in all gasoline, and that the extra penny Shell consumers spent at the pump paid not for platformate but for ads touting the virtues of platformate.

What made the documentary a thorny proposition was that Shell Oil was a significant funder of educational television. A Shell grant, for example, had helped fund a two-month experiment in 1966 whereby four stations on the East Coast (New York, Boston, Washington, and Philadelphia) ran live, simultaneous educational broadcasts.[52] According to one veteran public broadcaster, the NET platformate exposé cost a midwestern public television station a sizable donation from the oil giant.[53] (By the mid-'70s, the national public television system was receiving more than $7 million annually from oil companies, making such documentaries unlikely to air.)

PBL had similar trouble with its pointed anticommercials. One station, KLRN-TV in San Antonio, Texas, simply deleted the anti-ad material.[54] And the Television Advertising Bureau went so far as to petition the FCC, making the novel argument that such tongue-in-cheek attacks on commercials violated the Fairness Doctrine. The FCC rejected the claim, but *PBL* stopped running anticommercials not long after its debut episode. In the early 1970s, Ralph Nader himself produced *The Nader Report*, a series of consumer-oriented programs out of Boston's WGBH that were to include a dissection of a Mobil Oil commercial's claim that detergent gasoline contributed to cleaner air. The program's national distribution was held up for several weeks by PBS, ostensibly because more time was needed "to unearth necessary source material."[55] This delay happened to coincide with a million-dollar gift from Mobil Oil to the CPB for presentation of some English plays and for distribution of *Sesame Street*; the grant, intriguingly, had been negotiated not by a CPB officer but by the president and general manager of WGBH. The premiere episode of *The Nader Report* aired more than a month after originally scheduled, and did not include the analysis of the Mobil ad (although that analysis was eventually broadcast).

Even seemingly trivial attacks on modern marketing caused trouble. One *Dream Machine* segment—capturing the natural-foods, *Consumer Reports* flavor of the early '70s—featured comedian Marshall Efron "baking" a modern, supermarket-ready lemon cream pie. Dressed in a chef's hat and apron, Efron walked around a table, adding one artificial ingredient after another to a bowl. The final product, of course, bore no resemblance to a pie, and contained no eggs and no lemon.

The segment's producers had deliberately kept the manufacturer's name— Morton—in the skit; a week later, the producers received a "cease and desist" order from attorneys representing Morton (a subdivision of Continental bakeries, which was a subdivision of International Telephone and Telegraph, a powerful corporate ally of the Nixon administration). The producers verified the facts on the segment, and eventually ran it again. According to Efron, the president of Morton was dismissed not long after, and the company altered the pie recipe, substituting artificial flavoring with concentrated lemon juice.[56] (As we shall see in the next chapter, *The Great American Dream Machine*, which went off the air in 1972, also created more conventional political problems.)

In other cases, NET's anti-commercial impetus had more constructive impact. In the years between 1964—when the Surgeon General officially declared tobacco to be a health hazard—and 1971, when tobacco advertising was banned from television and radio, the commercial networks were hampered from doing critical stories on tobacco's health effects. This gap presented NET with an ideal opportunity, which it exploited in April 1967 with a documentary called *The Smoking Spiral*, which a critic labeled "the most stunning telementary yet on the health hazards of cigaret smoking." The film's most gripping section dealt with two men with advanced smoking-related disease (one with chronic bronchitis, one with emphysema). "If their disability and suffering as depicted by NET's cameras do not scare cig addicts," said the critic, "nothing will."[57] The program featured what was almost certainly the deepest discussion American audiences had ever seen about banning cigarette advertising from television's airwaves. Senator Robert Kennedy, pointing out that government health efforts were outspent 100-to-1 by cigarette advertisers, said in *The Smoking Spiral* that the FCC should make a "serious determination . . . whether cigarette advertising of any kind should appear on television." Numerous critics recognized that this documentary was unique; in the words of one, it "could tread where cigarette advertising–hungry commercial television wouldn't dare to go so forcefully."

Yet such controversy was bound to raise hackles. And while congressmen and corporate lawyers were occasionally eager to play the role of watchdog, the true power to keep NET programming off the air was in the hands of local station managers. Time after time, NET's more challenging material—from dramas to documentaries—dropped off the dial in one or more communities. Sometimes these omissions were innocent, with long-distance lines becoming unavailable at the last minute, or some local production preempting a broadcast, but quite often they were rejected for alleged obscenity or violations of taste or politics. An *NET Festival* profile of singer Nina Simone, for example, did not run on Michigan's WUCM because, as the station manager reported, "a certain segment would be offensive to our viewing audience." In a six-month period between 1968 and 1969, KETS in Little Rock, Arkansas, rejected more than 20 percent of the NET schedule, from all episodes of *Black Journal* to a production of Athol Fugard's *The Blood Knot* and most episodes of *NET Playhouse*. When KVLX declined to show the "Fidel" episode of *NET Journal*, it labeled the film "sugar-coated communism." Similarly, in 1967 the State Cabinet of Florida criticized its state's educational stations for broadcasting NET's "socialistic programs."

The charge that NET programming was too progressive and too opinionated came as often from NET affiliate stations as from anyone else, and it irked NET president John White. Speaking to NET affiliates in 1968—just days after the assassination of Martin Luther King, Jr.—White was defiant against his colleague-critics. "I remember occasions when a few of you said to us, in effect: 'You are programming too much on the issue of Vietnam, too much on civil rights and the problems of the cities. You are overbalanced in these areas, and besides the public is weary of hearing about these issues. Most people wish they would go away. There are other important things to treat.' Well, these issues have not gone away. It is crystal clear that these were and are the issues that require our deepest attention. In retrospect, we were underbalanced; we should have done more."[58] The station managers, however, tended to agree more with PBL's Barrett, and continued to use their academic and community standing as a way to enforce the standards of the gentleman's living room.

Thus, the political reputation of public television—as left-dominated, elitist, minority-radical—which would, by the mid-1990s, threaten its existence, was not only established before the Public Broadcasting Service was born but largely originated within the very community of educational broadcasters. Several television critics have portrayed the parochialism of university and educational broadcasters as the chief obstacles preventing NET (and later PBS) from establishing an effective network with national appeal. Journalist and television historian Les Brown has stated the stations' objections succinctly: "As the principal source of national programming, NET was too progressive, too given to muckraking, and too willing to create controversy for the comfort of most station operators. . . . They knew this: that the similarity between an expose and a Chamber of Commerce documentary is that neither would get a large audience, but the difference was that the expose would bring trouble and the other would win praise."[59]

It is irrefutable that local stations resisted and sometimes impeded the development of a nationwide network, but they were not always trying to protect segregation or push petty agendas. A full decade before Mobil Oil began dropping its name into *Masterpiece Theatre*, the local stations were raising polite objections to the use of educational airwaves for marketing purposes. In their 1960 annual meeting, the NETRC affiliates declared that "the Center should avoid underwriters who have direct interest in selling to an age group; for example, Coca Cola would be inappropriate for a teen-age or children's series." The affiliates unanimously voted to "convey to the Center the general dissatisfaction with apparent overt advertising connections, and suggest discreet modifications more in line with the educational atmosphere. The consensus was that there should be no suggestion [to the underwriter] that a program will have advertising value.[60] As educational television expanded beyond a strictly instructional role and got itself ready for prime time, such pledges of noncommercial purity would become impossible to meet.

3

INTERFERENCE PATTERNS

One cannot understand the Nixon administration's attempts to decimate public broadcasting without recalling that his was a White House obsessed with television. Popular history holds that a television debate cost Nixon the 1960 presidential election against John Kennedy; conversely, the Nixon White House believed that media coaching from onetime *Mike Douglas Show* producer Roger Ailes was decisive in Nixon's 1968 victory.[1] For Nixon, television was not only an intrinsically political medium—its every emission had potential campaign implications (witness, for example, Nixon's choice to head the Federal Communications Commission: Dean Burch, whose communications expertise derived from having run Barry Goldwater's 1964 presidential crusade and the Republican National Committee). Many memoranda and firsthand recollections reproduce the same scene: the President sitting alone, watching a news broadcast on television, and becoming so infuriated that he would pick up the phone and bark out orders to aides, believing that somehow he could change the image on the box to something more politically appealing.

At times the Nixon White House appeared more like a graduate seminar in media studies than the center of leadership in the free world; deputy assistant to the president Dwight Chapin once asked two aides to produce a "list of the top ten television shows, with a synopsis of each one, and how it fits in with social conditions of the country," with special emphasis on *All in the Family* and *Sanford and Son*. In the administration's early days, the White House press office produced daily and weekly accounts of how Nixon was faring on network news broadcasts, a naive approach that gave way over time to administration attacks on "nattering nabobs," angry phone calls to network brass, and furtive discussions about network antitrust suits.

As vicious as the Nixon-era attacks on public broadcasting were, public broadcasting was not the worst victim among electronic media of administration abuse; that distinction went to CBS. In 1972, CBS was responsible for making Watergate leap from a third-rate print story to TV, broadcasting a 14-

minute Watergate story in October 1972. After a lengthy, vituperative phone call from White House aide Charles Colson, CBS president William Paley urged his staff not to air a scheduled follow-up. The segment did run, but was cut nearly in half. Not long after the '72 campaign was over, Colson called CBS News president Frank Stanton, and vowed that because the network "didn't play ball" during Nixon's first term, the White House would now "bring you to your knees in Wall Street and on Madison Avenue." Colson threatened to take away CBS's five owned-and-operated stations, and vowed: "We'll break your network."[2]

It did not get quite that bad with public broadcasting.[3] The government connection to public broadcasting allowed Nixon to exercise more influence over the system than he could over commercial networks, but it also meant that there were times when he and his White House had to pretend to get along with it. The administration's policy toward public broadcasting, like so many of its policies, vacillated between hypocrisy and duplicity, sometimes spilling over into the Orwellian. Clay Whitehead, the White House's point man in the battle against public broadcasting (and one of the few in Nixon's crew who displayed a sense of humor), once made a revealing, self-mocking reference to Orwell, telling an audience of broadcasters: "I do not know if anyone has pointed out yet that the fiftieth anniversary of the Communications Act of 1934 is 1984."

Over the course of its multiyear harassment of the public broadcasting community, the administration articulated several incisive criticisms, expertly exploiting tensions already straining the system. How can a government-funded broadcasting outfit cover public affairs and controversies without raising prickly questions of censorship, fairness, and favoritism? Can a public programming "network" exist without trampling on the rights and needs of its community affiliates? Why should taxpayers be asked to pay for programming that a segment of the population finds inappropriate, or even offensive?

For all this intellectual candlepower, however, the historical record is clear that the administration's motivation for clamping down on public broadcasting was strictly political. Starting with Nixon's first year in office, the administration's goal was to eliminate, manipulate, or isolate elements within public broadcasting that it perceived as liberal or—a favorite in-phrase—"antiadministration." No matter how fine-tuned the arguments emanating from Whitehead's Office of Telecommunications Policy—OTP, the control center of the war against public broadcasting—they were always in service of base political goals, i.e., protecting the administration's political positions or punishing its perceived enemies.

For a time, the Nixon administration was able to coast on initial friendly-seeming gestures toward public broadcasting. The Johnson-appointed CPB had barely begun operations when Nixon took over in 1969, and the always image-sensitive White House viewed public broadcasting as, potentially, public relations. In a typically optimistic moment in May 1969—and the paper trail is sprinkled with such gems—Whitehead wrote to a presidential assistant that "I think it is desirable for the President to be associated in an affirmative way with public broadcasting."[4] The Nixon White House also won points from public broadcasters by agreeing to tackle the question of long-term financing (although, like the Johnson administration, it could not tolerate the proposed BBC-style excise tax on radio and television sets).

This seeming forwardthinking was at odds with Nixon's desire, clear from the very beginning, to put a conservative political spin on the public broadcasting structure. His first appointment to the CPB, just a few weeks after he was inaugurated, was Albert L. Cole, the business whiz behind the patriotic *Reader's Digest*. This was payback for a longstanding political debt: the kinship between Nixon and *Reader's Digest* went back as far as Nixon's undergraduate days at Whittier College in the 1930s, when he won the *Digest*-sponsored Southern California Extemporaneous Speaking Contest.[5] More significantly, in 1964 and 1965, Nixon used *Reader's Digest* to launch broadside attacks on the Johnson policy in Vietnam, and in 1968, Cole's *Digest* sponsored candidate Nixon's travels abroad and gave him liberal use of the company plane for speaking engagements and political rallies.

Cole was Nixon's beachfront into the CPB board of directors, from which he soon tried to launch a full-scale assault. In October 1969, Nixon and Cole dined at the home of Hobe Lewis, then the editor of *Reader's Digest*. These men were part of a tight-knit alliance of politics and money, with a curious connection to public broadcasting: Cole and Lewis would later turn out to be the funnel through which soybean magnate Dwayne Andreas made a $100,000 cash contribution to Nixon's reelection campaign, some of which helped fund the Watergate burglars; Andreas's company, Archer Daniels Midland, would become the country's leading agribusiness and, during the mid-1990s, the chief underwriter of PBS's *MacNeil/Lehrer NewsHour*.

Cole discussed with the President their plans for public broadcasting, which led to a White House meeting between the two and CPB chairman Pace. At that meeting, Cole and Nixon identified what would become a continuing thorn in the side for the administration: the Ford Foundation's role in public broadcasting. As noted in the previous chapter, the Republican right's friskier elements during the 1950s denounced the Ford Foundation's globalism and its forays into broadcasting as part of a grand pinko scheme; Nixon, who cut his national political teeth in the same circles, sought to continue the fight. Cole pointed out to the President and Pace that National Educational Television (NET) was funded largely by the Foundation. According to a staff memo, Cole felt this arrangement "was inappropriate in that 'He who pays the piper calls the tune.' The President entirely agreed and said that he was very anxious this not be the case."[6]

This fueled a campaign already under way in the White House to reduce or eliminate the influence of Ford Foundation money and ideas on public broadcasting (a direction that Ford's McGeorge Bundy had announced he wanted to head in, as the CPB became the system's primary funder.) The anti-Ford tack led to a strategic paradox: reducing the only public broadcastinging money the administration directly controlled—federal funding—threatened to increase the power of Ford-sponsored NET, which would rush to fill the vacuum. As an illustration of how the White House could argue itself in circles, as late as 1971 the administration considered raising CPB's budget, so long as it could be done in a manner that "reduces its influence over social thought."[7] White House functionaries were well aware of their dilemma, although they were out of office before they could resolve it. One helpful proposal offered by presidential assistant Peter Flanigan was to "support 'tax reforms' which will put the foundations out of business."[8]

The administration encountered other hurdles as well; it turned out that NET and Ford programming were not the only places in public broadcasting where enemies lurked. Suspect programs were everywhere, filled with what Whitehead labeled "liberal emphasis" and "antiadministration content." Direct CPB grants to stations, allowing them to produce programs that would compete with NET, were preferable, but could not be guaranteed to toe the politically correct line. As Whitehead laid out in an October 1969 memo:

> From the standpoint of the President's objectives, the grants to individual stations cut both ways: the people who run the educational and public television stations around the country tend to be relatively liberal, but the geographical diversification probably would promote an overall less liberal emphasis than the New York City centralized NET. Funding a separate production unit to "compete" with NET would not be a complete bed of roses either, since the liberal bent of people in the performing arts is well known. However, we could presumably have a hand in picking the head of such a major new organization if it were funded by the Corporation.[9]

Herein was the germ of the administration's strategy for bringing the system under political control. First, it would emphasize "localism," encouraging non-commercial stations to resist centralized, and putatively liberal, TV fare. At the same time, it would try to use the CPB to control programming. To do that, the administration had to have a compliant board, which meant, as Charles Colson put it, that the two men atop the CPB board, John Macy and Frank Pace, "must be removed."[10]

ANTIADMINISTRATION?

It is fully consistent for Nixon to have been convinced that public television was ripping his administration apart because it was populated with liberals. This is the President, after all, who felt that FBI chief J. Edgar Hoover, the architect of federal anticommunism, was too liberal to accept the administration's plans to infiltrate left-wing groups such as the Black Panthers and Weathermen, and who tried to circumvent the CIA because he believed it was staffed "by Ivy League liberals who . . . had always opposed him politically."[11] Furthermore, as historians have amply documented, the Nixon administration believed that the vast major ity of the press corps was filled with liberal adversaries. Nixon speechwriter William Safire claimed: "[Nixon] was saying exactly what he meant: 'The press is the *enemy*,' to be hated and beaten."[12]

But when wading through mucky White House paranoia about PBS's bias, it is worth stepping back to recall what public broadcasting actually looked like at the time. Most importantly, the system could not honestly claim to have a nationwide reach. As of December 1971—when the Nixon White House attack on public broadcasting was in full swing—tens of millions of Americans could not tune in to a single PBS program. At that point, 86 of the nation's largest 198 markets (43 percent) had no public TV stations.[13] The relative impotence of the public television "system" was amplified by the fact that, at any given moment, it was exceedingly rare for more than 2 percent of American households to have their dial tuned to a PBS or educational channel. (As of the mid-1990s, PBS was on average pulling in about the same percentage of viewers.)

What was that small audience watching? As the 1970s began, the administration's dreaded "fourth network" was producing, at most, about 10 hours of original programming a week (compared to hundreds of hours a week by the commercial networks). The vast majority of airtime on all the noncommercial stations during this early era was still devoted to children's and instructional programming, shown in perpetual reruns for maximum educational effect. A survey conducted in March 1970 found that in a sample week nationwide, more than two-thirds of public television broadcasts fell into the categories of "children's" (31.2 percent), "cultural" (16.8 percent), "entertainment" (10.4 percent), and "skills" (9.5 percent) programming. News, analysis, and public affairs together accounted for just 28 percent of airtime—and that figure included local public affairs programming, which presumably had the administration's blessing.[14]

The 28 percent of airtime for news and public affairs no doubt seemed high to Nixon's staffers, since the comparable figure for commercial networks in prime time was about 2 percent.[15] (By the mid-'70s, thanks to Nixon's intimidation, the proportion of the PBS schedule devoted to news and public affairs had been more than halved.) But it is impossible to overstate the degree to which public television's schedule, in the early '70s, differed from the rigidity of network broadcasting. Approximately 80 percent of the funds of local stations came from nonfederal sources, and were spent in an equally decentralized manner: what you saw on PBS depended mightily on where you were. Nixon's henchmen reacted to what they viewed on Washington, D.C.'s WETA, which has long been comparatively top-heavy with public affairs material. But most Americans tuned in to a menu of programming so regionally focused that it should have made White House advocates of PBS localism stand up and salute.

One way we know exactly what aired on PBS during the early Nixon years is that Nixon assistant Flanigan requested that CPB officials keep him "personally informed of programs of particular interest on a regular basis"—and some of those briefings survive. The first such cheery memorandum, from November 1969,[16] gave Flanigan a program guide, alerting him to potentially controversial specials on marijuana and police reform scheduled to appear on the PBS program *The Advocates*.

But for purposes of discerning a PBS "bias" one might just as well have focused on another program described in Flanigan's heads-up guide, one that ran on the South Carolina Educational Television Network (an early public broadcasting entity headed by Henry Cauthen, who would later chair the CPB). Titled *Job Man Caravan*, the program was an 18-episode series in which a "mobile job unit" rumbled across South Carolina to tell the locals about available jobs and how to get and keep them. At each stop, the employment listings were read by female college student volunteers, dubbed "The Jobettes."

Far from a medium devoted to ripping apart Richard Nixon, public television was turning inward and apolitical, like much of '70s American culture. Between 1972 and 1973, the most-requested program from the Public Television Library was *Hathayoga*, a 60-part series of various yoga exercises by a curvaceous woman named Kathleen Hitchcock, produced by WMVS of Milwaukee. Viewers elsewhere might have tuned in to a half-hour program called *I'll Get There as Soon As I Can*, described in PBS literature as "a humorous documentary on that special relationship between modern man and his plumber. The entanglements binding them together are examined, spoofed, and laid to rest." This film came courtesy of foundation support—not Ford, but the Nixon-friendly Reader's Digest Foundation. Indeed, the administration's focus on Ford programming obscured the fact that, overall, the NET influence was waning, and being usurped by that of PBS. In 1971, *Broadcasting* magazine called NET "the displaced king; once the pre-eminent leader in providing national programs for educational television and still the principal source of prime-time evening programming, it is no longer the heart of the national system."[17]

The Nixon critique was not wholly inconsistent with reality. There was some programming on public television in the early '70s that declared itself left-wing, and it was often made possible by the Ford Foundation. As noted in chapter 2, from 1969 to 1971, a black New York–based broadcaster named Ellis Haizlip hosted a weekly public television program called *Soul!* that wove political commentary into a black-themed variety show. In one 1971 episode, Haizlip interviewed Kathleen Cleaver; she was the wife of Eldridge Cleaver, the infamous author of *Soul on Ice* who was, at the time of the broadcast, living outside the United States to avoid prosecution. Haizlip introduced Cleaver as "a sister who is deeply involved in what I should call right-on revolutionary business . . . a member of the Revolutionary Peoples' Communications Network."[18] Cleaver, sporting a huge Afro haircut and smoking a cigarette, explained how she had evolved out of the international section of the Black Panther Party, how her daughter had been born in North Korea, and how the Nixon visit to China had confounded some of her comrades, causing "considerable consternation among all the forces still engaged in struggle."

While by no means omnipresent, such unabashedly radical rhetoric did appear on public television in its early days. Many Americans—the silent majority who weren't watching these programs when they aired—would probably have been outraged by these sentiments. Had the Nixon White House publicized Cleaver-type sentiments as an example of PBS's socialist tendency, it might have gained a significant political lever. It speaks, however, to the administration's actual disengagement from what was shown on public television that its attacks almost never referred to such ripe rhetorical flourishes as Cleaver's. Since the White House was certainly not reluctant to point out public TV's transgressions, one can only conclude that no one there was watching these programs.

Another factor left out of the White House's measurement of "bias" is the actions taken by public television managers not to broadcast certain material. The constellation of educational stations had a multiyear history of refusing to show material perceived as obscene, controversial, or "socialistic." When this ad hoc redaction continued into the Nixon era, it tended to mirror what the White House would want. The best example was the widespread cancellation of *Who*

Invited US?, a NET-funded documentary on American foreign policy produced by Al Levin. The film argued that "often economic self-interest is the controlling imperative in American foreign policy"; its examples included quotations from President Eisenhower that U.S. involvement in Vietnam was related to U.S. interest in expanding trade between Japan and southeast Asia, and it showed U.S. Green Berets training Latin American military leaders who protected North American coffee and agricultural companies. Journalist Geoffrey Cowan —who by the end of the decade would end up on the CPB board—wrote: "Some of the documentary was very tough. . . . Yet the film almost ended on a note of optimism, with President Nixon promising a re-evaluation of America's role abroad."[19]

Such subtleties were not enough: station managers in St. Louis; Norfolk, Virginia; and Austin, Texas, refused to show the film for its scheduled early 1970 release, and when Washington, D.C.'s WETA pulled it, the very people for whom *Who Invited US?* was intended were spared having to witness it.[20] William McCarter, WETA's station manager, called the documentary "distorted" and said that it was "actually an individual's statement under the guise of a station program presentation." Cowan noted that the WETA board was stuffed with corporate chairmen who had interests abroad, and that the board's chairman was the hawkish Max Kampelman, a foreign policy intellectual whose think tank had for years been supported by the CIA. Alas, the White House did not give public television much credit for such prudent tempering of hot material.

Nixon's assessment of public television's "bias" is also contradicted by the fact that his own Cabinet members and representatives appeared constantly on PBS programs. In a three-week period in late 1969, Attorney General John Mitchell, Secretary of State Bill Rogers, and Nixon aide Daniel Patrick Moynihan were all interviewed at length on a regular NET series called *The President's Men*. During the same time frame, a massive special PBS program was given over to a White House–sponsored conference on food, nutrition, and health. Through this program, public broadcasting provided the Nixon administration with a tremendous potential public relations coup, the "first national experiment in the use of television as a medium for two-way communication between the citizen and his government on a vital public policy issue."[21] In addition to two hours of prime-time network exposure, the food and health conference generated more than 48 hours of local station air time, and 15 hours of public and commercial radio. (Typically, even such unprecedented access to the airwaves did not pass the White House test for sanitized public relations; the president never saw a tape of these proceedings as promised because commentary from participants made the tape "not appropriate for viewing by the President.")[22]

Moynihan also explained the administration's welfare reform proposals on William F. Buckley, Jr.'s public television program *Firing Line* in October 1969; other Nixonites who appeared on *Firing Line* during Nixon's first year included Patrick Buchanan, Raymond Price, Donald Rumsfeld, and Clare Booth Luce.[23] While of course not all *Firing Line* programs could be expected to support every Nixon policy, public television support for the administration could be found even in unexpected places. Buckley and John Kenneth Galbraith, for example, recorded a Cambridge Union debate on the topic "Resolved: the market is a snare and a delusion," that first aired on PBS in November 1970. Galbraith— hardly a Nixon fan—nonetheless baited his opponent by calling Nixon's guaranteed minimum income "an excellent idea," and praising the President for nationalizing passenger rail transport.[24]

There were also instances when the White House was able to blunt criticism on PBS more indirectly. In 1971, when the administration began a stepped-up bombing campaign in North Vietnam, PBS's public affairs unit tried to pull together an extensive program about the goals and conduct of the war. "We were able to line up anti-administration spokesmen," said a PBS official later, "but the Administration would not provide us with a spokesman for their viewpoint. The program was killed."[25] There was even material appearing exclusively on PBS that the White House secretly liked; as late as 1972, after months of flaming rhetoric about PBS's anti-Nixon bias, an extensive internal White House analysis of a PBS special program called *Conservatives & 1972* concluded that "the show came off better for [Nixon] than one expected in advance."[26] While there were indeed "liberals" in public broadcasting who criticized the administration, the charge of PBS bias against the Nixon White House was spurious. As PBS veteran Robert MacNeil said in a 1973 speech: "Bias in their minds is any attitude which does not indicate permanent genuflection before the wisdom and purity of Richard Milhous Nixon." Despite public pronouncements, what Nixon's men generally sought was not to balance out the views of critics but to silence them.

"OBVIOUS LIBERAL BIAS"

Through early 1970, the Nixon White House believed it had struck a rough deal with the CPB. In return for phasing out NET's influence and minimizing airtime devoted to reporting and discussing politics, the administration made vague promises that it would boost the CPB's federal check. The loose agreement foundered, partly because the Bureau of the Budget—straining to pay for the massive commitment in Vietnam and trying to stem inflation—was not keen on spending more money for television. Principally, though, the problem was that PBS kept showing programs that sent the president and his staff into fits, even rage.

Despite public arguments about philosophical considerations, the historical record overwhelmingly shows that the White House war on public broadcasting stemmed from programming it disliked for political reasons. The chief hatchet man was usually Flanigan; this is how Flanigan instructed Whitehead to respond to an August 24, 1970, NET broadcast: "With regard to the question of the public hearing all points of view regarding Southeast Asia ... NET undertook to meet this responsibility by offering 12 Democrats and 2 Republicans, all doves, free time to reply to Nixon."[27] Flanigan was apparently unaware that NET's Washington bureau chief James Karayn had already publicly addressed the issue of the program's balance, telling the *Washington Post*: "NET has carried every speech and press conference by the President that dealt with Cambodia and Vietnam. Unlike the commercial networks, which have nightly news shows in which to air both sides, we do not. Therefore, we felt the senators were entitled to a forum in which to air their views." Contrary to Flanigan's mention of "free time," the senators had paid for the broadcast expenses.

For Flanigan, however, this telecast demonstrated bias, and was therefore potential ammunition: "I would like a somewhat more detailed description of how this came about so that I could hit [CPB president] Macy and [Nixon CPB appointee] Cole hard again on the NET question. In addition, we can use this to get a real blast against the Corporation for Public Broadcasting in the Senate which will hasten CPB's schedule for cutting NET's water off."

One event that kicked the Nixon White House's anti-PBS campaign into full gear was the November 1970 broadcast of a documentary entitled *Banks and the Poor*. This one-hour film, a NET production, was a multi-pronged attack on the refusal of American banks to invest in poor communities or lend to poor citizens. It began with a dissection of the Rockefeller family-dominated Chase Manhattan Bank's pledge to help Brooklyn's Bedford-Stuyvesant section. David Rockefeller was subjected to an on-camera grilling (a bold move for the producers, given that Rockefeller had played a crucial role in the 1961–62 establishment of New York's WNDT, PBS's flagship station). Despite promises that up to $100 million in loans would flow to revitalize this poor, largely black neighborhood, the documentary claimed that only $8 million had been committed, of which a mere $700,000 was Chase Manhattan's. One problem, according to the film, was that 80 percent of Bed-Stuy residents were ineligible for standard housing loans because they lived in dwellings housing four or more families. An attorney with the National Association for the Advancement of Colored People Legal Defense and Education Fund walked viewers through the streets of Bed-Stuy, slamming the banks' cynical promises as "another example of that vicious murder game perpetrated by the rich and the powerful on the poor and the helpless."[28]

From there *Banks and the Poor* took on the home financiers, sampling industry ads (such as the ubiquitous Beneficial "toot, toot" spots) that made credit look easy to obtain. A hidden camera followed a low-wage—$110 a week plus over-time—earner into a Beneficial office, which offered to loan him $800, on a 36-month payback schedule, for a total of $1,152—or a hefty 25.5 percent interest rate. The documentary pointed out that the same banks that had refused to loan this man money at a less usurious rate were ultimately the owners of, or financial sources for, companies such as Beneficial. The film then segued to a discussion of links between banking interests and U.S. congressmen, closing with an infamous segment where the names of nearly 100 congressmen and senators with banking ties scrolled up the screen, in front of a shot of the Jefferson Memorial, with "The Battle Hymn of the Republic" playing in the background.

This NET documentary, produced by Morton Silverstein, is frequently cited[29] as one that the administration perceived as an attack. While there may have been good reasons why Nixon's people didn't like it, it never—with the exception of Treasury Secretary David Kennedy, a 30-second mention—discussed the Nixon administration. *Banks and the Poor* had inflammatory moments and used occasional heavy-handed, agitprop techniques, but it was for the most part sober, giving all major targets ample opportunity for response. Oddly, as an antibank, anti-Rockefeller tract, it even tapped a strain of the bitter populism that Nixon was known for. In addition, the most prominent on-camera presence was a U.S. Congressman, and almost all its material came from official or established sources, such as the New York City Office of Consumer Affairs. (The film's pro-ducers at NET felt it should be nominated for an Emmy Award, but PBS, stung by the controversy, vetoed it.)[30]

To seek the seeds of Nixon's opposition in the film itself, however, is to over-analyze; the administration's battle against *Banks and the Poor* began before anyone in the White House had seen it. A *Washington Post* story announcing the documen-tary's existence was enough to set Peter Flanigan off. The *Post* article reported that the Texas Bankers Association had sent an advance protest letter to that state's five educational television stations, suggesting that the documentary pre-sented a biased view of banking in that state. While three stations said they planned to air the program as scheduled, San Antonio's KLNR postponed it, and Lubbock's KTXT canceled the broadcast.[31] For whatever reason, bankers seem to have had an easy time seeing the film in advance of its general screening. In Lubbock, local bankers were invited to watch a closed-circuit feed. In addition, although NET denied a request from the American Bankers Association to screen the film in advance, three ABA officials saw *Banks and the Poor* at "a semi-private preview" offered by the Corporation for Public Broadcasting. The *Post* claimed that "CPB officials were unclear about who had invited [the bankers] or why." The paper overlooked the fact that Michael A. Gammino, Jr., a CPB board member at the time, was president and chairman of the board of the Columbus National Bank of Rhode Island, and served on several committees of the ABA.[32] Gammino was also, not incidentally, among those listed in the documentary's banker hall of shame.

Bankers' preview privileges, however, were not Flanigan's concern. He sent a copy of the article to Cole, along with a terse letter calling the film "another example of NET activity that is clearly inappropriate for a government supported organization. Would you do me the favor of letting me know the extent to which NET has been supported by CPB in 1970 and the amount of the budgeted support for 1971." Flanigan was clearly sensitive to perceptions of White House interference, so he asked Cole to leave out the probe's high-level origin: "I am directing this inquiry to you in that I think it comes better from you to the board and the management of the Corporation than from the White House. Therefore, I'd appreciate you treating this inquiry in that light."[33]

Not long thereafter, the executives at PBS spontaneously decided that they needed a written set of journalistic standards. A PBS board member, Robert F. Schenkkan, the president and general manager of KLRN in Austin, Texas, was assigned the task. His list prohibited the use of secondary sources, called on producers to present the credentials and sources of all researchers, and gave PBS the right to screen and ultimately reject all programs. NET president James Day said at the time: "All the things that he was trying to prevent were things that had happened in the past. You could go through and write the names of the shows alongside. It wasn't the set of positive, ringing phrases that a set of standards should be. It was a lot of 'Thou shalt nots' and things that NET had done in the past, for the most part."[34] Day denounced the proposed standards as "flatulent" and "amateurish," and they were never formally offered for member stations' consideration. (By early 1973, however, Schenkkan would become chairman of the board of PBS.)

The administration's smoldering animus against public television was fanned into open flame when PBS formed the National Public Affairs Center for Television, which went by the awkward acronym NPACT. NPACT's function was to coordinate public television's already existing public affairs programs (such as *Washington Week in Review*), and expand into new areas, notably a weekly program on the 1972 presidential race. (In its later years, NPACT also dipped into documentaries, on subjects ranging from the parole system to male menopause; NPACT was eventually folded into Washington, D.C.'s WETA.) The firestorm that NPACT would cause was ironic, given that it was designed to give PBS's public affairs programming a professional gloss and steer PBS away from NET's feisty, subjective and risky documentaries.[35] Furthermore, the White House was invited to submit names for NPACT's board of directors. That degree of control was not enough. In September 1971, NPACT announced that it had hired former NBC reporters Robert MacNeil and Sander Vanocur to co-anchor its weekly news broadcasts beginning in 1972. Nixon exploded. The appointment "greatly disturbed the president, who considered this the last straw," according to aide Jon Huntsman.[36] The White House believed that these men were hopelessly biased against Nixon and against U.S. involvement in Vietnam and Cambodia, and assembled a list of supposed excesses. Actually, there is no record that the White House ever found any particular MacNeil utterance objectionable; the two administration charges of Vanocur's "bias" involved a claim that the Nixon government had used classification to hide "every kind of sin, arrogance and obscenity—and there is none greater than Vietnam," and an assertion that expanding the war into Laos and Cambodia was "stupidity."

One historian notes that Nixon's animosity toward Vanocur may have stemmed from an embarrassing question Vanocur asked Nixon during the infamous 1960 televised debate with John Kennedy.[37] Regardless, it was clear that, for the administration, trying to cooperate with public broadcasting officials was no longer enough: "It was requested that all funds for Public Broadcasting be cut immediately. You should work this out so that the House Appropriations Committee gets the word."[38] Nixon's watchmen got PBS president John Macy to divulge the annual salaries being paid to Vanocur and MacNeil ($85,000 and $65,000, respectively), which the White House labeled "a striking example of the abuse and misuse of government funds going to public television"; CPB president Pace was accused of "mismanagement" for hiring them.[39] As Whitehead recalled at the time: "After Vanocur and MacNeil were announced in late September we planted with the trade press the idea that their obvious liberal bias would reflect adversely on public television. We encouraged other trade journals and the general press to focus attention on the Vanocur appointment. . . . We then began to encourage speculation about Vanocur's and MacNeil's salaries."[40] In one example, the *Washington Daily News* published an editorial cartoon depicting a wildly suited man in front of a public television camera pitching bills out of a bag marked "Property of U.S. Treasury" into a bag held by Vanocur and bank guards, with the caption: "Who Says We Can't Compete With The Commercial Network Giveaways?" Subsequent news accounts also divulged Bill Moyers's $75,000 salary from NET, and the curious arrangement by which William F. Buckley's *National Review* magazine received more than $11,000 for every episode of *Firing Line*.[41] Even congressmen sympathetic to public television could not defend these sums, and the House Commerce Committee announced it would investigate.[42]

NPACT was blindsided. The assault against Vanocur and MacNeil began months before their weekly campaign-year program, *A Public Affair/Election '72*, had its first broadcast. Preoccupied with setting up operations, and trying to respond to administration attacks, NPACT principals were thoroughly unprepared to launch a public relations salvo as well. Not for lack of argument: although Vanocur's judgments about the "stupidity" of Nixon's extending the Vietnam conflict into Laos and Cambodia could indicate a bias, it is worth noting that none of the comments cited by the White House came from Vanocur's professional reporting; they were made in interviews where his opinion was solicited. Furthermore, news organizations are rarely swayed by the opinions of one or two anchors, and neither Vanocur nor MacNeil was hired to dictate NPACT programming. But there were legitimate issues at stake, and the public could hardly be expected to accept the seemingly inflated salaries without some explanation. In most instances, public TV officials ducked behind privacy and confidentiality agreements—a legally defensible strategy, but not one designed to win the system many friends. In the absence of any NPACT spirited public self-defense, the covert White House campaign was a reasonably effective diversion: instead of a discussion about PBS's editorial freedom to express antiwar sentiment now deeply felt in American society, a good portion of public debate centered on how much taxpayer money should line the pockets of television news anchors. (By February 1972, the CPB board, under considerable White House pressure, capped all public broadcasting salaries at $36,000 a year.)

Almost simultaneously, the federal government undertook its earliest direct attempt to remove damaging programming from public television. An eruption occurred in October 1971 over a segment of *The Great American Dream Machine* (*DADM*), NET's popular, innovative documentary and variety program that ran for two seasons in 1971 and 1972. While *GADM* was known primarily for humor segments (featuring then unknowns such as Chevy Chase and Linda Lavin) and documentary profiles on offbeat figures from Evil Knievel to Nina Simone, it also occasionally aired explicit political segments. A California-based reporter named Paul Jacobs, a self-described radical who had once run for office on a ticket with Eldridge Cleaver, had produced a story for *GADM* charging that the FBI and some local police authorities had tried to employ three young provocateurs to infiltrate left-wing groups and encourage them to commit murder, bombings, and arson.[43] Having gathered testimony from three such young men, Jacobs's *GADM* segment charged: "It seems clear now that at least some of the violence blamed on the New Left movement was actually the work of police and FBI undercover agents."

Given what has been subsequently learned about the FBI's extensive COIN-TELPRO (a program of infiltration and provocation of left-wing groups) efforts, this charge is not surprising, and aspects of Jacobs' story were reported at the time in the *Seattle Post-Intelligencer, Tuscaloosa Times,* and, eventually, *The New York Times.* Nonetheless, this was explosive stuff, and *GADM* wanted to ensure that it met basic journalistic standards. Both Jacobs and *GADM* co-executive producer Alvin Perlmutter—an NET and PBS veteran who today produces *Adam Smith's Money World*—tried to elicit response from the FBI. On August 19, 1971, none other than J. Edgar Hoover himself wrote to Perlmutter, declaring: "[I]t will not be possible to offer any comments on the individuals you mentioned, nor will it be possible for me or any of my representatives to give an interview on this matter."[44] That seemed final enough, and the show was scheduled to air over PBS stations October 6. Five days before, NET's general counsel received five letters from FBI officials, including response from the three FBI agents who'd been accused in Jacobs's story, each of whom denied the allegations and called them "malicious" and "libelous."

As if the postal threats weren't enough, on the afternoon of October 4, two FBI agents arrived in the NET office, bearing copies of the letters. One of the FBI men was John Malone, assistant director of the FBI in charge of the New York office. According to one journalist's contemporary account: "Malone explained that the visit was not intended to intimidate NET, only to indicate Mr. Hoover's concern that the *Dream Machine* get its facts straight."[45] Perlmutter, in a later interview, recalled their mission as more direct: "They went to see [NET vice president] Bill Kobin. They tried to persuade him not to put it on the air."[46] It was not put on the air, at least not initially, although the FBI did not yank the segment—PBS did. Arguing that the charges made by Jacobs were weak and journalistically unsupported, PBS took the segment out of the regular schedule, the first such action in PBS's brief history.

The incident drove not one but several wedges into public broadcasting. NET resented what it saw as PBS's censorship; PBS resented what it saw as NET's irresponsibility and aloofness; CPB resented that it would have to pay the political price for a decision over which it had no meaningful influence. The *Dream Machine* incident was so fractious that PBS president Hartford Gunn warned a public broadcasting convention that the system's pendulum was at risk of swinging away from producer freedom toward editorial control centralized in the office of PBS.[47]

At the same convention, Whitehead decided to go public with the more high-minded criticisms of public broadcasting he had spent months preparing. In an

October speech at the National Association of Educational Broadcasters (NAEB) convention, Whitehead practically taunted his audience: "I honestly don't know what group I'm addressing. I don't know if it's really the 47th Annual Convention of the NAEB or the first annual meeting of PBS affiliates."[48] While today that remark would hardly raise an eyebrow, Whitehead was stirring a cauldron of jealousy, infighting, and paranoia by suggesting to these broadcasters that their traditional and proper role was being usurped. Knowing that local educational broadcasters had resented the $12 million the Ford Foundation had spent on the Public Broadcasting Laboratory, Whitehead accused Ford of since having bought "over $8 million worth of this kind of programming on your stations." Knowing there was regional tension between local advocates of educational programming and the largely East Coast–based advocates of a "fourth network," Whitehead taunted his listeners for programming "for the Cambridge audience that WGBH used to go after—for the upper-middle class whites who contribute to your stations when you offer Julia Child's cookbook and Kenneth Clark's 'Civilisation.'" Whitehead even managed to stoke resentment of public television's already evident Anglophilia, claiming he hoped that CPB would one day have enough money "to fund programs on America's civilization and the Adams family instead of the Churchill and Forsyte families."

Whitehead's approach was scattershot, and in many ways his analysis was wanting. What if providing national public affairs programming was precisely what local stations wanted from PBS, because they lacked the resources to do it themselves? In fact, a Member of Congress who surveyed public TV stations found that their first preference for what CPB should spend money and effort to produce was national public affairs programming.[49] Furthermore, Whitehead argued that decentralization of public broadcasting was absolutely necessary, while at the same time he sought a single body of accountability to prevent further episodes like the FBI segment on *GADM*. Whitehead's occasionally dubious reasoning did not prevent his speech from having its intended devastating effect: it received tremendous press attention, and set into motion a strategy so effective that its divisions outlasted the people who were supposed to conquer.

At approximately the same time, comedian Woody Allen was putting into motion what would become PBS's first deletion of an entire scheduled program, thereby providing the most absurd battle during the Nixon war against public broadcasting. During the fall and winter of 1971, between shooting his films *Play It Again Sam* and *Everything You Always Wanted to Know About Sex but Were Afraid to Ask*, the comedian wrote and filmed *Men of Crisis*, a satirical imitation of an old cinema newsreel.[50] The idea had come from Allen, and was presented to Jack Kuney, a producer at NET. A thinly veiled arrow at the administration, the 25-minute film used a primitive form of a technique Allen would later perfect with *Zelig*: Allen did impressions of diplomat "Harvey Wallinger" thatwere juxtaposed against stock footage from various points in Nixon's career (Louise Lasser, Allen's regular female costar from this period, also made a brief appearance). Supplementing the film were interviews with Allen discussing satire and comedy; the one-hour finished product was called *The Politics and Comedy of Woody Allen*. Its humor was never intended to be universal: in one sequence, the Wallinger character asked the president's wife for a date; in another, Lasser plays Wallinger's ex-girlfriend, who describes the relationship "as something less than the wonderful first experience every girlfriend should have." Allen himself avowed that some of the humor was in "bad taste." On the other hand, the humor was more prescient than anyone in public television could have known: late in the film, someone asks Wallinger where that attorney general is, and is told: "Mr. Mitchell is busy—he's wiretapping Mr. Nixon's phone at the moment."[51]

The one-hour film was scheduled to run on PBS stations on February 21, 1972. It was pulled, however, and replaced by a show called *Come to Florida Before It's Gone*, starring comedian Myron Handleman. It has never been demonstrated that the Nixon administration directly ordered the show to be pulled off the air. The arguments that PBS used to can it, however, echoed internal White House sentiments; among other reasons, PBS president Hartford Gunn said that as a "30-minute attack on a single candidate," *The Politics and Comedy of Woody Allen* would, in an election year, violate television's guaranteeing equal time for political candidates. But the assertion is false: the program was too early in the election year to trigger equal-time rules, which, in any event, don't apply to programs clearly labeled satire. (Ironically, because the replacement show also featured comedian/quixotic presidential candidate Pat Paulsen, PBS received several frantic requests from member stations about whether this program, too, would trigger equal-time provisions; their attorneys determined that it wouldn't.)[52] Without having to issue orders not to broadcast one of America's best-known comedians, the Nixon White House had successfully created a mechanism of self-censorship within PBS.

4

THE PERSONNEL IS POLITICAL

Against a backdrop of infighting and fear of censorship, the Nixon White House prepared itself for an election-year showdown, culminating in the first veto of funds for CPB. The traditional weapon of criticizing public television's content was insufficient to the task: the White House learned to flex its ultimate power by shuffling the appointments on the CPB board. It thereby thoroughly politicized a board theoretically designed to deflect political influence—establishing a temptation that no succeeding president has been able to resist.

Speaking on National Public Radio in January 1972, the administration's telecommunications chief Clay Whitehead fired an opening salvo, declaring: "There is a real question as to whether public television . . . should be carrying public affairs and news commentary . . . the commercial networks, by and large, do, I think, quite a good job in that area." This was an extraordinarily disingenuous statement; by the end of the year, Whitehead would begin a ferocious attack on commercial newscasts.[1] Whitehead also knew that networks had been slashing their budgets and the amount of time they devoted to public affairs.

But most importantly, Whitehead knew that the White House was using all available tools to enforce an outright ban on public affairs programs on PBS. In a December 17, 1971, letter—not made public for nearly a quarter-century[2]—Nixon assistant Peter Flanigan wrote to Congressman William Springer, noting that the CPB board of directors would be voting at its January 21, 1972, meeting to consider its future involvement in funding public affairs programming. The administration wanted to ensure that this vote would go the way it wanted. CPB director Frank Schooley, a Republican from Illinois who had roots in educational broadcasting and was one of LBJ's initial appointees, threatened to get in the way. "Frank Schooley would be opposed to any limitation on the areas of CPB programming," wrote Flanigan to the congressman, a key member of the Commerce Committee who was also supporting Schooley's reappointment to the CPB board. "I think it is important that you talk to him and convince him he should change his position and that all the limitations [on public affairs programming, including eliminating interviews and panel discussions] are in the best interest of public television as a whole. Needless to say, our involvement in this should be kept confidential."

In January 1972, Springer did as the administration instructed. He phoned Schooley and told him "there was not a chance to get any appropriation of any kind . . . passed in the Congress . . . if [CPB] were to continue news, news commentary and news analysis by professional broadcasters." The congressman let the White House know that Schooley "has the message and I am sure understands what needs to be done."[3] On top of this backchannel pressure, Whitehead also relayed the administration's instructions in meetings with three CPB directors. Accordingly, at its late January board meeting, CPB voted not to fund news, analysis, or political commentary. This meant dropping from the PBS schedule not only NPACT's dreaded Vanocur and MacNeil but also *Black Journal*, William Buckley's *Firing Line*, Bill Moyers's *This Week*, the one-hour debate program *The Advocates*, and Elizabeth Drew's *Thirty Minutes With*.

CPB's retreat may be justified as dire pragmatism; it is no exaggeration to say that the very existence of public broadcasting was at stake. At this early stage, federal funds represented 25 percent of public broadcasting's operating budget—including the entire $9 million expense for the system's interconnection—meaning that their abrupt removal would have created dark screens across America. At the same time, however, the capitulation to administration pressure to remove public affairs programs raises the question of what, precisely, was being "saved" if public affairs were eliminated from public broadcasting. In a March 1972 speech in San Francisco, PBS president Hartford Gunn, citing mandates from the FCC and Carnegie Commission, concluded: "We in public television do public affairs programming because we are required to, because we have been asked to, and because as responsible citizens and professionals we want to."[4]

During the spring of 1972, as the administration prepared a CPB authorization bill, it also used an astonishing variety of covert measures to tug public television to its desired direction. Whitehead and his assistant Brian Lamb—who would go on to found the cable company-funded C-SPAN—held several meetings to try to get a CPB board that would respond more directly to White House orders (see below). Whitehead's OTP also provided Congressman Robert Michel with a set of questions that he should submit to members of the National Association of Educational Broadcasters (NAEB) as a way of pressuring them to accept the administration's strictures. As the House began consideration of a CPB authorization bill in June 1972, the administration drafted a number of commentaries to be read on the House floor by sympathetic Republican Members of Congress (including Michel, Sam Devine, and Jim Harvey). Despite these behind-the-screen maneuvers, a bill authorizing $65 million for fiscal year '73 and $90 million for fiscal year '74 passed both Houses of Congress by wide margins; in the Senate the vote was an overwhelming 82 to 1 (oddly, the lone opposing vote was cast by New York's James Buckley, brother of *Firing Line's* William Buckley).

What followed was a remarkable episode of official dishonesty. On the morning of June 26, Whitehead met with public television advisor Norman Cousins and members of his National Programming Council and pledged that the administration would do nothing to block this legislation. On the very same day, Whitehead wrote a lengthy memorandum to the President recommending its veto. Furthermore, Nixon and Whitehead met that same day in the White House with about 30 executives from commercial broadcasting, in a session clearly intended to win over their political support.

Among the topics that raised commercial broadcasters' hackles was the question of the FTC's proposed "anticommercial" time, in which NET programming had played a supporting role (see chapter 2). Nixon reassured the group that he opposed such measures, and appealed directly to their beliefs about private enterprise being the key to preserving free speech. He then lobbed a salvo at the fledgling public broadcasting system, telling his private audience that he had

> ... traveled abroad extensively and seen what government-run or government-sponsored broadcasting is like; and in spite of the growing reports of many people that government-controlled broadcasting produces high-quality programming, no commercials, etc., [Nixon] stated that no one should be fooled—that that was a bunch of crap.[5]

Remarkably, Nixon used this warning against the evils of a government-controlled communications system as precursor for arguing that what American public broadcasting truly needed was the strictest control. In Whitehead's recollection, Nixon said: "You never know who's going to be sitting in [the president's] chair next ... some presidents might be inclined to use Federal support of public broadcasting to their advantage." To prevent such abuse, "public broadcasting, particularly the use of Federal funds, should be kept under the strictest of control and not allowed to become too large."[6] OTP counsel Henry Goldberg was not alone in recognizing the glowing contradiction in the executive branch seizing control of public television to preserve its independence; he compared it to the infamous Vietnam dictum: "We had to destroy the village in order to save it."[7]

Nixon's veto message couched his objections in slightly different terms, playing on the arguments Whitehead had made in his NAEB speech. Nixon declared himself convinced that "the problems posed by Government financing of a public broadcast system are much greater than originally thought." Typically, while engaging in elaborate maneuvers to manipulate a relatively tiny government agency, Nixon sought to create the opposite public image, i.e., that he was unconcerned with public broadcasting. The night after his veto of the public broadcasting bill, CBS anchor Walter Cronkite charged that Nixon was trying to force "a direct muzzle" on PBS—an entirely accurate charge. Nixon encouraged his press secretary Ron Ziegler to respond that this was "ridiculous. RN doesn't see or hear it. He only has time to follow networks."[8]

The veto threw the public broadcasting world into confusion and despair. As one participant recalled: "Most of us expected the president to yield to the clearly expressed will of Congress."[9] In a definitive history of this battle, two communications scholars concluded: "The veto . . . served two functions: First, it was a political bone to commercial broadcasters in a presidential election year; and second, it was designed to send a message to public television, viewed with suspicion and contempt by the White House as a liberal leftover from Johnson's 'Great Society.'"[10] That message was received: on the day of the veto, Frank Pace informed the White House that he would not run for re-election as CPB chairman. Within a few weeks, CPB president John Macy also resigned, taking several top aides with him.

At some point in the summer of 1972, CPB director Thomas Moore met White House staffer Flanigan at Bohemian Grove, the all-male California retreat spot of the American elite.[11] They discussed a plan whereby former Congressman Thomas Curtis (see next section) would be appointed to the CPB board and elected chairman. In a follow-up letter to Flanigan, Moore proposed shifts in policy committees and a new CPB staff who would create a program schedule and budget request for 1974–76, "without public affairs, but heavy with music, drama, education, and new forms." Thus, Nixon could appear to have "saved" public television, and during his second term would "be repeatedly identified with the cultural and educational programming. He can well shape the character of the public television in such a way that the public affairs issues will never come up again. Welcome to the New Public Television."[12]

"GET THE HELL OUT OF PROGRAMMING"

The CPB authorization veto of '72 forced the administration to accept that it would never be able to effectively control the content of public television through the budget process. At the same time, however, the White House's political machinations cleared away a bevy of executives, confirming the administration's suspicion that the CPB's 15-member board could be appointed according to the president's political needs, which they would in turn enforce on PBS.

It is impossible to know if Nixon's interference with the CPB was inevitable or unique: had Lyndon Johnson served a second term in office, he might well have used his CPB appointments to try to stifle public television programming that he did not like. That is speculation, but Nixon's record is real: he deliberately plotted to use CPB appointees as spies, to use them to topple CPB chairman Frank Pace, and to use them to quash public TV content he and his allies disliked. Even more than his veto, Nixon's perversion of the CPB board was his most damaging and most lasting contribution to public broadcasting.

The CPB board was designed as a political "heat shield," intended to deflect Congressional pressure away from the system. Its legislative mandate requires that it operate "in ways that will most effectively assure the maximum freedom [of public broadcast systems and stations] from interference with or control of program content or other activities." Beginning with the Cole appointment, the Nixon administration saw the CPB board instead as a whip with which to bring public broadcasting into line. "It is only through this Board that we have any control over public television," said a White House functionary in 1970, "and we regard it as extremely important to get effective representation of the Administration." Administration searches went out for "five tough appointees" who would support the administration.[13] As for sitting CPB members perceived as nonsupporters— such as broadcaster Saul Haas—John Ehrlichman suggested that Whitehead "get an FBI check" on Haas's "very questionable political background."[14]

Not all of Nixon's appointee, once on the CPB board, behaved as predictably as the administration might have liked. Dr. Gloria L. Anderson, a professor of chemistry from Atlanta and a black independent, supported the administration position on some issues, notably the refusal to give PBS control of the system's interconnection. "It was generally known that I was an objective thinker," Anderson recalled nearly a quarter-century after her CPB appointment, "that I would look at both sides and made a decision based on analysis."[15] Anderson would also, however, become something of a CPB firebrand, issuing blistering criticisms of public broadcasting's treatment of women and people of color.

Yet for the most part, the Nixon appointees were specifically selected for their willingness to do the administration's bidding. Knowledge of broadcasting issues and valuable perspective were secondary. Whitehead made every potential nominee promise that he or she wanted to eliminate public affairs from the public television schedule and would support only cultural and educational programming. In a typical 1970 memo on CPB nominee Thomas Moore, Whitehead noted that he had headed a division of ABC and was then working on material for the 1976 bicentennial celebration. The best criterion, however was that "Moore was a staunch Nixon campaigner, having traveled during much of the campaign with the party. . . . It's important that we get someone who knows the business from the production end as well as the operating end if we are to carry out the President's plan."[16] This sort of litmus test for nominees is generally frowned upon; Whitehead, up for an ambassadorship in the Ford administration, felt guilty enough to ask the Office of Government Ethics to clear him for his role in "reminding" CPB nominees of the necessity of carrying out "the President's plan."

The president's CPB veto created several openings for Nixon's "personnel is political" brigade. On the day of the veto itself, Frank Pace told the White House and others that he would not run for reelection as CPB chairman in the fall. A little more than a month later, John Macy—who called the veto "shameful" and told friends that Nixon's reelection would be "the death blow to public broadcasting as I have envisioned it"—resigned the CPB presidency.[17]

After initially trying to arrange for conservative author Irving Kristol to get the CPB chairmanship, the White House replaced Pace with Thomas Curtis, whom the CPB board immediately elected as its chairman. Curtis's appointment began what would become a long line of curious White House reasoning—over many administrations—that the best background for a public broadcasting position was a career in politics. Curtis had been an eight-year congressman from Missouri, and had narrowly lost a Senate race in 1968 against Tom Eagleton (who would end up, briefly, as the Democrats' 1972 vicepresidential nominee).

Alas, after just six months on the CPB board, Curtis resigned on April 14, 1973, charging that the White House was trying to strong-arm the board. "I had the clear understanding that the President wanted us to so set up the Corporation for Public Broadcasting that public broadcasting could not be made a propaganda arm for the Nixon Administration or for any succeeding administration. . . . When it became clear that the White House was not respecting the integrity of the board, then I couldn't defend the integrity of the board the way I had. . . . I felt I better resign."[18] Curtis demonstrated his disdain for such politicization by promptly launching a second campaign against Eagleton (but Curtis was clobbered in the '74 election).

Henry Loomis, the White House's chosen candidate for CPB president, had greater longevity. Along with James Killian before him and Richard Carlson following him, Loomis was one of many men to come to public broadcasting with a background in propaganda, having worked for the Voice of America and the USIA (Loomis also hired his Voice of America deputy, Jack O'Brien, as CPB's director of public information). On the day of his appointment in the fall of 1972, Loomis had never seen a public television broadcast, and asked of the CPB: "What the hell is it?"[19]

One strange but fitting interlude of Loomis's early tenure was the aborted effort to use public television's interconnection to broadcast a NASA mission. Loomis approached the stations with a proposal to provide nearly an entire day's worth of live footage from the Apollo 17 moon landing. Space missions were rare objects that still attracted great public wonder, and NASA, particularly in the wake of some near-disastrous missions, was looking for improved public relations. There might well have been significant viewer interest in televising such a launch, but both NASA and Loomis handled the matter in a ham-fisted way that angered the public television bureaucracy. The stations complained that they'd been given insufficient time to prepare, and neither Loomis nor CPB gave much thought to whether the proposed presentation would duplicate that offered by the commercial networks.

There was also genuine concern about the propriety of broadcasting what could easily be interpreted as NASA propaganda: NASA was to provide the technical commentators, the on-screen props, and, initially, the production funding. Even one of Loomis's own underlings, David Stewart, feared that "unless a [public television] agency had strong editorial control, the project could turn into a NASA puff piece."[20] Worst of all, Loomis had utterly bypassed PBS; the NASA-USIA-CPB connection made perfect sense from the standpoint of the military-communications complex, but it confirmed fears that Loomis was trying to use the interconnection to run a domestic propaganda network. He was rebuffed by many station managers, including the one at KETC, St. Louis's public television station, whose brusque telegram said: "Get the hell out of programming and stay out!"[21]

One Nixon nominee who didn't make it to the CPB board was a charismatic young Republican evangelist named Dr. William Banowsky, who was the president of Pepperdine University and, significantly, the Los Angeles county chairman of the Committee to Re-Elect the President (CREEP) and a state chairman of the RNC (Republican National Committee). The administration was keen to reward him with a CPB appointment until June 1974, when they learned that his security clearance had been held up "due to a current California State's Attorney investigation of him regarding possible use of public and foundation funds for his personal living."[22] By the time the investigation went away, the administration had already chosen another nominee and Nixon had resigned. The Nixon White House seems to have deepened Banowsky's taste for public broadcasting, however; he served on the board of directors of Los Angeles's KCET from 1972 to 1979.[23] Banowsky also served on the Oklahoma Educational Television Authority, and in 1984 was elected as a lay member to the PBS board. While he served on the PBS board, Banoswky was charged with federal securities fraud and was forced to pay more than $750,000 in fines and penalties.[24]

The administration's chaos-sowing eventually created open warfare between PBS and CPB, not only over administrative questions but over programming. Not shy about their tactics or their allies, Nixon's CPB men tried to foist conservative politics onto PBS programs. One example from 1972 concerned *Population Growth and the American Future*, a two-hour documentary produced by Boston's WGBH on the issue of overpopulation. The program could not have had a higher political pedigree, as it was partly based on the report of a presidential commission. But the population topic is a classic hot-button issue for a sector of the American right, who sought to keep the program off the air because it advocated widespread use of birth control. A month and a half before the scheduled airing, Jim Lehrer, who was then PBS's public affairs coordinator, informed the director of a Pennsylvania-based organization called U.S. Coalition for Life that the show would air. "I am well aware of the fact that our decision to go ahead with this program will probably not please you and your organization," wrote Lehrer, who nonetheless encouraged them to represent their opinions to the producer, and offered to meet with them after the broadcast.[25]

A month later, John Golden, CPB's acting vice president, wrote to Lehrer, saying he thought he might have unearthed the source of "our public relations problem with the groups who are concerned about the program on population growth."[26] Citing Lehrer's letter, Golden asked: "Is it possible that your refusal to 'sit down and discuss' their problem until after the program is aired may be the source of our difficulty?" An angry, perhaps mildly paranoid, Lehrer fired back: "No, it is *not* possible. Period. . . . I have never refused to talk to anyone from any group protesting the population program or any other program, for that matter. It is not my way of doing business. If a polygraph or truth serum test is necessary to further relieve your mind, consider this an offer to submit. Sorry, John, but enough is enough."[27]

Lehrer was squarely within his rights. The CPB mandate pledged that it would "assure the maximum freedom of the non-commercial educational television or radio broadcast systems and local stations from interference with or control of program content or other activities."[28] Yet PBS during this period repeatedly had to fend off pressure from the supposedly balance-minded administration and its CPB allies who wanted the system to air friendly views. Around the time of Nixon's landslide November 1972 reelection, CPB sent PBS a documentary, produced by the hawkish Institute for American Strategy, entitled *Only the Strong*. Featuring what it claimed to be official Russian film footage about Soviet military might, *Only the Strong* was a sparsely veiled pitch for massive American strategic spending. A feisty Lehrer screened the film and wrote back: "I must confess genuine surprise that CPB would even suggest that such a film be considered alone for distribution. By itself, it clearly violates all basic guidelines for balance and objectivity. . . . [The lobby group's] view is certainly a valid one and deserves to be heard on public television. I seriously question, however, the desirability of public television's informing the public on this controversial subject by simply airing the lobby group's position."[29] It did not air.

For all Nixon's paranoid focus on public affairs programming, during this time PBS also experienced one of its earliest clashes over cultural material, stemming from a film adaptation of the play *Steambath*. An angry comedy indebted a bit to the existentialist theatre of Jean-Paul Sartre, *Steambath*, written by Bruce Jay Friedman, provocatively portrayed God as a Puerto Rican steambath attendant. Friedman recalls that he was approached by Norman Lloyd, and "we went over the script together to quiet it down a little bit—some of the language was a little raucous, even for PBS."[30] TV star Bill Bixby was cast, having been recommended by Friedman's 12-year-old son. Originally produced for public television by Los Angeles's KCET, the film version was called "one of the most brilliantly written, exquisitely performed, hilarious black comedies to be found in any medium."[31]

Despite such praise, both the station and PBS got cold feet, deeming the film "unsuitable for presentation on the interconnection." In a meek compromise, PBS stations were allowed to view the film via the interconnection but not to record it. The results were explosive. To Donald Taverner, president of Washington's WETA—who was under extreme administration scrutiny—the film fell outside the realm of public television's purpose. "We just don't feel that public broadcasting is here for this kind of a program," he said. "It possesses all possible elements of sex, obscenity and blasphemy." Echoing the standard of the gentleman's living room, Taverner continued: "It's the kind of thing you don't invite into your home. I'd say that 'poor taste' would be a compliment to it."[32]

PBS had to confront a dilemma, however: What if viewers want to watch programs that the system's elders deem immoral? Helped in part by the controversy surrounding its being muffled, *Steambath*, once it was finally shown on two dozen PBS stations in 1973, went on to be a huge hit. In Los Angeles, it received a stratospheric 8.5 Nielsen rating, by far the highest public television viewership at that time. Ten years later, KCET continued to air *Steambath* during fund-raising drives.

ENTER ROGERS

After all the programming and personnel battles, the Nixon administration was stalemated by a man who was by now a public broadcasting warhorse, James

Killian, whose presence on the CPB board implied some semblance of continuity and credibility. In May 1973, the Nixon-heavy CPB board elected Killian— who, after all, had been appointed by Johnson—as its chairman, signaling an end to administration interference. CPB board minutes indicate that Killian took the post only on several conditions, two of which were that there would be no more White House interference and that public broadcasting would reaffirm the central importance of public affairs programming.[33] Writing a letter some years later, Killian maintained that the administration knew that its days of monkeying around with public broadcasting were over. In Killian's telling, he announced this condition during his appointment press conference, and overheard a Nixon official saying afterward: "Well, we've lost this one."[34]

In addition to Killian's cavalrylike arrival, public television's continued survival during this period owes much to a former Texas Industries official named Ralph Rogers; in his book *The Vanishing Vision*, former NET president James Day calls Rogers "the man who saved public television."[35] Rogers, a lifelong Texas Republican who chaired the board of directors of Dallas's KERA, was probably the only individual with sufficient contacts and credibility to negotiate between the wounded camps of public broadcasters and the administration.

Rogers later recalled in an interview that in late 1972, he tried to capitalize on his donations to Nixon's campaigns by securing a White House meeting with the President to defend PBS. "I said, 'Well when Mr. Nixon wanted money to run for office, he never had any trouble finding me. I have been a Republican all my life.' And I said that I wouldn't have any trouble getting to him."[36] Rogers was wrong; Nixon refused to meet him, and so he had to try other means to influence the White House. Rogers had a longstanding political relationship with another Texas Republican, George Bush, then the administration's ambassador to the United Nations; in fact, Rogers was the finance chairman of Bush's first successful campaign to become a U.S. senator. Throughout 1972, Bush acted as an informal liaison between White House personnel and the group of public broadcasters whom Rogers represented. (In one typical letter shortly after Nixon vetoed the public broadcasting bill, Bush—employing his trademark prep-school locution—wrote to Rogers: "Seeing you all in Maine was a very special treat. . . . Sorry about the White House thing—Darn it!! I'll try again when you want.")[37]

One of Rogers's major accomplishments was to streamline the hydra-headed system through which public broadcasters made their voices heard in Washington. He was able to persuade the decades-old National Association of Educational Broadcasters (NAEB) and its division, the Educational Television Stations (ETS), to merge into PBS in return for being represented on that organization's board. In an even more Herculean move, Rogers was able to smooth over the battles between PBS and CPB, which culminated in a much-heralded "compromise" agreement.[38] That cease-fire, signed on May 24, 1973, was a complex piece of diplomacy, the full effects of which would not become clear for years. For example, while the compromise sought to reduce the CPB's role in programming by giving a higher share of federal funds directly to stations, it also allowed the CPB the ability to review and reject, prior to broadcast, all programs paid for with federal money. It was interpreted as a partial victory for PBS, mostly because the CPB had already given itself that power. But the victory was muddy; as the second Carnegie Commission report noted with some frustration in 1979: "PBS and CPB have never agreed on the precise meaning" of this agreement.[39]

WATERGATE: "OUR BEST PROGRAMMING"

The precise details of the PBS-CPB agreement were ultimately less significant than the fact that there was an agreement at all. By ending—at least temporarily—the mutual sniping, the two major public television organizations were able to reassert at least some independence from the White House that wanted to control them. Ultimately, Nixon's machinations in more far-reaching areas put an end to his machinations in public broadcasting. As 1973 drew on and Nixon's White House became increasingly mired in Watergate, the amount of time and energy the administration could devote to torturing a relatively tiny government-subsidized program dwindled. More visibly—and almost accidentally—public television made one of the most important decisions in its history: to carry extensive coverage of the Senate hearings into Watergate. In the end, there were 37 days of hearings between May 17 and August 7, 1973, constituting a whopping 237 hours of public television programming.[40]

In retrospect, it is easy to assume that public television officials were eager to air the Watergate hearings as payback for the President who had opposed them so severely. But virtually no one knew the eventual political impact of the hearings before they began; moreover, the system's inertia resisted such a sweeping experiment. The idea of broadcasting a series of Congressional hearings from "gavel to gavel"—today the trademark of the C-SPAN channels—did not originate with PBS; Pacifica radio and others had done so before Richard Nixon ever took office. But the PBS Watergate hearings were nonetheless a remarkable watershed, for the country and especially for PBS. Against many internal objections and with the thinnest margin of approval from local stations, PBS aired the Ervin Committee hearings, preempting precious daytime slots (between 150 and 160 stations also rebroadcast them at night). NPACT president Jim Karayn later claimed that he had to lobby PBS president Hartford Gunn "twelve weeks in a row, every single day, five days a week" to get him to approve gavel-to-gavel coverage of the hearings. "He wouldn't do it. I kept saying, 'Hartford, this is our issue. This is our real moment to make the whole world realize that we are *not* the government network.'"[41]

It worked. In many markets, public television broadcasts of Watergate hearings garnered higher ratings than the commercial networks' prime-time offerings—a first for public television (and a feat rarely repeated). An analysis of ratings data showed that after the networks began to rotate live hearings broadcasts among themselves, the public television coverage actually attracted viewers not normally attuned to daytime television.[42] Perhaps more important was the passion and fervor with which viewers responded. NPACT received more than 70,000 letters responding to its Watergate coverage. "Station feedback to PBS and viewer mail to stations and NPACT indicated that phenomena were occurring around the country which public television stations had rarely, if ever, experienced before," concluded an internal PBS report.[43] "Audience response, in the form of much needed dollars as well as enthusiastic mail and telephone calls, had never poured in so voluminously." (Actually, a fair amount of mail NPACT received was at least partially critical; although the decision to carry complete coverage of the hearings was almost universally acclaimed, many who watched felt that the commentary and wrap-up sessions were biased against the President.)[44] It was estimated that the Watergate broadcasts brought in $1.5 million in donations to local stations—a figure made more remarkable by the fact that nearly a third of the 220 public television stations didn't carry the hearings, including such significant markets as St. Louis, Houston, and Minneapolis.[45]

This surge in interest and viewer funding has led most historians comment on to the exquisite irony that the unfolding drama of Nixon's fall and resignation saved the very public television system he had tried to tear down. NPACT's Jim Karayn set the tone when he said: "Nixon vetoes the funding bill, cut our funding. Now he's given us our best programming. It's sort of like being reborn."[46] Echoing this perverse insight, TV historian Erik Barnouw wrote: "In the way that the Army-McCarthy hearings had given ABC-TV a blood transfusion, so the Watergate hearings gave public television a new lease on life. Some of its stations gained the highest ratings in their history. To many of their executives, it seemed ironic that the President's displeasure, and their resulting poverty, had pushed them toward their salvation."[47]

To end the tale of Nixon's campaign against public television with the Watergate hearings—however tempting that poetic closure may be—is to miss a crucial political lesson. There is a rich bipartisan tradition in the history of the American executive branch whereby ideological strategies prove successful, even where presidential tactics appear to have fallen short.

A prime example is Franklin Delano Roosevelt's famed attempt to stack the Supreme Court after it had issued several decisions that gutted his prized New Deal programs. Most American schoolchildren are taught that Roosevelt's efforts to add three permanent members to the Court failed, bringing scorn upon his administration. But as historian Alan Brinkley has pointed out,[48] Roosevelt won the political war at the expense of the tactical battle. Cowed by his attack, the Supreme Court began approving Roosevelt's regulatory schemes with little protest.

In the same fashion, Nixon's multiyear battle against public television forced the entire public broadcasting structure to regroup. PBS rewrote bylaws to allow itself to censor broadcasts at a postproduction level, for whatever reason it deemed necessary. NPACT was dismantled, and the amount of time PBS devoted to news and public affairs plummeted. Faced with the very real prospect that government funding could be taken away by a hostile White House, the CPB began soliciting massive underwriting from some of the very institutions that advertised on commercial television, such as oil companies; in the year Nixon left office, for example, the Exxon Corporation contributed a staggering $2 million to CPB.[49] (That was the largest one-year grant in public broadcasting's brief lifetime, accounting for more than one-third of the year's total nonfederal revenues.)

Although Nixon failed to close down the nation's public television network, and while he gave it a rejuvenating parting shot, he succeeded in weakening its operations in ways that have plagued the system ever since. As already noted, the amount of airtime devoted to public affairs dropped dramatically, in accordance with the administration's desires; on virtually all stations, the coverage of public affairs never returned to its pre-Nixon levels. The quarrels Nixon's White House stoked between CPB and PBS led to a "compromise" agreement between the organizations that took what had been isolated crises—the FBI sequence of *The Great American Dream Machine*, the Woody Allen satire—and froze them into a permanent structure of prebroadcast review. The degree to which producers have become intimidated or prohibited from creating controversial works cannot be measured, but as we shall see in later chapters, the trend has been primarily to erect gates to keep such offending material out.

The wake of the Nixon attacks also saw the rise of PBS's Station Programming Cooperative (SPC), the cumbersome, ostensibly democratic method whereby PBS stations choose which programs will be nationally distributed. Ratified in May 1974, the SPC gives one vote to each station, regardless of the size of its viewership; from a preselected list a majority of stations decides which programs will get funding for nationwide distribution. Many observers have argued that this system ratifies the proven audience-grabbers (such as *Masterpiece Theatre* and *Great Performances*) and weeds out programs that might have tremendous appeal among small audiences but lack nationwide appeal. Not surprisingly, that includes minority programs; in the first SPC-chosen season (1974–75), only 39 stations of the 152 public television licensees bid on *Black Journal*, and 127 on *Black Perspectives on the News*, a substantial drop in usage for both programs. More tellingly, not a single station chose to underwrite the distribution of *Soul!* Except for *Black Perspectives on the News*, "no minority-produced series obtained full series funding from the SPC from 1976 to 1978."[50] With even established minority programs struggling to stay on the public airwaves, there was little room for shows that challenged PBS's dominant culture. Increasingly, instead of trumpeting American voices that were underheard, public television's national programming decisions would celebrate the most common denominator.

Perhaps most importantly, the administration's tireless emphasis on "localism" and the 1972 authorization veto permanently altered public broadcasting's funding landscape. Because Nixon's people saw local stations as potentially more politically supportive than the national offices of PBS, they insisted that a hefty portion of federal money be given directly to local public and educational stations, in the form of Community Service Grants (CSGs). This funding method has certain strengths: it helps secure, for example, access to public broadcasting for areas—such as rural and minority communities—that might not otherwise be able to support themselves. As with other federal programs, spreading out the legislative largesse to virtually every state helps build a broad base of Congressional support—an essential pillar during the 1995 battle to retain federal support for public broadcasting. At the same time, the CSG funding mechanism has locked in a fragmented, patchwork approach that supports stations almost without regard to how well they serve their communities. The frustration is not simply on the national-planning level: because the matching formulae used to calculate CSGs changes from year to year, an individual station cannot know precisely how much money it is going to receive from the CPB, even as a percentage of the money it raises on its own.[51] The oft-championed principle of "localism" that formed the political rationale for the CSG program also created a system of Byzantine complexity and inefficiency. As public television began its dramatic growth of the mid-1970s, complexity and inefficiency would begin to gnaw away at the system's cohesion from the inside—a threat as dangerous as any that tried to crush public broadcasting from the outside.

5

SUCCESS AND ITS PERILS

At any instance in broadcasting history, there has always been a role for chance. Public broadcasters like to boast that they took a risk on future hit programs—most notably *Sesame Street*—that commercial networks were afraid to back. It is equally true, however, that some of public television's most enduring hits succeeded only after they had been killed by public broadcasters. In the early 1960s, National Educational Television (NET) initially rejected a Boston-based culinary program hosted by a woman named Julia Child. The rationale was that the cooking show was an outdated format from the '50s. Child was picked up by a regional outfit called the Eastern Educational Network, which was her eventual platform for international fame and fortune.

Similarly, although William F. Buckley, Jr.'s program *Firing Line* debuted in 1969, it was hacked off the national PBS schedule, along with most other public affairs programs, in 1973; his lifeline throughout the '70s was a regional network called the Southern Educational Communications Association (SECA). The shell-game financial arrangement has allowed Buckley, after nearly 30 seasons on the public broadcasting dial, to mouth the politically convenient canard that he receives no federal funds; instead, his distributor, SECA, receives the federal funds.[1]

Another PBS name brand that needed a bit of chance as it came of age during the early 1970s was *Masterpiece Theatre (MT)*. Alistair Cooke, the program's venerated first host, has called *The First Churchills*, the centerpiece of *MT*'s 1971 debut season, "a historical mishmash."[2] Cooke continued: "The first effort, if not exactly aborted, fizzled into orbit and limped to Earth after twelve anxious weeks. Somebody—the producer or the writer—was so disenchanted that the usual 13th episode was never written." Nonetheless, *Masterpiece Theatre* was sufficiently unlike anything produced for the commercial networks that it gave public television an identity and was quickly deemed a hit. By gathering attention for public television, *Masterpiece Theatre* helped promote the system even for those who weren't watching *Masterpiece Theatre*; between 1970 and 1972 the prime-time audience for public television jumped 30 percent.[3] (The promotional phenomenon of *MT* is discussed in greater detail in chapter 7.)

The early '70s success of *Sesame Street* was more direct, and provided public broadcasters precisely the evidence they needed to show that they could produce programs unlike anything on commercial television and still make them hits. Public broadcasting—much in the manner of commercial television—began cranking out variations. In 1971, the Children's Television Workshop produced *The Electric Company*, which was in many ways a *Sesame Street* spinoff aimed at an older audience. Like *Sesame Street*, *The Electric Company* featured a regular cast of children and adults, carried sketch comedy with instructional messages, and was punctuated with lively music and dance. *Mister Rogers' Neighborhood*, which began as an adaptation of a program on Pittsburgh's WQED, was added to the National Educational Television schedule in 1967, and remains a PBS staple today. Boston's WGBH came through with *Zoom!* in 1972, pitched to a still older and more sophisticated children's audience, with short films, brain-teasers, dissections of moods and fads, and so on. (It lasted only three seasons in its original incarnation, but CPB and WGBH announced in 1996 that they had made a pilot for a *Zoom!* revival.) Also premiering in 1972 was *Carrascolendas*, a bilingual children's program funded by the U.S. Office of Education and produced by KRLN-TV in San Antonio, Texas. Two years later, Exxon and the Department of Health, Education and Welfare teamed up to produce the daily half-hour program *Villa Alegre*, designed to help Spanish-speaking children make the transition from home to school.

Taken together, this represents an extraordinary amount of original programming for what was still a fledgling medium; even more extraordinary is that through the mid-1990s, *Sesame Street* and *Mister Rogers' Neighborhood* remained on the air, while their commercial contemporaries (such as *Captain Kangaroo*) have long since been replaced by network morning news programs.

The production of hit programs corresponded with the spurting growth of the public television system. With Richard Nixon out of office, Congress and the White House came as close as they ever have to agreeing on steady, multiyear appropriations for public broadcasting (an understanding that was short-lived). More and more public television stations were added to the system: National Educational Television had, at its 1968 peak, linked about 120 stations. By 1972 there were 216 public television stations, and by 1978 there were 280, meaning that over 80 percent of American households could receive a high-quality public television signal (only Wyoming and Montana had no public television stations in 1978).

But the success of these '70s hit programs, and the fact that they became associated with PBS in the manner of brand names, also provoked skeptical questions from those with a dissenting vision of what had been promised. There is nothing in the Carnegie report about an urgent national need for cooking shows or British drama (and there is only a brief passage referring specifically to children's programming). This is hardly surprising, since there is nothing intrinsically "public" about a cooking show. The domination of children's programming demonstrated priorities that were arbitrary and ultimately indefensible: Why should the children in Spanish-speaking households be served by a nationally distributed PBS program, but not their parents or older siblings?

Furthermore, the success of a few programs locked in specific genres, just as on commercial television. Although in their particulars *Sesame Street* and *Masterpiece Theatre* differed from the fare on commercial television, they employed essentially the same format. Unlike the experimentation of the Public Broadcasting Laboratory, for example, these PBS hits and their spinoffs did not attempt to change the relationship between audience and program: they are prerecorded and allow no viewer interaction. Whereas *PBL* tried to structure programming with breaks where local stations and audiences could react to capture the local effects of national issues, the PBS hits relied on central and uniform distribution, just like shows on the commercial networks. Their "success" was measured primarily in the traditional television terms of maximum viewership and identifiable celebrities: Buckley replaces Brinkley. Since they involved no true participation from viewers, there was virtually nothing that made these television programs "public," prompting critic Les Brown's cutting observation that "public television is a name without a concept."

As the nation and globe became awash in *Sesame Street* paraphernalia, heretics began to argue that, for all the money poured into psychological and educational consultants, children learned no more from *Sesame Street* than they do from any other television programs.[4] One researcher from Northwestern University, after combing through the original 1970 data that "proved" *Sesame Street*'s educational value, concluded: "The amount of learning gain was quite small. Kids who watched for a season gained about two letters of the alphabet."

PBS's children's programs do, however, possess one undisputed power: they are tremendous selling points for the system as a whole. Political enemies of public broadcasting—no matter how pure or tainted their motivations—have not, over the last three decades, been able to seize the rhetorical high ground from the characters of *Sesame Street*; few dare even try. As early as 1970, CPB board member Al Cole used *Sesame Street* to defuse pressure to defund the system from the Nixon White House—which had appointed him the year before—encouraging a Nixon aide to "get some of your kids to look at it."[5] A quarter-century later,

Congresswoman Nita Lowey, Democrat of New York, literally infantilized Congressional debate by donning hand puppets of *Sesame Street* veterans Bert and Ernie during a Republican-led House hearing into CPB funding. Even the vicepresident of the United States, Al Gore, ducked behind *Sesame Street*'s Oscar the Grouch in a March 1995 speech, arguing that a taxpayer would resent the spending of one federal dollar a year on public broadcasting only "if you live in a garbage can and you are an angry green male."[6]

"YOUR MAN AT GALLUP"

The "success" of public broadcasting in the mid-'70s derived largely from the power of independent production outfits (such as the Children's Television Workshop). The charm of *Masterpiece Theatre* and the mass audience of *Sesame Street* belied the fact that the organizational structure behind public broadcasting was in shambles. As Gerald Ford took office, public broadcasting—like much of the nation—felt relieved to put the Constitutional crisis of Nixon's reign behind it, but it was also battered, and somewhat paralyzed. The Nixon White House was so obsessed with the politics of public broadcasting that it very nearly crippled it. In the summer of 1974, there were actually more vacancies on the CPB's 15-member board than there were directors. One CPB board member said of this period that the divisions and vacancies "got to the point where it was so bad, the Board couldn't do business."[7]

Not three weeks after Nixon's resignation, James Killian, the grandfather of public broadcasting who had taken the reins of the CPB to end its crisis, wrote an urgent letter to President Ford "about the eight vacancies on this Board, some of long standing, which have not been filled." Killian pleaded with Ford to deal with the situation quickly "because the Board is grievously handicapped under present circumstances and can make no significant plans for the future."[8] He suggested that reappointing some of the sitting CPB directors—notably Robert Benjamin —might help resolve the matter expeditiously.

The problem of CPB appointments was not as simple as it appeared to Killian. Ford, of course, had far more pressing matters on his plate: the fallout from his Nixon pardon; wage and price inflation; the stillraging war in Vietnam; and the enormous, instant transition to a new White House that had lost most of the top personnel who made it hum. Ford did have an experienced team of staffers who were capable of tackling the policy challenges of public broadcasting, but they were simply too busy with other issues to become PBS activists in the mold of Douglass Cater or Clay Whitehead.

It is only a mild exaggeration to say that the Ford administration was over before it ever found someone who could focus on public broadcasting. Had Ford been reelected, he would probably have left a more permanent impression on the system, but since he occupied the White House for less than 30 months, his policy approach seems like one of prolonged distraction. Without the customary three-month warmup given to presidents who are elected to office, the administration let secondary policy concerns such as public broadcasting slip through the cracks of its attention span.

Examples of distraction abound. The Office of Telecommunications Policy had intended for Ford to promote a long-term public broadcasting bill in the "mini State of the Union" address that Ford delivered a month after assuming the presidency; it was omitted, according to a White House memo, "because nobody checked OTP until the last minute."[9] Ten weeks into the Ford administration, close Ford aides were still unclear about whose responsibility public broadcasting was: when film industry lobbyist Jack Valenti queried the White House about CPB, he threw Ford's staff into confusion. "I have checked to see who has the lead responsibility for the Corporation for Public Broadcasting," wrote one staffer to the president's scheduling chief. "Geoff Shepard is the man."[10] Shepard might have been the man, but he had already announced his intention to leave government for private practice. About a year into the Ford administration, a top presidential aide sent a handwritten note to a colleague, asking: "What is the president's attitude toward public broadcasting?"[11] This is not a question that anyone in the Johnson or Nixon White House would have needed to ask.

In one of the few historical attempts to answer the question, author Marilyn Lashley has suggested that "President Ford seriously considered elimination of the [Corporation for Public Broadcasting]."[12] She offers, however, only an anonymous interview for this claim, and a thorough search of available archive material turns up no support for it. Lashley makes a contrary and more important observation when she points out that the short-lived Ford administration—perhaps overcompensating for Nixon's attack—oversaw the highest percentage increases in the CPB's budget: a 26 percent hike in fiscal year 1976, followed by a 31 percent hike the following year.

These dramatic increases, however, reflected the needs of a growing system and Congressional priorities more than any genuine commitment from the administration. The few White House staffers who were concerned with public broadcasting in the confused summer and fall of 1974 were the ideologues held over from Nixon's shop. Although formally attached to the Ford White House for just a few weeks, General Alexander Haig was one who would not let a hectic schedule dull the ideological saber he wanted to rattle at CPB. Introducing potential CPB appointments in a memo to Ford, Haig and another staffer insisted that political enforcement at CPB was as important as ever:

> As you know, in the area of communications and the media, the CPB is second only to the FCC in terms of impact and importance. Because of its increasing authority and influence, it is very desirable that individuals of real substance and ability be appointed. In the past, the CPB has been controversial and only semi-supportive of the Administration's position in the public broadcasting field. For that reason it is equally important you appoint people who show your views in this important area and are politically sensitive. With the recent expiration of the last Johnson appointments, the CPB can become for the first time "our" CPB. It should become greatly more productive with the correct new appointments. [13]

Haig was intent on carrying Nixon's Procrustean public broadcasting views into the Ford White House.

The leading nonsupporter of the administration, in Haig's view, was Robert Benjamin, former chairman of United Artists and one of Johnson's original appointees. Haig had earlier approved another man, Amos Hostetter, to replace Benjamin, and his opinion did not change with the change in presidency. He called Benjamin a "liberal Democrat. . . . [H]e is not a supporter of the Administration and this is our first opportunity to clean the slate of non-supporters." Benjamin, in particular, was one who had to be cleaned from the slate, because of the dire possibility that he might advance: "Benjamin will undoubtedly be elected Chairman if reappointed and that isn't the place for someone of questionable support."[14] Ford concurred. That was in September '74; in March 1975, however, the administration ended up renominating Benjamin to the CPB; the Senate reconfirmed him, and he was indeed elected CPB chair.

The Ford administration did not always let political ideology or connections dictate its CPB appointments. There was some internal pressure to nominate Nancy Michael Chotiner, the widow of a close friend and advisor of President Nixon's who, even in Clay Whitehead's view, was thoroughly unqualified for the position. Ford tossed it out, picking instead a southern education activist named Lillian Herndon. In addition, Ford was stubbornly committed to Jack Valenti, the president of the Motion Pictures of America Association, against the equally stubborn position of transition guru Haig. "We mention [Valenti's] name only because of your expression of interest in him several months ago," said Haig in a memo. "As previously indicated, we think his selection would be a mistake for the CPB as well as for your administration, and especially would upset the moderate and conservative elements within the Republican party." Ford selected him anyway, although Valenti withdrew his name from nomination. [15]

But political patronage was never far from Ford's agenda. In mid-1975, Ford

sent a handwritten note to an aide: "Senator Pastore indicated there is a new vacancy
on Public Broadcasting Bd. He strongly recommend some Spanish speaking person. Has no one in mind. Can we find one?"[16] In 1976, Ford appointed Charles Roll
to the CPB board. Roll was a political pollster whose clients had included the influential GOP Senator Howard Baker and Nelson Rockefeller, Ford's vicepresident;
Roll had also accompanied H. Ross Perot on one of the businessman's prisoner-of-
war-seeking missions in the Far East, a vital public relations effort for the Nixon
White House.[17] Ford could hardly have chosen Roll for any great interest in public
or private broadcasting—since his career showed practically none—but his nomination had other dividends. About five weeks before Election Day 1976, when Ford
faced Jimmy Carter in his only presidential race, Roll wrote to the President:

> Please be assured that I intend to give this position my "all" and to strive in the solid
> and sound "Jerry Ford" tradition. Along this line, as your man at Gallup, I would
> like you to know, confidentially, that on the basis of preliminary figures in our
> weekend interviewing, post first debate and *Playboy* interviews, etc., you have
> seemed to narrow the Carter lead to approximately eight or nine points. This is
> sizeable movement when it is remembered how slowly public opinion moves in the
> absence of earthshaking events. It should be satisfying that the trend of this slow
> moving public opinion is in your direction.[18]

If Ford drew hope from these optimistic numbers, it was his own fault; in the fall
of 1964, Roll had also published an article entitled "Goldwater Can Win." At any
rate, Roll's public service on the CPB board outlasted President Ford's service to
the nation.

Ford's brief White House tenure also included some public broadcasting res-
cue efforts. In 1974 and '75, the buzzword among public broadcasters was "insulation": public broadcasters began pushing hard for multiyear federal funding to
take them out of the politics of annual budget battles. The Carnegie Commission
had clearly envisioned some version of such insulation, and the years of bald
intimidation and manipulation from the Nixon White House had given the point
some urgency. PBS launched a lobbying campaign in policy circles and the press,
including what was for them a slick brochure making "The Case for Insulation."[19]

The Ford White House was relatively sympathetic to the fight for insulation.
In part this was because the administration was trying to make peace with the
public broadcasting community, and in part because, blind to irony, it saw "insulation" policies as helping it maintain political control. "That legislation is our
quid pro quo for local station control of public broadcasting," wrote White House
staffer Geoff Shepard shortly after Ford took office.[20] The Ford administration's
1975 legislation reauthorizing public broadcasting was the first—and it would
turn out to be the only—bill to set out funds for a five-year period.

The "insulation" fight over the 1975 bill provided a strange, looking-glass moment when a Republican administration was championing the proclaimed interest of public broadcasters against the objections of a Democratic Congress. The House of Representatives equated insulating public broadcasting with eroding its own power, something Members of Congress—particularly those who sit on the Appropriations Committee—are loathe to do. They therefore accused CPB and PBS representatives of being unwilling to fight for their money like every other recipient of federal money, many of whom—it was argued—would love to be "insulated" from Congressional review. "Such respected institutions of higher education as Gallaudet College, Howard University, and the National Technical Institute for the Deaf receive most of their operating funds directly from the federal government through annual appropriations," said Congressman Dan Flood.[21] "Persuasive arguments could be made for insulating these institutions from potential political interference." Ultimately, Congress refused to give up its right to review CPB's funds every year. What Congress *could* offer public broadcasters was more money: the 1975 House bill planned for $634 million over five years—40 percent more than the administration had allocated. Ford declared himself "troubled" by the numbers, but signed the bill that his administration internally labeled "half a loaf."

The compromise did not please everyone, especially those Haig called "conservative elements within the Republican party," who responded with one part fiscal conservatism to two parts ideology. Patrick Buchanan, who had been sued for his interference with PBS during his White House service, wrote an acidic newspaper column assailing the Republicans' "collaborating role" in passing legislation that "would mean an increase for PTV of 450 per cent over seven years."[22] Buchanan labeled public television "an income transfer program, where working and middle class taxpayers are forced by the United States government to subsidize the entertainment of an affluent elite." Buchanan could only conclude that the Ford White House and Republican Members of Congress had sold out their cause "because there beats in the respectable Republican breast a terrible anxiety and fear of being labeled a philistine."

AIM EXCEEDS ITS GRASP

As outlined in chapter 2, educational television has had a reputation for liberal programming—even among many in its midst—that predates the regular commitment of federal funds. Because pre-PBS programming was generally too diffuse and viewed by so few, however, the attack on its putative liberalism was equally muted. The passage of the Public Broadcasting Act and the growth of PBS in the early and mid-'70s gave activists on the far right—those unafraid of being labeled philistines—a meatier basis for a sustained attack on public television and radio. At the forefront of this assault was Accuracy in Media (AIM), a corporate-funded Washington, D.C.–based watchdog group that seeks to identify and correct a liberal bias in the press. While public broadcasting has never been AIM's only, or even primary, focus, the group has for decades hammered on the accountability of this taxpayer-funded medium.

The Public Broadcasting Act of 1967 charged that noncommercial radio and television programming must exhibit a "strict adherence to objectivity and balance in all programs or series of programs of a controversial nature."[23] Despite AIM's tireless rants, that laudable, very American sentiment has proved difficult to define and impossible to enforce. What, for example, constituted "programs of a controversial nature"? Taken broadly, almost any subject had opposing views; as onetime PBS host Patrick Watson has famously said: "You don't balance out the astronauts with the Flat Earth Society."[24] How should a given program achieve "objectivity and balance"? Must, for example, a 15 minute interview with Fidel Castro be balanced with equal time from someone in the State Department? What about subjects on which there were more than two prevailing points of view? Or should public broadcasting merely strive to balance out views over the whole of its programming? And who was to decide these questions: producers? The FCC? Viewer groups?

The statute's resounding vagueness did not deter AIM, or its prickly leader, Reed Irvine (whom the Nixon White House once contemplated as a CPB board member). In the fall of 1971, two PBS programs prompted AIM to try to enforce its interpretation of the law. One was *The Three R's and Sex Education*, which some conservatives claimed "unfairly depicted the opponents of sex education in the public schools as uninformed or narrowminded." The second was a documentary called *Justice?*, dubbed by a U.S. senator "a propaganda effort on behalf of such radicals as Angela Davis and George Jackson made at a time when preparations for the trial of Angela Davis were going forward."[25]

AIM took its objections to the FCC, which declared in 1972 that the sex education program had afforded opportunity for alternative points of view, and that PBS had aired a variety of views on the criminal justice system that made the views in *Justice?* acceptable in context.[26] Addressing AIM's broader objections, the FCC decided that even if it could determine what "objectivity and balance" were, it was not necessarily the FCC's job to enforce them. AIM, dissatisfied, sued the FCC, and in 1975 the U.S. Court of Appeals decided that this section of the law was "hortatory" language, intended as "a set of goals to which the directors of CPB should aspire" rather than a strict legal requirement.[27]

This irked critics such as AIM who insisted that the language meant what it said. They began to take their battle to different arenas (all the while compiling a growing list of PBS's sins against balance). By 1977, when Senator Orrin Hatch introduced a bill he called the Public Broadcasting Fairness Act, AIM's roster of "one-sided propagandistic programs" had expanded to include:

- *The Children of China*, which AIM said "was such good propaganda for Communist China that it won praise from the Chinese Central Broadcasting Administration";

- *China Memoir*, produced by Shirley McLaine, which even PBS president Ralph Rogers acknowledged was "pure propaganda";

- *El Corrido*, described by the financial weekly *Barron's* as "a guerrilla theater piece on farm labor";

- *A Day Without Sunshine*, another documentary on farm labor, which an agriculture consortium claimed portrayed farmers as "heartless exploiters" and businessmen as "callouses opportunists."[28]

Hatch's bill charged the FCC with the daunting task of ensuring that PBS and NPR programming remained balanced. Under Hatch's scheme, whenever the FCC determined that an unbalanced program had slipped onto the schedule, it would command that the CPB "make available to the educational station or stations which have broadcast such programs adequate funding for a balancing program or series of programs."[29]

This centralized and potentially costly plan was a curious approach for conservatives, who generally advocate smaller and decentralized government actions. Perhaps stemming from that contradiction, and certainly as a measure of how few people in Washington took these arguments seriously in the 1970s, the bill languished and died. AIM, however, never gave up its fight: it would continue to paint PBS programming as pinko through the '80s and '90s, until a Republican-appointed CPB board was finally willing to listen.

PBS: THE COORS CHANNEL?

In 1994, the Colorado-based Coors Brewery Company began a winking television ad campaign designed to convince the viewer that he or she was watching a "Coors Lite Channel." One typical ad featured a mock soap opera called *Coors Manor*, which, after a brief melodramatic scene, faded into a "commercial" for

Coors beer. The series carried the tagline, "Coors Lite Channel—Always On," and was well received among the advertising intelligentsia for its knowing one-upmanship over the supposedly jaded cable viewer.

Few viewers could be expected to recall that 20 years earlier, the Coors Company actually had tried to create a television channel. Beginning in May 1973, Joseph Coors, the executive vice president of his family's brewery, founded Television News, Inc. (TVN), based in New York City. The fledgling media company made little attempt to distance itself from its brewing parent: the Adolph Coors Company was the majority stockholder (90 percent), and the board of directors, which included Joseph Coors, consisted entirely of employees of the Coors family.

The idea behind TVN was to create the visual equivalent of a wire service: each day, TVN staff would report and produce a dozen or so television news stories, which would then be distributed to subscribers, who could use as many as they saw fit. TVN's target audience was the potentially vast number of television stations that were "independent," not affiliated with any of the Big Three networks. TVN management optimistically viewed the news service as a stepping-stone to the creation of a fourth network that would operate via satellite technology, which was still tenuous at the time. A contemporary commentator noted: "It's an idea that would make TVN first with a dramatic new technology—a plan management hopes will make Coors as big a name in broadcasting as it is in beer."[30]

As is often the case with any Coors venture, there was also an ideological motivation behind TVN. Since the 1960s, the Coors family has been the single most generous underwriter of conservative and right-wing political causes in the United States. They have aided—or outright created—dozens of the best-known outposts of conservative activism, including the Christian Broadcast Network, the Heritage Foundation, the Hoover Institution, the Manhattan Institute, the Ethics and Public Policy Center, and the Free Congress Foundation. The Coors family's largesse does not stop at the limit of "respectable" conservatism: beneficiaries have included the John Birch Society, as well as individuals with links to racist organizations, Nazi collaborators, and neofascist outfits.[31]

The Coors family shared the Nixon/Agnew view that the national news media promulgated liberalism. Thus, much of Coors' ideological money—then and now—has gone to organizations that seek to promote a right-wing agenda on the U.S. media, including Accuracy in Media; the Center for Media and Public Affairs; Morality in Media; the American Spectator Educational Foundation (publishers of the right-wing *American Spectator*); and the Institute for Educational Affairs, which in the 1980s established a loose network of conservative newspapers on American college campuses, including the notorious *Dartmouth Review*.

Thus, it was hardly surprising that Joe Coors told a newspaper interviewer that he and his backers "got into it because of our strong belief that network news is slanted to the liberal left side of the spectrum and does not give an objective view to the American public."[32] In TVN's early days, the network's conservative ideology was kept in check, primarily because TVN had a professional news staff. Its first news director, Dick Graf, was a longtime newspaperman and former NBC employee (Graf was managing editor of *The 51st State*, a much-praised but short-lived public television daily news program in New York).

Within weeks of TVN's debut, however, Coors began tightening the political screws. TVN's ideological point man was Jack Wilson, an employee of the Adolph Coors Company who had also helped set up the Heritage Foundation. Wilson made his political presence known to TVN's staff mostly through a series of memoranda to Coors that tried to shape content through criticism. Shortly after the network's debut, Wilson complained about the coverage of Martin Luther King, Jr., whom Wilson labeled "an avowed Communist revolutionary." Graf resigned, and Wilson took control. His missives could be amusing and colorful, such as the one praising the network for showing Vice President Spiro Agnew "in a relaxed and human fashion." But more often Wilson exploded with conservative rage: "Our announcer says nothing about the problems of smut or in any way supports the Supreme Court of the United States, but rather picks out a fellow that says that smut is OK. . . . [O]n this issue alone several people should be fired!!" Wilson referred to the American Civil Liberties Union as "the legal arm of the extreme left if not the Communist Party in the United States," and tried to ban from TVN such figures as Ralph Nader and American Indian Movement activists. Joe Coors himself reportedly once asked his news staff: "Why are you covering Daniel Ellsberg? He's a traitor to his country."[33]

In its tug-of-war between being a straight news channel and a political outpost, TVN became a kind of farm team for conservatives who would later become significant broadcast figures. TVN hired Mike Douglas producer and Nixon media coach Roger Ailes and taught him how to work in a newsroom; following his career as a rough-edged Republican political consultant, Ailes would became in 1994 the president of the Consumer News and Business Channel (CNBC), NBC's flagship cable channel, and in 1996 the chairman of Rupert Murdoch's Fox News Channel. Another prominent TVN figure was Paul Weyrich, a longtime Coors political activist, who started National Empowerment Television (not to be confused with the Ford Foundation's NET). National Empowerment Television, which began in 1993, is in many ways a streamlined, next-generation version of TVN: a 24-hour conservative cable channel probably best known for carrying a weekly talk show hosted by Newt Gingrich (it was on this program that Gingrich first launched his attack on federal funding for PBS).

Though its quality was spotty, TVN filled a genuine need: at its peak, TVN's daily news feed was being picked up by approximately 40 stations across the country. Still, this was nowhere near enough to break even, and operations were costly: like PBS, TVN required the use of expensive AT&T coaxial cables. Even during its best times, TVN was losing close to $100,000 a week.[34]

And then something strange happened, which TVN's owners saw as a potential lifeboat. On August 7, 1974, as one of his very last acts as President, Richard Nixon nominated five people to fill openings on the board of the Corporation for Public Broadcasting. One of them was Joseph Coors (who, with his brother, had contributed $8,000 to Nixon's campaign). A moment's rational reflection would have shown this to be a doomed choice. Although he had bankrolled a startup news network, Coors had no experience in broadcast management. His record in public life was limited to being a trustee of a public university in Colorado (where he led a successful drive to force Students for a Democratic Society off the campus and handed out John Birch pamphlets at board meetings). In addition to bankrolling right-wing advocacy groups, the Coors company was notorious for its antiunion stance, and its discrimination against women and minorities. At the time Nixon nominated Joseph Coors, the federal Equal Employment Opportunity Commission was investigating Coors's workplace violations (the EEOC filed suit against the company in September 1975, just as Joseph Coors's CPB nomination hearings began in the Senate). The public broadcasting world was far too sensitive about allegations of its own racial hiring deficiencies to accept a man who was, in the eyes of millions, a renowned bigot.

But Nixon was on his way out, and left the Coors nomination almost as if thumbing his nose at the hated liberal Establishment that had forced him to resign. What better way to assuage the criticisms of a group like AIM than to place their hero and benefactor on the board of the CPB? Nixon could not be counted on for the logistical follow-through, however, and Coors's nomination to the CPB was hardly a high priority for the fledgling Ford administration; it languished for more than a year. For his part, though, Joseph Coors began acting as if he were already a board member. In late 1974, PBS was preparing to air a documentary called "Since *The American Way of Death*," directed by filmmaker Michael Hirsh as a follow-up to the groundbreaking book by Jessica Mitford.[35] This exposé maintained that the funeral industry, despite public outcry and reforms, continued to gouge some consumers and was riddled with deceptive practices.

Prior to the film's broadcast, a Colorado-based undertaker named Francis Vanderburg complained to his friend Joseph Coors that his industry was about to be maligned. Coors did not wait to be confirmed to intervene; he did not even wait until he'd seen the film. On January 10, Coors wrote to CPB president Henry Loomis: "It is, indeed, unfortunate if PBS is actually putting out a film which wrongly attacks this industry. I am not yet familiar enough with the interconnection between PBS and CPB to know whether you can do anything about this but it is the type of thing which I will be very interested in watching closely if I ever become confirmed on your fine board."[36]

Although there's no indication that this letter had any impact, it was a rather brazen attempt to steer public television toward Coors's agenda. But Coors had far greater plans for his new government role. Like PBS, TVN relied on AT&T coaxial cables to transmit its programs to affiliated stations. And—like PBS—TVN was exploring the possibility of replacing that system with a satellite system. In the eyes of the senators who eventually voted down Coors's nomination, this represented a conflict of interest. But to Coors, it was strictly a business arrangement: if he could be guaranteed that publicly funded TV signals would piggyback—for a price—on a satellite network that he was going to establish for TVN anyway, everybody would win. Even ardent free marketeers like a free lunch when it comes their way.

On July 24, 1975, six weeks before his scheduled confirmation hearings, Coors made his pitch in another letter to Loomis: "I would merely like to point out to you that at the present time PBS and the Corporation for Public Broadcasting are contracting with a commercial group, namely, American Telephone and Telegraph, for the distribution of their present programs. Would it not be just as feasible to contract for similar services with the additional flexibility and advantages of the earth stations? I can assure you that this can be done at a considerable financial savings over what you estimate spending at the present time, and what you indicated would be the carrying cost for the monies required to put in your own ground station system. In fact, I believe it would be much more acceptable to use this route than to expect commercial operations to contract with a PBS owned distribution system. [TVN president] Jack Wilson has been in contact with Mike Curzan [chief of staff of a public broadcasting satellite working group], but I would like to discuss this with you at some additional length before any firm decisions are made in regard to letting the contracts."[37]

To his credit, Loomis distanced himself from Coors's advance, responding with a clarification of CPB's satellite plans and saying flatly: "Regarding your suggestion that you and I discuss satellite-related matters, I would be pleased to do so, in general terms relating to matters already of public knowledge, but I am sure you will understand that it will not be possible to discuss specific proposals or transactions."[38]

Without this unseemly grab for CPB's satellite business, it is conceivable that Coors's six-year appointment would have been confirmed. But it came on top of Coors's embarrassing record on civil rights; in response to a question from a Republican senator at his confirmation hearing, Coors denied that he was a member of the John Birch Society, but offered that "I have at times supported them with funds and I support some of their thoughts and ideas." Senators also perceived a very real possibility that Coors would interfere with PBS programming, in addition to being generally underqualified, but it was the business conflicts that were too much for the Commerce Committee to swallow.

The White House tried to defend Coors's nomination by insisting, accurately, that the Public Broadcasting Act specifically exempts CPB directors from normal government conflict-of-interest rules. The Senate would likely have allowed Coors to keep his TVN stock, but he stubbornly refused to give up his TVN directorship if confirmed: "I don't plan in any way to disconnect myself with Television News and if I am approved for this appointment, I plan to put some very strong energies into the CPB. . . . [I]f the CPB stays out of the hard news area, it seems to me the conflict does not exist."[39] It should be noted that many Members of Congress were especially displeased with those Coors-funded political activities that were aimed at changing the makeup of Congress. In a revealing letter sent both to the White House and to the chairman of the Senate Commerce Committee, Congressman John Moss pledged that California's entire Democratic Congressional delegation had agreed to work against Coors's nomination. "I think it is interesting to note," wrote Moss, "that Mr. Coors has committed himself to fully supporting efforts to eliminate 100 Members of the present Congress as part of his move to remake this nation in an image more pleasing to himself. That Mr. Coors has the right to do as he pleases with his own money is not challenged by me nor any Members of the Delegation. Our only concern is that he not be given access through a sensitive public forum for the furtherance of his campaign to promote his own ideologies."[40] The Senate committee killed the nomination by a vote of 11 to 6, with all the Democrats and one Republican against. Ironically, by the time the committee voted, October 1975, TVN was essentially out of business because the Coors family decided it was no longer a worthwhile investment.

SATELLITE POLITICS REVISITED

Although Coors did not make it to the CPB board, his nomination was an early example of how the American right latched onto the view that the very apparatus of public broadcasting—from transmitters to satellites to spectrum space—is an asset that can and should be used for private sector gain. This, too, was a symptom of PBS's success. In its own ham-fisted way, Coors's attempt to skim some of the federal money being used for public satellite broadcasting was very much in keeping with government policy in the mid-'70s. Even though Fred Friendly's proposal in the late '60s to use satellite technology to subsidize public broadcasting was killed by opposition from COMSAT and the military, the desire to harness satellites for public broadcasting never disappeared. Like public broadcasting itself, satellite hardware was a technological panacea for its advocates in the '60s and '70s, reflecting a classically American belief that science could solve all problems and resolve all social contradictions. International cooperation on satellite communications was not, in Lyndon Johnson's words, merely a way to transfer information over vast distances: it was a method of contributing "to world peace and understanding."[41]

While public broadcasters generally had more immediate goals for satellite technology, they were equally fervent in arguing for the need to adopt it. Satellite broadcasting had major advantages over ground transmissions. It could bring television broadcasts to remote areas and to regions—such as the Rocky Mountains or Alaska—where terrain made telephone and cable lines impossible or prohibitively expensive to install. In 1971, as National Public Radio was gearing up, the radio broadcast circuits available from AT&T were, in the words of NPR president Lee Frischknecht, "inadequate to meet our needs, but they were the only ballgame in town."[42] The AT&T lines were low fidelity, and incapable of transmitting in stereo—a severe hurdle for NPR, which in the '70s operated almost entirely on FM, where high-fidelity stereophonic signals were the norm. The average NPR listener would notice a severe drop in sound quality as a station switched from a locally produced or prerecorded segment to an NPR broadcast, a situation Frischknecht labeled "somewhat of an embarrassment." Finally, although satellite technology required a substantial upfront investment, it offered potential cost savings over the long run, particularly if public broadcasters owned all or part of the airborne device.

These were the imperatives behind public broadcasting's move toward using satellites. Beginning in late 1974, a working group called the Public Service Satellite Consortium (PSSC) came into being. Inspired by powerful new NASA technology, PSSC believed that satellites could soon be affordable by small education and health providers. The PSSC board combined top representatives from public broadcasting (including Donald Quayle, CPB senior vice president for programming, and George Geesey, NPR's director of operations) with officials from the Federation of Rocky Mountain States. The PSSC had the blessing—and, soon enough, funding—of various departments within the Ford administration, including the Office for Telecommunications Policy.

Perhaps even more than the East Coast's inner cities, the mountainous western states were a place where public television was considered a vital educational tool. These states were home to minority populations little known in the East or Midwest: in the mid-'70s, some 30 percent of all Mexican Americans and 30 percent of all Native Americans lived in the western states. The Native American population was spread across vast territory: 234,000 people occupying 38 million acres of land. For geographical reasons alone, it was difficult even to communicate to these groups of Americans, much less provide them with government services or quality education. This was the source of a kind of inferiority complex for politicians of the region, who therefore greeted the potential satellite linkup through schools, hospitals, and public television stations as an unprecedented opportunity. Cecil Andrus, the governor of Idaho, said in 1972: "If we can truly provide a system of communication among the people of this region, we must be but moments away from the time when we can say we have helped solve the basic educational disparity between the community school and the fundamental principles of liberty, equality, and open opportunity for all people."[43] His statement and the satellite gold rush brilliantly epitomize a particular West Coast philosophy: what people need is not welfare or government-created jobs, but television.

The Satellite Technology Demonstration (STD) consisted of ground terminals in eight states (Arizona, Colorado, Idaho, Montana, New Mexico, Nevada, Utah, and Wyoming): 56 in rural schools and 12 at public television stations. In some of the schools, teachers would be able to select from a catalogue of 35-minute educational programs, which would then be beamed to their schools every day from a NASA ATS-6 satellite.[44] Students in the region whose schools did not have satellite stations could watch the programs when they were rebroadcast on public television. One STD brochure boasted: "Nothing quite like it has ever been attempted, building up from the ground floor a telecommunications system to broadcast educational television through a satellite thousands of miles in space. Actually, now established it is the largest non-military extraterrestrial telecommunications system in the world." In a later evaluation, analysts would conclude that these were clumsy educational methods: "The educational payoff was trivial when considered in terms of total cost."[45]

By 1975, more than 22,000 children—primarily in the seventh, eighth, and ninth grades—were watching programs such as the pseudo–science fiction show *Time Out* and *Crossroads Corners,* in which rural teens were depicted meeting at a career center. Much of the West Coast satellite programming focused on careers;

indeed, the STD annual report makes it clear that the satellite coordinators expected the technology to have as much impact on young minds as the content of the programs. Here the medium was the message, and the students were expected to adapt themselves to the space age. "Acceptance of social or technological change is revealed in our use of new terminology to describe our experience with innovation," asserted an STD annual report. "Words such as uplink, parabolic antenna, and down converter are a part of the vocabulary of students and teachers who have incorporated this new terminology in their lives."[46] To illustrate the point, the STD presented a photo of two early teens in front of a massive satellite dish, complete with dialogue.

> "Hey, how come you missed the bus home last night?"
> "Pointing exercises."
> "What exercises? I didn't know you were athletic."
> "No, I had to help Mrs. Foster align the parabolic antenna to pick up the ATS-6."
> "Scientific stuff, huh?"
> "Yeah, sort of. It's for the satellite class."
> "Why do you want to stay after school?"
> "I'm on the satellite pointing team; you know, kinda working for NASA."
> "You mean like Cape Canaveral? You're kidding!"
> "No joke. We had to point the antenna straight at the satellite to get a reading of at least 20 d.b.'s on the down converter so the picture on the monitor would be sharp for tomorrow's class. I got to talk to the scientists of Goddard Space Mobile on the ATS-3."
> "Far out!"
> "Yeah! It's wild."[47]

What children were learning from this episode in public broadcasting was less how to read and write than how to become junior communications bureaucrats. Interestingly, conservative critics who charge that PBS has pushed a liberal social agenda have been silent about this more blatant effort at social engineering. It is also intriguing to note that just a few short years after COMSAT used the clout of its space monopoly to kill the Friendly–Ford Foundation plan for public broadcasting's satellite use, this satellite–public television demonstration project was fully under way—with the crucial difference that this was NASA's satellite, which NASA controlled. Another difference is that while Friendly's proposal involved charging commercial networks, the STD was a private company supported by a battery of government funds. By 1975, the STD, headquartered in Denver, had received more than $11 million from three different federal agencies (as well as grants from the Alaska state government and the substantial investment by NASA); by the project's completion more than another $5 million in federal funds had been spent. This not insubstantial slice of satellite pork was conceived and carried out entirely under

Republican administrations. It is little wonder that Coloradan Joseph Coors saw so much potential in CPB's satellite plans.

Predictably, however, while a satellite system allowed for greater technical quality and an improved ability to reach remote areas, it could not address more fundamental public broadcasting questions. When Lawrence Grossman took the presidency of PBS in 1976, he showed little interest in satellite plans, insisting that the priorities should be "programming, programming, and programming. . . . Why build the greatest superhighway imaginable with nothing to put on it?"[48] Within a few months, however, PBS chairman Ralph Rogers convinced Grossman of satellite wisdom. His instinct was to put the technology to use, and the Senate confirmation hearings for incoming Carter cabinet members provided, he thought, an ideal opportunity. But not even the technical miracle of satellite transmission could overcome public television's post-Nixon antipathy to public affairs. "The system went berserk," Grossman recalls, and a movement arose to have him impeached. The problem was that the Senate hearings took place in the morning, and feeding them live via satellite meant displacing *Sesame Street* and *Mister Rogers' Neighborhood*. "The smaller stations didn't have the facilities to tape programs for future use," Grossman realized, "and they had contracts committed to run children's shows."[49]

PROMISES, PROMISES

By 1979, public television had contracted with Western Union to use the WESTAR satellite for its interconnection (public radio's conversion to satellite transmission occurred the following year). Today, as Grossman points out, the leaders of public broadcasting are often hailed as visionaries for following through on their satellite projects. But at the time, the preoccupation with future technology was also a retreat, a way of avoiding contemporary critics who insisted that the system had already failed in its mission to serve the underserved. This was increasingly the position of many on the American left—and within public broadcasting itself. The prolonged battle over Coors's nomination revealed that public broadcasting, like so many other American institutions, had become deeply polarized over identity politics. Dozens of major and minor civil rights, Latino, and women's organizations protested the Coors appointment: by letter, by telegram, and by appearing before the Commerce Committee. Some on the CPB board privately urged that the nomination be withdrawn, knowing that Coors's presence would have set back public broadcasting's attempts to dull criticism from such groups.

Because it is legally required to serve communities, and because it uses taxpayer money, public broadcasting has received far greater scrutiny and criticism than its commercial counterparts that its staff and programming do not reflect one or more aspect of American identity. To their credit, the stewards of public broadcasting on the national level have admitted that theirs is a unique duty. The CPB has set an extraordinarily high standard for itself, arguing that certain regulatory privileges can be justified only through public broadcasters' supposed accountability to communities. "Standards of community service must be higher than those for commercial broadcasters, and must be reflected not only in the ascertainment process but also in the quantity and quality of broadcast material designed to address community needs. . . . If it is appropriate to involve all willing elements of the community in the process of establishing station broadcast goals, it is all the more appropriate to involve them in the evaluation of station broadcast performance."[50] As far back as 1972, the CPB virtually begged to be evaluated by the standard of service to communities: "Licenses committed to public service do not regard community involvement in their efforts as an obligation imposed from above, to be tolerated every few years in order to satisfy a regulatory mandate. They welcome it. Their stations thrive on it."[51]

In practice, community service quite often means satisfying the representatives of one or more groups who claim to be underrepresented, and instead of thriving on community input, public broadcasters' open-arms rhetoric has returned to haunt them. The CPB, for example, was quick to acknowledge its duty to women and people of color, confessing that PBS's depiction of these groups was greatly lacking. "It is not a problem that is unique to public broadcasting," said the 1974 CPB annual report. "But it is one that public broadcasting is uniquely obligated to solve."[52]

Many steps, however, lie between the recognition of a problem and its solution; in bureaucracies those steps begin inevitably with the formation of a committee. Nearly every aspect of public broadcasting has been committeed and task-forced to the point of redundancy; none more so than its success or failure in minority hiring. In 1975, a CPB Task Force on Women in Public Broadcasting found "pervasive underrepresentation of women throughout the public broadcasting industry, both in employment and in program content," adding that the "disparity is especially marked at the decision-making levels in all aspects of public broadcasting."[53] The Task Force found that women held less than 30 percent of all jobs within the public broadcasting world. The jobs performed by women consistently paid poorly: 65 percent of women employees earned less than $9,000 a year, while only 25percent of men did. Only three women were making over $21,000 a year, while 60 men were making that amount or more.

The image of women that public broadcasting was projecting on the screen was not much better. Of the 28 adult programs studied by the Task Force in a week of public television, 11 had no women in them at all. Most of those all-male shows were clustered in public affairs: no women appeared on *Wall Street Week*, *Black Perspectives on the News*, or *Bill Moyers' Journal*. Thus, public television programming "directed to timely issues, dealing with events of major importance, such as the economy, government, and foreign policy issues, almost ignored women completely." The combination of feminist zeal and hard-numbers data was able to savage even public broadcasting's most praised accomplishments: among children's programs, *Sesame Street* "not only had the fewest numbers of female characters but also tended to present those females in traditionally feminine roles." Only one public television program—a weekly series called *Woman* —dealt specifically with what the Task Force labeled a "woman's issue." This pitiful record prompted the report's authors to conclude that "women are not 'stereotyped' on public television, they are overlooked."[54]

Having commissioned this caustic report, the CPB had no choice but to formally accept its recommendations: full integration of women into public broadcasting programming, equal pay for equal work, better recruitment of women, and a permanent Office of Women's Affairs within CPB. Two decades later, however, it is difficult to argue that these were anything but halfhearted measures. There remains no nationally known PBS program devoted to women's issues, nor any PBS-distributed public affairs program primarily hosted by a woman. (As we shall see in chapter 6, public radio has found itself on the wrong end of several lawsuits charging systematic discrimination against women.)

The issue of race in public television has been equally volatile, and the system's responses equally tepid. Most who have governed public broadcasting over the years have acknowledged that the medium has a special mandate to serve America's racial minorities and working-class citizens, since the Public Broadcasting Act specifically referred to those "communities not currently served by commercial broadcasting." Given that commercial advertisers generally prefer high-income families, it is hard to imagine, for example, a commercial network boasting—as PBS did in a 1977 press release—of new Nielsen surveys showing "a 15.4% increase in public TV viewership among households with a yearly income of less than $10,000."[55] PBS also proclaimed proudly that "the number of non-white households viewing public TV regularly increased 47.5% from a year earlier."

Blacks have probably been better represented on public television than any other "minority" group in America, beginning with the Ford Foundation commitments. That achievement, however, has hardly satisfied critics or representatives of black organizations. In a typical exchange in 1975, a House subcommittee chairman waited for CPB chairman Robert Benjamin to finish his opening statement, then immediately scolded him for the system's stagnation on meeting minority needs. "I am not being sarcastic," said Congressman Torbert MacDonald, "and I hope you don't take my remarks unkindly, but it reminds me of the musical 'Promises, Promises.' You have not taken much action—even on the hiring item."[56]

Black people within public broadcasting were even more critical. Tony Brown, one of public television's longest-running program hosts and its most visible person of color, has at times been especially militant in his criticism. In 1972, the CPB, acting on the Nixon White House's wishes, cut funds for Brown's PBS show *Black Journal* (along with almost the entire schedule of public affairs shows). When 100 black viewers picketed outside a CPB board meeting, the funding was restored. A triumphant Brown said: "They approved *Black Journal* because of the pressure from the Black community and from the Black press. . . . This proves that cohesiveness among Black people is our salvation."[57] The show's restoration, however, did not restore Brown's confidence in public broadcasting's commitment to black viewers or employees. In a 1974 Senate hearing, Brown lambasted the CPB for having established "a viable public broadcasting service for only one segment of our population—white America." Brown continued: "It is my firm conviction that this inequity is not the work of malice, evil, or prejudice. It is the result of those in power listening to and reinforcing those in power. And those in power are, naturally, because of the origin of our economic and political systems, predominantly white." Brown called the public broadcasting world (where, 20 years later, he still hosted a program) "a systematically, institutionally racist structure more frustrating than the old American bigotry of the South."[58]

The longevity of public broadcasting's failure to integrate either its staff or its programming is partly a subset of America's broader, de facto apartheid. But the race problem has been exacerbated by public broadcasting's peculiar institutions. For example, the leadership of the CPB for years rather shamefully insisted that—as a private, nonprofit corporation—it was not bound by the equal opportunity laws that governed federal agencies. In 1975, CPB chairman Robert Benjamin lamented that the CPB was "becoming the object of pressures from many parties who would have [it] behave like a Government agency or department," a goal which, he said, "would pervert the very philosophy of the Public Broadcasting Act and ultimately render the corporation useless."[59] (Not until 1978 was this responsibility spelled out in legislation.) And a great number of public television and radio stations employed so few people that they did not fall under the jurisdiction of the Equal Employment Opportunity Commission.

Even assuming, however, that the CPB wanted to launch an all-out affirmative action plan, it has always possessed powers too limited to do so. A commercial media outlet might be able to dictate that every other person hired be a person of color, or mandate that a certain number of visible program hours be given to minority producers (*USA Today* editors, for example, have a more or less firm order to carry a front-page photo of a nonwhite person in every day's paper, above the fold). But public broadcasting's insistence on localism makes such uniformity impossible. Indeed, the places where minority representation and programming might be needed most have, historically, also been the places where they are resisted most. Nearly half of public television stations are licensed to state governments or state universities—especially in the South and Midwest—and are thus unusually responsive to the state's political agenda. In the '60s and '70s, this arrangement meant that public television authorities were often the media enforcers of state segregation.

The longest-running and most notorious political program discrimination was practiced by the Alabama Educational Television Commission (AETC), a statewide network that, in the mid-'70s, consisted of eight stations. When educational broadcasting became public broadcasting in the late '60s, the population of Alabama was about 30 percent black, far greater than the national average. The state had witnessed the highest and lowest points of America's civil rights era (many of which were also crucial moments in television history): these included Rosa Parks's civil disobedience in 1955 and the ensuing bus boycott, and Martin Luther King's 1963 multicity crusade, culminating in Bull Connor's dog-and-fire-hose attack on peaceful protestors. It was from a jail in Birmingham, Alabama, that King wrote in 1963 one of the most powerful, resounding calls for immediate civil rights for blacks, and in a Birmingham church that a bomb killed four black children during Sunday services, bringing riots and the National Guard. Alabama also saw the 1965 mass arrest of King and almost 800 others in Selma, and the massive march to Governor George Wallace's statehouse in Montgomery.

It is no exaggeration to say that in Alabama, the issues of segregation and civil rights could incite some people to violence. The response, therefore, of the AETC was to avoid these issues, in nearly any form. The resulting irony was that on those occasions when educational and public television viewers across the nation were watching programs about civil rights battles in Alabama, the WAIQ viewer in Montgomery or the WBIQ viewer in Birmingham would generally not see them. Decades later, PBS would bring to public television viewers compelling images of civil rights marches in *Eyes on the Prize* and *Freedom on My Mind*, but while those events were actually transpiring, they were forbidden on southern systems such as AETC.

AETC's blinders strategy was made simpler by the fact that through the mid-'70s, the AETC had no black commissioners, no black professional staff, and no blacks on its program board. The programming offered by National Educational Television (NET) was laden with discussions—sometimes quite provocative—about civil rights and related race issues, and many of those programs carried into the early years of PBS. These programs might well have created controversy in Alabama—and thus they were not aired. In the blunt words of a 1974 FCC decision, NET "offered a substantial amount of [black-oriented] programming," but AETC "elected to broadcast virtually none of these programs. . . . In a state whose black population is approximately 30 percent, this obviously presents an issue of grave importance."[60]

In the early '70s, a coalition of church activists and communications attorneys challenged AETC's fitness to hold broadcasting licenses, arguing that it had utterly failed to serve the public interest. These protestors undertook a study to determine how often the stations broadcast what was labeled "integrated" programming, sampling five random weeks from a four-year period. In one week in 1967, a minuscule 0.7 percent of the network's programming fell into that category. By the end of the test period, a week from January 1970, the AETC had substantially upped its "integrated" programs, to 12.7 percent of broadcast hours. But, the FCC noted scornfully, "this increase was due almost entirely to the frequent broadcast of *Sesame Street*, a non-locally produced program for pre-school children."[61]

The Alabama television commissioners became quite creative in their rationalizations for rejecting racially hot programming. The network did not broadcast any episode of the series *Soul!*, arguing that its time slot conflicted with the broadcast of *Firing Line*; the AETC could have arranged to show *Soul!* at another time, but chose not to. Without explanation, the NET series *On Being Black* was not carried, and neither was a special on the Denver trial of a Black Panther. AETC deleted a segment of the program *Black Journal,* arguing that it contained "obscene material"; the segment included "damn," "go to hell," and a reference to "rats leaving crap in the corner." The FCC dismissed the "obvious lameness" of the AETC's obscenity rationale, and asserted that the AETC's "pre-emption decisions point irresistibly toward a conclusion of racial discrimination."[62]

The most outrageous example of the Alabama network's TV apartheid was its failure to cover a burning racial issue in its own backyard: the multiyear struggle to desegregate the schools in Alabama's Macon County. Beginning in 1964, a federal court had ordered Governor George Wallace to desegregate the state's schools, beginning in Macon County, and when he refused, teachers and parents struggled for years to force compliance in the mostly black county. When asked why AETC had omitted ever mentioning what was arguably the most important local issue of the decade, the general manager of the AETC, Raymond Hurlbert, testified before the FCC that he was only "vaguely aware" of the story, and that the AETC had taken "no steps to investigate the legal controversies" it brought up. The FCC could hardly contain its contempt, declaring it "literally incredible that a man in Mr. Hurlbert's position would be unaware of the situation which prevailed in the administration of the Alabama school system during this period." In a rare move for commercial or noncommercial broadcasters, the FCC declined to renew Alabama's television licenses, declaring that the AETC's "history of disservice" made it "impossible for us to find that renewal would serve the public interest, convenience and necessity." (That decision was later softened in a compromise, and in 1980, the state regained control of all eight of its public TV stations.)[63]

Although Alabama was an extreme case, black and other minority organizations insisted that public broadcasting consisted of a series of mini-Alabamas. Their legitimate distrust of the public television establishment sometimes spilled over into protests that—with different intent—had a similar effect in narrowing public television's representation of black Americans. In 1975, the CPB gave a $23,000 grant to New York's WNET to purchase and package a Swedish documentary called *Harlem: Voices, Faces*, a bleak and somewhat exploitative portrait of the black neighborhood's pathological side. The station produced a 90-minute version, and scheduled a 30-minute panel discussion of two black academics and a political activist, moderated by Roger Wilkins, then on the *New York Times* editorial board.

After Tony Brown read a press release about the scheduled broadcast, he organized a nationwide protest of black civic groups, and petitioned the panelists to withdraw. In a letter to PBS president Hartford Gunn, Brown called the documentary a "racist statement," and predicted that if it were shown, "the bigoted sector of white America will have its prejudices frozen in place and reinforced, and so many black people . . . will be even more psychologically destitute."[64] The would-be panelists withdrew, and the film was yanked off the station's schedule. Wilkins—who thought the film "awful"—nonetheless lamented that "we are entering a period of neoracism where only the exceptional Negroes are given coverage and the pathology is denied. People are saying, 'We've *tried* to solve those problems,' and now they are giving up."[65] This neo-racism is partly attributable to the phenomenon that would later be deemed political correctness, but in this and so many other episodes the response of Brown and his allies bespoke a seething frustration with a public medium detached from the public it proposed to represent.

As with the underrepresentation of women, a Task Force on Minorities in Public Broadcasting was convened, and its 1978 report, *A Formula for Change*, reached nearly identical conclusions. It found "what appears to be a vicious cycle designed to exclude minorities from public broadcasting." The report claimed that not a single African American or other minority member was in a primary leadership position at either CPB or PBS, and that people of color were similarly excluded from local stations. Of the country's nearly 300 public television stations, only one was controlled by a person of color. The Task Force concluded that public television was "asleep at the transmitter."

It says a great deal about the lack of high-level representation of women and minorities in public broadcasting that the same person—Gloria Anderson, a black female CPB director—chaired both task forces. Anderson recalls that on the day she presented a report to the CPB board, the board had spent the "whole day discussing plans for the system's first satellite. I presented the recommendations, they said thank you, and it was over in five minutes."[66] No questions were asked; the board had no debate or even discussion of these issues that were giving public broadcasting a bad name in Congress and among community leaders. "There were things that were done," Anderson acknowledges, eventually including minority training programs, under which CPB would pay up to 50 percent of the salaries of qualified minority employees at stations around the country.

But even the most dedicated CPB directors never bothered to familiarize themselves with the system's racial record. Ralph Rogers, the man credited with saving public broadcasting after the Nixon-induced crisis of 1973–74, once told Anderson that he "didn't believe there was any discrimination in public broadcasting. He said to me: 'If I hear of anything like that, we will get in my jet, and we will go to the station, and we will tell them they can't discriminate against women or minorities.'"[67] Even though the reports Anderson submitted to CPB documented far-flung discrimination, no such jet-hopping ever occurred. "Either he didn't understand CPB's mandate," Anderson concludes, "or he ignored it."

6

RADIO WAVES

"It seems to me as if you are talking as if you felt that public radio
is sort of a poor relative to public TV?"
"Yes. Well, I think it is clear just from the facts."
—MATTHEW COFFEY, PRESIDENT OF AMERICAN PUBLIC RADIO STATIONS, ANSWERING
A QUESTION FROM CONGRESSMAN TORBERT MCDONALD, APRIL 9, 1975

Radio's status as the neglected child of the public broadcasting family dogged it
even before federal funding began. The Carnegie report, entitled *Public Television:
A Program for Action*, does not mention radio. The original draft of the Johnson
administration's public broadcasting bill, according to Johnson aide Douglass
Cater, referred only to television. "When we drafted our legislation, we didn't
have anything on public radio. [I realized it] less than 24 hours before the bill was
supposed to go to Congress. I phoned in to the budget bureau, and we injected
public radio. It was nearly a mishap."[1] While that recollection may be a simplifica-
tion or exaggeration of real events, there is no question that federal funding and
national programming for radio was essentially an afterthought.[2]

Nonetheless, as public broadcasting came into being in the late 1960s, public
radio possessed several distinct advantages. There were more noncommercial
radio stations than television stations, and most of those stations had been operating for a longer period. Because of radio's relatively low cost and mobility, it provides a sense of immediacy and flexibility that most television, including public
television, avoids. As an NPR official wrote in 1974: "[R]adio programming tends
to become a continuing process into which can be fitted units of almost any length
without drastic upset of predisposed listener expectation. In fact, listeners are
coming to expect the unexpected, the real, the 'now,' from public radio stations."[3]

It is hard to overstate how thoroughly decentralized American public radio is.
Today, NPR's best-known programs, *Morning Edition* and *All Things Considered*
(*ATC*), are current affairs programs that are almost always used at their original
airing time. That seeming uniformity, however, belies the reality: the average

115

NPR affiliate station—there are about 600 nationwide—devotes only about 15 percent of its schedule to NPR programming. The remainder is filled by a variety of material: music chosen by local disk jockeys, community talk or news shows, syndicated programs from the BBC, Public Radio International, or even *Newsweek on Air*. In this decentralized not-quite-network, generalizations are hard to come by. Complicating American public radio even further is the smaller Pacifica network. Although it consists of only a half-dozen stations in five markets nationwide, Pacifica Radio, like NPR, receives federal funds from the CPB (as of 1995, approximately $1 million annually) and is substantially older than National Public Radio. (About 40 additional stations not formally affiliated with the Pacifica Foundation pick up some of Pacifica Radio News; in 1996, the Pacifica news service also expanded its potential "listenership" by establishing an audio-based Worldwide Web service.) Over the years, Pacifica has drawn audiences as loyal—and in some cases nearly as large—as NPR's, as well as a disproportionate share of political criticism.

Despite the difficulty of making generalizations, in several measurable ways, public radio comes closer than public television to achieving public broadcasting's loftier goals, particularly its commitment to community service. The format of *All Things Considered* and *Morning Edition*, NPR's most popular programs, allows local stations to cut in and provide news and information relevant to local listeners, a capability national public television generally makes available only during pledge periods. NPR programs have long been, to use the '90s jargon, "interactive": they regularly read letters over the air or play voice recordings of listener feedback, a privilege national public television generally denies its viewers. Some of NPR's national programming, such as the daily *Talk of the Nation*, includes live nationwide caller input, a populist trait absent in public television.

At the same time, NPR, perhaps more than public television, has suffered from a decades-long identity crisis. In part because of its loose structure, and in part because of a fluctuating sense of its role as an "alternative" versus a "primary" news provider, the Washington headquarters of NPR has long been a site of internal squabbling, personnel struggles, and wars waged by memoranda. In 1983, this already volatile situation was punctuated by a bankruptcy that forced drastic reorganization; the service remained alive only via a favorable loan from the CPB. Conceived as an alternative radio presence but used by many listeners in ways similar to a newspaper or wire service, NPR has been dramatically torn between national and local needs, between hard-news advocates and aural pioneers, between fundamentalists who stress the primacy of programming and pragmatists who see noncommercial airwaves as a great place for commercial activity.

"THE FEEL AND TEXTURE OF THE DAY"

National Public Radio, a nonprofit corporation, was formed in 1970; it began providing national programming for noncommercial stations in the U.S. and territories on April 1, 1971. Its quirky mission statement stabs at the coarseness of modern American life; it reads almost as if it were written by a team of existentialist psychologists. NPR pledged it would "serve the individual: it will promote personal growth; it will regard the individual differences among men with respect and joy rather than with derision and hate; it will celebrate the human experience as infinitely varied rather than vacuous and banal; it will encourage a sense of active, constructive participation rather than apathetic helplessness."

NPR's mission statement refers to both a "cultural mode" and "journalistic mode," with the former designed to "provide listeners with an aural esthetic experience which enriches and gives meaning to the human spirit." As for journalism, it is not enough for NPR simply to get the stories; it conceives of itself as the building block of democracy: "The programs will enable the individual to better understand himself, his government, his institutions and his natural and social environment so that he can intelligently participate in effecting the process of change."[4] The NPR mission draws deeply from the liberal humanist tradition; surely it is the only launching pad for a mass medium service that cites Susan Sontag.

The most dominant figure in shaping this statement was William Siemering—who was also the driving force behind *All Things Considered*. Siemering had grown up in Wisconsin in the '40s and '50s, impressed with how educational station WHA was able to bring news and culture to his farmer neighbors. That and his experience with community radio in Buffalo shaped the scope and goals of the early NPR.[5] The first broadcast of *All Things Considered*, on May 3, 1971, sounded like nothing that had been on American radio before. It coincided with a massive anti-Vietnam demonstration throughout Washington, D.sC. More than 6,000 protestors were arrested that day; having attempted to shut down the workings of the federal government, the demonstrators succeeded primarily in clogging Washington's local criminal justice system. *ATC*'s coverage was almost certainly the most comprehensive of any nationally available medium. After host Robert Conley delivered an overview of the day's arrests and confrontations, he gave what would become a kind of mission statement for the program: "Rather than pulling in reports from all over town, we thought we might try to take you to the event, the feel and texture of the day, through a mix of sounds and events."[6] What followed was a lengthy hodgepodge of recorded stories and interviews, through which listeners could hear army surveillance helicopters, the sounds of police officers arresting people, demonstrators clapping and chanting, "Stop the war now!" and so forth. A roundtable discussion followed with reporters from the *Christian Science Monitor*, which then segued into a reading—courtesy of the Canadian Broadcasting Corporation—of two antiwar poems from the World War I era, set to military music. Rounding out the evening was a dispatch from a barber shop in Ames, Iowa, where barbers had taken to shaving women's legs to compensate for lost revenues created by longer men's hairstyles. Finally there was a harrowing portrait of a onetime nurse named "Janice" who was addicted to heroin, followed by a discussion with Allen Ginsberg and his father about the merits and pitfalls of drug use.

As with so many public broadcasting staples, *ATC* was not an immediate hit, and was misunderstood by the very entities it today supports and defines: local public radio stations. "A month after *ATC*'s debut," according to one internal history, "the first Public Radio Conference was held and the reaction of station managers to the program was uniformly negative. The program was criticized for being ragged, unprofessional, and too liberal, among other things. Some thought the program 'artsy-crafty' and even counterculture oriented; others objected because it did not sound enough like commercial radio."[7] One author notes that *ATC*'s long, almost antiformat approach "often drew complaints from local stations whose listeners would get bent slightly out of shape by the occasional 'fuck' or 'shit' emanating from NPR interviews."[8] There were related tensions within NPR itself, and soon the *ATC* format was juggled. Susan Stamberg and Mike Waters were brought in as hosts; by 1972, most station managers had come around to support the program.

Compared with public television, public radio suffered very little from the Nixon-CPB wars.[9] The paper trail from the Nixon White House shows very little concern for public radio, regardless of its political orientation or its failure to adhere to principles of localism. This benign neglect probably helped NPR get off the ground with a minimum of interference; on the other hand, as the second Carnegie report noted in 1979, "with no increase in federal funds as a result of the [1972 CPB authorization] veto, the growth of public radio was slower than it might have been. And in resolving the conflict between CPB and PBS, little attention was paid to the needs of radio. It is curious that public radio—also criticized by Whitehead, in his NAEB speech, for what was in fact a far more centralized program production process—survived the period virtually unaffected by the political battles. Perhaps this was because public radio, underfinanced and with few outlets, posed little real political threat."[10]

Even without the Nixon-driven disdain, NPR suffered its own crisis about how much of its airtime should be devoted to the "journalistic mode." Although NPR was theoretically structured to purchase and rebroadcast reports from its member stations, in its early years the local stations were unaccustomed to preparing such tapes, and thus the broadcasts leaned heavily on material from the NPR central office in Washington. Inevitably, the definition of news from the Capitol Hill area sounded, to many, like the traditional media definition of news: Congressional hearings, press conferences, cabinet secretary interviews, etc. Under Robert Zelnick and Jim Russell, NPR's National News and Information Bureau became an aggressive journalistic outpost. *ATC*'s ability to run news pieces as long as 10, occasionally even 20 minutes freed NPR reporters to explore stories with unusual depth, and they used this freedom to explore such risky topics as urban poverty, presidential politics, national security, and American foreign policy. There were rumblings at the time that, as with public television, reporting on such topics occasionally became too aggressive for those holding public radio's reins: among the NPR stringers deemed controversial was Morton Halperin, a onetime Nixon aide whose writings in the area of national security have irritated the American right for decades.

The tension within NPR between hard news and cultural production has been so fierce and lasting that it infects even the organization's memories of itself. Through the mid-'70s, NPR's lengthier, non-news productions were almost as well known as *All Things Considered*. A weekly documentary series called *Options in Education*, for example, presented an hour-long exploration of issues in that field, gathered into reports and discussions from around the country.[11] Radio-adapted drama and fiction were NPR staples, and a series called *Voices in the Wind* brought performing arts to a reasonably large radio audience. The pinnacle of NPR's humanistic thrust was the 13-part *A Question of Place*, a National Endowment for Humanities project that explored the work of William Faulkner, Simone de Beauvoir, Michel Foucault, W. E. B. Du Bois, and other twentieth-century luminaries. And while many NPR veterans and former staffers recall these as the organization's golden days of experimentation, others deride the indulgent "ear candy" of aural experimentation. "People talk about the 'golden days,'" says Neal Conan, "but they forget that in the old days we had a few very good things but put an awful lot of crap on the air because we had nothing else."[12]

In April 1976, NPR president Lee Frischknecht circulated a 45-page memo outlining proposed changes in the operations of the national NPR office. The memo was particularly hard on NPR's National News and Information Bureau, charging that it focused too much on "political and economic affairs," that it ignored "analysis and background which are clearly stated within our goals," that it paid insufficient attention to the views of women and minorities, and that it

relied on "predictable sources."[13] Regardless of whether the charges were valid
—and they were disputed in a blistering 5,000-word memorandum written by
Bob Zelnick, who then headed the bureau—they represent the continuing and
often painful tension between the goals of a news-gathering organization and the
demands of stations. Explaining his reshuffle to *The New York Times*, Frischknecht
said he was responding to the demands of NPR's member stations, who wanted
more jazz; more programs for women, minorities, and the elderly; less current
affairs; and more of "the kinds of things that used to be called human interest."[14]

Frischknecht's reorganization plan and his decision to hire an outside consultant to study NPR's operations provoked impassioned and widespread resignation threats. *ATC*'s Susan Stamberg, who would go on to become one of NPR's
best-known personalities, wrote Frischknecht that she would "have to leave" if
his proposed reorganization went through. "The staff will fall like a house of
cards, unable to function," she handwrote on a memo. "There will be no point in
staying to pick [up] pieces that have been put so laboriously into place—at such a
great intellectual and psychological cost—over these years."[15] The tension
apparently rose to the point of fisticuffs; White House correspondent Richard
Holwill was disciplined because, according to Frischknecht, he had "seized NPR
staff member Jay Kernis by his clothing and violently propelled him." Holwill
maintained the incident was "harmless horseplay," but was suspended for three
days without pay. (Holwill left NPR shortly thereafter, and ended up working for
Ronald Reagan, who nominated him to be ambassador to Ecuador.)

Nina Totenberg, considered today to be one of NPR's biggest talents, came
close to being fired. A supervisor concluded: "Nina Totenberg did take a copy of a
confidential memo from Bob Zelnick to Lee Frischknecht from Zelnick's desk,
which she then passed to the [now-defunct *Washington*] *Star*. This is an act of
theft, a criminal act on the NPR premises, and grounds for suspension under
NPR policies and procedures."[16]

Almost certainly part of the backdrop to these suspensions and reprimands
was a pending vote on whether or not the staff would unionize with the American Federation of Television and Radio Artists (which they did, later that year).
There is also some reason to believe that Frischknecht was trying to make NPR
more corporate-friendly. Around the same time as the flare-up, NPR officials had
their first-ever meeting with potential corporate funders—hosted by Gulf Oil.
According to a Texas public radio broadcaster who resigned during this period
from NPR's program advisory board, Frischknecht had said in early 1976 that he
felt NPR's occasional forays into advocacy journalism "made it hard to attract
needed outside funding."[17]

Regardless of what specifically led to this 1976 crisis, the hard reality is that

During a newspaper strike in the 1940s, famed populist Republican mayor Fiorello LaGuardia took to the city-owned radio station WNYC to read daily comic strips to hundreds of thousands of New York City children. Half a century later, Republican mayor Rudolph Giuliani, who claimed to model himself after La Guardia, sold WNYC's television station to media conglomerates, decimating programming aimed at the immigrant communities La Guardia championed.

Nixon aide Clay Whitehead led the charge against public broadcasters, charging them with anti-administration bias and accusing them of practicing "ideological plugola."

Thomas Curtis, Nixon's hand-picked candidate for the chairmanship of the Corporation for Public Broadcasting, lasted only six months, charging the White House with "not respecting the integrity of the board."

On the day in 1972 when Henry Loomis was appointed to head the Corporation for Public Broadcasting, he asked: "What the hell is it?"

Carter media advisor Barry Jagoda resigned his post following Senate criticism over his scheduling of a Vladimir Horowitz concert on public television.

One of the longest running public affairs programs on public television is William F. Buckley's *Firing Line*. Buckley has boasted for years that he receives no money from the federal government, glossing over the fact that Firing *Line's* distributor, the Southern Educational Communications Association, takes hundred of thousands of dollars in federal funds. Here, Buckley interviews convicted Watergate conspirator E. Howard Hunt.

$2.50

EXTRA!

A Publication of FAIR

Inside:
Election Survey,
Syndicated Columnists,
October Surprise

June 1992
Vol. 5, No. 4

PBS' Missing Voices

pages 15-18

COMING UP NEXT: A GATHERING OF PUBLIC TV HOSTS DISCUSS THE INVISIBILITY OF **CONSERVATIVES** ON PBS STATIONS...

MORTON KONDRACKE SPONSORED BY OLIN, BRADLEY FOUNDATIONS

JOHN McLAUGHLIN SPONSORED BY GE, MET LIFE, PEPSICO

MACNEIL/ LEHRER SPONSORED BY PEPSICO, AT&T

TONY BROWN SPONSORED BY PEPSICO

LOUIS RUKEYSER SPONSORED BY WALL STREET

WILLIAM F. BUCKLEY SPONSORED BY OLIN, MOBIL, PAINE WEBBER

As cartoonist Tom Tomorrow demonstrated on the cover of *Extra!*, no matter how many corporate-sponsored conservatives appear on public television, right-wing critics continue to charge that they are underrepresented on public broadcasting. In fact, the publication that has singlehandedly most influenced the content and management of public television is the conservative *National Review*.

While occasional controversial PBS program like *Tongues Untied* or *Stop the Church* generate attention from Members of Congress and conservative activists, the bulk of public television screentime is devoted to far tamer fare. Quilting shows are particularly prized: the Florida PBS affiliate WCEU, for example, carries no fewer than four regular programs devoted to the quilting craft, including *Quilt in a Day*, starring Eleanor Burns, pictured here. *Quilt in a Day* runs continuously on more than 100 stations, and is especially popular in the South and Midwest.

Footage courtesy WPBA; photo by Linda Marrow

Despite Gingrich's repeated insistences that he would zero out the federal money for public broadcasting, Atlanta's WPBA enlisted the House Speaker in its spring 1995 pledge drive. Gingrich praised Ken Burns's documentaries and *Sesame Street*, and urged viewers to call in. "Tell them Newt Gingrich told you that it's important that PBS stays on the air," said the Speaker.

During a January 1995 subcommittee hearing, New York Congresswoman Nita Lowey donned hand puppets of the well-known *Sesame Street* duo of Bert and Ernie to voice her support for continued federal funds for public broadcasting. The muppets seemed indifferent to the infantilization of Congressional debate.

Photo by Bob McKeown; courtesy AndersonGold Films

In this still from the documentary *Out at Work*—which examined the fallout from three people who told fellow workers that they were gay or lesbian—one of the film's main characters denounces the anti-gay policies of his employer. During the spring of 1997, PBS refused to allow *Out at Work* to be shown on the *P.O.V.* series, claiming that the documentary's funding by labor unions violated the conflict-of-interest provisions of PBS's underwriting guidelines. A PBS spokesman claimed that unions would not be allowed to fund programming related to workplace issues, even though corporations are routinely given that privilege.

NPR's national management during this time had overwhelming external re-
sponsibilities that made it impossible to effectively oversee the content of NPR.
Many headaches were strictly financial: while federal funds allocated for public
broadcasting were growing dramatically so that the entire nation could receive its
signals, the *division* of money between radio and television consistently short-
changed public radio, or so public radio's bosses have always maintained. Between
1970 and 1976, the federal CPB appropriation ballooned by 423 percent, and the
size of the average grant to television stations grew by nearly 1,000 percent; the
size of the average grant to radio stations increased by only 276 percent.[18]
(Through the mid-'70s the portion of the CPB operating budget going to radio
was between 10 and 18 percent; today it is legislatively fixed at 25 percent.) Thus,
Congressional begging and cajoling was a constant necessity, but garnering
greater sums from Congress required solving a chicken-egg dilemma: even sympathetic Members of Congress wanted some tangible evidence of listener interest
before allowing more federal money to be spent, but without being able to reach
more listeners, NPR found it hard to generate interest.

Although it seems mundane today, one of the most important legislative battles that NPR leaders had to fight was to get the government to mandate that all
radios sold for more than a certain price be wired to receive both AM and FM signals. Since a substantial number of NPR affiliates were FM stations, this was a
lobbying priority; Congress did not pass the law until 1974 (and did so by a very
thin margin). Moving to a system of satellite transmission was also an acoustical
and logistical priority that took up a great deal of managerial time. The attempts
to streamline the nation's public radio bureaucracy (through an eventual merger
with the American Public Radio System) also taxed NPR's management. So while
the atmosphere at NPR's national office in these early years can legitimately be
described as chaotic, it is something of a wonder that the fledgling network got as
far as it did. By 1977, approximately 60 percent of the U.S. population could
receive an NPR station signal—a remarkable achievement in less than a decade.

"A FAILURE OF MANAGEMENT"

As it did with public television, the Carter administration tried to heal and nurture the public radio system. In some cases, this support bordered on political
co-optation, as when a Democratic National Committee official attempted to
get White House aides Hamilton Jordan and Barry Jagoda to influence the
choice for the presidency of NPR following Frischknecht's 1977 departure.[19]
Although the DNC's attempt was unsuccessful, the NPR presidency went to

Frank Mankiewicz, a longtime public relations functionary associated with the Democratic Party. Mankiewicz's early years are sometimes portrayed as a time when resources were shuffled toward hard news, which in part meant recruiting stars from mainstream commercial organizations (as opposed to the network of university and Pacifica stations that had filled many of the slots in the early '70s). One NPR innovation during the Mankiewicz era—successful at least in terms of building support for NPR on Capitol Hill—was that in early 1978, it carried live broadcasts of the Senate hearings on the Panama Canal Treaty, which sparked listener enthusiasm arguably analogous to public television's Watergate hearings; an official CPB publication declared in February 1978 that "live coverage is a hit."[20] Mankiewicz was also willing to venture out on a funding limb, proposing that public radio be paid for through a permanent tax on the revenues of commercial broadcasters. This was, as *Congressional Quarterly* dryly suggested, "a concept totally opposed by commercial broadcasters."[21]

The "professionalization" of NPR during Mankiewicz's stewardship also meant studying NPR listeners as consumers, albeit "noncommercial" consumers. Even more vehemently than their colleagues in public television, employees of public radio have long had a passionate hatred for the use of ratings and market research. "The reason commercial radio is a stinkhole is because of ratings," said Larry Josephson, former station manager of Pacifica's WBAI station and host of the NPR program *Bridges*, at a 1979 conference.[22] A manager of WPBX in Spokane expressed the same sentiment: "The moment we ask research to answer metaphysical questions, and help us find cultural integrity, that is the moment I believe we become commercial broadcasters."[23]

But by 1980, NPR dropped any resistance to blatant, in-depth market research, and hired one of the nation's leading firms, Simmons Market Research Bureau, to survey and measure its audiences. Their findings included "psychographic data," material that purports to measure how NPR listeners feel about themselves in an attempt to understand their behavior. Using the confoundingly circular logic practiced by marketing experts, when the survey found that only 30 percent of the NPR audience thinks advertising presents "a true picture of the products of well-known companies," the NPR promoters did not despair that advertisers would thus resist trying to reach listeners who didn't respect them. Instead, NPR argued that this situation had a silver lining. If underwriters used some of their advertising budget to support public radio, argued one study, NPR could "encourage them to include in their print advertising the fact that they support station WXXX. That will have the dual impact of adding to the credibility of their advertising message—it might help build the local public radio audience, which in turn, will mean more people will hear their underwriting credit on the air."[24]

The production of such gibberish only served to deepen the gulf between public radio's self-styled realists and fundamentalists. The realists now believed they had reams of hard data on which to make programming decisions (74 percent of NPR women listeners describe themselves as "amiable, affable, benevolent"! Fifty-two percent agree that "all products that pollute the environment should be banned"!), while the fundamentalists were convinced that NPR, under the influence of Reaganite values, was straying from its idealistic mission.

The 1979 debut of *Morning Edition* deepened the same rift. *Morning Edition* was designed as an accelerated version of *ATC*, involving many of the same stories and reporters but in abbreviated form, without the leisurely pace and with less of the "alternative" flavor. Although it, too, was initially poorly received, by 1989 *Morning Edition*'s audience surpassed that of *ATC* (4.9 million weekly listeners versus 4.6 million) and has retained its eminence ever since. The two news-driven programs required still more tinkering with the setup of NPR's natsional office, which evolved into a system of news "desks" like those of commercial stations and newspapers. This, in turn, created a need for reporters and writers, and thus NPR in the early '80s plucked many of its hires from the world of print journalism, moving public radio a step closer to a "hard-news" organization.[25]

Whatever NPR officials' enthusiasms were for ratings and potential underwriting revenues, they might have done better in the early '80s to examine the way money was being spent and accounted for. By 1983, an accounting firm's report showed that the nonprofit entity was $6.5 million in the red—an extraordinarily high debt, given that the annual budget was $26 million, about $20 million of which was federal funds. The accounting firm Coopers & Lybrand determined that NPR "may be unable to continue in existence."[26] More embarrassing than the debt itself were the explanations for how it came about, which showed not just an unfamiliarity with business techniques but utter ineptitude. NPR was weeks and months late in sending out hundreds of thousands of dollars in bills, used bad accounting software, misestimated income by registering many grants twice, and kept horrendously sloppy records of travel and entertainment expenses. Between 110 and 125 American Express cards had been issued, and staffers ran up travel and entertainment bills of more than a half million dollars.[27] NPR had also illegally withheld more than $800,000 in federal and local taxes, an amount that auditors predicted would earn substantial penalties and fines.

Right-wing commentators had a field day. What better proof could be offered that public radio was a superfluous government entity run by an effete group incapable of surviving in the private sector? In a syndicated column, Pat Buchanan dubbed NPR "an upholstered little playpen of our Chablis-and-brie set." Public broadcasters and their political supporters weren't pleased either, predicting that the incompetence would reflect poorly on the entire system. Ward Chamberlain, president of Washington's WETA television and radio stations, called NPR's financial management "disgraceful," adding: "It's unbelievable and pretty hard to know how you can run up a $4.5 million deficit on a $26 million budget and have people claim they didn't know what was going on." John Dingell, a key Congressional ally, agreed, criticizing NPR's "cavalier" attitude toward its public monies.[28]

NPR's service came within days—some say hours—of shutting down. In mid-1983, Frank Mankiewicz resigned, willing to take the fall for the debacle, though often sounding notes of defiance: "Hell, we're only talking about a few million dollars. The United States government is going to have a deficit of $250 billion, and their president's not resigning."[29] (Mankiewicz remained, however, on the NPR payroll as an $80,000-a-year consultant.)

On top of these cuts, a massive appeal to listeners, called "The Drive to Survive," pulled NPR through this crisis; in three days of soliciting over only about one-third of NPR's affiliates, the campaign raised more than $2 million. NPR also took the bold step of allowing its audience to listen in on internal conversations about the crisis and the mismanagement that brought it about. *ATC* reporter Scott Simon got the assignment to describe the financial abyss; in one broadcast he stated plainly: "These are the very worst times in the thirteen-year history of National Public Radio, and they are occurring in a time, ironically, when the network's audience has never been larger, its programming more extensive, or its reputation for excellence greater."[30] When Simon brought Mankiewicz in for an on-air interview, the result was an extraordinary exchange, painful and candid for any broadcast medium. Mankiewicz, who by this point had already resigned, said: "What happened, of course, is that we underestimated the length and depth of the recession." Simon's response bordered on irreverence: "How could someone who not only listens to the two daily news programs that National Public Radio does, but also has a hand in them, be surprised by that?" After a humble gulp, Mankiewicz responded: "There you have a failure of management for which I'm not only willing to take the blame, but already have. We simply lacked either the people or the tools to track it."[31] It is impossible to imagine so frank a conversation taking place on national public television.

Part of the strategy to keep NPR alive despite its own mismanagement involved using Congressional clout. Mankiewicz had sought to make NPR's news services well known on Capitol Hill, a political marker that came in handy. Congressman Tim Wirth of Colorado (who was chairman of the House Subcommittee on Telecommunications, and would later hold a high position in the Clinton State Department) intervened in the tense discussions between NPR and its financial masters at CPB. After 12 hours of negotiating, NPR agreed to use its hard-won satellite transmission equipment as collateral for $7 million in a series of loans from the CPB (including one $500,000 loan completely interest free, and others at exceptionally low rates).

Thus did NPR begin an austerity program that corresponded gloomily with the broader Reagan cutbacks in federal funds for public broadcasting (see chapter 8): NPR's 1984 budget was cut by more than a third, to $17.65 million, and staff was cut by 30 percent. NPR's programming hours were slashed in half, with culture and arts programming virtually eliminated. Douglas Bennet, another functionary from Democratic politics, was brought in to take Mankiewicz's place, and he installed a firm system of cost controls.

Ironically, although Lee Frischknecht had expressed the fear in 1976 that NPR was too news heavy, the financial crisis pushed the service further in that direction. In addition, whatever possibility existed of keeping NPR a commercial-free environment was now eliminated. The early '80s had already seen Congress approve the Temporary Commission on Alternative Financing (TCAF), which experimented with corporate underwriting. Now public radio was desperate and opened itself wide to commerce, on both the national and local levels. As former NPR programmer Thomas Looker noted in his book *The Sound and the Story*, individual stations had previously used government and foundation money to cover basic operating expenses, and used their listener contributions to cover their relatively modest dues to NPR. But the cutbacks in federal funds meant that "public radio stations of the 1980s found themselves spending a lot of their time trying to squeeze money from the public which they were trying to serve. On-air membership drives proliferated and became more insistent. . . . Corporate underwriting became an important part of public stations' financial base, and suddenly the public airwaves, which for a couple of decades had provided a haven from the sales pitches of commercial broadcasting, began including a couple of minutes each hour of 'business.' "[32]

During this period NPR adopted the questionable practice of accepting donations to cover specific topics. Both *All Things Considered* and *Morning Edition* solicited and accepted grants from corporations for single-issue coverage. By one late-'80s count, nearly a third of NPR's news budget came from approximately 30 companies and foundations for specified programming, e.g., the John D. and Catherine T. MacArthur Foundation paying for national security coverage; the United States–Japan Foundation for coverage of Japanese affairs and U.S.-Japanese relations. The practice is unusual in American journalism: an individual reporter who accepted money for covering a story at a U.S. newspaper or radio station would likely be fired. Commercial networks and stations accept donations for separate programs, but a commercial network that hired out its regular news staff to report on a specific issue would certainly come under fire for putting the news up for sale.

In 1989, Richard Salant, the former CBS News president who sat on NPR's board, publicly criticized this practice in a dispute with NPR president Douglas Bennet; his concerns were echoed by *Morning Edition* host Bob Edwards. Salant ultimately resigned over the issue: "You can't say 'I'm going to be unethical just because it costs me too much to be ethical.'"[33] In fairness, the payment for reporting often results in stories that go significantly deeper into topics than most media coverage, commercial or noncommercial. Nonetheless, the practice is fraught with potential conflicts of interest,[34] and is one of the leading edges of corporate control over the medium.

PACIFICA

Although NPR is the largest and best-known public radio network, there are several other levels of public radio activity, including hundreds of tiny 10-watt stations, community radio stations, and large NPR-type services, such as Monitor Radio (a division of the *Christian Science Monitor*) and Public Radio International (which began as American Public Radio in 1981 and changed its name in 1994). Straddling the divide between localized "community" radio and broader "public" radio is the small Pacifica network. Although Pacifica-controlled stations operate in only five markets nationwide, Pacifica Radio, like NPR, receives federal funds from the CPB (as of 1995, approximately $1 million annually) and is substantially older than National Public Radio.

Founded in 1949 by a radical Quaker pacifist broadcaster named Lew Hill, Pacifica's charter pledged "to study the causes of philosophical, religious, racial and national antagonisms in the interest of world peace; to disseminate news and analysis that was being suppressed in commercial media; and to foster new art forms."[35] The original Pacifica station was Berkeley's KPFA-FM. The station, as one writer summarized, "quickly became one of the era's few expositors of radical politics and culture. Opponents of the Korean War, Alan Watts' lectures on Eastern mysticism, open discussions on the burgeoning marijuana culture, and interviews with Beat poets Allen Ginsberg and Lawrence Ferlinghetti all aired on KPFA during the early '50s."[36] In 1957, the station won a Peabody Award for its anti-McCarthy broadcasts.

Later Pacifica additions were Los Angeles's KPFK-FM, New York's WBAI-FM, Houston's KPFT-FM, and Washington, D.C.'s WPFW-FM, a huge 50,000-

watt station launched in 1977 after a 10 year legal battle with a Christian broadcasting group over the frequency's allocation.[37] WPFW has been a major cultural force: during the early 1980s, WPFW became the largest and
most-listened-to black community station in the United States, with a program
of jazz, Latin, and world beat music, and extensive coverage of black,
Caribbean, and Latin American politics.

Pacifica's employees and listeners often disagree passionately about how successfully Lew Hill's goals have been met; Pacifica seems to operate in a constant
state of crisis and redefinition. Its stations rely heavily on volunteer program
hosts, low-paid staff, and equipment that is often a generation behind the state
of the art. Nonetheless, its impact has been substantial: Pacifica is generally
credited with having initiated the on-air listener support drive and, although its
audience is limited, it is by far the public broadcasting entity with the highest
degree of individual listener financing. Long before live Congressional hearings
came over C-SPAN, they were a staple of Pacifica's political coverage. More than
any still-operating mass media outlet, Pacifica has documented the activities and
struggles of civil rights and black power organizations, the women's movement,
antinuclear and radical environmental groups, poor people and their advocates,
anti-Vietnam protestors, and gays and lesbians.

Although the Pacifica-operated stations are in large cities unassociated in the
popular mind with Native American populations, Pacifica's "unique commitment
to the unconventional and innovative, and its distinctly nonconformist (if not
antiestablishment) posture provided entree to the airwaves for many would-be
Native broadcasters,"[38] including Frank Ray Harjo and Suzan Shown Harjo,
whose dispatches on Indian politics aired on Pacifica stations in the '60s and
'70s. Pacifica's unique niche also extends beyond America's borders: when the
Indonesian-backed military conducted a massacre in East Timor in late 1991, the
only American journalists who witnessed it were Allan Nairn (affiliated with *The
New Yorker*) and Amy Goodman of Pacifica; Goodman's work on this story brought
widespread attention to Pacifica's reporting and won her broadcasting's prestigious Dupont Award.

Pacifica's ongoing commitment to radical politics might appear anomalous in
an era of corporate-controlled media with right-wing or shock-jock radio
celebrities. But it could also be argued that Pacifica's fervent commitment to
free speech—including speech that many Americans would label "dangerous"—
paved the way for the outrages of Howard Stern, Rush Limbaugh, and even the
militia-tinged radical radio of Chuck Harder. New York's WBAI, for example,
fought a protracted battle against the FCC in the late '80s for the right to read
passages from James Joyce's *Ulysses* in their steamy entirety on Bloomsday, and

was also the station involved in the landmark obscenity ruling that inaugurated the legal battle for broadcasting George Carlin's comedy routine "The Seven Words You Can't Say on Television." Pacifica's commitment to risky programming sometimes lands it in absurd positions. When, in 1990, the National Endowment for the Arts made grant recipients adhere to a policy of not using the money to create or promote "obscene" material, Pacifica had to consider returning a $20,000 grant designed to preserve 40,000 tapes from its own history.[39] It seems likely that Jesse Helms, author of the NEA's obscenity amendment, would have found something objectionable in the archived interviews with Allen Ginsberg, Jack Kerouac, Lenny Bruce, Huey Newton, and Abbie Hoffman.

Pacifica's stated commitment to programming that is more adventurous, more politically vibrant, and more community based than NPR's has not, however, kept it immune from the broader public broadcasting crises of the 1980s and '90s. On the contrary, Pacifica's militant and marginal commentators have frequently attracted the loudest criticism from congressional and conservative groups. Joel Hefley, a Republican Congressman from Colorado, helped spearhead a legislative attack against Pacifica. In 1993 and 1994, Hefley offered amendments to federal legislation that would cut back $1 million in federal money from the Corporation for Public Broadcasting—the amount that helps fund what he labels "the sensationalist hate programming that Pacifica is known for."[40] According to Hefley, Pacifica stations are responsible for airing such stories as the following:

- Jewish doctors are injecting black babies with the AIDS virus;

- There is a plot to "genetically annihilate" the black race;

- The U.S. government funded a 40-year experiment with syphilis on the entire black population;

- A recent measles epidemic was a "genocidal plot" by whites against the black community;

- The white Jewish population in America is "establishing the impoverishment of Black people."

All of this was brought to you with the help of federal subsidies!

Rarely during such attacks is any attempt made to determine whether such material is representative of Pacifica's overall programming, and the Congressional leaders who assemble attack hearings rarely invite Pacifica representatives to defend their broadcasts or their free speech rights. (This is not to say, however, that Pacifica has lacked Congressional supporters.)[41] More surprising than salvos like Hefley's is that the '80s and '90s have seen numerous criticisms of Pacifica from its traditional allies on the left—and indeed from within Pacifica itself. There are numerous causes for this tension, some related to broader splinters within left movements, and some specific to Pacifica. The tremendous growth and success of NPR, for example, created competition for literate, motivated listeners where Pacifica had once enjoyed local monopolies. This set off a series of probing identity crises. Former KPFK program director Clare Spark has outlined several such crises,[42] the most fundamental of which is: Can a community Pacifica station serve as an instrument for avowedly leftist social change, and at the same time serve as a forum for local community access?

Not only has Pacifica failed to resolve these warring impulses, but the chasm has arguably widened with recent events. During the 1990–91 Gulf War, Pacifica alienated some listeners by opening its airwaves to activists whose antiwar stance might have seemed consistent with the no-blood-for-oil position many progressives took, but who were in fact far-right figures with links to neo-Nazi organizations. According to Sara Diamond, an author who specializes in tracking far-right and hate groups: "Pacifica radio stations, long known as reliable sources of alternative public affairs broadcasts, promoted Bo Gritz, Craig Hulet and other luminaries of the far Right as if they were reputable analysts for the Left. Out of ignorance, Pacifica programmers misread the far Right's opposition to the Gulf War as a green light for a putative alliance."[43]

At KPFA in Berkeley, paid professionals who favored programming with mass appeal identified themselves as "populists" and canceled shows featuring alternative and leftist views, condemning them as "elitist." New York's WBAI dropped some of its programs hosted by established local leftists (such as *Left Business Observer* editor Doug Henwood) in favor of nationally syndicated shows from Jerry Brown and Julianne Malveaux. After donations dropped precipitously at WORT in Madison, Wisconsin, and as much as a third of the station listenership evaporated between the mid-'80s and early '90s, a kind of coup occurred, whereby volunteers dubbed "rabid ne'er-do-wells" overthrew a group of "professionals" and elected an entirely different board. Confronted by financial decline and internal debate, a station volunteer asked a question that framed one of public broadcasting's eternal dilemmas: "Is it more important to become more like commercial radio to gain a larger audience, or is it more important to continue to offer programming that cannot be heard elsewhere, acknowledging that the station may remain small and poor to do so?"[44]

For all its allegiance to the cause of free speech, Pacifica was more active in keeping any discussion of this crisis off the airwaves than NPR was during its dark days of 1983–84. At New York's WBAI, on-air hosts were barred from airing their grievances on their programs; the censorship only enhanced their frustration. During one of Pacifica's board meetings in New York in late September 1996, the avowedly left-wing radio network was picketed by members and supporters of the electrical workers' union, who charged that Pacifica had spent $30,000 on a union-busting law firm. In California, a group of volunteers and supporters of Berkeley's KPFA formed Take Back KPFA. They accused Pacifica of shifting its focus away from its community roots and listener sponsorship toward a national network more like NPR, changes they said "constitute fundamental deviations from Pacifica's longstanding claim to be 'the voice of the voiceless' and to serve as a genuine alternative."[45] These dissidents charged Pacifica with abandoning its commitment to free speech by holding its 1995 and 1996 board meetings in secret, a prima facie violation of CPB rules and state laws. Take Back KPFA claimed it could not even obtain minutes of the Pacifica board meetings, a policy the group said "is not only not in keeping with a network that claims to be 'First Amendment Radio,' it is also against the law."

LEAVING "ALTERNATIVE" BEHIND

If during the mid-'90s marginal or minority voices were becoming more difficult to air on Pacifica stations, they had become essentially impossible to find on NPR. Following NPR's return from financial ruin, the service grew into a major media player, both in news and in cultural programming. Garrison Keillor's *A Prairie Home Companion*, originally rejected for distribution by NPR, became a huge hit. Two chattering men who called themselves Click and Clack made a smash out of *Car Talk*, a call-in show combining two quintessential American elements: self-reliance and an obsession with the automobile. By 1990, the weekday audience for NPR's news programs reached more than 3.5 million; NPR had hit prime time, leaving behind its "alternative" image like an outgrown cocoon.

In a seminal 1990 *Columbia Journalism Review* article, Bruce Porter, a journalism professor at Brooklyn College, documented the tension between NPR's alternative history and mainstream present. "NPR has taken on some of the trappings of the establishment," wrote Porter, "most particularly the Washington establishment, into which several NPR correspondents, like their counterparts in the national press corps, are fairly well plugged."[46] (Porter's evidence, curiously, was to cite the family connections of three female NPR reporters: Cokie Roberts, daughter of longtime Louisiana Members of Congress Hale and Lindy Boggs; Nina Totenberg, wife of former Senator Floyd Haskell; and Linda

Wertheimer, wife of longtime Common Cause president Fred Wertheimer.)
NPR editorial director John Dinges justified the resources devoted to making *All
Things Considered* and *Morning Edition* into news-dominated operations: "People
out there who have nothing to read but the Fort Dodge *Messenger* are desperate
for quality coverage and deeper levels of the news than what they can get out of
their increasingly mediocre newspapers."

While Dinges's comment, strictly speaking, is hard to refute, it suggests an
organization measuring itself by a declining standard, rather than one seeking to
challenge or expand journalistic norms. The fact is that NPR in the '90s came
more and more to resemble well-established, mainstream news organizations. At
the extreme end of this phenomenon, NPR figures crossed over into commercial
media; notably, Cokie Roberts became a fixture on ABC evening news broadcasts
and on its Sunday morning program *This Week with David Brinkley* as well as a syndicated columnist with her husband, Steve Roberts. More commonly, NPR began
searching for news commentators with mainstream (especially conservative)
views, as if they would enhance the service's legitimacy. In some cases, NPR's
commentator choices seemed chosen for obvious strategic reasons. In 1986,
journalist Fred Barnes, then of *The New Republic*, wrote an early and oft-cited
attack on the supposed liberal bias of NPR news, called "All Things Distorted"; by
the mid-1990s, Barnes had been snapped up as a regular NPR commentator.

In at least a few cases, the choices corroded NPR's editorial legitimacy. A regular feature of *Morning Edition*'s coverage of the Congressional debate over health
care reform in 1993–94, for example, was a debate between two former Members of Congress, Tom Downey and Vin Weber; because one was a Democrat and
one a Republican, the discussions were presumed to be "balanced." NPR failed,
however, to tell listeners that both men professionally opposed the Clinton
health plan, since both were paid lobbyists for various health insurers! Downey,
in an interview with WNYC-AM radio host Brian Lehrer, even admitted that as a
Member of Congress, he had supported a single-payer insurance system, but
since leaving government his views had changed. Lehrer (who is not related to
Jim Lehrer of PBS's *NewsHour*), asked Downey: "Is it so cynical . . . to look at
your sequence of beliefs and say, 'Gee, when you were a Democrat from Long
Island you believed in the single-payer system in Congress and now all of a sudden your paycheck is coming, in part, from Met Life and suddenly you have this
new faith in the market mechanism?" Downey's response began: "Yeah, I guess
you could believe that."[47]

That Downey's views had evolved according to who signed his paycheck is
hardly startling; that NPR would consider him a legitimate commentator without disclosing what he admits is a proindustry bias, however, indicates a capitula-

tion of public radio to the established views of private lobbyists. As the progressive media watchdog group, Fairness and Accuracy in Reporting (FAIR) asked in a *New York Times* advertisement: "Can't [*Morning Edition*] producer Ellen McDonnell find anyone without a personal financial interest to debate health reform?"[48] Similarly, NPR allowed journalist James Fallows to continue his weekly commentaries on politics throughout the election year of 1996, even though Fallows had been appointed by the Clinton White House to a trade advisory committee, about which NPR listeners remained ignorant.[49]

For the most part, however, NPR reporters seem very content with their role as power brokers. "I'm not nostalgic for [the old] days at all," Linda Wertheimer told an interviewer.[50] "I don't want to be a sidebar to the world anymore, or an intellectual magazine that twelve people read." As such commitment to mass audience grows, however, it will crowd out other stated goals of public broadcasting—notably diversity in employment and in on-air views. As with public television, diversity has remained a stubbornly elusive goal for public radio. Because so many NPR affiliates have tiny staffs (often fewer than 10 full-time employees), they have been exempt from federal equal employment laws; even those stations that meet the legal requirements have so little turnover that diversity remains a paper commitment. A prominent NPR minority hire, Adam Clayton Powell III, left the organization in 1989 after less than two years as news directo, because his news judgment and management philosophy clashed with NPR's news staff.

Throughout the '90s, NPR's failure to diversify the "public" airwaves erupted into legal problems. In 1995, Katie Davis, a prominent host of NPR's *Weekend Edition*, sued her employer, claiming that she had been consistently paid less than her male counterparts, and that NPR discriminated against her because it did not want female on-air hosts. She maintained that NPR refused to pay her a salary commensurate to men performing similar work, and that, based on her gender, NPR had denied her a permanent reporter position. Davis left the network in March 1995, despite a letter signed by 12 colleagues urging NPR to "make every attempt to resolve its differences with Katie." (NPR called Davis's allegation that she was denied a permanent position "completely false.") In her suit, seeking $1.2 million in damages, she alleged that an NPR official criticized her voice for not sounding "authoritative" enough; she claimed that NPR managing editor Bruce Drake told her that "being more 'authoritative' meant sounding 'like Walter Cronkite.'" Davis's case was settled out of court for an undisclosed amount in late 1995.

The Davis suit seemed to set off a chain reaction of politically charged lawsuits. In June 1995, a former NPR librarian sued NPR, claiming that she'd been wrongfully dismissed and that the network violated the Americans with Disabilities Act, and in November Mozell Stelley sued NPR, claiming that she'd been fired because she is black and because she had complained to network management that she was overlooked for promotions because of her race.[51] In May 1996, a recording engineer suffering from vaginal cancer sued NPR, charging another instance of disability discrimination; and in early 1997, NPR's Cairo bureau chief Sunni Khalid sued the network for racial and religious discrimination, charging, among other things, that an NPR senior editor repeatedly referred to Arabs as "ragheads" during an editorial meeting. An NPR spokeswoman denied that the network discriminated against anyone, but confirmed that the "ragheads" incident had occurred.[52]

"BECAUSE OF HIS POLITICAL ASSOCIATIONS"

The meatiest lawsuit filed against NPR in the '90s also delineated how limited free speech in America can be when one's speech is opposed by the police and by Congress. In 1994, NPR contracted with Mumia Abu-Jamal for a set of commentaries. Abu-Jamal was serving time on death row in a Pennsylvania prison for the 1981 murder of Philadelphia police officer Daniel Faulkner. Abu-Jamal was an inspired choice as a commentator, in part because he symbolized America's growing love affair with the death penalty (and its disproportionate use against blacks who kill whites), but also because he was surely the most seasoned radio journalist on America's death row. Prior to his conviction, Abu-Jamal had worked for Philadelphia's NPR station WHYY; he had even won a prestigious Peabody Award, and had been profiled by *Philadelphia* magazine as "a neighbor to watch."

To stem off potential complaints that public radio was giving a platform to a convicted cop-killer, NPR and Abu-Jamal agreed that his three-minute commentaries would not address his individual case, but discuss the broader world of prison life and the death penalty. In one particularly provocative piece, Abu-Jamal discussed how Supreme Court Justice Harry Blackmun's rejection of the death penalty was received by those condemned to die. Reversing his decades-old support for the death penalty, Blackmun pledged: "From this day forward, I no longer shall tinker with the machinery of death."[53]

Abu-Jamal was not impressed with Blackmun's retirement conversion. "If Blackmun's denunciation of his benchmates seemed bitter," he opined, "the response from some on death row seemed equally acerbic." Blackmun, Abu-

Jamal reminded listeners, provided the crucial fifth vote in the 1976 case *Greg v. Georgia*, which restored the death penalty to America, and his conversion "comes almost a quarter of a century too late for many in the shadow of the death house. . . . Blackmun's dissent, though remarkably impassioned discourse, is of negligible legal force, and will save not one life."

NPR listeners, however, never heard those powerful words, nor any of Abu-Jamal's commentaries. The weekend prior to Jamal's scheduled debut, a coordinated effort between Philadelphia's Fraternal Order of Police—a longtime advocate of Abu-Jamal's immediate execution—and Senator Bob Dole succeeded in reversing NPR's choice of commentaries. Ellen Weiss, the executive director of *All Things Considered*, had praised Abu-Jamal as "a good writer [who] brings a unique perspective to the air." But after the Congressional pressure was applied, NPR managing editor Bruce Drake declared that he had "serious misgivings about the appropriateness of using as a commentator a convicted murderer seeking a new trial. . . . After reviewing the commentaries, I did not find them of such a compelling nature as to overcome these misgivings."[54]

NPR never bothered to tell Abu-Jamal that it had spiked his recording; awaiting his May 16, 1994, debut in his cell, Jamal listened, only to hear an audio essay by a Hudson Valley man who slugged his horse after it stood on his foot. "She took her punch philosophically," said the radio commentator. Abu-Jamal, in a later interview, could not resist a sneer: "That was the relevant, compelling material they had to run."[55] Following its clampdown, NPR refused even to release the commentaries Jamal had recorded (although they were later published in Abu-Jamal's book *Live from Death Row*). Abu-Jamal's jailers also took the opportunity to prohibit his other radio work for Pacifica—and indeed to cut off all personal interviews.

Senator Dole was more pleased at the prospect of Abu-Jamal's being silenced. Criticizing the $150 per commentary Abu-Jamal was to be paid, Dole cracked on the Senate floor: "The last time I checked, we were trying to fight crime, not promote the fortunes of convicted murderers through taxpayer-supported public broadcasting."[56] To Dole, NPR's cancellation was a vindication of his own 1992 legislative efforts to strengthen public broadcasting's commitment to "objectivity and balance," although he declared himself disturbed that "NPR had apparently forgotten until the last minute" that it needed to balance the Abu-Jamal essays. (Typically, "balance" was achieved in this case by simply removing the commentaries.) To ensure that such outrages would not occur in the future, Dole proposed: "One way we can make certain is to have closer oversight by the Congress"—precisely the kind of political control that public broadcasting's founders had hoped to avoid.

The Abu-Jamal cancellation was a sterling parable for the new, mature NPR. At the time when NPR canceled his commentaries, Abu-Jamal had done a great deal of radio work heard on Pacifica stations, which—despite Pacifica's taxpayer subsidy—prompted little more than local Philadelphia protest. Through some unexplained media-political alchemy, those same commentaries became unacceptable when their potential audience was six million *ATC* listeners. Explaining the Abu-Jamal decision on a New York public radio program, NPR's editorial director John Dinges expanded on the reasoning behind Abu-Jamal's airwave expulsion: "We in fact made a decision not to go ahead with those commentaries because we thought it was not good journalism to put somebody on the air in the role of a kind of Anthony Lewis on public radio,"[57] referring to the veteran *New York Times* columnist. Dinges went on to say that Abu-Jamal's "unique political position because of his crime and because of his political associations" made him taboo.

These were remarkable statements. By declaring "Anthony Lewis on public radio" to be bad journalism, Dinges could hardly have meant that individuals with strong records of political advocacy were inappropriate for NPR; after all, around this time NPR seemed happy to air the views of former Bush speechwriter Tony Snow, former Republican Congressman Vin Weber, and the right-wing journalist David Frum. The practical effect of NPR enforcing "objectivity and balance" circa 1994, however, appeared to be eliminating anti–death penalty discussions from *ATC*, and—if Anthony Lewis was verboten—lopping off the entire left wing of American political commentary. This was, it should be noted, several months *before* the Republicans took over Congress.

In March 1996, Abu-Jamal and the Prison Radio Project filed a $2 million law-suit against NPR, charging breach of contract and a violation of his free speech rights. Bill Buzenberg, NPR's vicepresident for news, explained the organization's rejection of Abu-Jamal by saying: "Here is a person who is the focal point of a polarized, politicized controversy and he has a legal case which is on appeal. We do not feel that was the place for a commentator's role, and we do think he was an important person and should have been part of a story. We've produced a 17-minute radio documentary in which he and his voice were part of that documentary, and we've also followed his case very specifically about the death row issues in Pennsylvania."[58] In fact, NPR had done and continues to do very few news stories on the Abu-Jamal case; in 1996, for example, when a key witness who had testified against Abu-Jamal admitted under oath that she'd been pressured by police to lie, NPR failed to report it. (Both Abu-Jamal's death penalty appeals and his suit against NPR were pending as this book went to press.)

ANY CD IN PRINT!

Among the crucial distinctions between public television and public radio are that through the 1980s and 1990s, although commercial radio experienced a remarkable renaissance, the medium of radio witnessed no transforming break-through comparable to the cable explosion. Rush Limbaugh, Howard Stern, and dozens of others brought a tremendous commercial vitality to talk radio and caused hundreds of stations nationwide to switch to talk formats. But the funda-mentals of radio remained the same: the spectrum retained an upper limit for the number of powerful stations, and a handful of formats—talk, sports, music, reli-gion, news—continued to dominate the dial. Consequently, public radio did not face an identity crisis comparable to that faced by public television in the wake of the proliferation of niche cable channels.

In fact—and this is a second crucial distinction—it was public radio during this period that was proliferating. While National Public Radio remained the largest service provider, the '80s and '90s saw the expansion of public radio ser-vices.[59] While it would be naive to expect that the competition between public radio services would produce wholly positive effects, the multiple services pro-vide many listener benefits that would be hard—and expensive—for a single entity to provide. For example, Public Radio International makes available *National Native News*—a daily five-minute news broadcast concentrating on tribal and Native American issues—to 145 public stations nationwide.

Thirdly, and few are brave enough to raise this point, NPR and public radio in general devote almost none of their resources or broadcast time to children's programming. Individual stations, such as New York's WNYC-AM, produce their own weekly children's programming, and a small portion of public radio's instructional programming is designed for children. There is nothing on radio, however, comparable to the multibillion-dollar commitments of *Barney*, *Sesame Street*, and *Puzzle Place*. The resources are largely devoted to services for adults, and adults have responded with according enthusiasm.

At the same time, what Larry Josephson has called "high church" public radio has, like its television counterpart, become overtly and hungrily commercial. On a daily basis, public radio listeners of some 330 public radio stations nation-wide—most are NPR and PRI affiliates—may hear on an hourly basis a spot for a service called Public Radio MusicSource.[60] An offshoot of the entrepreneurial Minnesota Communications Group, which also operates Minnesota Public Radio's KSJN and KNOW stations in the Twin Cities, Public Radio MusicSource offers to find listeners "any CD in print" via an 800 number, "delivering the music you want right to your door." Behind this benign boast lies one of public broadcasting's most aggressive attempts to cash in on its listeners. Begun in 1993, MusicSource gives participating stations a cut of up to 10 percent of sales every time one of their listeners places an order. MusicSource vice president Rolf Hansen, while declining to provide figures for total sales, did say that member stations collectively earned $300,000 from MusicSource in 1994.

"There's room for growth," Hansen said, "but it can only go so far. We figure it'll probably plateau at $500,000 in total revenues for the stations."[61] Besides the money, stations also get a list of their listeners-turned-customers—a rich resource for future pledge drives. "Stations have said they generate more new members with our lists than any other source," says a MusicSource official. And, despite claims to the contrary, stations are well aware of what's selling: New York City's public radio station, WNYC, goes so far as to publish listeners' "top 10" favorites in its monthly program guide.

Even those two resources understate the impact MusicSource has had on the radio and classical music industries. To public radio's commercial competitors, MusicSource looks like a threat. Shortly after MusicSource started operations, the Minnesota Broadcasters Association filed a complaint with the FCC, calling for the recision of KSJN's license as a "non-commercial operator." (The FCC, however, dismissed the complaint after a brief investigation.)

In the world of classical music, meanwhile, MusicSource has had a measurable impact. Public radio's championing of the classical format has long provided the genre its greatest public exposure. When the public broadcasting funding debate peaked in March 1995, *Billboard* magazine devoted its lead article to how public radio's death would affect the recording industry. As Carol Yaple, vice president at classical label Elektra/Nonesuch records, bluntly admitted, "it would be devastating."

But three weeks later, a letter to *Billboard* from record store owner Samuel Reifler showed the other side of the story: "We used to underwrite one of our two local public radio stations, WAMC. . . . However last year WAMC, along with every other public radio stations I know of, went into the retail CD business via the 800-number-based 'Public Radio Music Source.' Almost overnight, public radio became our heaviest competition for the classical music collector who had been keeping our shop in the black."

For the nonprofit MusicSource to wield such power in the exceedingly for-profit music industry might seem inconsistent with public radio's origins. According to Nelson, MusicSource offers public radio several benefits: first and foremost, it "provides a service to our listeners," who are curious—and slothful enough—to opt for dialing an 800 number and paying a premium to get that CD. Second, there are the relatively meager royalties returned to stations.

Finally, MusicSource "makes the stations more important to record companies," Nelson said. "They know they count in terms of selling records, so the labels are willing to provide demos or promotional albums for the stations." Thus selected, public radio stations are therefore twice subject to the whims of the marketplace: first by industry hype and solicitation, second by knowing that if they play something palatable to a wide audience, the station's share of royalties will grow. While acknowledging that such risks exist, Hansen denied that such influences were determining program content. "Stations have asked us are we going to tell them what to play. The answer is always 'no.' Certainly the envelope can be pushed, but I don't think we're doing that."

MusicSource will not end up enforcing, song for song, what is played on public radio. But the organization's acknowledgment of "pushing the envelope" means that it perceives how marketing and public relations can be used to influence the content of this supposedly noncommercial medium. In its increasingly dire drive over the last fifteen years to secure funding, public radio has willingly constricted the freedom and variety that it once enjoyed. As we shall see in subsequent chapters, the distinctiveness and even the mission of public broadcasting has evaporated as private companies push the underwriting envelope to the limit—and beyond.

7

UNDERWRITING POLITICS

"We'd love to do a program on the history and role of business in America.
But who will underwrite that?"
—BARRY CHASE, PBS VICEPRESIDENT OF NEWS
AND PUBLIC AFFAIRS, 1985[1]

In the spring of 1995, as Congressional Republicans were trying to pry public television off the public payroll, New Yorkers who watched *The Nightly Business Report* and *The MacNeil/Lehrer NewsHour* saw a 15-second advertisement for a bank called Menatap.[2] If the name seemed unfamiliar to most, it was probably because the bank is located in Russia, not a well-established source of support for American public television. The bank had paid WNET $66,000—more than the annual contribution of Bloomingdale's or Salomon Brothers—for the privilege of promoting itself during this peak viewing time slot.

Not long before these WNET spots began, a CIA report had identified Menatap as one of the most corrupt banks in Russia, with close ties to the Russian mafia. Technically, it was illegal during this period for any American bank to do business with Menatap. Luckily, nothing prevented Menatap from giving money to public television's largest station. From the bank's perspective, the CIA had not accused it of any specific illegal act, and the contribution to WNET was a gesture meant to demonstrate that it wanted to be a good corporate citizen. For its part, WNET was simply operating by the unwritten rule behind all corporate underwriting: it makes no economic sense for the beggars of public television to be choosers.

Menatap was probably unaware that by using public television donations to advance a political agenda, it was behaving in a great American tradition. Although McDonald's today is considered a global success story, the path to that success has not been one unbroken golden arch. In the late 1960s and early 1970s, the growth of McDonald's was threatened on several fronts. One threat was the industrywide problem that *The Wall Street Journal* referred to, with char-

acteristic tact, as "the increasing reluctance of Negroes to take menial jobs."[3]
McDonald's, like all the growing fast-food chains, relied almost exclusively on
part-time teenage employees. By 1968, union grumbling about the chain's
refusal to pay starting employees more than the minimum wage had turned into
demonstrations and ministrikes that startled the burger magnates.

This was especially a problem in San Francisco. In the spring of 1972, a group
of union leaders came before the city's Board of Permit Appeals to denounce
McDonald's as an "unfair competitor engaged in exploitation of young people for
profit and personal gain."[4] Their fury over $1.85-an-hour wages persuaded the
five-member board to deny a McDonald's permit to open a franchise in the city's
Marina District. The company retaliated with a lawsuit, but McDonald's was further humiliated later that year by public revelations that it forced its teenaged
employees in other San Francisco outlets to take lie detector tests.

Another headache came from federal government investigations. In 1971,
McDonald's added to its menu the Quarter Pounder, a hefty chunk of beef advertised as twice the size of its normal burger. One of the great consumer advocate
pastimes of the 1970s was exploding such claims by actually weighing the meat
(a scale test would have made an ideal segment for PBS's *The Great American
Dream Machine*). The Department of Agriculture did put the burger to the test,
and found it wanting by more than an ounce; a New York congressman asked the
Federal Trade Commission to investigate what he called the Quarter Pounder's
"inherently deceptive" brand name.

Perhaps McDonald's biggest problem was inflation. Certain that inflation was
going to force a raise in the minimum wage, McDonald's supported legislation—known as the "McDonald's Bill"—that would allow companies to hire full-
time students and sixteen- and seventeen-year-olds for 80 percent of the federal
minimum wage. The bill actually passed the House in 1972, but stalled in the
Senate. On the price side, responding to cost pressure, the McDonald's Corporation raised its prices in late 1971 on the Quarter Pounder and Quarter Pounder
with cheese. This fell afoul of the federal Price Commission, charged with
enforcing Nixon's anti-inflationary price-freeze policy of the time. The Price
Commission ordered the burger chain to reinstate its lower prices.[5]

McDonald's chairman Ray Kroc responded to these political challenges with a
barrage of tactics, some highly creative, some pedestrian. The company launched
a sweeping, nontraditional advertising strategy, featuring sponsorship of the
Ice Capades and "Hamburger Olympics." Another, more heavy-handed technique
was political contributions. Kroc's first-ever political contribution was a $1,000
gift to Richard Nixon's 1968 presidential campaign. Seeking to expand his influence for the 1972 reelection, Kroc simply expanded his donation—

to $250,000. (The gift was later investigated by Watergate special prosecutor Leon Jaworski.)

It was during this stressful period that McDonald's also discovered public television. Never having given to the medium before, the burger behemoth began shoveling large amounts of cash into public broadcasting. In 1974, McDonald's was the third-largest donor to the Corporation for Public Broadcasting (behind the Exxon Corporation and the ever-faithful Ford Foundation). Its $565,000 gift accounted for more than 10 percent of CPB's nonfederal contributions. McDonald's was especially interested in a program called *Zoom!*, watched by thousands of preteens who, within a few years, would be considering employment at McDonald's. When *Zoom!* went off the air, however, the burger company's philanthropic interest in public television waned. It gave nothing to public television for at least another decade.[6]

MILIEU CONTROL

When trying to make judgments about the relative purity or corruption of contemporary public broadcasting, it is easy to forget that noncommercial television in America has never been completely without commercial sponsorship. A glance at the 1958 annual report for Pittsburgh's WQED, for example, shows that one of the station's most-watched programs, *Understanding the Stock Market*, was sponsored by the Investment Bankers Association of Western Pennsylvania; other programs came via grants from the U.S. Steel Corporation and Westinghouse.[7] While Ford Foundation money was the driving force behind the NET offerings of the 1960s, NET also took money from dozens of big businesses, including Humble Oil, U.S. Steel Corporation, *TV Guide*, Hills Brothers Coffee, Xerox Corporation, and Met Life.

Although private industry helped fund educational broadcasting even before the federal government did, the era of massive, nationwide corporate underwriting of public television programming can be traced to instability in the system brought on late during the Nixon administration. Corporate money filled the void left by the vagaries of the federal budget-and-veto process; in the short period between 1973 and 1976, for example, business support for public broadcasting leaped from just over $11 million to more than $29.1 million; the 163 percent increase made this by far the fastest-growing sector of support in the entire system (state funding, by way of comparison, rose approximately 40 percent, federal funding approximately 55 percent).[8] As public television moved from a medium dominated by National Educational Television to the Public

Broadcasting Service (PBS), it dramatically expanded the role of private funding; by the mid-'70s, a full one-quarter of the funds used to produce national PBS programs came from 39 corporations.[9]

In a universe as complex as public television, there is no single reason why businesses choose to underwrite the medium. First, and probably least important, is that the expense is taxdeductible. Second—as is obvious on both the local and national levels—there is a promotional agenda. Underwriting provides a unique marketing opportunity, saturating the presumably upscale public broadcasting audience with the underwriter's product or service.

Promotion has been an especially prominent underwriting agenda since the restrictions on advertising were loosened; the year that PBS decided to allow full-fledged commercials to run on noncommercial television was, appropriately enough, 1984. Once confined to dull, tombstonelike on-screen promotions, PBS underwriters were in 1984 set free to give locations of stores or offices, and to provide "value-neutral" descriptions of their wares. Perhaps most important, their logos and product symbols were liberated to appear on screen; in a spot, for example, that ran at the beginning of *The MacNeil/Lehrer NewsHour*, the various product symbols of Pepsico—including Pepsi, Frito-Lay, and Pizza Hut— jumped out of a paper grocery bag; for years, a regular viewer could anticipate seeing this ad more reliably than any on commercial television.

Also beginning in 1984, viewers started seeing advertisements remarkably similar to, if shorter than, those aired on network television, although these ads went under the euphemistic name of "enhanced underwriting credits." The few restrictions retained by the FCC and PBS were designed to prevent advertisers from drawing comparisons to their competitors; in 1996, Representative Jack Fields proposed lifting even those minimal limits in his "self-sufficiency" bill.

The advent of advertising in public broadcasting represented a multidecade triumph for corporations in colonizing this ostensibly off-limits medium. The pattern of corporate giving to public television, however, was firmly in place a decade before these brazen pitches were allowed; McDonald's shelled out half a million dollars in a year without expecting that Ronald McDonald would get to appear in spots between *Sesame Street* and *Mister Rogers' Neighborhood*. Thus, sociologists and critics have tried to isolate what specifically makes public broadcasting attractive to funders. The record of corporate contributors—particularly in the early days of public broadcasting—suggests a correspondence between donations to PBS/CPB and a desire to get something out of the federal government, out of the media, or out of public opinion. As highlighted by the Menatap example, the underwriter purchases an image of prestige and civic-mindedness by being associated with the "good cause," or the content of public broadcasting—

the donation is a form of reputation laundering. And even more than traditional advertising, an underwriting grant—particularly a sustained grant to public affairs programming—carries with it the clout to influence debate on a specific issue, and to help guide the terms used by America's policymaking elite. Collectively, these motivations constitute what technology sociologist M. David Ermann calls "milieu control."

THE THINKING MAN'S GASOLINE

Perhaps because its contributions disappeared over time, McDonald's attempt at milieu control through funding public broadcasting attracted little notice. Not so the oil companies, whose omnipresence on the PBS dial for the last quarter-century prompted the joke that its initials stand for "Petroleum Broadcast Service" (or, noting the underwriters' Anglophilic bent, "Petroleum's British Subsidiary"). The correspondence between the oil crisis of 1973–74, the huge profits reaped by oil giants in the mid-70s, and their sudden interest in public television has been a constant criticism, not limited to marginal Marxist cranks. In a 1975 Congressional hearing, Congressman Torbert McDonald—whose Commerce Committee oversaw funding for public broadcasting—observed: "If you notice, Mobil and other oil companies such as Gulf—they were never terribly interested in public news programming or anything like that before the Arabs and before this criticism in Congress."[10]

The congressman was exaggerating—but only slightly. Almost no historical studies exist that analyze public television donors by industry sector; however, the oil companies' predilection for public broadcasting in the early to mid-'70s is easily documented. One sociologist analyzing contributions between 1973 and 1976 found that "mining firms, for instance, allocated only one-tenth of one percent of their [philanthropic] contributions to public television and radio, compared to an enormous 10.5% allocation by petroleum and gas firms."[11] Although the oil companies had little taste for news programming until the mid-'70s, one company, Mobil Oil, had made a substantial investment in public broadcasting as far back as PBS's second season, underwriting what would become one of public television's longest-running hits, *Masterpiece Theatre* (Mobil had also provided a small start-up grant for *Sesame Street*).

Masterpiece Theatre's premiere episode, on January 10, 1971, was a production of *The First Churchills*, and featured Alistair Cooke and an announcement that the evening's entertainment had been "made possible by a grant from Mobil." The connection between this corporation and costume drama has remained intact—

indeed has expanded—for more than a quarter-century, generating both publicity and controversy. In the '70s, some in public broadcasting were horrified when Mobil Oil was allowed to begin using a typeface similar to its official logo; the cry of protest was: "Next we'll be allowing them to use a red O!"[12] Today, the company not only uses the red O but features a segment copied directly out of Mobil's commercial network advertisements. In PBS promotional literature and in some on-screen promotions, the program is actually called *Mobil Masterpiece Theatre*.

The relationship between Mobil Oil and recycled British drama—generally from the Victorian or Edwardian period—is not immediately apparent. In 1970, when WGBH president Stan Calderwood phoned Herb Schmertz, Mobil's vice-president for public affairs, to inquire about funding a PBS production of *The Forsyte Saga*, Schmertz confesse that he had never watched a single episode of the BBC series.[13] He was, however, attracted by the prospect of being able to purchase 39 hours of television at the bargain-basement price of $390,000.

The economics of underwriting favor the underwriter so overwhelmingly that in at least one well-known instance, PBS accepted a Mobil-sponsored program even though PBS officers didn't want to air it. Schmertz told the second Carnegie Commission that the "entire public television establishment was opposed to" acquiring *Upstairs, Downstairs* when it first became available, and that Mobil was "just as adamantly in favor of it." Schmertz used a bit of hardball negotiating: "If you're not going to acquire it, we're going to acquire it anyway, and find some way to run it on American television whether it's commercial or public." This was an offer PBS could not refuse.[14]

Over time, Schmertz and Mobil became convinced that they had tapped into an effective alternative sales scheme known as "affinity-of-purpose marketing." (Schmertz, who is generally viewed as one of corporate America's most effective mind-benders, calls *Masterpiece Theatre* "easily the most spectacular and successful project I've been involved in.")[15] The theory is not especially complex, and today is widely practiced. It argues that a small but substantial group of consumers have grown indifferent, even hostile, to the traditional TV sales pitch, and must therefore be pursued more subtly. "Very often," notes Schmertz, "the people in this group are upscale viewers with the discretionary dollars to buy, for example, premium gasoline for all three of their cars."

The idea is to use sponsorship to associate one's product or service with programming or causes that this lucrative target audience values. Schmertz asserts that "cultural excellence generally suggests corporate excellence. Invariably your support of first-rate programs in the arts and culture will significantly enhance the image of your company."[16] The imageenhancement is made possible by hefty amounts of outside promotion; although prior to 1984 an underwriter's on-screen acknowledgment was limited, there has never been a limit on how much an underwriter could spend to promote a program off the screen. In 1978, for example, Mobil spent $3.5 million for public broadcasting programs, and another $2 million to advertise them. When Gulf Oil sponsored *National Geographic Specials* the same year, it actually spent more on advertising than on the programs themselves.[17] In 1988, Mobil began sending money directly to individual PBS stations so that they could publicize their own broadcasts of *Masterpiece Theatre*.

Of course, only programs held in esteem will serve this image-enhancing function, and hence the common complaint that big business supports only a narrow slice of "safely splendid," ostensibly highbrow fare. PBS research from the mid-70s confirms that while small (less than $100,000) corporate donors supported a wide variety of programming, large grants ($250,000 and over) were "heavily concentrated in the performing arts": nearly 80 percent supported drama for adults and children, music, dance, and feature films. The vast majority of large grants came from oil companies, and three-quarters of these petro-grants supported "cultural programs in performing arts."[18]

Schmertz also believes that buying so many hours of public television has helped Mobil purchase credibility for its larger agenda. He promises that cultural underwriting presents an "opportunity to present your top management not as narrow-minded experts, but rather corporate statesmen whose concerns go beyond the bottom line," telling other public relations people that "your chairman and president will be seen as broad-based and far-reaching in their concerns—and intellectually entitled to be listened to on vital public-policy issues." Peter Spina, Mobil's general manager of corporate relations, describes the long-term benefits of underwriting public television as a "halo effect."[19]

While claims of enhanced prestige are difficult to prove, there's no question that top policymakers have always taken note of Mobil's commitment to public broadcasting. A month before *Masterpiece Theatre* hit the screen, no less a public broadcasting fan than Richard Nixon wrote to Mobil's chairman of the board to offer his praise. "Mobil's commitment in excess of $1,000,000 to support programming by the Corporation for Public Broadcasting is an excellent and needed demonstration of private support to further the quality of the nation's cultural life," wrote the President, who clearly preferred private funding over public.[20] "I commend Mobil for this significant investment."

The "corporate statesman" image was a special priority for oil companies during this period, because their more traditional methods of gaining influence were under ferocious attack. In 1974, Senator Henry Jackson called the heads of the nation's seven largest oil companies before his Permanent Subcommittee on Investigations and labeled their profits "obscene." Culminating months of Congressional investigation, Jackson proposed that oil companies be licensed and controlled by the federal government.[21] Other Congressional committees had disclosed that the oil giants, along with other multinationals, had lavished millions of dollars in bribes on political parties in Italy, Canada, Bolivia, and South Korea. Exxon alone, through Italian affiliates, secretly contributed $27 million to that country's political parties between 1963 and 1972 (in some cases supplementing the CIA's contributions).[22]

Schmertz makes the even more far-reaching claim that Mobil's multi-year funding of public broadcasting has translated into increased gas sales in high-income markets. He cites a 1982 Mobil-commissioned survey of 300 "upscale college graduates in the Boston area." Claiming that many of these presumed liberals in the Harvard sphere of influence disagreed with Mobil, Schmertz insists that they nonetheless appreciate Mobil's public TV underwriting. "Asked which company was identified with quality TV programming, people . . . chose Mobil by a large margin—even though Exxon spends much more money than we do. In fact, we often get letters thanking us for Exxon's programs!"[23] When then asked what gasoline they buy most often, 31 percent said Mobil, 16 percent Exxon, 15 percent Gulf, and 10 percent Texaco. Mobil's pollster, impressed by these results, declared: "Mobil must be the thinking man's gasoline."

Assertions about public broadcasting's ability to deliver a market for Mobil gas or any other product must be viewed skeptically. (Some sociologists believe that, aside from a small number of marginal cases, it is impossible to prove that any advertising has a direct effect on consumer behavior.)[24] But enough companies believe in some version of affinity-of-purpose marketing that, in any given year, hundreds donate to PBS, and countless more underwrite programs on local public television and radio stations. The precise figure of corporate underwriting to public broadcasting may go up and down—both as an absolute figure and as a percentage of all CPB revenues—but the fact remains that by the late 1980s virtually no national PBS programs are aired without some degree of corporate aid (as in so many other categories, *Frontline* is an exception).

KEEPING UP APPEARANCES

Curiously, *Masterpiece Theatre* has not always had the overwhelmingly British accent that today identifies it. As one student of *Masterpiece Theatre* has noted: "The first three seasons dedicated themselves to the high bourgeois novel, reproducing as closely as possible the masterpieces of Balzac, Dostoevsky, and James."[25] It is only in the mid-'70s that *Masterpiece Theatre* shifted toward original screenplays set in Britain, which provided the show with some of its greatest hits: *The Six Wives of Henry VIII*; *Upstairs, Downstairs*; *Flickers*; *Elizabeth R.*; and the *Duchess of Duke Street*.

Such "instant classics" complemented the wealth of genuine British material that began airing on PBS in the '70s and continues to dominate the dial. The continued success of *Monty Python's Flying Circus* in the U.S. is attributable almost entirely to its airing on public television stations in the '70s. *Monty Python* ensured a bright future for other British comedy series, including *Fawlty Towers*, *Blackadder*, *Are You Being Served?*, *Keeping Up Appearances*, *Mr. Bean*, and many others. Drama series have not fared as consistently well, although there have been notable exceptions. While not generally recognized as such, *East Enders* is one of the longest running nighttime soap operas on American television, and *Prime Suspect* has received high praise from critics and a fervent, if small, audience.

By the mid-'70s, the British invasion of American public television programming had become a mainstay target for American critics, who generally adopted a posture of reverse snobbery and an implicit nationalism. "Audiences for American public television soon grew accustomed to gorgeous displays of the Union Jack as programs opened," one critic has said of PBS in the '70s. "Inexplicably, American audiences were delivered, as part of their educational experience, left-over video tapes of week-old English soccer matches—Leeds 1, Birmingham 0."[26] The influential *New Yorker* critic Michael Arlen, praising not only *Upstairs, Downstairs* but *A Family at War* and *Monty Python's Flying Circus*, felt compelled to ask: "How does it happen that the best entertainment series on American public television is an essentially British import from England?"[27]

There are many, often intertwining reasons why British programming has been so overrepresented on American public television. One is simply financial: unlike the commercial networks, neither CPB nor PBS operates their own national production company. Hence all public TV programming must either be uploaded from a member station or purchased from an independent production source. Of course the system spends millions of dollars every year on programming produced by American firms, but minute for minute, it is cheaper to co-produce with—or purchase a ready-made program from—a foreign provider. Naturally, English-speaking countries have a tremendous advantage in the U.S., as their programs do not require costly dubbing or translating. As former PBS president Larry Grossman famously quipped: "I can't imagine where American public television would be if the British didn't speak English."[28] And programs that have already run their course on British television are discounted accordingly.

(This cozy transatlantic situation could be threatened with the arrival, scheduled for mid-1998, of an American cable BBC channel.)[29]

Such programming can of course be justified on the grounds that depictions of "classic" literature have an educational value. Surely, though, there are classic literary works written in countries other than Great Britain, and written in a period other than 1760 to 1910. It is a curious definition of public service that the viewer of fictional programs on American public television sees more about daily life in nineteenth-century London than about daily life in twentieth-century New York or Kansas City or Miami.

As with any other industry, public television's heavy reliance on a foreign producer effectively displaces domestic providers. Labor unions operating in the TV business—which include writers, directors, and many different technical unions—have tried to press this point on public television executives for decades. Not surprisingly, the unions regard the PBS-BBC alliance as an end run around their clout in broadcasting, one that has the effect of sapping American jobs. Despite labor's long history of supporting educational broadcasting— recall that United Auto Workers president Leonard Woodcock was a board member of the original Carnegie Commission, and that his union pledged $25,000 to support the first year of public television—very few dramatic series have been produced for American public television in this country. *The Adams Chronicles*, the well-received 1976 PBS series, was an exception; not coincidentally, it was also one of the few PBS dramatic series to have an American theme and setting.

Because American public television is chronically underfunded, the allure of cheap programming cannot be understated. All television programmers are motivated to find low-cost programming; yet no other networks or cable channels carry British programming nearly every evening. And as literary critic Timothy Brennan has pointed out, most of the current offerings on *Masterpiece Theatre* are not dramatizations of "classic" novels; they are "original dramas based on schemata from the nineteenth-century British novel."[30] What is important for *Masterpiece Theatre* is not British literature but "a literary aura—the paraphernalia and the atmosphere of literary life." By projecting the feel and flavor of British literature onto the crass mass medium of American television, Brennan argues, "*Masterpiece Theatre* is training us to read the 'literary' in a TV culture—to see in America the recurring parable of rugged American success; to see in England the continued value of good breeding; and to imagine, as is only possible in the confines of a living room, that a TV literature can raise select groups above the thousands of others who simply aren't tuned to the right channel."

The stratum created by American public TV's Anglophilia, the use of British tradition, is a marketing strategy for public TV itself. False snobbery is public broadcasting's brand recognition, the code that allows viewers to quickly distinguish the content of public television among the clutter of a multichannel universe, but more importantly it gives public television viewers a way to distinguish *themselves* from other television audiences. The development of the "PBS identity" is an aesthetic stance that is, in vital respects, independent of other class-determining factors, such as income, education, and class upbringing.

The elite PBS identity is occasionally at odds with public television's other goals: since it is forever trying to refute charges of elitism, PBS is surely the only American media organization that constantly produces survey data to show how poor, undereducated, and blue-collar its viewers are. But this identity is an assertion nonetheless designed to separate the PBS-watching class from the masses. The French sociologist Pierre Bourdieu refers to such choices as "elective distinctions," and notes: "Aesthetic intolerance can be terribly violent. Aversion to different life-styles is perhaps one of the strongest barriers between the classes. . . . [A]esthetic stances adopted in matters like cosmetics, clothing or home decoration are opportunities to . . . assert one's position in social space, as a rank to be upheld or a distance to be kept."[31]

The distance between the contemporary viewer and PBS's repeated nineteenth-century British fare is not exclusively sociological. British costume drama also exacts an important opportunity cost: by preoccupying viewers with long-dead social situations, PBS avoids dealing with the thorny modern politics that nearly brought on its untimely demise. "More than one hundred years after the events, gorgeously costumed dramas based on Trollope's novels examined the social consequences of the 1867 Reform Bill before Parliament," notes a sarcastic critic. "England's nineteenth-century reforms were not too 'controversial,' objectively speaking, for twentieth-century American audiences."[32]

PBS's predilection for British or British-seeming programming fits snugly into the countless other classassertions in all elements of public broadcasting: public broadcasting constantly uses words such as "civilization" and "tranquillity" to differentiate itself from commercial broadcasters. Thanks to grants from petroleum giants, it puts a premium on opera, ballet, and classical music, which appeal disproportionately to the nation's elite. And nowhere is public broadcasting's identity with the lifestyle trappings of the ruling elite more apparent than in its fundraising pleas: in the mid-'80s, an on-air solicitor on New York radio station WNYC one morning urged the listener to "put down your cappuccino, put down your croissant, pick up the phone, and call us."

DEATH OF A DOCUDRAMA

It goes without saying that an audience that consciously or semconsciously uses public television to identify itself as a civilized elite will hold tremendous appeal for corporate marketers. The aura of "cultural excellence" exuded by *Masterpiece Theatre*'s pseudoliterary dramas is precisely the distinction that Schmertz hopes will rub off on Mobil's otherwise ordinary product. What Schmertz—and very few in public broadcasting—ever explicitly ask is what fundamental differences might exist between the agenda of public television and that of a multibillion-dollar oil company seeking to penetrate an upscale market. Public television was founded in part because of measurable disgust with commercial advertising and the kind of programming it can support. While there may be common ground between what Mobil wants and what public television producers and viewers want, they are also likely to clash.

One of the fiercest clashes took place in 1980, over the PBS airing of a docudrama called *Death of a Princess*. This two-hour film, directed by Anthony Thomas and initially aired on the BBC, was the dramatization of the public execution of an Arab princess and her lover. Although names had been changed and identities obscured, the film was clearly based on a 1977 case that had taken place in Saudi Arabia. The dramatization took the form of a journalistic detective story, with the main character, a British reporter, attempting to get at the true story through a haze of competing, *Rashomon*-like recollections, almost all of which are second- or thirdhand. Woven throughout are discussions of Arab politics and the battle between keeping Islamic tradition and the onslaught of Western values. The young woman's love affair, a violation of her arranged and largely theoretical marriage, is portrayed as "the story of 200 million people; it's the whole Arab predicament." None of the scenarios offered for her execution are flattering to the Arab government, and some are disdainful of Western governments as well; one Arab character speaks of CIA complicity in a mass murder, and tells the reporter:"This regime is your responsibility. The West took over after the Turks, and you've always sided with the enemies of progress, because you want to control us."

Such sentiments did not please the Saudi government. Following *Death of a Princess*'s broadcast on British television, the Saudis expelled the British ambassador, one of the few diplomatic flaps to be caused by a television broadcast. The Saudis threatened to repeat the performance in the U.S.: in his 1995 book *The Electronic Republic*, Lawrence Grossman, who was president of PBS at the time, recalled:"The Saudi royal family did everything possible to prevent PBS from broadcasting the film. . . . The Saudis, the biggest oil supplier to the United States, let it be known that they were prepared to shut off the supply or raise oil prices precipitately."[33] Four days before the scheduled broadcast, Jimmy Carter's acting Secretary of State, Warren Christopher (who, 13 years later, would become the official Secretary of State), sent a letter to Grossman urging him to "give appropriate consideration to the sensitive religious and cultural issues involved."[34] Although Christopher's letter claimed that the government did not want to play censor, Grossman concluded "the import of his letter was clear—kill the show. . . . [Christopher's] letter was unprecedented, as far as I know, in putting on paper the interest of the United States government in killing a television program."[35]

For Mobil, billions of dollars were at stake in protecting access to Saudi oil. (Toward that end, Mobil had in the '70s underwritten a book called *The Genius of Arab Civilization*.) Thus, Mobil took up the Saudi cause, using its regularly purchased space on *The New York Times* op-ed page (another Schmertz innovation) and elsewhere to attack the film prior to its U.S. broadcast. While careful not to call specifically for *Princess*'s withdrawal, Mobil's ad skillfully referred to the film's "proposed showing." Attempting to separate dramatized broadcasts from those protected by the First Amendment, the Mobil ad declared: "The public will have to decide whether a 'free press' is acting responsibly if it presents a fictionalized story of 'events' and thereby demeans another nation's religion and possibly jeopardizes U.S. relations with that nation." As Grossman has pointed out, Mobil's logic here was convoluted: if Mobil got its way and *Princess* never aired, how would anyone be able to decide whether the press had acted responsibly? In its ostensibly patriotic conclusion, Mobil pleaded with "the management of the Public Broadcasting Service [to] review its decision to run this film, and exercise responsible judgment in the light of what is in the best interest of the United States."[36] No one in the public television community could fail to miss the import of such a command coming from a multimillion-dollar funding source. It is also remarkable that Mobil invoked the United States' "best interest" as a PBS programming criterion; not even Richard Nixon had been that brazen.

Mobil was not the only oil company that wanted the program pulled. Grossman recalls receiving a phone call from Admiral Thomas Moorer, former head of the Joint Chiefs of Staff and a member of Texaco's board of directors. He predicted that the broadcast would bring about a second Arab oil embargo, and reminded Grossman that Texaco was a major underwriter of PBS's broadcasts from the Metropolitan Opera. He then offered Grossman an incentive to not air *Death of a Princess*. "He said, 'I realize that you spent money to get the program,' which of course we didn't, . . . 'and a whole bunch of us in Texas put money together to make you whole as long as you don't run the show.' I said, 'I can't believe that you're talking this way.'"[37]

The docudrama aired on most PBS stations on May 12, 1980, on a now-defunct program called *The World*. The greatly feared boycott did not occur, and although a few angry speeches were delivered in Congress, public television and the oil industry survived. Intriguingly, the *Death of a Princess* controversy far outlasted the documentary itself. Several public TV stations—notably the Alabama Educational Television Commission and the station licensed to the University of Houston, both regions where oil company arguments are taken seriously—refused to show the program. This blackout prompted a lawsuit arguing that the stations had canceled the program for its political content, thus violating viewers' First Amendment rights. In what must be considered a victory for would-be censors, a federal appeals, ruled in 1982 that public television viewers have "no right of access to compel the broadcast of any particular program."[38] Thus, Mobil's anti-*Princess* agitation helped indirectly define the upper limit of how much public input would be allowed on public television. More immediately, PBS producers learned that they could avoid such headaches by sticking to fare that would not raise the hackles of the Saudi government or other global powers.

Mobil officials claim that in subsequent crises, they have been able to use their *Masterpiece Theatre* connection to sway public television to their advantage. Peter Spina, Schmertz's successor as vicepresident for public affairs, boasted to an interviewer in 1991 that PBS stations were a vital public relations tool in the period leading up to the 1991 Gulf War. Because oil companies were "being beat up again as an industry, as we were in the '70s," Spina wrote to local station managers with a letter saying: " 'You have such a close identification with Mobil. I can just imagine you're getting some heat with all these claims of gouging. Now, here's an ad we just ran in *The New York Times*, and here's our explanation of the crisis. We are not gouging, in fact we are losing money, etc., etc.' Some of these stations even put it in their [program] guides . . . You talk about credibility!"[39]

"ITS ADVERTISING OF PRODUCTS
IS MORE SUBTLE"

From the mid-1980s to the 1990s, corporate-sponsored public television programming entered into a broader new phase. Just as commercial advertisements from firms such as Benetton broke onetime taboos by featuring hot-button issues like AIDS and racism in their spots, so too did public television's corporate sponsors leap directly into current affairs programs with aggressive underwriting campaigns. The move toward identifying underwriting with specific public affairs issues could hardly have been accidental. According to two CPB officials, a noticeable shift in funding patterns took place in the late '80s as private funders stopped giving to public broadcasting out of their charity/philanthropic arms; instead the "donations" to public television came out of the companies' advertising and marketing divisions.[40]

To accommodate the needs of corporations who sought to use public broadcasting underwriting to promote specific programs, PBS had to change its rules. Through the late 1970s, PBS guidelines still tried to keep underwriters from using PBS programming as an advertisement or editorial pronouncement on their industry. "Underwriting of a program will not normally be accepted from an organization having a *direct* and *immediate* interest in the content of a program," insisted PBS's 1976 underwriting rulebook. "For example, underwriting of a program about the benefits of gardening would not be accepted from a seed company; underwriting of a program about the alleged dangers of sugar substitutes would not be accepted from a sugar manufacturer; and so on." Here was a statement of general principle:

> PBS will not accept a program on the history of the computer by a computer manufacturer. The interest is less that the connection will lead to the potential of control of the content of the program (though this danger may indeed be present), but that the program is so self-serving of the interest of the funder that a reasonable public could conclude that the program is on public television principally because of the existence of the funding or that public television is in fact no different than commercial television, but simply that its advertising of products is more subtle.

By the 1990s, such guidelines seemed quaint, even nostalgic. As if to thumb its nose at these forgotten prohibitions, in 1992, PBS broadcast a history of the computer, called *The Machine That Changed the World*, which was paid for in part by a $1.9 million grant from computer manufacturer Unisys. The concern behind the 1976 principles—i.e., that noncommercial television had vital integrity that needed to be safeguarded—had all but evaporated. On those occasions when PBS did enforce its underwriting guidelines, it did so at the expense of those who might question the corporate agenda; in 1997, PBS refused to accept a documentary for the *P.O.V.* series about gays and lesbians in the workplace solely because labor unions had been prominent funders.[41] This rationale flew in the face of PBS conflicts of interest that had become so numerous that they seemed the rule rather than the exception. Some examples from the 1980s and '90s:

- In 1991, PBS aired *Eat Smart*, a prime-time special program on the American diet, hosted by Judy Woodruff and sponsored by the Kellogg Foundation and Nestle.

- Beginning in 1979, public television began airing *Nightly Business Report* (NRB), produced by Miami's WPBT, and in 1981, expanded it to a half-hour. Through much of the '90s, *NBR* was underwritten by Digital Equipment Corporation, A. G. Edwards and the Franklin/Templeton Group, both major investment houses. In local markets, the *NBR* presentation is usually paid for by a bank or large local business, who of course have their own interest in highlighting business news.

- A 1991 series called *Childhood* showed how children grow up differently in different societies. The series was underwritten by HIP, a large health mainte- nance organization. According to HIP's vice-president for marketing: "We were looking for a different way to communicate our message about how well we were doing in the child care area."[42]

- In 1996, San Francisco's KQED was embarrassed by media revelations that it had accepted a large grant from California wine magnate Robert Mondavi to produce a documentary about his life.[43]

Schmertz's initial insights into using public television for corporate promotion had become commonplace, and in fact had been expanded. Not only had these companies abandoned the lowprofile by using public broadcasting for public relations, they had one-upped Schmertz by underwriting programs that specifi- cally touted issues of the day that the companies wanted in the public eye. Because of its interest in single-topic programs, public television became the best place for a company to shape a policy message without its being cluttered by other advertisers. Instead of creating a noncommercial alternative to network television, public television had created a link between underwriters and their series that, in the view of two sociologists who studied the medium, more closely resembled "the early days of network television, the so-called golden age when advertisers were commonly sole sponsors of programs."[44]

BUYING SILENCE

These unvarnished admissions that PBS programs are thematically used to pro- mote the agendas of the corporations that underwrite them are disturbing enough. In order to get a full picture of how corporate underwriting warps pub- lic television programming, however, it's essential to look at what *doesn't* get pre- sented on public television.

There is no better example of the blinders that accompany corporate under- writing than the performance of PBS's premiere public affairs program, the weekday evening *NewsHour*, in reporting on its major funders. In his book *Public*

Television for Sale, sociologist William Hoynes examined the coverage of the March 1989 Exxon *Valdez* spill into Alaska's Prince William Sound on the program that was then called *The MacNeil/Lehrer NewsHour*. (In the early 1980s, Exxon was actually a *NewsHour* underwriter.)[45] Reviewing every relevant episode in a six-month period, Hoynes concluded that the *NewsHour* aired "extremely limited perspectives" on the disaster, and generally presented "a largely reassuring view of the impact of the accident."[46] While spokesmen for Exxon frequently appeared on the *NewsHour* for interviews, at no point during Hoynes's study period did the *NewsHour* have an environmentalist as a guest to discuss one of the decade's worst environmental accidents.

This one-sided approach led to some laughable misinformation. On one program, Exxon's Alaska coordinator, Don Cornett, told viewers that "people tend to forget that oil is biodegradable," and said that by using chemical dispersants, Exxon would be able to "handle a great deal of the spill before it ever touches the shoreline of Prince William Sound." This claim turned out to be false. Because *NewsHour* hosts MacNeil and Lehrer, who pride themselves on their "civil interviewing" styles, rarely challenged such hopeful corporate boasts, Exxon representatives who had declined to appear on ABC's *Nightline* agreed to appear on the PBS program. In this instance, the news service provided by PBS was an "alternative" to commercial television primarily by being friendlier to the oil giant's perspective.

The *Valdez* spill was an international story too big for the *NewsHour* to ignore. In other cases of scandal involving PBS funders, the *NewsHour* has responded primarily with silence. The most egregious example concerns Archer Daniels Midland (ADM), the Illinois-based agricultural giant that is one of the world's largest producers of soybeans and various grain by-products. ADM chairman Dwayne Andreas has a colorful history of buying influence through politicians; some of his $100,000 cash contribution to Richard Nixon ended up paying for the Watergate plumbers. In the 1992 presidential election, he gave more than $1.4 million to both major political parties, and another $350,000 to Congressional candidates.[47] During the 1980s, ADM also funneled millions of dollars into television sponsorship, making its slogan "Supermarket to the World" something of a household name. Like General Electric's sponsorship of *The McLaughlin Group*, ADM focused its ad dollars on public affairs programs: ADM has been a heavy advertiser on ABC's Sunday morning program *This Week with David Brinkley*.[48] In 1993, ADM extended this influence when it became the chief corporate underwriter of *The MacNeil/Lehrer NewsHour*. Before every night's broadcast, a luscious spot can be seen of a reaper over a golden corn field; this placement has cost ADM approximately $6,867,000 a year, taxdeductible.[49]

Such media connections came in handy in 1995, when ADM was accused of conspiring to fix more than politicians: a high-ranking ADM official named Mark Whitacre said that he had been instructed by company officers to meet with competitors in the lysine market (a corn-derived amino acid used in swine and poultry feed) in order to fix prices. When he went public in 1995, Whitacre claimed that, with Justice Department cooperation, he had recorded such ostensibly illegal price-fixing chats on hundreds of hours of video- and audiotapes. He claimed that Dwayne Andreas's son Mick frequently said that the company philosophy was: "The competitor is our friend, and the customer is our enemy."[50]

Naturally, the Whitacre/ADM tale was one of the biggest business-political stories of 1995, receiving front-page treatment in *The Wall Street Journal*, *The New York Times*, and the cover of *Fortune* magazine. The scandal led to the resignation (and, later, indictment) of a high-ranking ADM official, and inspired a lawsuit against ADM by several of its lysine clients. Yet the story received virtually no attention from the *NewsHour*; the program waited until ADM made a counter-charge against Whitacre to run its sole, one-paragraph mention of the scandal, and never returned to the price-fixing allegations. Instead of being liberated from the constraints on commercial news broadcasts, PBS's premier public affairs program was actually less likely to explore the scandal because of its ADM ties.

The blinders were not limited to the question of pricefixing. ADM receives a tremendous bounty of subsidies from federal taxpayers: it buys corn at subsidized prices to make sweetening products subsidized by the federal sugar program, and uses the remainder to make the gasoline substitute ethanol, on which it receives a 54-cents-per-gallon tax credit. ADM has been the single largest recipient of Congress's corporate welfare; the value of federal subsidies to ADM has been estimated at approximately $4 billion a year. In the 1980s and 1990s, ADM benefited from some three dozen Congressional resolutions exempting ethanol from federal taxes and regulation. (Most of these resolutions, interestingly, were introduced by Kansas Senator Robert Dole, a serial nemesis of public broadcasting who has boasted that he voted against the original 1967 Public Broadcasting Act.)

Asked in early 1996 by *Variety* to respond to a charge in *The Village Voice* that ADM's sponsorship of *The NewsHour* helped steer the program away from any discussion of charges against ADM or the massive federal subsidies it receives, host Jim Lehrer exploded. "It's utter bullshit to suggest we're being bought—no formal charges have been made against [ADM]," Lehrer claimed. "When Exxon was an underwriter and had legal troubles we covered it. There are people out there who may have a problem with what we cover and don't cover, but it has absolutely nothing to do with who is and who isn't an underwriter, and that's been the case for 20 years."[51]

Lehrer's choice to frame the ADM scandal solely in terms of whether "formal charges" had been brought is an ideal example of how gingerly the *NewsHour* handles issues that affect its funders. Throughout 1995, when the Justice Department investigation into ADM was front-page news, Congress and many public interest groups—left and right—were railing against "corporate welfare." The term loosely describes the billions of dollars in federal monies that flow to corporations in the form of tax breaks, research subsidies, specialized tariffs, monopoly protections, and so on. The microscope placed on the corporate dole was a natural extension of the GOP Congress's dissection of nearly all federal expenditures—not least of which were those that help pay for public broadcasting.

Following Congress's lead, in 1995 the *NewsHour* held in-depth discussions about proposed cutbacks in education, aid to the poor, and medical subsidies. But corporate welfare—without which ADM, the *NewsHour*'s chief private contributor, could hardly exist—was never discussed. Asked to respond specifically to this omission, Lehrer declined to give an answer.[52] Not until October 1996—when ADM was hit with a $100 million criminal penalty for pricefixing, seven times the amount of the next-highest such penalty—did the *NewsHour* devote a full segment to this scofflaw corporation. The segment that finally addressed the issue featured Charlayne Hunter-Gault interviewing a journalist and an antitrust expert, but at no point did it note that the massive federal subsidies to ADM continue, despite its record-setting illegal acts.

THE POLLUTERS' PENANCE

Political scientist Thomas Ferguson has suggested an "investment" theory of political contributions in which large corporate donors use their gifts to political parties and elected officials to move the field of electoral politics away from a conception of "the public good" toward the fulfillment of specific private gain.[53] This is a useful model for public broadcasting: the underwriting process is an investment in a forum that theoretically represents the many so that it will reflect the views of a wealth-and-power elite. These groups may not seek—and cannot gain—outright control; they desire primarily the maintenance of a relatively friendly policy climate. ADM could not bribe the *NewsHour* into ignoring the ADM scandal altogether, but its underwriting serves to narrow and contain the parameters of discussion on public television.

Public broadcasting contributions can thus be seen as part of a broader corporate communications strategy, through which American-based multinationals

help shift public debate away from their own misfeasance. Indeed, the environmental activist group Greenpeace has suggested that contributions to public
television constitute a "penance," whereby polluters can buy forgiveness for their
sins by underwriting PBS programs. The best programs for such expiating donations are, of course, ones that extol the importance of natural habitats and environmentalism. Thus, Chevron, California's largest petrochemical polluter,
sponsors *National Geographic*, Dupont pays for *Discover Underwater*, and Waste
Management International helps remind viewers that there is *Only One Earth*.[54]

The overwhelming role oil companies play in funding national public television makes them the most obvious purchasers of the medium's silence. Although
the level of American public outrage toward oil companies has been generally
lower in the 1990s than in the 1970s, the '90s have hardly been a period that has
lacked for petroscandals. Internationally, for example, Shell Oil became the target of protest and denunciation for its role in destroying the environment of
Nigeria's Ogoniland, and for its at least tacit role in the execution of Ogoni novelist and activist Ken Saro-Wiwa. Although the U.S. media did not treat the
hanging of Saro Wiwa and his allies with as much urgency as their counterparts
in Britain and elsewhere, the story was nonetheless prominent; ABC News even
named Ken Saro-Wiwa as its "Person of the Week" after he was hanged. In most
media outlets, there is no difference between reporting the execution of Saro-
Wiwa and Shell's rapacious approach to Nigeria: the novelist's family has called
for a Shell boycott, Shell has been in sued in U.S. court for destroying
Ogoniland, and, in the words of *Newsweek* Africa correspondent Joshua Hammer,
because of Shell's support for the ruling Abache junta, "it is nearly impossible to
overstate Shell's role in Nigeria."[55]

By contrast, on public television, it is nearly impossible to state any connection between Shell and Nigeria at all: the few times that Saro-Wiwa's execution was mentioned on the *NewsHour*, there was no reference to Shell, and
Shell's actions in Nigeria have never been explored on the *NewsHour*, *Nightly
Business Report,* or, as can best be determined, any nationally available PBS public affairs program.

The Shell-Nigeria disaster is but one of many oil company scandals from the
1990s. In 1994, 30,000 Ecuadorans sued Texaco in United States federal court
for similar environmental damage in that nation. In 1996, the Project on
Government Oversight (POGO)—a watchdog group that played a leading role
in exposing Pentagon waste in the 1980s—produced a thorough report showing
that major U.S. oil companies had failed to pay some $2 billion in drilling fees to
the Department of the Interior. Later that year, two public interest groups analyzing data from the Environmental Protection Agency found that Mobil was one

of the top firms responsible for toxic discharge into U.S. waters.[56] Any and all of these topics would make compelling subjects for television documentaries; none have ever received any significant attention from American public television.

Although public television stars such as Bill Moyers and Jim Lehrer continue to mouth the shibboleths of objective and fearless journalism, their stated values have long been recognized as irrelevant when measured against the imperatives of public television's corporate sponsors. "The already small number of corporations that fund the financially strapped medium have assumed the role of programmers, and dictate what types of broadcasts they will underwrite and support," concluded *Variety* in 1985.[57] Local stations are "helpless in watching a facet of journalism—the serious, hard-hitting documentary—become extinct on the very medium that was supposed to save and nurture it." When General Motors and Mobil insist that fictional television should be about nineteenth-century England, and nonfiction television should be about business news, the U.S. civil war, and villain-free celebrations of the animal kingdom, who is PBS to object?

8

THE INVENTION DID NOT WORK

As modern public broadcasting approached its tenth anniversary in 1977, criticisms of the system were reaching a crescendo. The near-utopian optimism that accompanied the birth of public television had disappeared, replaced by bitterness and frustration. A three-part *TV Guide* series charged that infighting among public television leaders created "a chronic infirmity that is sapping its strengths, exasperating its partisans, and shortchanging the viewing public."[1] The system's sole attempt to maintain a liaison with public interest and advocacy groups—the Advisory Council of National Organizations (ACNO)—was under boycott by many of its own members. By the end of the year ACNO would dissolve itself, its chairwoman denouncing CPB board members as "part of the political patronage system [who] often have no sense of what public broadcasting is about."[2]

There were pressing fiscal questions: despite steadily advancing federal budgets—now up to more than $100 million annually—no one could satisfactorily explain why just $13 million went to national programming. And there were stubborn programming objections as well: right-wing critics maintained that public affairs programs violated legal obligations to objectivity, while left-wing critics found the system engaged in a "vicious cycle designed to exclude minorities," and charged that "most public television stations produced few programs that would qualify as hard-hitting, investigative broadcast journalism of any form."[3]

There was nonetheless some political reason for hope from above, because no president had taken office with as outspoken a commitment to public broadcasting as Jimmy Carter. During the 1976 campaign Carter, speaking to *TV Guide,* pledged: "I would do what I could to strengthen the autonomy of public television. I think this is one of the fine opportunities in our country that hasn't been adequately realized. I watch public television a great deal and have always been very impressed with the educational contributions, at the classroom level and also for the general public." For added effect, Carter's son, Chip, quite publicly volunteered at Atlanta's WETV.

Within the first few weeks of taking the White House Carter told an interviewer: "My daughter Amy loves television. She learns a great deal from it. She
watches *Electric Company* and *Sesame Street* and knows all the characters. And I
think that's part of her education."[4] Two months into his presidency, Carter took
part in a one-hour television call-in program, which CBS newsman Walter
Cronkite called a "unique . . . new approach to communication between the
President and the people of the United States."[5] Although the CBS television network broadcast the program, it was, significantly, rebroadcast in its entirety a
few hours later on National Public Radio. Later in his presidency, Carter also
taped a segment of PBS's *Black Perspectives on the News*,[6] a gesture neither of his
GOP predecessors had made.

The Carter White House's motivation was not entirely altruistic; his aides saw
the growing NPR and PBS audiences as fertile ground for political support
(although a poll at this time showed those audiences to have a slightly higher concentration of Republicans than the general population).[7] As much as Nixon—but
without the bile—Carter advisors believed in broad political symbolism. This
did not go unnoticed; in response to symbolic gestures of frugality such as a
reduction in the number of White House limousines, Garry Trudeau's *Doonesbury*
slyly created a Carter White House Secretary of Symbolism. The character was
based on real-life, TV-centered men, such as public relations consultant Barry
Jagoda. These men generally had multiple roles: at one minute they were the
President's image molders, the next they were helping shape the administration's
policy toward public broadcasting. Thus, for Carter, visible support for public
broadcasting was a relatively cheap way to appeal to the medium's growing audience, and a subtle reminder of past Republican excesses and misdeeds. In a message to Congress, Carter pledged: "This Administration will not try to stifle
controversy on public television and radio. No President should try to dictate
what issues public broadcasting should cover or how it should cover them."[8] Just
as Carter's election was interpreted as a national repudiation of Watergate, so,
too, was support for public broadcasting a slap at Nixon's sins.

Although intended as symbols, Carter's gestures toward public broadcasting
were not fabrications; he had, for example, strongly supported public broadcasting as governor of Georgia. The administration felt that public broadcasting
needed an overhaul after the Nixon debacle, and thus worked hard on a long-
term bill of support. Carter was also one of the only Presidents to hire public
broadcasting experts to set public broadcasting policy. He brought onto his team
Frank Lloyd, one of public broadcasting's fiercest and most knowledgeable
critics; just a few months before he joined the Carter White House, Lloyd

co-authored a massive study called *Public Broadcasting and Equal Employment Opportunity Regulation—Where Does the Buck Stop?*[9] This broadside accused the entire public broadcasting structure of evading its legal obligations for minority hiring; enforcing them soon became an administration priority.

To a limited extent, the Carter advisors also tried to rectify the stodginess of public radio and television programming by opening the system to independent producers. Noting that independent producers had "complained about the parochial bias of PBS and NPR," the administration supported those at PBS and NPR who wanted a percentage of CPB funds set aside for independent and experimental work. The legislation Congress eventually passed, the 1978 Public Telecommunications Finance Act, did contain a new provision instructing CPB to earmark "a substantial amount" for producers working outside public broad- casting's established institutions. It also tried to shake up the system by reducing CPB's role in choosing programs, and by explicitly stating—over the objections of top public broadcasting officials—that employment discrimination laws applied to all stations or recipients of CPB grants. As media historian Ralph Engelman has noted, these and other achievements of the 1978 Act were attrib- utable in large part to an impressive coalition of media activists working with women's, minority, labor, consumer, and religious organizations.[10]

Perhaps because it relied so heavily on insider experts, the Carter administra- tion spent a great deal of energy on public broadcasting reforms that, while help- ful, were essentially housekeeping duties. One was to pare down the vines of federal spending for public broadcasting. As the reach of public television and radio grew, more and more executive branch offices found the electronic media a winning method of educational outreach. By the mid-'70s, according to some estimates, as much as $40 million of federal money a year that did not go through the CPB was being spent on public broadcasting. Most significantly, the Department of Health, Education and Welfare (HEW) retained the grant pro- gram, established in 1962, to build new broadcasting stations and improve facili- ties. Under the Emergency School Assistance Act, the executive branch received a specific mandate to produce racially integrated children's programming; this resulted in federal money going to *Sesame Street* and *Electric Company*. (By 1977, nearly $34 million in HEW funds had been given to the Children's Television Workshop, which developed and produced both programs.) Some half-dozen other agencies (including the National Sciences Foundation, the National En- dowment for the Arts, and the National Endowment for the Humanities) also provided money directly to public broadcasting. In one instance, Congress essen- tially ordered the Administration on Aging (a division of HEW) to provide initial production money for *Over Easy*, a PBS program targeted at the elderly.

This practice clearly bumped up against the principle that the federal government should stay out of programming; a Ford administration study had concluded that because the federal government was essentially dictating what appeared on PBS, agency financing "had already subverted the intent of the Public Broadcasting Act of 1967."[11] Ironically, the agency-to-screen funding pattern expanded rapidly under two Republican administrations that proclaimed themselves enemies of government influence on public broadcasting. Indeed, direct agency funding could be viewed as one of the Nixon administration's weapons in changing the mix of public television: since agency funding is heavily weighted in favor of science, arts, history, and children's programs, that leaves less time and fewer resources for public affairs. Convinced that this situation "compound[ed] the disorganization [and] has resulted in agencies using grants to improperly dictate program content,"[12] the Carter White House set out to shepherd all federal authority for public broadcasting activities into the CPB.

One of the boldest proposals considered by the Carter White House—though not made publicly—was to eliminate public broadcasting's "balance and objectivity" requirements. Frank Lloyd advised his colleagues that the presence of section 396 would provoke "continued mischief," such as Orrin Hatch's bill that would empower the FCC to enforce objectivity and order the CPB to provide "balanced" programming wherever violations were found. Even if that effort failed, Lloyd predicted in 1979—with impressive accuracy—that "individual Congressmen will continue to use the clause as a justification for closer CPB control of internal journalistic program judgments and close Congressional oversight of those decisions."

THE WHITE HOUSE'S PIANO MAN

Not surprisingly, the Carter White House did not receive credit for its efforts to divorce the executive branch from PBS programming. On the contrary: the administration found itself accused of manipulating public television—not because of an incendiary documentary like *Banks and the Poor*, or a program containing even the mildest taint of controversy. It was instead a Sunday afternoon concert given in February 1978 by the renowned pianist Vladimir Horowitz. The circumstances seemed innocuous: at the request of the White House social secretary and the First Lady's press secretary, Horowitz agreed to give a concert before a small audience of invited guests in the White House. Carter media advisor Barry Jagoda decided that Horowitz's gifts should be shared with the American public, and he contacted WETA-TV, Washington, D.C.'s public television station, to handle the job. Horowitz, according to *The Washington Post*, was not paid for his appearance, and had turned down "lucrative offers from commercial stations" for what was only his second performance ever on television.[13] (The 73-year-old pianist had some promotional motivation, since the appearance coincided with the RCA Records release of a recording Horowitz had made with the New York Philharmonic.)

WETA applied for and received a $50,000 grant from the CPB to produce the Horowitz concert. "We consider it quite a coup for us," declared WETA vice president Gerald Slater. "The commercial stations have been trying to get him for some time."[14] President Carter introduced Horowitz, reminding the audience that he had become a classical music buff by listening to Horowitz records while a midshipman at the U.S. Naval Academy. "My roommate and I would take all our slender earnings and spend it on classical records," said the President, praising "the tremendous brilliance of [Horowitz's] playing, his technical perfection, how well he could interpret the intentions of great composers."

Amid hundreds of tulips and hyacinths in the White House's East Room, Horowitz played selections from Chopin, Schumann, Rachmaninoff, and his signature version of pieces from Bizet's *Carmen*. Paul Hume, one of the few critics who attended the concert in person, called the performance "sheer enchantment," but suggested nonetheless that "both the administration and Horowitz consider the recital's importance far greater as a media event."[15] The concert was broadcast three hours later on most of the nation's public TV stations (and some public radio stations), and was generally hailed as a success.

On one level, there is nothing wrong with such an event; as one television critic wrote: "A genius sat down to play the piano for a nation, and the triumph was everybody's—TV included." Nonetheless, the Carter administration was behaving a bit like Mobil and the various oil companies who underwrite so many of the classical music segments on PBS. Akin to Mobil's affinity-of-purpose marketing, the Carter strategy might be called affinity-of-purpose politics—if you like our taste in music, you'll love our Panama Canal Treaty. Republicans soon began grumbling, accusing the administration of using the concert "to bring the Carter cultural philosophy to the American people" via a federally funded broadcast system. It did not help matters that PBS president Larry Grossman and WETA president Ward Chamberlain had sent Carter a telegram, pledging that "a variety of program formats could be designed that would, simultaneously, help to open direct communications between you and the American people and also contribute to our goal of serving the people with independent broadcast journalism."[16] There was also considerable internal grumbling that the program had been provided to PBS stations with the unusually strict proviso that it be broadcast when it was fed or not at all.

Although the charge of White House cultural thought control was stridently partisan and hardly a national crisis, the symbol men in the White House had lost control of the symbolism; conservatives created a whisper campaign pointing out that state-funded broadcast systems like those in the Soviet Union also devoted a great deal of airtime to classical music played by men named Vladimir. Senator Barry Goldwater, a hard-core Republican who sat on the communications committee that decided how much federal money went to the CPB, charged that Jagoda was wearing too many hats. "The request for coverage of the Horowitz concert came from Barry Jagoda," noted Goldwater on the Senate floor.[17] "Mr. Jagoda . . . was involved in drafting authorization legislation affecting public broadcasting's future, development of the President's budget with respect to public broadcasting, and assisting in the selection of nominees for the board of the Corporation for Public Broadcasting." (All this was true.) "Of course, at the same time, Mr. Jagoda was in charge of polishing the President's tarnished media image." At Goldwater's request, Democrat Ernest Hollings asked Jagoda to appear before his Subcommittee on Communications, declaring himself "disturbed" by the "apparent conflict" in Jagoda's roles. Jagoda insisted that he had been misunderstood, and that he agreed with the senator's broad point: "I think it is absolutely improper for government officials to be involved in programming, particularly in the publicly-financed system of broadcasting."

Even if his intentions were innocent, however, getting "involved in programming" was precisely what Jagoda had done—the administration that set out to remove White House politics from public broadcasting had ended up reinserting them. Goldwater introduced a bill requiring that any government event made available to public broadcasting would also have to be made available to commercial broadcasters. Jagoda did not accept Goldwater's invitation to testify on the Hill, and not long after, he abandoned the post of presidential media advisor. His replacement, Gerald Rafshoon, was instructed by White House superiors to promise Goldwater that he would not repeat Jagoda's booking indiscretion.[18]

Not all of Goldwater's thrusts against supposed administration domination of public broadcasting were as effective. Angered that WETA had sent out to stations nationwide a portion of a Senate Foreign Relations Committee debate on the administration's proposed Middle East arms package, Goldwater thought he smelled a conspiracy. David Aaron, who worked under Zbigniew Brzezinski in the White House office of national security affairs, was married to Chloe Aaron, senior vice president for programming at PBS. Concerned that public television's coverage of Congressional matters "could be slanted," Goldwater demanded that PBS disclose what role, if any, Chloe Aaron had in making the tape available. It was pointed out to the senator that Chloe Aaron had begun working at PBS before Jimmy Carter was even a presidential nominee; the idea that she was an administration plant was a bit of a stretch.[19] The matter was dropped, but—because such a minuscule coincidence would never prompt such questions to a commercial broadcaster—the event illustrates the degree to which partisan Congressional politics translated into micromanagement of public broadcasting.

"A STORM IS BUILDING"

If Goldwater overly politicized his role in oversight, however, he was only mirroring the Machiavellian maneuvers emanating from the White House. Although the Carter White House made some quality appointments to the CPB, several of its nominees were clearly political chips, meant as markers in a larger strategic poker game. The Carter administration squandered a large chunk of its good will in public broadcasting—as well as segments of the black community—by nominating Irby Turner, Jr., to the CPB board. Turner had been a state legislator in Mississippi in the '60s, and had gone on to head the Mississippi Authority for Educational Television (MAET).

Carter could hardly have picked a worse time to try to place a public broadcaster from a southern state on the CPB board. The man Carter had chosen to develop administration policy on public broadcasting, Frank Lloyd, had spent years documenting and fighting racial discrimination in places like the MAET. The programming decisions made by state governments who held the public television licenses in many southern states frequently reflected gubernatorial and local politics that, in Mississippi in the '60s and '70s, were permeated by racial containment notions. As in Alabama, the Mississippi system where Turner had worked was essentially all white, and civil rights groups accused Turner of keeping black programming off the MAET. Through Lloyd, the administration was well aware that lack of minority control was a problem well beyond Mississippi: contemporary data showed that only three public TV stations out of 257 (1.16 percent) were minority-owned or -controlled, and none of those were in the continental U.S.; similarly, only seven out of 887 public radio stations (0.78 percent) were minority-owned or -controlled, and six of the seven were Spanish-language stations.

Turner's chief attraction for the Carter White House, however, was that he was backed by Senator James Eastland, a southern Democrat whose votes, in the very tight Senate politics of the late '70s, were vital to the White House. When Turner was not among the first round of Carter CPB nominees in early 1977, recalled two White House staffers, Senator Eastland was "very hurt," and "made it quite clear that . . . nothing else meant as much to him and that this was his only personal request to [Carter]."[20]

The White House believed Eastland was part of a select group of malleable conservative southern Democrats whom it could not afford to alienate. "Looking down the road at the Panama Canal Treaty, SALT agreements, and other things," White House aides Frank Moore and Hamilton Jordan told the President, "Eastland, Stennis, McClellan, Randolph and Sparkman fall into a special category, and you are the only person who can persuade them to do things that their personal philosophy or constituencies indicate they not do."[21] There was but one solution: Eastland had to be promised that his candidate Turner would be nominated when the next CPB vacancies came up.

Eastland got his promise, and Turner got his nomination in October 1977. Because the nomination was a fait accompli, the White House failed to get as thorough a background check on Turner as they might have. Turner had already appeared before the Senate Commerce Committee when the thunder of the black media activist community hit. "A storm is building rapidly over the nomination of Irby Turner to the Corporation for Public Broadcasting," reported a top White House aide in November 1977. "[Turner] is being attacked by the Congressional Black Caucus, the NAACP, and various public interest groups as having a racist background. Charges center on anti–civil rights votes in the state legislature and support for an all-white school."[22]

Within a few days, the vagaries of Turner's racial history began to seep into the media. Carter was asked a question about Turner at a presidential press conference—an unusual degree of attention for a CPB nominee. A reporter queried whether Carter was aware that his "most recent nominee to the Corporation for Public Broadcasting was a very active member of the White Citizens Council in Mississippi, and worked very hard to keep schools from being integrated down there? If that is true, would that make any difference to you in making that nomination?"

Carter said he knew nothing of the charge and would look into it. As a good born-again Christian, he tried to strike a conciliatory note: "I always think it is good to give people a chance to change if they will."[23] But the nomination was clearly in doubt, and when the NAACP finally delivered its specific charges, they were highly damaging. Turner had been a state legislator during Mississippi's most tumultuous civil rights period, and had sponsored or cosponsored dozens of bills obviously designed for racial containment: outlawing passive resistance in civil rights demonstrations, establishing curfews, trying juveniles arrested in civil rights demonstrations as adults. Even more embarrassing was the staggering volume of Jim Crow legislation Turner had supported: bills requiring a voter to be "of good moral character," allowing boards of elections to dispose of election form applications, poll taxes, literacy tests—even a resolution praising the Robert E. Lee Hotel for closing after the Civil Rights Act passed, rather than admit black guests.

For a moderate-to-liberal southerner like Carter, such explicit racism was a liability. Joining the NAACP in its outraged opposition were the United Auto Workers and just about every minority journalism group in the nation; these groups would make Turner's life very difficult through their role in CPB's Advisory Council of National Organizations. Yet Turner had his supporters within public broadcasting, including the sainted Ralph Rogers and Henry Cauthen, and so the administration stuck to its nominee. A series of embarrassing damage-control statements followed, such as one to a trade magazine claiming that, contrary to reports, Turner's involvement with Mississippi's Klan-linked White Citizens Council was limited to attending one meeting and paying $10 in dues.[24] His nomination was eventually withdrawn, nearly a year after the controversy first arose.

Although not as overtly offensive, the Carter CPB choices who were approved were not always more qualified. One CPB candidate appointed strictly for political purposes was Paul Friedlander of Seattle. A successful jeweler, Friedlander sat on the board of Seattle's KTCS–Channel 9, but of greater interest was the fund-raising Friedlander did for both Washington senators, Scoop Jackson and Warren Magnuson. Internally, administration aides were candid about Friedlander's scant qualifications. "Senator Magnuson has been pushing a Seattle businessman named Paul Friedlander (a major fundraiser for Jackson's campaign and for local campaigns)," warned one memo to Hamilton Jordan.[25] "He is only marginally qualified to be on the Board, but Magnuson may ask for some gestures toward him." Another reported that Friedlander "says he fully supports the Administration's public broadcasting bill, but our discussion with him indicated that he knows little about the Bill or about the major issues in public broadcasting."[26] Despite these gaping weaknesses, Friedlander was appointed and confirmed to the CPB board. A state public broadcasting official scolded the White House: "Rather than appointing distinguished authors, performers, historians and academicians, we are dipping into the political pay-off bucket to make up the CPB board, and I find this offensive."[27]

"BADLY IN NEED OF REPAIR"

As the 1970s came to a close, America's public broadcasting received the equivalent of a parental rebuke. A second Carnegie Commission had convened, setting sights on the future of public broadcasting, and issued its report, *A Public Trust*, in January 1979. Although it carried the weighty name of the progenitor of public broadcasting, the second Carnegie Commission had a different makeup, as it included leading figures from the now-established public broadcasting community (such as children's television guru Peggy Charren and CPB board member Virginia Duncan) as well as a representative from commercial television (the chairman of Cox Broadcasting). Carnegie II also filled in spaces its predecessor had left blank, offering plans for public radio and other telecommunications. The biggest difference, however, was the report's pervasive critical, even pessimistic tone. Public broadcasting's "financial, organizational and creative structures [are] fundamentally flawed," the report declared in its introduction. "The invention did not work, at least not very well," said the report, deeming the various institutional forces "out of kilter and badly in need of repair."[28]

The report's particular charges stung harder. Corporate funding of public television "has undoubtedly skewed the total schedule in the direction of cultural programs which are popular among the 'upscale' audiences that corporations prefer," thus placing documentaries, minority programming, controversial drama, and public affairs programs into a "near-Darwinian competition" for money that often forced them into extinction.[29] The Commission discovered "a widespread and growing perception among many groups on the periphery of public broadcasting that it is a system which is closed, unwilling to change, and afraid of criticism and controversy."[30]

The second Carnegie panel's reform recommendations were as sweeping as its criticisms. It called for the CPB to be replaced by a National Telecommunications Trust, that would fund and set goals for the system while maintaining political autonomy. The report calculated the system's financial needs at $1 billion a year, of which nearly $600 million was to come from the federal government— approximately a 500 percent increase over then current spending levels.

More than any other single factor, that particular budgetary recommendation condemned the Carnegie II report to oblivion. The Carter White House, while more receptive than most to cultivating public broadcasting, was attempting to stick to a fairly strict fiscal regimen. A few members of Congress were willing to take up the cause of reform, though they would likely have been overwhelmed by lobbying from commercial broadcasters who were none too pleased with Carnegie II's call for a spectrum use fee.

Regardless, the recommendations of earnest reformers like the second Carnegie commissioners would have been no match for the public broadcasting reforms envisioned by a different, more powerful entity: Ronald Reagan's White House. Reagan brought aboard many key staffers who had worked in the Nixon administration, including some who had helped orchestrate that era's public broadcasting crisis. Nixon speechwriter Pat Buchanan, for example, who had referred to public television as "a cargo preference act for the cultural elite," joined the Reagan staff in 1985, and helped choose Reagan's appointees to the CPB panel, even though his stated position was to eliminate government involvement in public broadcasting. Although conservative hostility toward PBS in the '80s was essentially the same as it had been under Nixon, Reagan's methods were subtler—he did not issue edicts to shut the system down—and ultimately more effective. By maintaining a public face of cooperation with public broadcasting— Nancy Reagan even hosted a two-part PBS series on drug and alcohol abuse—by playing budgetary hardball, and by using his CPB appointees as ideological enforcers, Reagan was able to move public broadcasting in the desired direction. As with Nixon, however, the combination of monetary cutbacks and political pressure threw public broadcasting into chaos.

"ANTI-WESTERN DIATRIBE"

Reagan and his advisors believed, as Nixon did, that the media was biased against them and their causes, with public broadcasters on the frontline of hostility. An often-heard phrase during the early Reagan days was "defunding the left"; based on the belief that federal funds supported a wide range of activities that harbored left-wingers—environmentalism, legal services for the poor, product regulation—"defunding the left" was a strategy to use the federal budget as an ideological scalpel. To a great extent, public broadcasting fell into this category: Reagan's first budget tried to cut CPB funding in half, but Congress resisted. The result was a multiyear financial stalemate. Money already planned for public broadcasting through 1983 was rescinded; not until 1989 did the CPB budget reach $220 million, the amount it was scheduled to get for 1983.

Beginning with the NPR bankruptcy hit (discussed in chapter 6), public broadcasting during this period seemed almost cursed. In October 1984, a fire broke out in the basement of the U.S. Postal Service, where PBS was renting space, damaging $12 million worth of transmission equipment and scattering employees to four separate locations around the Washington area. Shortly there-after, Reagan vetoed a three-year, $775 million public broadcasting authorization bill, labeling it a "budget buster";[31] there would be no further authorizations until 1986. As a result, for the first half of the 1980s, "public broadcasters had to live with the very real fear that federal funding might be totally eliminated."[32] In addition to actual cutbacks in programming and services, the financial uncertainty made long-term planning essentially impossible.

The road to this budgetary breakdown was bumpy; the Reagan White House encountered many political potholes, notably when it decided to reappoint Sharon Percy Rockefeller, a Democrat, to the CPB chairmanship. The Reagan man who handled White House appointments later said: "Our intention had been to remove her as chairman, just as we tried to do with every other agency. But when we announced our intention, her father, Senator Charles Percy, was out-raged. He went storming over to the White House and told the President: 'If you want my cooperation on the Foreign Relations committee, you'd better reap-point my daughter.' So we did."[33] The administration and its CPB appointees ended up spending much of their energy trying to work around Rockefeller.

Even where the White House could make its own appointments, they didn't always work out as planned. Lloyd Kaiser, president of Pittsburgh's WQED, disap-pointed the White House's true believers by often supporting the public broad-casting status quo. To an extent, Kaiser's appointment reflected the dueling power structure inside the Reagan White House. Despite charges of lavish expenses and financial irregularities at Kaiser's station, Kaiser was appointed primarily because he had produced *The Chemical People*, the two-part PBS antidrug series that aired first in November 1983, hosted by Nancy Reagan.[34] Indeed, the First Lady's use of public broadcasting to promote her anti-drug campaign—Mrs. Reagan's press secretary Sheila Tate went on become a CPB board member—partially interfered with the administration's desire to curb the system's influence.

Nonetheless, the White House found ways of undermining Rockefeller, notably by appointing to the CPB board several veteran Republican political con-sultants, including William Hanley, who headed the 1980 Reagan-Bush campaign in Connecticut, and Kenneth Towery.[35] Richard Brookhiser, the *National Review* editor whom Reagan appointed to the CPB board in 1982, took a $1,000-a-month consulting job with the Republican National Committee a few months after his nomination, where his duty was to write speeches for Vice President George Bush;[36] no one seemed to think this conflicted with his role as an over-seer of public broadcasting.

Sonia Landau, a Reagan campaign veteran who worked with Republican media advisor Stu Spencer, took the most active role on the CPB board: Landau was elected CPB chair over Rockefeller in 1984, the year she simultaneously headed Women for Reagan-Bush. Landau knew more about politics than broadcasting; in addition to her work on Reagan's campaigns, she had also once run unsuccessfully for Congress. According to one fellow CPB board member, Landau's campaigning for Reagan inside the CPB was just as intense as her Reagan campaigning at large. "When Reagan appointees hit the board," said Carter appointee Jose Rivera, "for the first time we heard things like, 'the administration's view is not being totally represented.' We never heard talk like that before. Our concern was whether public broadcasting was being funded, and all of a sudden it was whether the White House was being heard."[37]

One example of the White House making itself heard was with the propaganda film *Let Poland Be Poland*. Produced by a division of the United States Information Agency, this slick, celebrity-packed documentary was designed to stir international support for Poles living under martial law imposed by Poland's Communist leaders. (One of Reagan's CPB appointees, Kenneth Towery, had been a deputy director of the USIA.)[38] Its mixture of broadstroke politics and show business was a perfect reflection of the movie star turned president: along with taped messages from various world leaders, the film featured Orson Welles reading John Donne poems and Frank Sinatra singing "Ever Homeward" in Polish. Just as Nixon's people had pressed to have a NASA mission broadcast on public television, the Reagan administration campaigned hard for *Let Poland Be Poland* to be shown on American television. A longstanding U.S. law prevents Americans from being subjected to their own propaganda, and although the resistance to government-funded communications is a staple of conservative PBS critics, it was Reagan's conservative government that convinced Congress to waive the law for this USIA film. *Let Poland Be Poland* went out on the national PBS satellite; stations were, however, given the option not to carry it. Stephen Kulczycki, the Polish American vice president of KTCA in Minneapolis, declined to broadcast the film: "It clearly violates our programming and journalistic standards. We turn down hundreds of requests a month to broadcast someone's propaganda."[39]

Several years into her CPB tenure, another Landau project was to commission a "scientific content analysis" of PBS programming. Richard Brookhiser said that he got the idea not from perceiving a bias on public television—"I watch very little television," he said—but from reading a copy of the Carnegie Commission report and Public Broadcasting Act.[40] Coming across the stated goal of "objectivity and balance," Brookhiser said: "I thought, 'Wait a minute, nobody ever mentions this,' and we have no way of even talking about it. . . . People who are upset with us will criticize us, but they never do it in a comprehensive fashion, and so why don't we take a look at this?"

The proposed "content analysis" was, in many ways, a quixotic pursuit. It was, for example, directly opposite to the tack that the Reagan administration and the right-moving Supreme Court were taking regarding private broadcasters; the so-called Fairness Doctrine, which required broadcasters to air opposing points of view on controversial subjects, was essentially eliminated by Reagan's second term, opening the door for such lopsided broadcasters as Rush Limbaugh. Furthermore, Brookhiser was proposing a CPB study to verify or refute the charges that Accuracy in Media and Reed Irvine had made since the '70s, using the same statutory basis that the FCC and courts had declared useless (see chapter 4). While Irvine was an ally of Landau's, Brookhiser said that he never discussed such a study with Irvine, and in fact "didn't know" the unsuccessful history of AIM's complaints about objectivity and balance. "My notion of who should do it were Bob and Linda Lichter," who work for the conservative Center for Media and Public Affairs.[41]

Landau had a stronger personal impression of bias, pointing to several mid-'80s public television productions, including *When the Mountains Tremble*, a documentary on Guatemala, and *Cuba in the Shadow of Doubt*.[42] It is interesting to note that, with the exception of Vietnam commentary, the PBS programs that attracted the ire of Nixon were about domestic politics, whereas Reagan-era conservatives were most often upset by documentaries about other countries. For a mere CPB chair, Landau took an unusual interest in American foreign policy; she frequently made official trips abroad, serving, for example, as special ambassador under Elliott Abrams as part of the U.S. delegation to the inauguration of the president of Bolivia in 1985.[43] That Landau later ended up as the State Department's coordinator for International Communication and Information Policy strongly suggests that her views on how public broadcasting should handle foreign affairs were coming directly from the Reagan administration.[44]

Another international issue that got PBS in trouble was a 1985 documentary called *Hungry for Profit*, exploring the role of agribusiness in perpetuating Third World hunger. Visiting 10 nations on five continents, the film found a pattern of multinational companies displacing peasant farmers to buy up cheap land to grow food for export to wealthier nations. In Costa Rica, for example, the documentary showed rain and cloud forests that had been cleared and turned into pasture for beef cattle, not to feed Costa Ricans but for the U.S. fast-food industry. "The average Central American," the documentary stated, "now eats less beef than the average U.S. pet cat."[45] This was too much for PBS's corporate backers. Gulf+Western, the conglomerate now called Paramount, cut off its support of New York's WNET, PBS's largest affiliate. In a letter to WNET, Gulf+Western's chief executive officer wrote that the station's actions had "not been those of a friend," and that the film was "virulently anti-business, if not anti-American." For its part, WNET claimed that it "did all it could to get the program sanitized."[46] Even one of PBS's boldest public affairs specialists, Jonathan Kwitny of the excellent but short-lived *The Kwitny Report*, felt pressure from his superiors at New York City's WNYC to tone down his broadcasts. Shortly after Kwitny called the anti-Communist Angolan rebel Jonas Savimbi "just one more blood-stained autocrat on the U.S. taxpayers' payroll," his program was canceled.[47]

The most wildly controversial public television broadcast of the Reagan period was *The Africans*, a nine-part series that aired in the fall of 1986. Narrated by Ali A. Mazrui, a native Kenyan who came to the U.S. in 1974, *The Africans* sought to tell the history of the continent "as seen through the eyes of the Africans." Mazrui, who received a doctorate from Oxford University and taught political science at the University of Michigan, spent four years on the documentary, which took him to 18 countries on three continents—the kind of vast, historical undertaking that PBS made possible. The film was co-produced by Washington's WETA and the BBC, and had received $600,000 from the National Endowment for the Humanities. That grant nearly became the documentary's undoing, because prior to its U.S. broadcast, NEH chairwoman Lynne Cheney assaulted the work as "narrow [and] politically tendentious," scolding WETA that: "Worse than unbalanced, this film frequently degenerates into anti-Western diatribe."[48] Cheney demanded that NEH's name be removed from its credits, and withheld $50,000 that had been promised for film publicity.

Cheney excoriated one segment of the film that, she said, "strives to blame every technological, moral and economic failure of Africa on the West." She complained that, after showing a group of Liberians carrying out a political execution, "the blame is cast on . . . the guns used by the executioners rather than on the Africans pulling the triggers." Defending his sequence, Mazrui told an interviewer that "the transfer of technology from the West to Africa has been very shallow. And then I show things which don't work: television, water taps, door knobs. The West takes a lot of resources that are relevant for its own development, such as chrome, cobalt, coal or whatever, and the West sometimes claims it brings in know-how. The only form of technology which seems to have more effect is the West's technology of destruction. The only forms of technology which work, because we buy large-scale arms, are the weapons."[49]

What really set conservatives off was a portion in *The Africans'* final installment that, according to Cheney, "extols the virtue of Moammar Gadhafi." The sequence, which takes up 150 seconds of a nine-hour film, compares Gadhafi to the late president Nasser of Egypt—noting that both were demonized by the West—and cites the Libyan leader as an example that "it is not enough just to stop being pawns in the games of the powerful. We [Africans and Arabs] must become global players in our own right." The visual accompaniment was footage of Gadhafi visiting children in a hospital following the U.S. bombing raid on Tripoli.

A Washington-based group called Citizens for Reagan asked WETA for an hour of airtime to rebut the program; they were turned down. In his defense, Mazrui said that he never claimed to be objective, and that his 15 books and dozens of articles were fully available to NEH and PBS officials when he proposed the film. Asked if he considered Gadhafi a terrorist, a feisty Mazrui told *The Los Angeles Times*: "Only in the sense Reagan is. That is, both subsidize instruments of violence. Congress has just reconfirmed support to the UNITA movement in Angola . . . and support to the contras is the same. One man's terrorist is another man's liberation fighter, you see." That equivalence had been explicitly drawn in the film's British version; it was "softened" for the American release, and carried the subtitle "A Commentary by Ali A. Mazrui" for American viewers, a move that Cheney praised as "truth in labeling."[50]

Most of Reagan's appointees—Brookhiser, Landau, and businessman/political consultant Robert Hanley—supported the idea of a content study and thought they could pull it off without much flak. "We proposed doing this, and we tried to rush it through, which was a tactical mistake," recalled Brookhiser. Brookhiser said he was unaware that the law required the CPB to assure the "maximum freedom" of public broadcasting "from interference with or control of program content." At a meeting of public broadcasters in Boston, Brookhiser proposed the Lichter content study and it was heartily voted down. At this point Republican Members of Congress got into the act. Led by Representative Don Ritter of Pennsylvania and Senator Barry Goldwater, 56 members of the House and Senate sent a letter to the CPB urging it to establish an "auditing system" to analyze the content of CPB-funded public affairs programs. In the wooden language of the bureaucrat, Ritter said he wanted "an ongoing and systematic content analysis, performed under a methodology designed to provide an objective evaluation and subject to peer review."[51] While the initial idea for a CPB study was merely a nuisance, Ritter's suggestion bordered on Orwellian. It seems unlikely that his proposed "content analysis" would have been rigorously scientific, since he had not been troubled by an outright propaganda film like *Let Poland Be Poland* running as PBS fare, but wanted to label independently produced documentaries as biased because they expressed opinions contrary to the administration's. Furthermore, a peer review mechanism would add another bureaucratic layer onto to the already cumbersome process of getting a program on public television—a peculiar position for conservatives. For her part, Sharon

Rockefeller denounced the content analysis as "yet another link in the chain. . . . I hope it will not have a chilling effect on public affairs documentaries on public television."[52]

Nonetheless, within weeks of Ritter's call for a content review, PBS president Bruce Christensen announced that he would undertake such a study. "This step is necessary at this time because there are some who seek to discredit the programming on PBS," Christensen said.[53] "Nothing is more important to public television than its program and editorial independence."

Reagan's White House was a brilliant manipulator of Cold War imagery, and that, too, was used as a lever against public broadcasting. Edward Pfister, formerly the head of Dallas's KERA, became president of CPB in the early '80s. In 1985, during a CPB meeting in San Francisco, Landau unexpectedly attacked a trip Pfister had planned to make to Moscow. Pfister was to lead a delegation to explore the possibility of exchanging programming with Soviet television. Landau declared it unacceptable that "an institution that operates on federal money is dealing with the Soviet government," a surreal charge, since there was always some level of contact between the two nations; within a few months, President Reagan and Soviet leader Mikhail Gorbachev exchanged televised New Year's Day greetings to each other's citizens. Landau added that "we shouldn't be influenced by the Soviets," a notion seconded by Brookhiser, who said that it would be "disastrous" to "open the door to Soviet ideas on history."[54]

The board voted 6-4 to withdraw CPB sponsorship of the trip, causing Pfister to resign. He later delivered a speech to a gathering of public broadcasters, warning them of the threat to their independence; Landau accosted him afterward, shouting: "Ed Pfister. . . . You don't know the meaning of the word honest! You don't give a damn about this organization!"[55] It took eight months for CPB to find a replacement; within 10 months, he, too, resigned. As under Nixon, such turmoil and division made it nearly impossible for the executives of public broadcasting to get their work done. This time, however, the White House would have greater success in using the division to change the content of public television.

9

NIXON'S REVENGE

If the public television apparatus was breaking down, right-wing critics, boosted by allies in the administration and on the CPB board, were happy to fill the void. Angered by the 1983, 13-part PBS series *Vietnam: A Television History*, Accuracy in Media had produced a one-hour rebuttal, narrated by Charlton Heston and—since AIM was always willing to use dreaded government funds when they served its purposes—funded by the National Endowment for the Humanities. "We have seen what can only be called communist propaganda aired on that network," said an AIM officer. The rebuttal film aired on PBS stations in 1985, as part of a two-hour presentation called "Inside Story" that also featured a dissection of the original documentary's history and a panel discussion. The AIM film, according to one commentator, "spent far less time pointing out errors in the PBS program than it did impugning the motives of those who made it."[1] In a blistering attack on *The New York Times* Op-ed page, Anthony Lewis labeled the AIM response film "propaganda dressed up as journalism," and scolded: "The fact that public television broadcast a doctrinaire harangue posing as a news documentary raises worrying questions about political pressure and public television's will to resist it."[2]

Lewis's attack underscored an important point: AIM had finally trumped the very network it had spent 15 years demonizing, on an issue—the propriety of the U.S. war in Vietnam—that had plagued public television from its very start. It was as if PBS had been worn down from constantly fending off AIM's attacks. AIM chairman Reed Irvine crowed. "It marks the first time that a network [would] air a criticism of its own program," he told an interviewer. "It will set a precedent for airing professionally produced critiques of TV shows on the same system that aired the original program."[3] There is nothing intrinsically wrong with PBS carrying a rebuttal to its own broadcast. Irvine, however, was wrong: his triumph did not set a precedent. PBS has never, for example, allowed comparable access for its critics on the left.[4]

NATIONAL REVIEW BROADCASTING SERVICE

While AIM's triumph was visible, it was only one of many organizations with a conservative agenda to get its views on PBS during the '80s. General Electric (GE), a multibillion-dollar military contractor that, in the 1950s, had employed Ronald Reagan as a spokesman, created a hit with *The McLaughlin Group*, which premiered in 1981. GE—which also purchased the NBC network in 1986—understood that the best way to get a program on public television is to pay for it yourself, and send it for free to PBS stations. General Electric also promoted *The McLaughlin Group* in a series of magazine ads, billboards, and television spots. The program, noted for grafting the atmosphere of professional wrestling onto discussions of public affairs, had a decided right-wing edge: its regular panelists—who included Pat Buchanan, Jack Germond, Morton Kondracke, and Robert Novak—generally defended controversial Reagan policies, such as aid to the Nicaraguan contras and cuts in welfare programs. One of its specialties was that each panelist made a prediction at the end of the program; a magazine survey found these predictions to be inaccurate more than 75 percent of the time.[5]

In truth, *The McLaughlin Group* never had many viewers; like so many PBS programs, it wasn't broadcast at the same time on every station, which makes national audience difficult to measure, and in many markets it aired at low-viewing times, such as Saturday mornings. But for public television, the mere fact that *McLaughlin Group* panelists appeared to have clout with the Reagan administration and that the show was discussed in Washington political circles qualified it as a hit. It made a national celebrity out of McLaughlin, who was a *National Review* colleague of CPB board member Brookhiser; McLaughlin went on to host a program on the GE-owned CNBC. The rise of conservative programming on PBS sometimes made it difficult to tell who was acting as a mouthpiece for whom; just watching the revolving door between public broadcasting, conservative institutions, and the Reagan White House was enough to make one dizzy. *The McLaughlin Group* made PBS into a national television platform for Pat Buchanan, who had tried to kill federal funds for PBS; Buchanan left the weekly PBS perch in 1985 to go work in Reagan's communications department.

Another frustrated Nixonite who found success on PBS in the '80s was Neal Freeman. Once a producer for *Firing Line* and a consultant to the PBS program *The Advocates*, Freeman had served briefly on the CPB board during the '70s, and in 1981 founded a TV production company called The Blackwell Corporation. (He also sat on the board of the *National Review*; considering the varied and high-level success of Buckley, Brookhiser, McLaughlin, Freeman, and William Rusher, no single publication has had as large an impact on the management and content of American public television as the *National Review*.) Using large grants from conservative foundations such as Olin, Bradley, and Smith Richardson, Blackwell became a veritable fountain of PBS programming throughout the '80s and '90s. From the four-part documentary series *Crisis in Central America* (which the *National Review* called "a great leap forward for integrity and objectivity in television documentaries") to the 1987 documentary *The Conservatives* (the Associated Press said "no one is going to accuse [PBS] of liberal bias" for showing it), Blackwell produced hit after hit for PBS. (In the early '90s, Freeman began hosting his own PBS show called *Technopolitics*, on which he promoted telecommunications and cable giants as great democratizing forces.)

Blackwell's weekly series *American Interests*, which aired from 1988–92, was hosted by Morton Kondracke, a neoconservative who promoted probusiness and hard-line foreign policy views. In 1988, for example, *American Interests* hosted contra leader Alfredo Cesar, who pleaded for continued U.S. support to overthrow the Sandinista government; in 1991, the program hosted South African Zulu leader Gatsha Buthelezi, who argued that Nelson Mandela was "captive" to Communists within the African National Congress. Other *American Interests* guests included Margaret Thatcher and Brian Mulroney; the program almost never reached out to Labor Party governments or nationalist leaders who might have opposed international free trade agreements.

Perhaps the crowning moment for *American Interests* came in the spring of 1990, when Kondracke interviewed Richard Nixon. In a magazine essay, Kondracke, who had once been on Nixon's famed enemy list, confessed that he'd "changed his mind a lot about Nixon," and that because "he was no danger to anybody now . . . he ought to be forgiven." One acerbic press critic provided a list of words that were never used during Kondracke's 90-minute puffball interview: "Cambodia, Watergate, Constitution, ITT, psychiatrist's office, Pentagon Papers, CREEP, unindicted and coconspirator."[6] Like Reed Irvine, Richard Nixon, the man who tried to destroy public television, was now welcomed into its neoconservative bosom, and treated with the utmost deference as a foreign policy master.

RED HERRINGS AND RED BAITING

One curious facet of PBS's love affair with conservative programming is that much of it was underwritten by a handful of right-leaning foundations that also backed the media activist groups who were constantly denouncing PBS leftist bias. This oddity was documented in a 1992 report from Fairness and Accuracy in Reporting. A prominent example is the Committee for Media Integrity, which uses an acronym with a clever red-baiting echo, COMINT, and is run by David Horowitz, the onetime radical editor of *Ramparts* who moved rightward in the 1980s. COMINT is part of the Center for the Study of Popular Culture, which in the late 80s was heavily funded by the Bradley and Olin Foundations, and spent much of its time attacking *South Africa Now* (*SAN*) and other putatively left-wing PBS programs. At the same time, Bradley and Olin had supported *American Interests*; Olin was the lead underwriter for William F. Buckley's *Firing Line*.[7] Similarly, the Heritage Foundation, which published an influential study by Laurence Jarvik calling for the privatization of public broadcasting, has received huge grants from these foundations, as well as from the Sarah Scaife Foundation, which had given generously to a PBS documentary on black conservatives.

Thus, these foundations have been able to launch a powerful double-pronged attack: they fund programs with a conservative bent that appear on public television, and pay policy intellectuals (sometimes quite well) to attack competing programs, hoping to browbeat public broadcasters into airing more of the kind of programming they favor.[8] The steady stream of funding for such studies helps explain why the charge of liberal bias would not go away in the '80s and early '90s, even as conservatives began to dominate PBS's public affairs programming.

It has never been difficult to locate "liberal" programming on public television (particularly given that most of these groups also find CNN and network news captive to "liberal" ideas). The charge of overarching bias, however, has remained elusive; the closest these organizations have come to substantiating it was a study issued in 1992 by the Center for Media and Public Affairs (CMPA). Dissecting some 225 documentary programs that ran on Washington's WETA between 1987 and 1988, the study found that the "balance of opinion tilted consistently in a liberal direction."[9] One of the more nuanced points made by the study was that many documentaries, even where they attempt to represent various sides of an issue, start by defining issues that appear to conservatives as left-determined.

"Consider," said the report's conclusion, "that the preponderance of opinion questioned justifications for armed conflict and nuclear development, supported the primacy of environmental concerns over human needs, asserted that American society discriminates against women and minorities, upheld liberal interpretations of constitutional rights ranging from gay rights to search and seizure provisions, and condemned the failings of America's allies far more frequently than its Marxist opponents, at a time when the cold war was very much alive. This set of issue positions bespeaks a liberal sensibility, if not a liberal agenda."[10] Leaving aside the question of whether this summary accurately reflects PBS programming—and whether there should be a place on public television for, say, documentaries denying the plentiful evidence that American society discriminates against women and minorities—it is not hard to imagine an inverted set of definitions that would appear to many as conservative. Should there be affirmative action at all? Why can't the capital gains tax be cut or even eliminated?

That, however, is precisely what PBS programs like *MacNeil/Lehrer* or *Wall Street Week* often look like to critics on the left; the CMPA study conveniently did not include such regular PBS programs in its study. In 1992, for example, a guest on *Adam Smith's Money World* said: "Average hourly earnings is a gauge of how much people are getting in pay increase in their paycheck. It's up 3 percent. It's the smallest increase since the 1950's. It's great for inflation. If you're on the receiving end of it, you sure don't like it, but it is great for inflation. And in a global sense it makes the U.S.—it's the brightest spot the U.S. has because it makes the U.S. gain competitiveness."[11] The assertion that keeping wages low is the "brightest spot" in the U.S. economy was not challenged, which "bespeaks a sensibility" quite different from liberalism.

It is worth noting that the CMPA study also found that the documentaries "fell short of the standard of diversity by failing to give voice to excluded groups," an opinion with which progressives would certainly agree. Indeed, in the '80s and '90s progressive organizations maintained that they *were* the excluded group. In the late '80s, a small New York production company called Globalvision began producing *South Africa Now*, a weekly update on the antiapartheid struggle in South Africa and its frontline states. In its three seasons (1988–1990), *SAN* displayed remarkable footage from inside South Africa, mixing cultural reporting with its political dispatches, virtually all of which had no outlet on American television. Although the program eventually aired on 72 PBS affiliates—about a fifth of the stations—it received no support from PBS or CPB.

But even with the taxpayer-support argument removed, local station broadcasts of *SAN* were too much for conservative media activists. COMINT's Horowitz said: "I had gone to Stephen Kulczycki, the station manager [of Los Angeles's KCET], and said that this show is an embarrassment, and that he should either balance it with a more reasonable show—that is, one that was not simply a mouthpiece for the terrorist wing of the [African National Congress]— or label it an opinion show—because it was presenting itself as a news show—or take it off."[12]

Once again, Horowitz raised the reasonable and legally based challenge that public broadcasting's controversial programming should be "balanced," but without offering any practical mechanism for doing so. Counterprogramming might appear to be a solution, but neither local stations nor PBS nationally have a structure for determining exactly which broadcasts would require balance or how to achieve it: does a half-hour Morton Kondracke interview with a Zulu leader "balance" an episode of *SAN*? Should every PBS program hosted by someone from *National Review* be followed by one hosted by someone from *The Nation*?

It is often assumed that only public affairs programming will be deemed controversial, but gay sex themes in fictional works such as *Steambath* in the '70s and *Tales of the City* in the '90s generated as much ire as any political programs (and more viewer interest!). Could PBS be required to show works of fiction depicting homosexuality as wicked and depraved? If a station did determine that a program was unbalanced, it would rarely be in a position to produce or find a "reasonable" alternative to a program such as *SAN*. If a balancing program could be discovered, it might turn out to have a bias in an unanticipated direction, and stations could theoretically end up with an endless series—which, although possibly informative, is practically impossible. The possible regressions behind the balance and objectivity requirement may seem absurd, but it is precisely because public broadcasters are illequipped to deal with such questions that their practical response to such pressure is to censor. Whether responding to Horowitz or not, KCET in 1990 announced plans to take *SAN* off the air, as did Boston's WGBH. Both stations restored the program in the wake of community protest, but *SAN* ceased production shortly thereafter.

The right-wing balance and objectivity argument also gave public broadcasting a strong incentive to avoid putting anything on the air in the first place that might provoke such an attack. PBS has the dubious distinction of refusing to broadcast, for three years running, films with a liberal reputation that had won the Academy Award for best documentary. In 1991, the award for best short documentary went to *Deadly Deception: General Electric, Nuclear Weapons and Our Environment*, while the best documentary feature went to *In the Shadow of the Stars*, a film featuring the players in the San Francisco opera. In 1992, *The Panama Deception*, a skeptical exposé of the U.S. account of the 1989 invasion of Panama, won the best documentary feature award, and in 1993 best short documentary went to *Defending Our Lives*, a film about battered women who fight back against their attackers.

Of course, the mere fact that a documentary has won an Academy Award does not and should not guarantee it a screening on public television. But these were films dealing with important, timely subjects, reflecting points of view outside the mainstream; since more Americans have heard of the Academy Award than have heard of the films, the award have been used to attract an audience.

But these were not the terms on which PBS refused to show the films. In rejecting *Defending Our Lives*, PBS programming officials cited a guideline that "programming must be free from the control of parties with a direct self-interest in that content." Because *Defending Our Lives* was produced in collaboration with a domestic violence group called Battered Women Fight Back, an organization also quoted in the film, PBS deemed the film unacceptable. Similarly, *Deadly Deception* was rejected because it had been funded by INFACT, a corporate accountability organization that sponsors a nationwide General Electric boycott. *The Panama Deception* was said to violate PBS "fairness" standards; it was released theatrically and also shown on Cinemax.

Other PBS outcasts from this period include *Building Bombs*, a documentary about America's nuclear arms buildup and its environmental effects. In 1990, PBS rejected the documentary because it "does not give adequate voice to those who are proponents of nuclear arms."[13] After three years of struggle and protest and after a version was shown on the Discovery Channel, *Building Bombs* was finally broadcast on *P.O.V. (Point of View)*. Approximately ten minutes of the film were cut in the PBS version; they dealt with broader issues of the nuclear buildup, and included an estimate from a physicist who claimed that America's stockpile of hydrogen weapons had grown to 30,000 bombs. Coproducer Mark Mori told an interviewer that the sequence was cut for "fear of offending nuclear interests." Another film—*The Money Lenders*, a documentary about the World Bank and International Monetary Fund, directed by Robert Richter—displayed, according to a PBS officer, a "bias in favor of poor people who claim to be adversely affected."[14]

In 1993, the producers and directors of these films joined with progressive media activists to form the Coalition vs. PBS Censorship, which occupied the difficult position of supporting the ideals of public television against conservative attack, while simultaneously lambasting CPB and PBS leadership, and lobbying—occasionally with success—to have their own work broadcast. While right-wing critics focused on balance and objectivity questions, the Coalition vs. PBS Censorship appealed to the Carnegie Commission's vision of public television as "a forum for controversy and debate," and its role in helping "us to see America whole, in all its diversity."[15]

Since its members had substantial contacts within public broadcasting, the Coalition became a pesky gadfly, knowing where the system was weakest. Citing a City University of New York study of two years of PBS programming, the Coalition noted that for every hour of PBS programming focused on working people, there were nine hours about the wealthy and upper classes. Of the 27 hours of programs on working people, 19 were about British workers, and only about 20 minutes a month about U.S. workers on American public television. (An AFL-CIO officer had told Congress in 1991 that the best-known workers ever depicted on American public television were the household help on *Upstairs, Downstairs*.)

What's more, the Coalition pointed out that massive portions of the regular public television schedule were underwritten by companies with conflicts of interest at least as grand as those that had been cited to keep films like *Defending Our Lives* off the air. *Adam Smith's Money World* is financed by Metropolitan Life; *Nightly Business Report* by Digital Equipment Corporations and the investment groups A.G. Edwards, and the Franklin/Templeton Group; and so on. In some cases the conflicts were explicit, like a *Nova* episode, underwritten by Chevron, that advocated a less critical attitude toward companies responsible for chemical and environmental hazards. PBS also aired a documentary on a famous *New York Times* columnist called *James Reston: The Man Millions Read*, which had been partially funded and produced by the *Times* and directed by Susan Dryfoos, a member of the Sulzberger family, which owns a controlling interest in the New York Times Company. An angry 1994 letter from the Coalition to PBS said that the Carnegie Commission "made no mention of providing a voice for *The New York Times* or Prudential Securities, and it made no mention of guidelines that could be 'flexibly interpreted' to include those wealthy enough to buy a forum anywhere, while excluding those 'that may otherwise be unheard.' "[16]

These criticisms were deeply wounding; a top PBS official acknowledged to the Coalition that "it is not surprising that an outside observer may feel one decision is inconsistent with another."[17] Some films the Coalition lobbied for were broadcast, either locally or in those markets that chose to air them, but rarely did they make the PBS national schedule. In 1994, for example, KCET agreed to broadcast *Por La Vida*, a documentary about the harassment of Los Angeles' Latino street vendors, after Coalition protests. There was still plenty of material, however, for the 1995 Coalition-sponsored "Banned by PBS Film Festival," hosted by actor Alec Baldwin.

A CRAZY-QUILT SCHEDULE

The person who received most of the blame for PBS's apparent double standards was Jennifer Lawson, who, when hired in 1989 as PBS's executive vice president of programming, became the highest-ranking African American in American television. Her rejection of work such as *The Panama Deception* represented a logical outgrowth of her stated, innocent-sounding goal of systematizing PBS's programming to bring it closer to an actual network. This was a far more gargantuan task than it appeared from the outside. Many people mistakenly believe that the "S" in PBS stands for "System" (as it does in the CBS network). It actually stands for "Service," a more accurate description, since public broadcasting in America has never been systematic. Despite PBS's successes in building a national audience and reputation for some of its programming, the "system" remains stubbornly decentralized. The fact that a television station has a public broadcasting affiliation is a poor predictor of what it is likely to broadcast at any given moment. To an extent this fragmentation is a result of Nixon's attack on PBS, with its enforced localism, but politics, technological limitations, and the system's educational roots have always stood between public broadcasting and the coherence needed to merit the label "fourth network."

The PBS schedule's lack of uniformity is not accidental. The Carnegie Commission envisioned a broadcast entity that would not be "rigidly planned and scheduled," but would instead provide a medium for "the unpredictable, the sudden events and unique occasions where actions and reactions are not known in advance, where there is suspense, excitement and the actuality of life." Similarly, the Carnegie commissioners rejected the "stifling restrictions . . . imposed upon artistic and imaginative freedom in television by the necessity to shape aesthetic forms and program content and length to economic considerations." Instead, public television programming "should free the creative artist and technician to explore the full uses of the medium, allowing them to give priority to the aesthetic motive, to the moral and intellectual quest."[18]

Despite those lofty imperatives, most PBS programming comes in the same half- and full-hour chunks as commercial programs, and the national PBS schedule today tolerates few disruptions. The chief exception is Congressional hearings; the success of PBS's Watergate hearing broadcasts encouraged a reflexive pattern. One of the few displays of national PBS flexibility in the '80 and '90s were preemptions of daytime broadcasts for Congressional hearings: 1987 hearings on the Iran-contra scandal 1994 Whitewater hearings and, in early 1995, hearings over future federal funding for public broadcasting. (All of those hearings were also carried on either CNN or C-SPAN, although not always live.) According to PBS officials, those interruptions, no matter how infrequent, provoke great wrath from station managers who would prefer the normal daytime kiddie lineup.

Some local stations have been even more rigid; years can elapse between instances of New York's WNET suspending its programming for a special broadcast about New York City. Between 1990 and 1995, the only preemption occasion a WNET press representative could recall was the 1992 arrival of the Tall Ships in New York Harbor on the Fourth of July. "It would take a mayoral assassination for WNET to interrupt a *Great Performances* episode," says one producer, "and even then they'd probably wait until Pavarotti had stopped singing."[19] Although Los Angeles's KCET can respond to spontaneous events—such as riots—with its weeknightly news program *Life &Times*, the station estimates that it preempts its regular schedule approximately two times a year, one of which is the Christmas Eve concert at the Los Angeles County Music Center.[20] Smaller stations, with limited or no production facilities, have even more difficulty capturing "the unpredictable, sudden events and unique occasions."

But the fact that individual PBS stations cling guardedly to their own schedules does not imply that all stations are airing the same thing at the same time. Part of that incoherence is built in: instead of a network, PBS is more like a club offering different tiers of membership. Through mid-1995, approximately 60 of PBS's 341 stations enjoyed a "limited use discount" (LUD) allowing them to use the PBS logo and some of its programming provided that they broadcast no more than 60 percent of the PBS national programming service. (In July 1995, that number went down to a more restrictive 20 percent).[21]

One such LUD station is WCEU, established in 1988 on the campus of the University of Daytona in Florida. The station's surroundings do not immediately suggest public broadcasting's highbrow reputation; just a few hundred yards away is the famous Daytona Speedway, and on certain weeks of the year the insectlike whine of racing car engines is quite audible just outside the office door.

The central Florida resident who has read about the latest *Frontline* or *P.O.V.* controversy would be left in the dark, since those series have never aired here; the incurious viewer watching WCEU might well not realize that he or she was tuned in to a PBS station. There is no *Barney*, no *Sesame Street*, and no *NewsHour*. There are a few familiar signposts: a local Ford dealer underwrites the Miami-produced *Nightly Business Report*, and ITT Community Development ensures that *The McLaughlin Group* is shown; there are also delayed versions of *Washington Week in Review* and *Wall Street Week in Review*. WCEU's relative estrangement from the national PBS schedule is two-way; as of 1995, it had produced only one program that had been accepted by a national distribution service: *For the Love of Manatees*, a one-hour documentary that combines "the position of the conservationist with that of the boaters and fishermen to tell the story of man and manatee's fight to co-exist."[22] Another WCEU-produced film, *Ten Days in March*, a documentary about Daytona's annual Harley-Davidson festival, was not considered to be of sufficient national interest.

Stations like WCEU represent a part of public broadcasting rarely addressed in national debates over funding and programming, because they behave more or less the way the Nixon White House wanted them to behave: WCEU's public affairs programs are heavily skewed toward local issues, and it steers clear of tackling current national political controversies. Ironically, a Republican-led total shutdown of federal dollars for public broadcasting would hurt stations like WCEU more than the big-city stations whose programs vex conservatives. In 1994, WCEU received a $439,000 grant from the CPB—quite large for its viewership, and representing about one-third of its total budget.

A WCEU official says that losing that grant would be "definitely disastrous,"[23] and that the station's educational role would be jeopardized. Just over one-third of WCEU's programming hours are college courses for credit, intended to help viewers receive Associate of Arts degrees. The "telecourse" curriculum includes such classes as "Understanding Poetry," "Introduction to Business," "College Algebra," and "U.S. History: 1865 to Present." Enrolled students—approximately 500 per semester—pay a few hundred dollars, watch their class lecture one hour per week, read assigned texts, and attend one or two on-campus classes in order to earn their course credit. Also sprinkled through WCEU's daytime hours are craft shows—*Quilting for the '90s*, *Quilting from the Heartland*, *Strip Quilting with Kaye Wood*, *Best of the Joy of Painting*—shows about country and western music, and cooking programs, all of which a station employee cheerfully offers as "alternatives to soap operas."[24]

"LIBERAL CHEERLEADING"

The fractional PBS station is not limited to smaller towns like Daytona or even to university stations. Until the sale of New York's municipally owned WNYC in 1995, the New York metropolitan area featured six different PBS-affiliated stations. In the morning, the viewer of Long Island's WLIW can find the familiar *Sesame Street*, *Barney*, and *Reading Rainbow*, and in the evening can actually catch the *NewsHour* at 6 p.m., a half-hour earlier than much of the rest of the country. But there's no *Charlie Rose*, no *American Playhouse*, no *Frontline*, no *Wall Street Week in Review* or *Washington Week in Review*. For those programs, the Long Islander must tune into WNET, the region's largest PBS affiliate. None of the major commercial networks would tolerate an affiliate who shot these gaping holes in the national schedule (and in most cases, such deviance wouldn't be in the local station's interest).

Public television's do-it-yourself approach was the chief barrier between Lawson and a uniform schedule, and thus a conservative force: if you can't get all the stations to broadcast *Charlie Rose*, you certainly can't get them all to broadcast *The Panama Deception*. Today, an individual station's decision not to broadcast a particular program from the PBS menu is often financially motivated: the membership fee paid to PDBS s adjusted to reflect the amount of national programming used. In other instances where signals overlap, stations will divvy up parts of the schedule, in essence agreeing not to compete with each other's limited audience (or for certain special broadcasts, agreeing to air them at different times). WLIW's president says that the station's LUD status allows her station and the giant WNET "to work closely, try not to overlap, and offer different programming for the greater community."[25]

But historically there have been more political reasons for a regional station not to sign up the national programs. In early 1968, for example, a NET documentary about Cuban president Fidel Castro was rejected by several stations, many of whom shared the opinion of KLVX in Las Vegas, which labeled the film "sugar-coated communism."[26] Some censorious decisions also represented station survival skills: a *Black Journal* program featuring civil rights activist Julian Bond was not carried by WGTV in Athens, Georgia, because it contained criticism "about Governor Lester Maddox at a time when he was commenting negatively on the Ford Foundation and public broadcasting."[27] As discussed in chapter 6, many southern stations chose to show little or no programming dealing with volatile race issues.

The present-day equivalents of those station managers were Lawson's true audience, and it was their collective taste that helped shape the national program service Lawson managed. In the early 1990s, programs devoted to gay and lesbian issues became a political flashpoint for public broadcasting, much in the way that programs about racial issues were for NET and PBS in the '60s and early '70s. In July 1991, the PBS documentary series *P.O.V.* aired a film by the late acclaimed black filmmaker Marlon Riggs. Called *Tongues Untied*, the film explores the lives of black gay men, precisely the kind of "community that may otherwise be unheard" the Carnegie Commission hoped public television would spotlight. But of the 284 PBS stations that normally carry *P.O.V.*, nearly two-thirds refused to air it, including 18 of the nation's 50 largest markets.

Similarly, a month later, PBS canceled outright a scheduled 24-minute *P.O.V.* documentary called *Stop the Church*, a video account of a 1989 demonstration by the AIDS Coalition to Unleash Power (ACTUP) at New York's St. Patrick's Cathedral. Explaining the decision to zap the film from the airwaves, *P.O.V.* president David Davis said that in the wake of the previous month's problems with *Tongues Untied*, it would be "irresponsible, with so little notice, to expect stations to handle the level of press interest and viewer response *Stop the Church* is likely to generate."[28] This may have been the first time in television history that a program was canceled because viewers might have been too interested in it. To make sure that something this provocative didn't make it through the system again,

Davis promised that "PBS will take steps to beef up review efforts to ensure that similarly objectionable material is weeded out before it is scheduled."

The controversy and cancellations that greeted gay-themed programming represented public television's own conservatism coming back to haunt it. By relying so heavily on children's programming, public television made it harder to fulfill those parts of its mission that might not be suitable for children. (It is worth repeating that neither the Carnegie report nor the original Public Broadcasting Act dwell much on children's programming; its domination of the public television dial is largely due to the success of *Sesame Street*.) This contradiction left a wide hole for conservatives to exploit, not always honestly. In 1992, Senator Robert Dole gambled that public funding of television might become the politically explosive issue that public arts funding through the National Endowment for the Arts had been. Latching onto *In the Life*, a gay and lesbian variety show that had yet to be aired, Dole announced that PBS "apologists are hiding behind Big Bird, Mister Rogers, and *Masterpiece Theatre*, laying down their quality smokescreen while they shovel out funding for gay and lesbian shows, all those doom and gloom reports about what is wrong with America, and all the other liberal cheerleading we see on public television."[29] A few critics objected, noting that neither CPB nor PBS had given a cent to support *In the Life* (and fewer than two dozen stations aired the pilot show anyway).

Taken more broadly, however, Dole had a point. The public television system was too cowardly to properly support or even defend its more controversial programming, and therefore pinned its hope for public support on its blander, surefire brand names. When attacked, PBS was all too willing to jettison the offending program. In 1994, PBS's *American Playhouse* broadcast Armistead Maupin's *Tales of the City*, an ambitious, six-hour dramatic series set in San Francisco in the '70s and starring such well-known box-office draws as Olympia Dukakis and Chloe Webb. Few would pretend that *Tales* was much more than a racy soap opera, but the show was a smash success, attracting some 14 million viewers, marking *Tales* as PBS's most popular dramatic series ever.

As with *Steambath* in the early '70s, however, the fictional depiction of the free-wheeling California lifestyle was too much for religious antimedia activists, who declared themselves appalled by the series' "nudity, drug use, passionate homosexual kissing and bed scenes of homosexuals doing their thing, profanity, and adultery."[30] The Reverend Donald Wildmon and his Mississippi-based American Family Association denounced *Tales*, and produced a 12-minute highlight tape that Wildmon offered to show to Members of Congress. Intriguingly, Wildmon urged his contributors not just to attack *Tales*, but to ask their Members of Congress to close down PBS altogether: "PBS promotes the homosexual agenda. PBS attacks the family. PBS mocks traditional Judeo-Christian values."Wildmon also attacked the system at its most vulnerable level: state legislatures, which, in many states, control the licenses for public television stations. In response to the Wildmon campaign, Georgia's state legislature passed a resolution condemning Georgia Public Television for broadcasting the series—and removing nearly $20 million in state support for a new Georgia Public Television facility.[31]

In the end, these voices of protest echoed louder than the series' millions of viewers: PBS declined to fund a planned sequel. (In 1997, the cable channel Showtime and the BBC commissioned a sequel.) An angry Maupin declared: "I have no doubt whatsoever that this sudden decision was made in response to homophobic protests from the religious right," and called PBS's president "either a bigot or a coward."[32] Once again, public television had boxed itself into the worst of both worlds: it wanted to support popular, soap-opera programming under the guise that the material was culturally challenging, but as soon as the cultural challenge was accepted, PBS backed down.[33]

Even Bill Moyers, favorite target of the right, did not have absolute clout within the public television universe. In 1987, Moyers produced an 11-part series on the Constitution to celebrate its two hundredth anniversary. He found, however, that station managers were insufficiently patriotic to want to broadcast the program in prime time. David Othmer, station manager of WHYY in Philadelphia—a city that might be assumed to have an interest in the Constitution—announced: "We've grown beyond the point of doing things because they're good for people—castor-oil television—and saying, 'You've got to watch this.' We have got to make television that people want to watch."[34] In what would have been Moyers's prime-time slot, WHYY aired an episode of Jacques Cousteau instead.

THE RESISTIBLE RISE OF LAWRENCE WELK

Othmer was speaking for a good number of his fellow station managers: in the 1980s public television decided it should devote itself to what people wanted to watch. In some cases, this was done consistently with public television's educational role, such as The Civil War, Ken Burns's epic eleven-hour documentary, which won widespread critical acclaim and is the most widely viewed public television program of all time. In many other cases, however, "what people want to watch" meant "whatever we can get away with."

There are two ironies behind the political attacks on programs such as *The Africans*. One is that heaping abuse on a program prior to its airing almost always ensures that more, not fewer, people will watch it; the second is that the politicians were flailing away at the kind of programming that was attracting fewer and fewer people to the medium. The increasing depth and sophistication of public television's market research and the growing need for membership dollars to compensate for federal cutbacks combined to reproduce, on a smaller scale, the ratings chase of commercial television. Where networks monitor Nielsen ratings, public television stations monitor programs that bring in membership dollars; networks run blockbuster movies and extra-sensational news items during "sweeps" months, while public television stations bring out surefire winners during pledge drives.

During the '80s, many public TV stations moved away from auctions and toward programming gimmicks, interrupted by requests for money. Marathon sessions of *Monty Python's Flying Circus*, back-to-back Frank Sinatra concerts, best-of gardening shows, the ever-reliable *Three Tenors*; these were the kind of public television programs having the biggest public impact. (An interesting side effect of pledge-week programming is that local public affairs tended to get bumped, because research found it attracted few new members.[35]) As they adjusted themselves to the desires of viewers, some stations found that "viewer demand" meant more than they'd anticipated. The New Jersey Network (NJN) in Trenton, for example, leaned heavily on the cult hit *The Uncle Floyd Show* for a fund-raising session during 1986. "They had the *Uncle Floyd Show* people go on and say 'Keep *The Uncle Floyd Show* on the air for another year, become NJN Members today!', according to a NJN volunteer.[36] "This was scripted by the network and put on the Teleprompter for Uncle Floyd to read." The appeal garnered some $15,000 in donations to NJN, surpassing that brought in by national PBS warhorses such *Masterpiece Theatre* or *Mystery!* Within a few weeks, however, NJN canceled the program. After irate viewers protested and the Uncle Floyd Fan Club filed a suit with the FCC, NJN became the first public television station forced to return money to its contributors (NJN also refunded money to those who contributed to keep reruns of *Dark Shadows* on the air).[37]

At least *The Uncle Floyd Show*, during its NJN tenure, had the virtue of being unique to public television. The ratings-consciousness of the '80s led many stations to broadcast just about anything they could get cheaply, even if it was simply a commercial television retread. During the late '80s, reruns of *The Lawrence Welk Show* became the fastest-growing program in public television, despite the fact that the bubble-festooned band leader represented everything in commercial television that the Carnegie Commission had tried to move away from. (One Welk special is on the list of the most-watched public television programs of all time.) Much like the commercial cable station Nickelodeon, public television stations began using "nostalgia" as a justification for such programming, even though it was blatantly commercial. *Leave It to Beaver* is a quintessential commercial network sitcom, but call it an artifact of lost Baby Boomer innocence and it becomes acceptable public television fare. PBS programming "czar" Jennifer Lawson set herself the goal of "eliminating programs that might blur the [public medium's] identity."[38] But even she could not resist the power of what sold; in a 1992 interview she defended PBS's proliferation of *The Lawrence Welk Show* as "heartland culture."[39]

Broadcasting commercial offcasts was not the only way that public television began to abandon the quest for uniqueness in the '80s and early '90s. PBS likes to boast that its long-running *Washington Week in Review* is watched by more than two million households every week, an impressive number comparable to CBS's *Face the Nation* and significantly higher than CNN programs such as *Capital Gang* and *Sunday Late Edition*. What they don't say, however, is that in order to reach that audience they offer opinion and analysis that—rather than seeking to expand on the journalistic mainstream—merely reproduces it. Sampling the *Washington Week in Review* guests over six months, one magazine found that the news outlet most frequently represented on the program—almost twice as often as the second most represented—was *U.S. News & World Report*, about as perfect an example of journalism's center-right as can be imagined.[40] (The second- and third-most=represented outlets were *The Los Angeles Times* and *Newsweek*.) As *Forbes MediaCritic* commented: "Journalists from media outlets with a distinct ideological slant, such as *National Review*, *The American Spectator*, *The Nation*, *The Progressive*, and *In These Times* almost never appear."[41]

Oftentimes PBS's fare was so dismal that it left viewers begging for programming that was merely redundant. In a gesture that managed to combine elitism and mediocrity, some public television stations began carrying a weekly Ivy League football game on fall Saturday afternoons. Using Hollywood producers as consultants, Boston's WGBH developed a prime -ime quiz show called *Think Twice*, a *Jeopardy!*-style game show. CPB and PBS spent $1.5 million for 22 episodes of *Think Twice*, but the program was yanked from PBS's national schedule after four dismal weeks in 1994.[42] Like most critics, Howard Rosenberg of *The Los Angeles Times* savaged the show, calling it an example of PBS's "fading uniqueness." Inits attempts to mimic network pandering to viewers, public television often ended up with the worst of both worlds: popular programming that no one wanted to watch.

Arguably the most embarrassing and least defensible controversy in PBS's history was the 1992 broadcast of a documentary called *The Liberators: Fighting on Two Fronts in World War II*, as part of the *American Experience* series. The subject was fascinating: the film traced the history of two American battalions—the 761st Tank Battalion and the 183rd Combat Engineer Battalion—and their role in liberating the concentration camps at Dachau and Buchenwald in 1945. What made this portrait exceptionally moving was that these were all-black units, giving the film a sense of a mission to prove a since-lost cooperation between blacks and Jews. *The Liberators* made an explicit connection between the plight of these black soldiers —who lacked at home the rights they were ostensibly protecting in Europe—and the Nazi persecution of Jews. (The existence of these black liberators had, for years before the film was released, been a staple of Jesse Jackson speeches.)

In part because *The Liberators* carried this aura of civil rights liberalism—one critic said it was designed as "an important tool in the rebuilding of a black-Jewish alliance"—the first attacks on its accuracy were launched in small, right-wing papers.[43] Through journalistic inquiry, veterans emerged whose recollections differed sharply from the oral histories in the film. Official military records, too, told a conflicting tale: although the 761st had played a role in liberating a concentration camp, it was a far less-known one at Gunskirchen. Records also showed that on the day Buchenwald was liberated—April 11, 1945—the 761st Battalion was some 60 to 70 miles away. It would be a serious but forgivable error if the filmmakers—William Miles and Nina Rosenblum—had been misled by the shaky memories of events nearly a half-century old. But they had made their situation far worse by taking their subjects to Buchenwald and filming them giving a walking tour of places they had never been before.

When, in February 1993, complaints over the film's inaccuracies reached a crescendo, WNET pulled the film from PBS stations and requested that it not be shown again, pending an inquiry into its veracity. WNET-sponsored investigators said six months later they could "not substantiate" the presence of the two battalions at the camps the film claims they liberated. Filmmakers Miles and Rosenblum denounced PBS's "censorship" but, tellingly, were not able to back up their film's claims. As Congressional and other conservatives have repeatedly pointed out,[44] the book and videotape versions of *The Liberators* are still available in books and libraries throughout the country, a black eye on history for which PBS has never fully atoned.

10

EMBRACING THE ENEMY

"I have to explain again to my colleagues on the other side of the aisle:
CPB, the Corporation for Public Broadcasting, the public taxpayer–
financed component of public broadcasting, will be gone by 1998. . . .
It is history, guys. Open your eyes up. We are talking about
letting the private sector run it as it always should have."
—CONGRESSMAN PHILIP M. CRANE,
MARCH 15, 1995

As it did with so many aspects of American public life, the 1994 Congressional election shook the premises on which public broadcasting had operated for decades. Although it was little surprise that the budget-cutting Republican "virtuecrats" would want to slash or eliminate public broadcasting's federal funds—this had been a brewing Republican issue for some years—few would have predicted that the Republicans would choose public broadcasting as their first and most feverishly pursued target. House Speaker Newt Gingrich calculated that, in the new era of government frugality, public radio and television could easily be exposed as the government service that was most unnecessary. Gingrich's choice gave a free pass to every conservative who'd ever spoken out against PBS and NPR. No longer could the tendentious microscopes of right-wing critics such as David Horowitz and Reed Irvine be avoided; their arguments were front and center in every public discussion about public broadcasting.

One highly symbolic event took place in January 1995, just days after the Republicans had officially seized control of the legislative branch. The House Appropriations Committee, which in the past would have held perfunctory hearings or concentrated on PBS budget minutiae, instead opened its doors to right-wing critics who eviscerated the system. A panel of six PBS critics—including, bizarrely, a representative of the National Rifle Association—spent more than an hour ripping into the network's politics, programming, and very existence. A libertarian scholar named Sheldon Richman—not widely known as a commentator on media or public broadcasting—argued that it was intrinsically unconstitutional for the federal government to use taxpayer dollars to fund the expression of any opinion with which any taxpaying citizen might disagree. Because of the hearing's cattle-car structure, Richman left the testimony table before any representative had the opportunity to ask why his constitutional argument failed to cite any portion of the Constitution.

That, however, was far from the hearing's strangest moment. In the voluminous history of morally driven American censorship, from Anthony Comstock to the Reverend Donald Wildmon, there are repeated scenes in which the vehemence of the censor appears to betray his own prurient interest, and this hearing provided a classic of the genre. Seeking to refute the notion that PBS programming is a "sea of tranquillity" in a violent media environment, L. Brent Bozell III, chairman of the Media Research Center, read into the official record an excerpt from Marlon Riggs's *Tongues Untied*. "I would like to note that maybe C-SPAN will be able to carry this," said Bozell. "This will not make the evening news tonight because any network trying to cover this is going to have a very huge Federal problem." Bozell continued:

> Anoint me with cocoa oil and cum so I speak in tongues twisted so tight they untangle my mind. I walk the waterfront curbsides in my sister's high-heeled shoes, dreaming of him, his name still unknown to my tongue. While I wait for my prince to come, from every other man I demand pay for my kisses. . . . Wet my pillow, part your eyelids. Wet me with the next lie, the resounding refrain of grown men in love. We stop kissing tall, dark strangers, sucking mustaches, putting lips, tongues everywhere. We return to pictures, telephones, toys, recent lovers, private lives, now we think as we fuck.[1]

This was a very different Congress indeed.

One of the initial objections to the airing of *Tongues Untied* was that it risked exposing children to gay-themed material. After the right's campaign against the documentary, it aired on only 110 stations—less than a third of PBS affiliates—often very late at night. By contrast, Bozell's testimony, which took place in the afternoon, was carried live by several large PBS stations, where it was readily available to children who might have missed its first airing.

Although Republican attacks on public broadcasting were by now familiar, they had in the past generally been orchestrated by the executive branch, which worked most effectively behind the scenes by pressuring its CPB appointees; these Congressional foes, by contrast, chose to carry out their mission in front of cameras and microphones, using television and radio to attack public television and radio. Congressional relations with public broadcasters—which historically remained respectful even when critical—became contemptuous, mocking, venomous. Because the actual CPB appropriation was only 0.02 percent of the federal budget, and because opinion polls showed that few Americans wanted to cut off money for public broadcasting, they needed to attack it symbolically, seeking any argument that would demonize it. House Speaker Newt Gingrich fired the first salvo, using an anti-elitism tack reminiscent of Spiro Agnew: "Lyndon Johnson created this little sand box for the rich, and they give out the money to the particular producer they want, the particular show they favor. . . . It's a very tiny group of people, self-selected, basically. In the age of cable—where you have C-SPAN and C-SPAN2, and Arts and Entertainment, and CNN, and Headline News, and you're now going to have a History Channel and you have the American Movie Channel—there's a point here where you say to them, grow up. And if you got a good product, people will donate. If you don't have a good product, why are you forcing working taxpayers to subsidize your plaything?"[2]

Senator Larry Pressler—Republican of South Dakota and chairman of the Commerce Committee, through which public broadcasting's federal funds must pass—spun these themes into more arcane arguments. Borrowing a line that Bob Dole had used a couple of years earlier, the senator announced on *Nightline* that "Barney made a billion dollars last year,"[3] as if he envisioned a populist revolt against one of the most beloved characters in television history. Pressler claimed that PBS had a "liberal bias," even down to the unlikely example of Ken Burns's *Baseball* documentary: "I was watching this nice baseball series [on PBS] and, God, every night I'd have to listen to Mario Cuomo tell about his boyhood. It seems that all [PBS's] favorite people are from the left."[4]

The charge of liberal bias—always dubious—was particularly strange, given that the CPB was so thoroughly dominated by Republicans. Since 1992, the president of CPB had been Sheila Tate, a corporate lobbyist and former press secretary to Nancy Reagan. Tate was particularly adept at intermingling these roles; in 1994, for example, she appeared in a panel discussion on *The MacNeil/Lehrer NewsHour* about attacks on Hillary Rodham Clinton, stemming from the First Lady's role in health care legislation and in Whitewater. Somewhat predictably, the Republican Tate argued that attacks on the Democratic First Lady were not motivated by partisan politics but were entirely legitimate. "I think Hillary Clinton made a decision early in her husband's presidency to assume a policy making role," said Tate. "And I think that what she is experiencing right now is the consequences of that decision. She has to answer questions just like anyone else in a similar position."[5] At no point did the *NewsHour* mention that Tate was a paid lobbyist for industries fighting to defeat the Clinton health legislation; neither did it disclose that Tate sat on the board of the Corporation for Public Broadcasting, which helps fund the *NewsHour* itself.

Pressler's grandest overreach had genuine McCarthyite overtones. Seeking personal information that would embarrass PBS and NPR celebrities the way that high salaries and reputed liberal bias had effectively tarred Sander Vanocur and Robert MacNeil a generation before, Pressler produced an enormous questionnaire, demanding that anyone receiving CPB grants divulge a host of personal information, including employment history, political affiliations, salaries, and work efficiency. William F. Buckley, the syndicated columnist and PBS *Firing Line* host, who was sympathetic to removing CPB's federal subsidy, nonetheless found Pressler's methods offensive, damning the senator's questionnaire as "Orwellian persecution, pure and simple."[6] After five of Pressler's initial 168 questions were dropped, CPB answered the questions; a CPB official estimated that the task took 1,800 staff-hours and cost $92,000.[7]

Conservative critics, some of whom had been pushing these issues for decades, thought they could smell victory, and furiously began reissuing old articles and arguments. As always, Bill Moyers made an irresistible target for the right: the Heritage Foundation's Laurence Jarvik charged that Moyers was making "far more" than $1 million a year from public broadcasting, and he estimated "the total Moyers empire totaling approximately $100 million."[8] Jarvik also charged that a 1994 Moyers special on the health care crisis was part of a series of PBS documentaries designed to promote the Clinton health care plan (an argument that, if true, would speak less to PBS's bias than to its impotence, given that the Clinton plan never passed).

Inevitably, every protracted political battle will yield absurd elements. A preacher in North Carolina, author of *Barney: The Purple Messiah*, determined that Barney was a satanic cult figure: "Barney is much more than just a fun creature of children's imaginations. He is a politically correct teacher of everything on the liberal left's agenda, from New Age evolution to radical ecology." In late 1995, *The Washington Post* uncovered what appeared to be a sexual harassment case against 61-year-old CPB board member Martha Buchanan, a Democrat who had been appointed by George Bush. At a Dallas broadcasters' meeting in January 1992, according to CPB memos obtained by *The Post*, Buchanan bought a T-shirt for CPB vicepresident Fred DeMarco that bore the slogan "I Only Sleep with the Best." Later, she is said to have asked him: "What is an older woman to do to get men to date her? No one wants to date mature women. . . . What is an older woman supposed to do, only go to bed with her cat?"[9] After a more direct unsolicited—and rebuffed—kiss, Buchanan began lobbying for DeMarco to be fired. This caused a rift between board member Sheila Tate—who wanted the matter investigated and resolved—and Henry Cauthen, who wanted it to go away. Tate wrote an angry memo, saying: "For our board to be left open to political as well as legal liability for failing to address this issue in a direct and forthright manner is irresponsible, and, on my part, intolerable." The matter appeared to recede when, in March 1996, Buchanan's term expired and she resigned.

"TELL 'EM NEWT SENT YOU"

By making public broadcasting the Fort Sumter of their war against the federal budget, the Republicans tapped into several genuine flaws in the public broadcasting system (albeit in ways that were frequently dishonest and silly). It was more than coincidence that Pressler was one of the system's leading critics; because he represented South Dakota, he perceived that public broadcasting's programming carried a lingering East Coast flavor, a complaint left over from the '60s and '70s. The only public television stations that produce more than 100 hours a year picked up for nationwide distribution are New York's WNET, Boston's WGBH, and Washington, D.C.'s WETA; only a handful of others provide more than 10 hours a year, and 300 stations produce no programming at all for the national schedule.[10] It follows that these and other large stations eat up a significant chunk of the system's money; Pressler charged on the Senate floor that a single station, WNET, "gets at least 20 times as much federal money as my huge geographic state gets."[11]

Although such discrepancies may be defensible, they nonetheless raise hackles; it is undeniable that PBS's *NewsHour* and NPR news programming, for example, define the news largely as what happens in Washington, a definition that is often unresponsive to what South Dakotans want and perceive. Public broadcasting's guardians cleverly played off this attack by claiming that the elimination of federal funds would likely wipe out scores of rural radio and television stations. KCTF-TV in Waco, Texas, and WJWJ-TV in Beaufort, South Carolina, for example, rely on CPB grants for more than half of their operating revenue.[12] This argument effectively marshaled support in places like South Dakota and West Virginia, but did nothing to address the systemwide domination of a few large stations.

Similarly, Gingrich correctly argued that cable had made many—perhaps most—public television offerings redundant. And although "Barneygate" was ludicrously exploitative, the questions—raised for years by conservative critic Laurence Jarvik—of public broadcasting's alliances with private enterprises were perplexing, and the system had no comprehensive strategy for handling them.

The Republican would-be slashers, of course, lacked their own comprehensive strategy: they wanted the federal subsidy eliminated, and had little time to investigate its unintended consequences. As of 1995, 6.7 percent of Americans nationwide contributed to PBS, providing about $280 million, or one-seventh of the public television budget. Presumably, if federal funds were removed, that number could be enlarged by a factor of one or two percentage points. But examining the breakdown by regions, it becomes very clear where the highest financial support for PBS is (and therefore who would likely fill the void of federal funds): the Northeast seaboard from New Hampshire to northern Virginia, and a handful of big cities and retirement areas. The lowest areas of donations are throughout the south and most of the Midwest (except around cities, including Chicago, Denver, and Kansas City). Obviously, population density and income have great influence over who gives and does not give to public broadcasting; by betting that donors would make up for federal funds, the right-wing critics might well have created a system that enhanced the power of the urban eastern liberals they wanted to disempower.

Happily for the conservatives, rather than engaging these issues, the national officers of public broadcasting quite properly denounced the partisan invective, and then did what they had been doing for years: they caved in. CPB—publicly on notice to trim expenses and under Gingrich-led scrutiny for encouraging public television viewers to contact their representatives—decided that a wise way to silence right-wing critics would be to give them money. CPB issued a $100,000 consulting contract with GOP representative-turned-lobbyist Vin Weber, a close personal friend of Speaker Gingrich and a cofounder of Gingrich's Conservative Opportunity Society. The choice seemed particularly strange, since Weber, at the time a commentator for National Public Radio, had expressed the opinion—heretical within the public broadcasting sphere—that privatization was inevitable, even desirable. "My view is that Congress is going to zero out public broadcasting," Weber said, defending his contract. "The question is, do they want to take control of their destiny and guide the path towards becoming an unsubsidized entity or just fight to protect the subsidy?"[13]

The CPB is prohibited by law from lobbying Congress, and thus the Weber contract disturbed Bush-appointed board member Vic Gold, who said: "I've been in this town 35 years, and I know lobbying when I see it. This was lobbying."[14] His comment put CPB president Richard Carlson in the unenviable position of saying that although he had hired a lobbyist, he had not hired him to lobby. "We didn't hire him to be a lobbyist," Carlson told The Washington Times. "He was hired to give us strategic advice."[15] Weber's strategic duties appear to have consisted solely of a dinner with Gingrich. When Weber's contract was brought before the CPB board, it was rejected, with one board member, an Arkansas friend of Bill and Hillary Clinton, reported to be "viscerally opposed" to hiring Weber. (Shortly after losing this contract with public broadcasting, Weber went on to take a high position within the Dole presidential campaign, which promised voters it would eliminate federal money for public broadcasting.)

But the Weber lobbying contract was only the crassest way for public broadcasting to pacify angry Republicans. Like a weathervane in a thunderstorm, PBS and NPR had turned themselves to the prevailing wind and stuck hard. The early and mid-'90s saw an onslaught of conservative commentators, hosts, and consultants in public broadcasting; it were as if there was a quota system for anyone with right-wing credentials. Onetime Reagan administration fixture William Bennett got a two-part contract to adapt his neo-Victorian *The Book of Virtues* as a PBS cartoon. Former Reagan/Bush speechwriter Peggy Noonan got a three-part series, *Peggy Noonan on Values*, to discuss her views on "the family, faith, and culture" (CPB grant: $100,000). In April 1993, PBS began running a documentary series called *Reverse Angle*, hosted by the center-right journalists Fred Barnes and Morton Kondracke (CPB grant: $399,285). Another Bush speechwriter, Tony Snow, was signed up in 1993 to produce a documentary called *The New Militant Center* (CPB grant: $75,000), and in 1995 to moderate a two-hour special on welfare reform (CPB grant: $80,000). Add to these Snow's regular appearances as a commentator on NPR and he emerges as a one-man Republican public broadcasting industry. CPB publicists make sure to remind journalists that Snow is "Rush Limbaugh's favorite substitute host"; Snow was also chosen by Rupert Murdoch's Fox network to host its weekly Sunday morning news program, a job that did not appear to conflict with his public broadcasting work.

A continuing conservative presence on the new public television is Ben Wattenberg, host of PBS's weekly *ThinkTank*, and recipient of a $250,000 CPB grant for a documentary on the history of third parties in America and a $300,000 grant for something called *Values Matter Most*. When it is not serving as an outright platform for conservative views, *ThinkTank* serves to defang populist issues by placing a corporate frame over them. For example, *ThinkTank*'s response to the 1996 national debate over multinational downsizing and excessive executive salaries was to interview Michael Novak about his book *Business as a Calling*. Novak denounced greed in general, and was mildly critical of companies who choose to close or relocate American businesses that are marginally profitable, but the entire discussion was framed as a moral dilemma faced by a CEO. It is simply inconceivable that *ThinkTank* would carry on such a discussion with a factory worker, a union official, an advocate against foreign child labor, or anyone whose criticisms of the free market's limitations went beyond the theoretical.

Appearing before a Senate subcommittee in 1994, PBS president Ervin Duggan proudly proclaimed Wattenberg and Noonan as examples of PBS's "good faith effort" to respond to conservative critics.[16] (Duggan did not produce any examples of PBS programming meant to answer critics on the left.) These "good faith" efforts supplement the wealth of other conservative material on public television, including William Buckley's long-running *Firing Line* and *The McLaughlin Group*.

An outside observer might well have been baffled: Why was there so much shouting and name-calling between Republicans and the public broadcasting officials who were doling out millions to Republicans? As if to blur the lines altogether, in early March Gingrich himself recorded fund-raising pledges for Atlanta's WPBA and for PBS nationwide. "As we move to balance the federal budget, public television needs your help," Gingrich told viewers. "Tell 'em Newt sent you." In a variation on the challenge grant technique, Gingrich promised he'd donate $2,000 a year for the next five years and said: "If everyone writing letters to Congress about public TV matched me, they'd have the money they need."[17] If they had been less eager to use the speaker's image for political gain, PBS officials might have pointed out that according to their research figures, the average public TV viewer does not have $10,000 to spare.

The message this spot sent to public television viewers was decidedly scrambled; Gingrich's image was meant to scare viewers into thinking that public television was threatened, but he was also used as the generous voice of authority. Perhaps it worked, since the $44.2 million raised during PBS's nationwide March 1995 membership drive was 15 percent higher than the previous year's. The programs that brought in the most dollars during this extended pitch period—garnering "particularly enthusiastic viewer support" according to PBS's upbeat press release—were "The Eagles in the Spotlight," "John Tesh Live at Red Rocks with the Colorado Symphony Orchestra," and "Lawns and Gardens with Jerry Baker."[18] No liberal bias or cocoa-oiled homosexuals there; Gingrich and Pressler should have been pleased, or at least mollified.

In the end, perhaps they were. The shouting, the accusations of bias and elitism, the embarrassing press leaks, and the wailing pleas for private donations produced little more than a fairly simple—if painful—budget cut. The CPB budget for fiscal year 1996 was approved at $281 million—a cut of $37 million—for fiscal year 1997 at $266 million, and fiscal year 1998 is scheduled to be $250 million. These are substantial, unprecedented cutbacks, returning the system to its 1991 funding levels, despite higher costs and wider commitments. Discussions about the future were essentially put off until the future. Public broadcasters and Members of Congress alike now speak of keeping public radio and television on a federally funded "glide path" through at least fiscal year 2000. Beyond that, it is widely assumed that the federal government will no longer directly fund public television or radio, but nothing close to a single plan exists about how the federal funds should be replaced. In effect, the most vocal debate over public broadcasting in decades produced no more consensus about how public radio and television should be funded than it did over what exactly was wrong with the system.

SELF-SUFFICIENCY OR SELF-DESTRUCTION?

One reason it was difficult to engage the Republicans' more penetrating criticisms of public broadcasting is that they were widely perceived as a Trojan horse, hiding a fairly naked power grab by the nation's communications companies. Inspired by the deregulatory environment promoted by both the Clinton administration and Congressional Republicans, the American communications industry went through a delirious orgy of mergers and acquisitions during the mid-1990s. In a single month in 1995, three multibillion-dollar media mergers were announced: Westinghouse and CBS joined forces, creating a massive network of television and radio stations; Disney acquired Capital Cities/ABC, becoming the world's largest media company; and Time Warner announced that it would acquire Turner Broadcasting, an unprecedented marriage of cable giants. The January 1996 passage of a sweeping telecommunications "reform" bill removed—among other things—all limits on how many radio stations an individual company could own, effectively putting a "For Sale" sign on every small radio station in the country; a flurry of radio station sales ensued.

With television and radio giants freed for a massive shopping spree, the assets of public broadcasting suddenly but inexorably became prime real estate. Cable companies, which had heretofore been more or less gentlemanly competitors, immediately became predators, having off-the-record discussions with Congressional committee chairmen about "takeovers" of public broadcasting. Discovery Communications, the company whose Discovery Channel nature documentaries had made it one of public television's primary "competitors," was in early 1995 talking about helping PBS pick up the slack for programs such as *Nova*, should Congress cut off federal funding—provided, of course, that they would be shown on Discovery cable networks first. Jamie Kellner, the president of the WB network, suggested that public television stations could raise money for themselves by selling blocks of prime-time programming to up-and-coming commercial networks like his own.[19] "I wouldn't want to see it end," Kellner said. "But I think the way to prevent the ending is to be realistic about what you need, and what you need is a revenue stream."

Telephone companies, too, felt they could help themselves to a slice of the public broadcasting pie. Senator Pressler declared on a network talk show that he'd spoken to representatives of Bell Atlantic, who'd generously offered to take the CPB off the government's hands, as long as it got bidding dibs on PBS's affiliate stations.[20] "There are a lot of companies that would love to buy CPB," Pressler said. This takeover bid was bold to the point of silliness. Neither CPB, PBS, nor NPR holds the licenses of affiliated stations, and therefore no national organization was positioned to sell public broadcasting assets in any takeover, hostile or friendly.

Of course, a Republican Congress could theoretically remove that limit, too, if it desired. In February 1996, Texas Congressman Jack Fields introduced what he called a public broadcasting "self-sufficiency" act. Among its provisions was a section declaring that public broadcasters would be "allowed to surrender" their licenses to the FCC, and receive a portion of the proceeds.[21] Since Fields offered no evidence of a massive desire among public broadcasters to "surrender" their licenses, many in public broadcasting suspected that he was trying to secure a new area of the broadcast spectrum where Bell Atlantic could try to stake its claim. Henry Becton, president of Boston's WGBH, promptly dubbed Fields's proposal a "self-destruction act."

In New York City, the country's largest media market, the question of Republican-driven "license surrender" moved from the theoretical to the real. Rudolph Giuliani was elected in 1993 as New York's first Republican mayor in a quarter-century, invoking the legacy of Fiorello La Guardia, an earlier Republican whose earthy Italian roots made him a populist hero. One of the most lasting images of La Guardia's administration was from the city's 1946 newspaper strike, when every afternoon La Guardia used the city-owned radio studio of WNYC to read *Dick Tracy* and other comic strips to the city's children. Giuliani, saw a different political purpose in the municipally owned broadcast station (which now included a powerful AM station, an FM station, and a television station).

Shortly after he won the election, Giuliani suggested that WNYC would do well to hire a more conservative radio show host (this was at the height of the popularity of commercial right-wing radio bullies such as Rush Limbaugh and Bob Grant). Giuliani had in mind Curtis Sliwa, the macho, idiosyncratic founder of the vigilante police auxiliary group the Guardian Angels, who also hosted a commercial radio program (and, coincidentally, had supported Giuliani's campaign). Since the president of WNYC served at the pleasure of the mayor, Giuliani's suggestion was interpreted as more than a passing comment; before Giuliani had a chance to name a new WNYC president, Sliwa was hired for a daily three-hour call-in program. Many on the station's staff were appalled, pointing out that Sliwa had confessed to such questionable stunts as staging crimes that his Angels would then "solve." After less than a year on the air, Sliwa's WNYC contract was not renewed.

After this experiment in municipal propaganda fizzled, Giuliani—facing a multibillion-dollar budgetary shortfall—decided that the WNYC stations' civic value was not as high as what they could fetch on the market. In 1995, Giuliani announced that he was putting the stations up for sale. Immediately the radio listeners revolted: WNYC was New York's only NPR outlet, and the FM station one of its only remaining classical music stations. Caving in somewhat to the elite radio audience, Giuliani announced a deal whereby the radio stations would be sold (on bargain-basement terms: $20 million for two stations in the nation's largest market, payable over six years) to the nonprofit WNYC Foundation, which would continue to operate them unchanged.

The television station, however, did not get the same protection. WNYC-TV had always been overshadowed by the mammoth WNET, which freed it to concentrate on community programming. A 1993 study of five multistation public television markets (Atlanta, Boston, Los Angeles, New York, and Washington, D.C.) found that a huge amount—17.1 percent—of WNYC-TV's airtime was devoted to local programming; the comparable figure for WNET was 0.0 percent.[22] The prospective closing of WNYC thus had tremendous community ramifications, but while more than 14,000 viewers protested the sale, they were primarily from various immigrant communities who lacked the political clout to save the station.

Eventually, WNYC-TV was sold for $207 million to a partnership between Dow Jones (the parent company of *The Wall Street Journal*) and ITT (the multinational conglomerate that had also recently purchased the New York Knicks and Rangers franchises, Madison Square Garden, and the associated MSG cable channel) for a channel renamed WBIS+, featuring business news by day and sports at night. One planned feature of WBIS+ was for the New York Stock Exchange to build the station a glass-encased "skyroom" over its trading floor to guarantee coverage of its activities throughout the programming day; that fell through.[23] A coalition of ethnic broadcasters petitioned the FCC to block this sale on the grounds that no other station with WNYC-TV's reach was willing to pick up the 60 hours of programming they leased from WNYC. These programs—representing the rainbow of New York's Chinese, Haitian, Polish, Italian, and Indian communities and others—were often in their native languages, and because large sectors of the served community would tune in, garnered ratings as high as many programs on the national PBS schedule.

The FCC, under the Congressional deregulation spell, was torn between not wanting to interfere with media takeovers and recognizing that the public interest must at least be addressed, if not always served. In a March 1996 Congressional hearing, FCC chairman Reed Hundt was asked how the public interest was served by replacing this unique community programming with largely redundant sports and business broadcasting. "This is a very difficult question," said Hundt, before ducking behind a boilerplate assertion that "the actual use of the airwaves would be up to the owners and not up to us."[24] Two months later, the FCC approved the WNYC sale. The FCC held no hearings on the sale of this unique public asset; neither did the New York City Council. Gita Bajaj, who headed the coalition of community broadcasters tossed off the air, denounced the ruling and the sale, charging Giuliani with "ethnic cleansing of the airwaves."[25] New Yorkers, who were already served by two all-business cable channels and as many as four all-sports channels, began getting WBIS+ in the beginning of 1997. A similar downsizing began in Pittsburgh in the spring of 1996 when WQED, a venerated station that was nonetheless $12 million in debt, decided to sell its smaller sister station, WQEX.[26] Not surprisingly, the Pittsburgh area will continue to receive the larger station's national PBS menu, while losing WQEX's local and public interest programming.

THE MALLING OF PUBLIC BROADCASTING

One of the few figures in public broadcasting willing to publicly question the alliance of Republicans and cable companies against public broadcasting was Bill Moyers. Speaking via satellite to a group of television beat journalists in January 1995, Moyers said he found it "intriguing" that Gingrich had chosen C-SPAN as the site of his lengthiest attack on public broadcasting. "C-SPAN, which I admire greatly," said Moyers, "is the creature of the cable industry, run by friends of the new speaker of the House."[27] (He might have added that the man interviewing Gingrich, C-SPAN founder Brian Lamb, had been an aide to Clay Whitehead when the Nixon administration tried to shut down public broadcasting.) Moyers added: "I think there is a correlation between this ideology of publicly supported politicians in the service of a commercial industry that, frankly, would like to see public television not exist."

But if Moyers was one of the few to speak up, it was largely because the cable-communications takeover of public broadcasting was already in progress. The '90s flurry of corporate media acquisitions also involved the purchase of major pieces of public broadcasting. The role of commercial media companies in public broadcasting has evolved well beyond the seed money of the '70s or the underwriting of the '80s: they now use the public broadcasting system to promote their own media products. In many cases, private media companies have become some of the major profiteers of the nonprofit system. As of 1996, there was almost no major American media company that, in one manner or another, had not established a major beachhead in public broadcasting. While no comparative financial figures exist, the symbolic leader of PBS privatization is certainly General Electric, producer of nuclear plants and light bulbs; owner of the NBC network; and, as of 1994, America's sixth-largest military contractor. General Electric made a PBS star out of *National Review* columnist John McLaughlin, who went on to host programs on General Electric's CNBC channel. When NBC began airing *The McLaughlin Group* on some of its affiliates, the average viewer could easily confuse PBS and GE/NBC political programming.

Public radio seemed almost to celebrate the confusion; as it crescendos behind the identification of corporate sponsors, the theme song for *Marketplace*, public radio's nightly business affairs program, merges into GE's familiar advertising jingle: "We bring good things to life." By 1992, the mingling of General Electric-—owned media and public television became an on-screen merger when the two networks announced that they would team up to cover the Democratic and Republican conventions. PBS president Bruce Christensen boasted: "You get the news gathering of NBC plus the perspective Robin [MacNeil] and Jim [Lehrer] give to those activities. It's a wonderful match and marriage."[28] Part of the wonderful marriage was cross-promotion of convention coverage by both PBS and NBC, meaning that for the first time, the system designed to provide an alternative to network television provided free advertising for network television.

The primary service of growing information giant Bloomberg is business stories and data, but as it expanded in the '90s, it found a ready audience among news-starved public television stations for end-of-the-hour, five-minute summaries of local news, broadcast on split screens with market updates. Among the various services displayed in a 1996 ad campaign, Bloomberg ads promoted "business news," "information services," and—to no noticeable outcry—"public broadcasting." Bloomberg's New York facility also became the site where PBS host Charlie Rose produced his nightly program, after he abandoned a studio at New York's WNET. (Although the WNET studios were apparently too expensive for Rose, WNET did lease a studio to *The Montel Williams Show*.)

Indeed, Rose, who in the early '90s became one of the best-known faces of adult public television, was by the mid-'90s using public television only as a distributor. His program was produced in Bloomberg facilities, and underwritten by the USA Network, which was jointly owned by communications giant Viacom and the MCA unit of Seagram's. PBS's most popular news feature, *The NewsHour with Jim Lehrer*, is produced by the Washington-based MacNeil/Lehrer Productions, which, in late 1994, sold two-thirds of itself to Liberty Media Corp., a subsidiary of TCI, the country's largest cable provider. TCI, which also holds a stake in Time/Warner/Turner is controlled by media magnate John Malone, a man Al Gore once referred to as "the Darth Vader of telecommunications." In his very public 1995 defenses of PBS, Gore praised the *NewsHour* as one "of the crown jewels of public broadcasting"; Gore did not mention that Darth Vader now owned a majority of the jewel.[29]

Telecommunications companies, too, are major players in the world of public broadcasting. AT&T, which subsidized public broadcasting even before the federal government did, was for several years the primary underwriter of the *NewsHour* in the '80s and '90s. USWest hooked up with the CPB in 1995 in an on-line services project. In March 1995, PBS president Ervin Duggan proudly announced that PBS was teaming up with communications giant MCI to merge PBS programming with Internet, on-line, and CD-ROM media services. PBS was quick to point out that this was not the first joint venture with a commercial media company: Turner Home Video had paid a reported $20 million for the contract to distribute PBS videos, and Disney/Buena Vista had the right to air the children's program *Bill Nye the Science Guy* on commercial and public stations. NPR caught the Buena Vista bug as well: in 1997, it was reported that Buena Vista was negotiating with NPR to coproduce a television game show to be called *Wait, Wait . . . Don't Tell Me!*, which was proposed to be sold to commercial television.[30]

The growing presence of commercial media companies on the public broadcasting dial created a political and rhetorical problem during the 1995 crisis. Would-be supporters of public broadcasting's federal funds argued that PBS and NPR were losing their distinctiveness, while those who wanted to kill federal funding argued that private media companies would obviously pick up the slack. This dilemma forced public broadcasters back onto the system's oldest and most principled stance: its noncommercial status. America is generally uncomfortable with criticisms of its consumer culture, but public broadcasting's very existence is predicated on the idea—expressed by prestigious Americans—that television's commercial obsessions are antithetical to quality programming. The Carnegie Commission politely but firmly insisted that commercial television was inherently incapable of producing the broadcasting excellence the Commission envisioned. "A public affairs program or a news analysis sometimes will deteriorate as it passes through the various stages of production," wrote Dr. Hyman Goldin, the FCC veteran who served as the Commission's executive secretary, "because the producer is seeking desperately for some device to increase its rating. . . . In the end, commercial television remains true to its own purposes. It permits itself to be distracted as little as possible from its prime goal of maximizing audience."[31]

Nearly 30 years later, to defend public television against scathing Congressional attacks, PBS president Ervin Duggan echoed the same sentiment. In his grand southern rhetorical style, Duggan insisted that those calling for PBS's privatization sought actually to impose a scheme of commercialism, the very outlook of which would destroy public television. "If to privatize means to zero out—and no clear plan exists to replace that seed capital—then to privatize perforce means to commercialize. Take away public broadcasting seed funding, starve it financially of its own venture capital—however small—and you force it headlong, blinking into the alien world of ad agencies and ratings and cost per thousand and merchandising, rather than the world of teachers and historians and journalists and community volunteers."[32]

The threat that public broadcasting might be thrust into the hostile world of commercialism and merchandising is a stirring emotional rallying cry. It is also an effective fund-raising appeal. The two largest money drives in public radio's history were held by WNYC in New York; in both cases, the on-air funding pitch was based almost entirely on the possible elimination of local or federal funding (in February 1994 and February 1995, respectively).

But contrary to Duggan's supplications, there is virtually nothing about commercialism or merchandising that is alien to public broadcasting. In fact, the forces of commercialism have been heavily cultivated during Duggan's tenure and can legitimately be said to have taken over. Today, a visit to the American commercial mecca—the shopping mall—may well involve an encounter with PBS. Visitors, for example, to the Stamford Town Center in Stamford, Connecticut, can find a store that acts as a direct outpost for New York's WNET. Between the Rodier Paris store and Casual Corner, and two stores down from a Warner Brothers merchandise outlet, is a store called Learningsmith. It carries both the PBS and WNET logos, and describes itself as a "general store for the mind."

Inside is a smorgasbord of self-advertised brainy materials, from placemats that depict the periodic table to books by Stephen Hawking. There is a unique amount of public broadcasting tie-in material, including books by Carl Sagan and Bill Moyers, a video called *My Heart, Your Heart* hosted by Jim Lehrer, and any imaginable product with a *Sesame Street* character. Playing on three huge Mitsubishi screens in the store's rear during one visit was a PBS video called "Peter, Paul and Mommy," featuring the aging folk trio singing the refrain, "Don't ever take away our freedom." But the store does not discriminate against non-PBS merchandise: here one may also purchase videos of Nickelodeon's kid hero *Doug*,

CNN: The Game, and a video on tornadoes that is often promoted on the Weather Channel. In keeping with good marketplace thinking, PBS is just one more product on the shelf.

Learningsmith was founded in Boston in 1991. (Los Angeles's KCET created a similar shopping venue called the Knowledge Store.) WGBH, the Boston PBS station that is one of the system's top programming producers, helped found the store; Eric McNulty, Learningsmith's director of marketing, described WGBH as "an equity investor" in the enterprise.[33] As of 1995, there were 27 stores nationwide, of which 16 had direct public broadcasting affiliations. Besides WNET's stores (in Stamford and on Long Island), there are stores for WGBH, WETA (D.C.), and WCNY (Syracuse). McNulty explains that Learningsmith stopped having affiliations with individual stations because it was "cumbersome to have each local station having authority." He declined to divulge the percentage of gross sales that each station receives, calling it "confidential." (Commercialization apparently helps take the public out of public broadcasting.) McNulty did allow, however, that the company's nationwide gross sales in 1994 were $40 million.

Shortly after the debut of its hit kids' show *Puzzle Place*, PBS announced an unusual marketing agreement with Toys R Us, *Family Circle,* and *Child* magazine. As of August 1995, according to *Inside Media*, all 619 Toys R Us outlets have permanent floor space dedicated to *Puzzle Place*. The toy chain's founder, Charles Lazarus, "is personally involved in this, which shows how committed they are to this promotion and the *Puzzle Place* line."[34] Among others, toy giant Fisher Price has been awarded a licensing contract for *Puzzle Place* tie-ins.

Individual PBS stations, too, have been scrambling to merge their mission with shopping and marketing. Some 10,000 members at KVIE in Sacramento have gold membership cards that give them discounts at local stores. The station not only shows commercials on the air, it produces them in house for local businesses. Los Angeles's KCET, one of the system's largest stations, gets an astonishing 14 percent of its revenue—$6.7 million for fiscal year 1995—from product sales.[35] No longer content with doling out underwriting credits, in Grand Rapids, Michigan, station WGVU has pioneered "Business Television." Local businesses contract to use the station's studio and satellite uplink in return for a donation. According to assistant general manager Chuck Furman, the businesses use their time to broadcast meetings, which can then be viewed by those at remote sites. "It's kind of the Cadillac of teleconferencing," said Furman. Business Television has been around for about five years, he said, and as of 1995 brought in approximately $200,000 a year, about 4 percent of the station's annual budget. Although Furman declined to name the businesses who use these facilities, he said one of the station's regular clients is a Fortune 500 office furniture store. The content of these private, encrypted broadcasts is usually sales and marketing, but Furman said Business Television can also be effective for crisis management. "One client used it to help resolve a strike situation," he boasted.[36] Asked if community or nonprofit groups were ever given an opportunity to use the studios for their own purposes, Furman said he'd never considered it. On the national level, PBS Enterprises also provides teleconferencing and satellite data services for private clients such as Bell & Howell and *Washington Post–Newsweek*.

Maybe the most dramatic sign of public broadcasting's commercial power is that commercial broadcasters are increasingly wary of the new competition. Thirty years earlier, the commercial networks were vital supporters of public broadcasting; CBS put up $1 million to help the fledgling network's early years. But today they can smell a competitor. After reading two potential funding plans published by public broadcasting, the National Association of Broadcasters (NAB) could barely mask its scorn. "Revenue from commercial broadcasters appears to be a major element in their plans to achieve 'self sufficiency,'" said an NAB press release. "One thing you have to give these people is when they dream, they dream big."

Part of the big dream is to hitch public broadcasting's wagon to the communications supernovas. Whatever his stated qualms about the alien world of "ad agencies and ratings," in a teleconference with reporters, Duggan boasted that PBS was "the most powerful, most recognized non-profit brand name" in the country. (He was not exaggerating: in June 1995, *Advertising Age* included PBS in its annual survey of America's top 100 marketing schemes—along with the Republican Contract with America.)[37] Seeking to capitalize on that power, Duggan pledged that although MCI's initial investment in this new media venture was only $15 million for the first five years, the $12 billion communications giant had its "eye on the future."[38] That future was left vague but optimistic: "Children might interact on-line with their favorite educational characters, for example, and adults might view on demand the latest segments of signature PBS programs, providing, in turn, their own real-time views on relevant issues."

Just as with the very tool of television in the '60s and satellite equipment in the '70s, the American public was being promised that technology itself would break down barriers and finally create the universally accessible educational utopia that initially inspired public broadcasting. The difference in the '90s Internet version, however, was that few bothered even to pretend that it should be done as a separate noncommercial project. Public broadcasters and legislators accepted the monumental technical advantages held by communications companies as a given, as a force to ally with rather than a force to overcome. While that approach may have short-term pragmatic benefits, it is supremely naive to believe that these alliances will themselves move the programming in a direction that fulfills public broadcasting's mission. "It's all about technology, and nothing about content, which is the curse of Washington," says former PBS president Lawrence Grossman. "The last thing anybody thinks of, the thing that everybody least likes to support is the stuff that goes through it."[39]

All historical evidence indicates that when commercial companies are involved with producing and distributing public broadcasting programs, they will reproduce the constrictions found in commercial broadcasting. There is already enough pressure on the system to choose programming that will attract member dollars. The more PBS and NPR rely on commercial tie-ins and merchandising, the more their programming will be determined by what is merchandisable. The best example is the fate of *This Old House*, the well-known public broadcasting series on carpentry and home renovation. In March 1989, the program's original host, Bob Vila, was fired after a dispute with his producer over Vila's endorsement of commercial products. By 1996, however, the series itself was a commercial product. WGBH and Time Inc. had created *This Old House* magazine, an every-other-month publication with some 300,000 readers. That was a first step toward marketing the program itself on commercial television stations, which WGBH and Time Warner began doing in the fall of 1996. An executive at Telepictures, a division of Warner Bros., explained the attraction of *This Old House*: "It's a 17-year brand that appeals to the most valuable, sought-after demographic—someone who owns his own home, has children and disposable income. That's the promised land for advertisers."[40]

"LISTEN TO CORPORATIONS"

There is good reason to question whether that promised land will ever be reached. Suffering from the intoxication of privatization, public broadcasting's entrepreneurial gurus seem to have ignored some elementary aspects of commercial ventures—beginning with the fact that they often fail. At San Francisco's KQED, the station converted its program guide into *San Francisco Focus*, a slick lifestyle magazine whose advertising helped fund the station. (The project somewhat recalls Britain's BBC magazine series on a smaller scale.) That worked well, until the magazine suffered from the plagues that hit most American print media in the mid-'90s: flat circulation and skyrocketing paper and postage costs. A March 1996 *San Francisco Examiner* story reported that the magazine was "six months behind in paying vendors and freelance contributors," and with declining ad sales, was about to turn into a money-loser for the already financially strapped station.[41] A few weeks later, KQED was forced to sell the magazine and its much-hyped publishing and new media divisions at prices far lower than what they were worth.[44] Similarly, the timing of the major league baseball strike severely deflated the impact of Ken Burns's September 1994 PBS film *Baseball: The American Epic*; a local station business plan relying on sales of *Baseball* T-shirts, hats, mugs, trading cards, duffle bags, umbrellas, keychains, or "9-player pin sets" was likely to find itself stained with red ink.[43]

More important, however, is the question of how such enterprises distort the mission of public broadcasting. That the programming, supposed to represent the soul of public broadcasting, is inherently unmerchandisable is the very reason the system was devised in the first place. On some level, the public television audience appears to grasp that conundrum; an October 1995 CPB poll found that 62 percent of public TV members agreed with the statement: "If public broadcasting needs bigger audiences to attract sponsors, public broadcasting programs will become more like commercial programs." It is not hard to imagine what the future will look like if marketing and merchandising become the norm. *Frontline*, as television's only weekly documentary series, is already an endangered species; if its federal funds dry up, they are not likely to be replaced by revenues from the sale of *Frontline* T-shirts.

An ideal example of the limits of the malling/merchandising approach is the public television series *Rights & Wrongs*, hosted by Charlayne Hunter-Gault. Every week the program explores human rights violations and issues around the globe; some episodes are the only American television broadcasts of human-rights related documentaries that run on the BBC or ITN. In its fourth season debut (spring 1996), for example, *Rights & Wrongs* sent a producer and a Chinese American newspaper reporter to investigate the "snakeheads," the Chinese slave brokers who sell teams of slaves abroad. The damning footage they obtained included officials of the Chinese government who offered to hook the journalists (who posed as U.S. employers) up with a team of slaves.

In theory, there is nothing to prevent *Rights & Wrongs* from publishing a magazine, and given the interest in human rights, such a publication might well establish a medium-sized readership. But major advertisers are as likely to stay away from such a project as they are from the program itself. Noting the China program, producer Danny Schecter said: "We went to 40 different corporations to try to get funding for the program. But everybody's trying to open up the Chinese market, and doesn't want to make that government mad."[44] Because CPB and PBS have also declined to support *Rights & Wrongs*—PBS programming vicepresident Jennifer Lawson infamously declared that human rights is an "insufficient organizing principle" for a series—the program has been able to be broadcast on public television stations only through a chain of hand-to-mouth foundation grants.

Tying public television programs to stores and merchandising will also likely accelerate the extinction of local programming. Local production is notoriously expensive, because it is usually the only programming that requires the use of cameras, studios, and production facilities. The average public television station spends about 65 to 75 percent of its total program costs on local programming, even though it accounts for only about 7 percent of broadcast hours.[45] These costs are a principal reason why, by the mid-1990s, most public television stations no longer bothered to produce a nightly news program. WNET in New York abandoned its quirky and highly regarded *Eleventh Hour* in 1990; a year later its replacements—the much cheaper call-in programs *Thirteen Live* and *Live Wire*—were also canceled. A similar axe fell in Boston in May 1991 when WGBH canceled its *Ten O'Clock News*.

Sponsors—even local businesses—prefer to underwrite better-known national programs, because they are more predictable and usually have larger audiences. Furthermore, as author Pat Aufderheide has noted, "ongoing coverage of local events can't be resold on the national market," thereby giving individual stations a further disincentive.[46] In those cases where businesses are willing to sponsor local programming, they have the same depoliticizing effect that they do on the national level. Robert Lipsyte, the *New York Times* columnist who hosted *The Eleventh Hour*, WNET's canceled nightly news program, says: "You end up asking yourself 'What kind of audience does Tri-State Honda want?' . . . After a while you started to realize that shows about Karen Finley and Donald Trump tended to do better than the school crisis."[47]

This risk ripples through the national system. Many critics and public broadcasters themselves have noted that not all relevant "local" programming must be locally produced; the community in a given city "may be better served by a program, say, about child sexual abuse produced in Chicago or one on illiteracy produced in Pittsburgh than by locally produced programs that attempt to address similar themes with a pittance of production or promotion resources behind them."[48] But moving toward a system of sponsored programming virtually guarantees that public television will be as unlikely as its commercial counterparts to tackle unglamorous or unpleasant issues, because private corporations will be controlling the images and agenda. "We used to be very producer-driven until six months ago," said a WNET official in 1991. "But to be more market-driven we have realized we need to listen to corporations and come up with projects that suit their needs."[49]

Obviously one primary corporate need is to deflect attention from any issues that call into question corporations' own shortcomings. As discussed in chapters

6 and 7, funding agreements between public broadcasting and private firms generate gaping conflicts of interest for public broadcasting's current affairs programs. *The NewsHour* and others generally handle these conflicts by avoiding critical reporting on funders. As public broadcasting continues to make vital partnerships with media conglomerates such as Disney/Capital Cities/ABC and Time Warner/Turner, all historical evidence predicts that they will be frozen out from any critical reporting on these corporations as they become leading engines of the U.S. economy and major political forces in their own right. Because they already control most commercial media outlets, these merged behemoths can use "alliances" with public broadcasting to silence some of the few mass media outlets positioned to conduct critical investigations of them. An equally likely scenario is that, just as NPR programs already plug GE and WNET's annual report was used to promote Nabisco cookies, the assets of public broadcasting will be used to promote the "synergies" of their media partners.

The media companies will join the ranks of those businesses once criticized on public airwaves who now pay for silence. It is impossible to imagine PBS airing an updated equivalent of *Banks and the Poor*, with its ferocious criticisms of the Rockefeller family and Chase Manhattan Bank. (Actually, it's even impossible to imagine PBS rerunning the original inflammatory documentary.) But this is not because the issues of redlining or the lack of affordable housing in New York or Washington have disappeared. The Rockefeller family has become a leading star in public television's firmament (Sharon Percy Rockefeller served for years on the CPB board and now chairs Washington's WETA), while Chase Manhattan underwrites New York's broadcast of *Wall Street Week* and is a vital corporate contributor to its hometown station, WNET.

DOWNSIZE FITS ALL

It is a measure of how deeply privatization has colonized American political thought since the days of the Great Society that these concerns over the mission and integrity of public broadcasting's programming could hardly be heard during the great debate of 1995. Rather than recognizing such commercial traps, most in Washington have encouraged public broadcasters to go further in the malling direction; this includes the very leaders of public broadcasting, who didn't need Big Bird to help them read the writing on the wall. In May 1995, public broadcasters presented to Congress two possible plans to wean themselves off the public payroll. The Corporation for Public Broadcasting plan turned not to some '90s version of the Carnegie Commission but to Wall Street and Lehman

Brothers to evaluate alternative funding sources. Although it noted in a single sentence that advertising "in the traditional sense . . . violates one of the core principles" of public broadcasting, the $150,000 Lehman study saw the risk posed by advertising primarily in financial terms.[50]

And with good reason: station experimentation with commercial messages has already reached the point where it creates viewer backlash. During pledge drives at Sacramento's KVIE, the studio set and on-screen graphics have been redesigned to the point that they are "unabashedly emulating the Home Shopping Network,"[51] which turns at least as many viewers away as it might attract. During an "open phones" segment on a popular WNYC-AM talk show, a caller berated host Brian Lehrer, inquiring why the station promoted an Internet provider that was notorious for bad service. Audience members like these are bound to cease donating to a public broadcasting service that relies on advertising or other commercial schemes. CPB research indicates that about seven out of ten public TV and radio audience members see "enhanced" ads as an appropriate fund-raising gimmick;[52] still, public broadcasters are loathe to alienate 30 percent of their audience.

Though the Lehman study—entitled *Common Sense for the Future*—found that for these and other reasons, advertising would be a "net money loser," the plan did recommend a "carefully controlled voluntary experiment for stations interested in pursuing" advertising. A second plan from a coalition of broadcasters went beyond the experimental stage: it advocated opportunities for what Jeff Clarke, general manager of Houston's KUHT, called "super-enhanced underwriting."[53] The precise recipe has yet to be decided, but it seems clear that public broadcasting's future will have heavier dollops of advertising, provoking the flight of a good portion of listeners and viewers, who may or may not be replaced by a more commercially tolerant audience.

Also at risk are the privileges public broadcasting has enjoyed over the years, such as tax-deductible donations and discounted transmission rates. Conservative critics have already asked the legitimate question of why private media companies should have to compete for programming with "public" stations and networks that are engaged in just as many commercial activities yet receive the often lucrative privileges of the nonprofit world. The number crunchers who produced the Lehman report recognized the tax dilemma, but they were not prepared to abandon commercial revenues in order to save a deduction.

Perhaps the saddest agreement between Congressional critics and public broadcasters was a reduction in vision. Prodded by efficiency studies and pestered by legislators, public broadcasting looked at itself and reached the quintessential '90s corporate conclusion: it decided it had to downsize. Beginning with a Boston Consulting Group study in 1991, many national public broadcasters seized on "station overlap" as one of the system's villainous inefficiencies. Although estimates vary, approximately 40 percent of public television stations have signals that overlap with another public television station. In the New York City area, for example, many viewers, even without cable, could, through 1996, receive up to six public television stations: WNET; the municipally owned WNYC; Long Island's WLIW; WNJN (the New Jersey Network); Stamford, Connecticut's WEDW; and Brooklyn's educational station WNYE. In many cases, the schedules of these stations vary quite little, often only in the particular time slots when they show the PBS national schedule.

This type of inefficiency aggravates systems analysts and private sector bean counters. In one of his floor attacks, Pressler used station overlap as key evidence that "public broadcasting is mired in waste and duplication." For impatient Republicans, the solution to overlap was to sell: the self-sufficiency legislation introduced into the House in 1996 specifically allowed for "the sale of an overlapping station as a commercial station," with proceeds going to local educational operations of the station that survived.

Public broadcasters indicated that they agreed: throughout 1995, contingency plans were drawn up in Florida, Connecticut, and other places to combine stations. Although it did not specify the number of stations it would eliminate, the self-sufficiency proposal drawn up in May 1995 by a coalition of public radio and television providers detailed how existing licenses could be transferred to the FCC, and eventually sold, with a portion of the sale to fund a Public Broadcasting Trust Fund (discussed at greater length in chapter 11). And the CPB's own plan called for it to fund only one station in each market, providing that it share some programs and services with lesser stations.

When under fire from Congressional committees, CPB officials pleaded that budget cuts would force the closure of smaller stations. But by the end of 1995, those same officials were offering "common sense" plans that would accomplish the very same shutdowns.

11

CAN IT BE SAVED?

Although it failed to reach its ultimate goals, the 1995 Republican attack on public broadcasting forced would-be supporters to return to first principles. Is there, in the information maelstrom of America's late twentieth century, a genuine need for a public/educational system of broadcasting? If so, why should it be supported by taxpayers in an epoch when far more vital programs—starting with welfare assistance—are being slashed and eliminated?

For all public broadcasting's shortcomings and backsliding, the first question can still be answered with an emphatic yes. There are critical television theorists who might argue that saving and reforming American public television is a fruitless pursuit. Some have maintained, for example, that television is necessarily a hegemonic instrument, serving primarily to reinforce social norms and dominant values. Television, George Gerbner has argued, "is an agency of the established order and as such serves primarily to extend and maintain rather than alter, threaten or weaken conventional conceptions, beliefs, and behaviors . . . its chief cultural function is to spread and stabilize social patterns."[1] In this view, public television's drift toward the mainstream could therefore be seen as an inevitable adjustment according to type. Others, such as Douglas Kellner, reach a similar conclusion, but situate its solidification in the 1980s, a period of such overwhelming conservative hegemony that broadcasters were swept up in reinforcing the interests of capitalism and the state: "They . . . promote the conservative interests that own and control them, thus precipitating a massive crisis of democracy and journalism in the United States."[2] Even the quasi-independent system of public broadcasting could not escape this hegemonic tidal wave. Still others, notably Neil Postman, argue that television's very mode of presentation undercuts the ability to think and analyze rationally, and therefore its presence necessarily erodes the values of democracy and education.[3]

While these arguments all have their merits, their conclusions are simply false. This book has provided dozens of historical examples of educational and public television programming that has provocatively challenged status quo thinking. That such programming has consistently produced calls for censorship or "balance" only underscores its importance to genuine democratic debate. As communications scholar Robert McChesney argues: "On occasion stories slip through and programs get produced [on public broadcasting] that would never clear a commercial hurdle. This is especially true on public radio and with some of the more progressive community stations that would suffer the most without any federal grant money. And this is precisely why it is so important for those who believe in journalism, free expression, and democracy to fight on behalf of public broadcasting."[4]

If recent history is a proper guide, public broadcasting's stated commitments to free expression and diversity will not soon be overtaken by any of the dazzling technologies that have flourished over the last decade. The 1990s have been crammed with utopian predictions for multimedia information sources, promises that the power of telephone lines, computers, satellites, and cable television can be used synergistically to produce hundreds of thousands of information and entertainment sources. Early glimpses of this future—particularly the rapid maturation of the Worldwide Web—show promise of imminent fulfillment.

For all the media developments that chipped away at public broadcasting's mandate, however, it is striking that none have the structure or desire to take on the entire project. The power—potential and real—of the Internet is irrefutable, but its devotees often gloss over its birth in an intrinsically undemocratic swamp. In a familiar overemphasis on novelty and technology—one that has periodically plagued public television's advocates as well—those who tout the Internet as an ideal tool of communication and education fail to recognize that machines will not instruct those who can't or won't get to them. It is easy for sophisticates creating online magazines and fretting over modem speeds to forget that in many poor American neighborhoods, up to 25 percent of residents do not have telephone service, to say nothing of personal computers and the training to use them. Public service advocates have labored hard to ensure public school and library access to the Web and its future incarnations, but even if realized, this method will not deliver—especially for adults—an access comparable to that available through television or radio.

Moreover, the recent flood of media mergers and the encroachment of advertising and corporate support suggest that the Internet—a medium once fiercely anticommercial—will evolve into the twenty-first century's most sophisticated and ubiquitous commercial and promotional engine. The very phrase "content provider"—used in new media circles to denote those who, as opposed to technology workers, traffic in information and culture—hints that the machine's ability to gain access to information has, thus far, outstripped demand for most

of the information available through it. Given the present conglomerate structure of American telecommunications, it seems probable that this vacuum will
be filled by media monoliths who see it as the best medium through which to
promote their software, sitcoms, recording artists, and other commercial products and services. When the Internet becomes a truly mass medium, a few
geniuses will find ways to effectively tap its unique powers; a tremendous,
unprecedented, and somewhat unruly amount of information and interaction
will be available to a relatively small number who seek them out; and the vast
majority of its content will be updated versions of very familiar cultural forms
dominated by a few huge multinational entertainment firms. It will act, in other
words, like a much-expanded version of the current cable television box.[5]

To date, the cable television box, despite its tremendous expansion and varied
services, has shown an uneven appetite for a truly public television. As argued
throughout this book, numerous cable channels have encroached on the once-
exclusive territory of public television, perhaps none as importantly as C-SPAN.
In several vital respects, C-SPAN outperforms public television, especially in fulfilling the Carnegie-mandated tasks of broadcasting "the great debates in public
life, the crucial hearings." PBS advocates like to point out that many of C-SPAN's
techniques—from gavel-to-gavel convention coverage to the live transmission of
newspaper or magazine editorial board meetings—were first done on public
television, which is as much an admission of creeping redundancy as it is a boast.[6]
Unlike PBS, C-SPAN is relatively flexible, capable of reacting within a programming day to a breaking news story (so long as that news story can be adequately
related through a speech). C-SPAN is participatory, at least to the mild extent
that many hours a week are devoted to airing and answering viewer calls, faxes,
and electronic mail.

C-SPAN practices an almost obsessive evenhandedness, bringing its cameras
into auditoriums whether they are filled with radical black nationalists or members of the Christian Coalition; in so doing, it explodes—however infrequently—
the common mass media fiction that all important political discourse takes place
within the confines of the two major parties. And while *The Charlie Rose Show*
hosts a fair share of book authors, public television officials have explicitly said
that they have no room for a program devoted exclusively to books,[7] even though
such book chat programs are a staple of European publicly funded television. By
contrast, C-SPAN's *Booknotes*, though limited to public policy and history books,
represents one of national television's few regular nods to the world of letters,
adult scholarship, and debate.

At the same time, C-SPAN—even in the expanded forms of C-SPAN2,
C-SPAN3, and so on—has limitations that make it an inadequate substitute for a

truly public television. Most obviously, C-SPAN is available only to cable sub-scribers and satellite owners, media that exclude tens of millions of Americans, and also (under present technology) make local tailoring of schedules impossi-ble.[8] It is not fully available even to all cable subscribers—between 1993 and early 1997, more than five million Americans lost access to C-SPAN because their cable systems dropped or reduced service.[9] C-SPAN carries no cultural, science, or documentary programming; it doesn't even have a true staff of news reporters (although on some occasions—notably during the 1996 party conven-tions—C-SPAN rebroadcasts reports from the BBC or ITN, rather like some PBS and NPR programs). While C-SPAN has made some admirable efforts to take its cameras on the road, the predominance of programming from Washing-ton, D.C., is almost stifling.

C-SPAN—today the most commercial-free nationally available cable chan-nel—benefits from essentially hidden subsidies. Its annual budget—approxi-mately $30 million—is admirably low, in part because C-SPAN does not, like some other cable stations, pay carriage fees to cable operators. Indeed, it is paid for by cable operators themselves; as noted in the previous chapter, PBS host Bill Moyers underscored this point at the height of the Gingrich attack on public broadcasting: "C-SPAN, which I admire greatly," said Moyers, "is the creature of the cable industry, run by friends of the new speaker of the House."[10] Moyers added: "I think there is a correlation between this ideology of publicly supported politicians in the service of a commercial industry that, frankly, would like to see public television not exist."

One need not share this mildly conspiratorial view to understand that C-SPAN represents a partial privatization of a public domain. To paraphrase the old conservative saying, there's no such thing as free TV; whether through an extra charge on their cable bill or through the tax system, both PBS and C-SPAN are viewer-subsidized. Generally speaking, C-SPAN does not make avail-able viewership numbers, but on a per-viewer basis, the federal subsidy of public television is not significantly more expensive than C-SPAN. (It would be interesting—and possibly disheartening—to see how the nation's cable viewers would react if they were given the option that Newt Gingrich wanted to give taxpayers regarding PBS—i.e., remove the subsidy, and offer C-SPAN as a pre-mium channel costing slightly more only to those who elected to watch it.) This is but one example of the sleight-of-hand economics used in the debate over government funding of public broadcasting (see section below).

Another public opportunity made possible through cable television is the pro-liferation of local public access channels (the most precise term is public, educa-tional, and governmental [PEG] channels, since the institutions allowed to use the channels vary between communities). Historically, many municipal governments have required cable operators to set aside a portion of the cable spectrum for PEG channels that are noncommercial, although since a federal 1984 cable regulation law, many cities have removed this mandate; recent estimates are that fewer than half of America's cities require any level of access. Typically, the programming on such channels depends entirely on local producers, many of whom have limited experience in television production and even more limited resources, leading to fare that is often rough-edged and idiosyncratic. Nonetheless, as media scholar Ralph Engelman has recently documented,[11] there is a decades-long history of radical and community activists who have attempted to cultivate this medium. Among the better-known efforts of such groups is *Paper Tiger TV*, a program that began in New York in 1981, consisting initially of media critics sitting in a studio and (literally and analytically) ripping up copies of *The New York Times*.

Later work by related producers included the *Gulf Crisis TV Project*, a five-hour dissection of the U.S.-led Gulf War of 1991, with particular scrutiny of mass media's role in promoting the war. It may be the most widely viewed political home movie of all time, having aired on more than 100 PEG stations; many PBS stations; and Canadian, Australian, and Japanese television; even five years after the war's conclusion, episodes were still being rerun on some PEG stations. Engelman sees this as a major democratic accomplishment: "Two major objectives of community television—grassroots participation and the presentation of diverse, alternative perspectives—were achieved in a context in which local video productions were shared on a national and international level."[12] While such breakthroughs are still rare, they suggest that a better-funded, better-coordinated system of PEG producers could help fill the void in compelling national programming left by PBS.

The other cable channels offered as proposed substitutes for public television have their own shortcomings. While broadcast networks have lost almost all taste for the serious documentary, the genre has been admirably kept alive on such specialized networks as the Discovery Channel, the Learning Channel, and the History Channel. Yet such channels have demonstrated more clearly than any public broadcasting advocate could that the task of educational television is too important to be left strictly to private broadcasters. In 1996, details of a planned History Channel series, *The Spirit of Enterprise,* were revealed in press accounts. Each episode was to focus on an individual American corporation, telling its history in an eerie admixture of nostalgia and propaganda that would blend in neatly with the advertising the station planned to show. The corporations—AT&T, American Express, Boeing, Dupont, and General Motors had all signed up—also had an editorial role in developing the programs, and were to own the rights to the programs after broadcast. After negative publicity, the *Spirit of Enterprise* series was pulled. Similarly, the History Channel took great liberties with a program on the American presidency that had originally been produced by Gore Vidal for Britain's Channel Four. Without notifying Vidal, the History Channel executives convened a panel of journalists and historians to defang Vidal's treatment of U.S. imperialism, corruption, and the legacy of slavery. A History Channel spokeswoman told the press that "Vidal is so opinionated that we had to have real experts on." In an essay published in *The Nation*, Vidal argued that his films had been butchered precisely because of its attacks on General Electric and Disney—two of the parent companies that own the History Channel. [13]

FALSE ECONOMIES

There is no question that public broadcasting has opened the airwaves for high-quality, essential programming that is unlikely to appear elsewhere over the electronic media. Too often, however, the best programming is sporadic and actually unavailable to large sectors of the American public. The challenge for public broadcasting's fourth decade is how to structure the system to ensure more distinctive and higher quality programming, and to strive for universal availability. How, then, can a site in the cable/satellite/Internet future be secured where cultural and public affairs programming can be produced with a minimum of corporate interference? No method of funding for public broadcasting is without some pitfall. Federal funding remains the best revenue source, although it is extremely unpopular to say so because the debate over public broadcasting has been hamstrung by dishonest rhetoric and distorted analytical categories. Congressional Republicans spent the early '90s demonizing federal subsidies in myriad forms, a political investment that allowed them in 1995 and 1996 to put the entire system of public broadcasting on the defensive.

Consequently, public broadcasters have failed to use the simplest but most powerful argument at their disposal—namely, that the American "free market" of telecommunications has always rested firmly on a bed of subsidy. America cannot have an effective debate about the merits or flaws of public broadcasting if it maintains the illusion that commercial broadcasters are thoroughly "private"—i.e., that their profits are gained free from government subsidy. For decades the U.S. government has provided tax breaks and indirect subsidies of all kinds to commercial broadcasters. In some cases, these goodies have been focused on a broader social purpose, such as the tax break provided to companies that sell stations to minority-controlled companies (a loophole the Republican Congress eliminated in 1995, after two decades of tax breaks worth billions to giant communications companies). More often, the public funding of the communications industry is little more than corporate welfare. When the FCC, for example, came up with rules for "digitizing" the broadcast spectrum in April 1997, consumer advocates charged that the holders of broadcast licenses received a 10-year, interest-free loan worth as much as $70 billion—an amount that dwarfs the sum that the federal government has spent on public broadcasting since its 1967 inception. FCC chairman Reed Hundt, though a key supporter of this bargain-basement approach to the digital spectrum, called it "the biggest single gift of public property to any industry in this century."[14] Congressional supporters of the "free market" in communications did not raise their voices in protest.

Even the U.S. government's simple regulation of the television and radio dial since the early twentieth century is itself an indirect gift to broadcasters. As the U.S. Court of Appeals noted in 1977: "The fact is that public support is not limited to noncommercial stations; by providing and policing the exclusive channels and frequencies of commercial stations, the Government—and thus the taxpayers—provide a benefit to commercial stations which in all likelihood is many magnitudes larger than any benefits provided to noncommercial stations."[15]

If they wish to regain the rhetorical edge and protect their modest government subsidy, public broadcasters must produce a realistic version of the sundry ways that federal taxpayers subsidize the communications industry. One line of attack almost never used by public broadcasters is to compare their federal grant to the ones that subsidize U.S. broadcasting to other nations. If, as conservatives have argued, public television and radio are a stale relic of Great Society thinking, what should taxpayers make of the Voice of America and Radio Free Europe, surely relics of the Cold War? In fiscal year 1995, the U.S. government spent more than $500 million to carry U.S. culture and news to tens of millions of non-Americans.[16] It hardly seems unreasonable for U.S. taxpayers to spend half that amount to fund a system that United States citizens can see and hear.

Beyond finding a persuasive political argument for why it should be subsidized, the public broadcasting community needs to devise strategies for *how* it should be subsidized. As shown in the early chapters of this book, the current method of using repeated Congressional appropriations to fund public broadcasting is nothing short of a historical accident, a three-decade oversight. Presidents Johnson and Nixon both promised that they would devise a long-term funding method for public broadcasting, though neither delivered one. Since Carter, presidents have not even bothered paying lip service to the idea that they would change the illogical and increasingly less popular system for funding public broadcasting.

What is desperately needed is a renewed commitment to finding a funding plan that makes sense, that takes advantage of America's Golden Age of media and helps provide a genuine and intelligent alternative. There are many advocates and analysts who call for a return to the Carnegie Commission's original funding scheme: an excise tax on television sets.[17] The scheme has many attractions: it would be renewable and relatively independent from Congressional control. An excise tax is, as the original Carnegie commissioners pointed out, modeled after the BBC's funding mechanism.

The reality, however, is that the antitax sentiment in Congress is far more fervent today than it was in 1967, when the Johnson White House rejected the excise plan as unlikely to win support. The British plan—which involves an annual license fee to operate a television, the proceeds of which fund the BBC—has come under ferocious attack in recent years, despite a populace that prides itself on the quantity and quality of its public television and radio. In 1994–95, the BBC collected 1.75 billion pounds through the license fee, or 31 pounds (nearly $50) per citizen—a hefty fee at which Americans would surely balk. If an excise tax were used to support American public broadcasting, it would have to be considerably smaller, and would likely not cover the majority of expenses.

Another idea that has been proposed—often by public broadcasters themselves—is using the income tax form to solicit contributions for public broadcasting (in some versions, this would be coupled with contributions to the NEA and NEH). This plan has the intrinsic appeal of the voluntary tax: no longer would those who find public broadcasts immoral or unappealing be "forced" to pay for them. Removing that argument, however, may be the only significant accomplishment of a tax checkoff scheme; the sums that could be collected through a line on the tax return are not likely, by themselves, to replace the federal appropriation. Moreover, the inspiration for this scheme—the checkoff system on tax forms used to finance presidential campaigns—is no longer a trustworthy model; far fewer taxpayers choose to give to this fund than when the program was initiated in the 1970s. Finally, such a scheme might have the effect of siphoning off support for local public television and radio stations.

Former PBS president Lawrence Grossman, recalling the original Congressional declaration that airwaves belong to the public, suggests a tax on networks and other commercial broadcast operators. "In any other situation where you use a public resource, you pay a fee," says Grossman.[18] "If you drill for oil on public land, you pay a fee. If your cows graze on public land, you pay a fee."

The notion of a public broadcasting trust fund—which by late 1995 had attracted a large number of supporters in Congress and among public broadcasters—is appealing on several levels. It could be administered with a minimum of interference; the CPB or some comparable agency would serve as a disburser of funds, and could be stripped of all or most programming roles. If the fund's principal were large enough, the money flowing to public broadcasting could surpass the roughly $300 million annual levels of federal support current in the '90s. It seems doubtful, however, that there will be enough support to create a trust fund so large that it could encompass the system's overall expenses—in 1996, $1.8 billion—without resorting to downsizing strategies. The Fields legislation (discussed in chapter 10), for example, proposed a $1 billion trust fund, which would generate an annual sum smaller than the one Congress now appropriates. The trust fund also raises a number of challenging questions that public broadcasting has not had to face: What institutions will guard the money? If a bank handling the trust is also a programming underwriter, what potential conflicts of interest exist?

The most logical funding scheme for advertising-free broadcasting would be the system of advertising itself. In 1993, total advertising revenues in the United States were a whopping $138.1 billion, of which 22.1 percent ($30.5 billion) was spent for television advertising.[19] During a single annual televised event— the Super Bowl—approximately $75 million in advertising expenses changes hands (an amount that does not take into consideration the millions spent to produce the spots). This massive industry relies on a federal subsidy that almost never makes the hit lists drawn up by federal lawmakers in either major political party. Advertising seems like a natural expense to tax, even for conservatives; after all, money spent on advertising doesn't produce anything useful. The idea has some political precedents: Canada and a handful of states have experimented with taxing advertising, and the Bush administration briefly considered limiting the tax deductibility of advertising expenses.[20] As noted in chapter 6, NPR president Frank Mankiewicz once suggested taxing commercial radio as a way of paying for public radio, a notion that did not sit well with commercial radio. The power of the advertising and marketing lobby is the most obvious political obstacle to any such plan, but a 1 percent tax on television and radio advertising "buys," earmarked for public broadcasting, would generate a steady stream of revenue as large as that today appropriated by Congress.[21] Another plentiful and relatively painless source of revenue could be found in a small percentage of the sale of the digital broadcast spectrum, scheduled to occur in 2006.

One area where public broadcasters ought to be able to reach common ground with their critics is that the system is preposterously inefficient. Since the post-Nixon rearrangement, the CPB has funneled money to local stations in the form of community service grants (CSGs); those stations also receive money from member dollars, universities, corporations, foundations, and state and local governments. The stations must in turn pay PBS and pay for their national programming, while spending hundreds of millions on fund-raising and juggling the national schedule for their own needs. The Boston Consulting Group study, released in 1991, produced a chart (see page 227) of how money flows through the veins and arteries of public broadcasting, a ridiculous plan that would have made Rube Goldberg blush.[22]

Surely a less convoluted structure would serve all parties better. If a greater portion of national funds went to a national program distributor (PBS or its successors), then the stations would be less dependent on CSGs, and PBS less dependent on their subscription fees. Such a restructuring may require substantial legislative tinkering, but nothing more radical than some of the other plans on Congress's agenda in recent years.

A MULTICHANNEL FUTURE

The creation, made possible through cable, of the multichannel environment has been the single greatest external threat to public television. Simultaneously, however, cable's maturation may hold the key to solving PBS's chronic irrelevance, even if public television officials have failed to exploit it. For if the chief argument offered by contemporary conservatives is that the need for government-funded television has been eliminated, that implies that one of the strongest earlier objections—the fear of an overpowerful government-funded television system—has also been eliminated. In the 1960s television environment of three networks, a genuine, publicly funded fourth network could theoretically have constituted a dangerous propaganda vehicle. Thirty years into the experiment of public broadcasting, however, when even noncable viewers have six commercial networks to choose from, when cable subscribers and Internet mavens can tap into thousands of information sources, and when the average public television broadcast does not reach more than 2 percent of the viewing public, the notion of government brainwashing via public television is not only far-fetched, it is downright silly.

On the fringe right, there remain charges of interference; that the Clinton administration, for example, has used PBS broadcasts to support its policies (not surprisingly, these groups found other topics to occupy their time when similar spin was practiced by the Reagan White House). Government has at times exercised a pernicious influence on public broadcasting under both political parties, but most often that influence serves to keep controversial programs off the air, rather than PBS or NPR acting as administration shills. Even granting,

BUDGET CATEGORY ANALYSIS
The Structure of Public Television
(Millions Of Dollars - 1989)

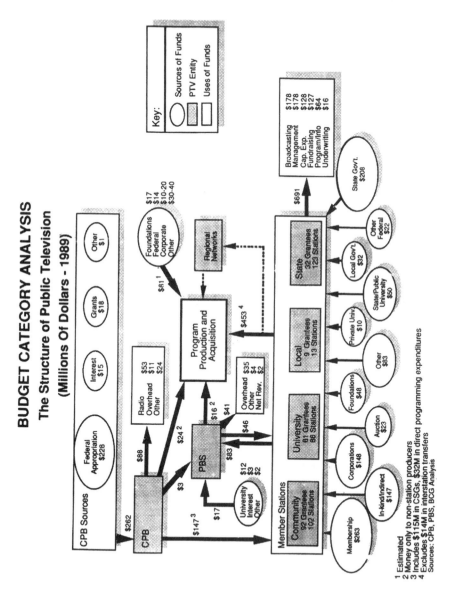

Key:
- Sources of Funds
- PTV Entity
- Uses of Funds

CPB Sources
- Federal Appropriation $228
- Interest $15
- Grants $18
- Other $1

CPB
$262

Radio
- Overhead $53
- Other $11
- $24

$88

$24 [2]

$3

$147 [3]

University Interest Other
- $12
- $3
- $2

$17

PBS

$83

$16 [2]

$41

Overhead $35
Other $4
Net Rev. $2

$46

Foundations $17
Federal $14
Corporate $10-20
Other $30-40

$61 [1]

Program Production and Acquisition

Regional Networks

$453 [4]

Member Stations

Community
52 Grantees
102 Stations

University
61 Grantees
86 Stations

Local
9 Grantees
13 Stations

State
32 Grantees
123 Stations

$691

Broadcasting $178
Management $178
Cap. Exp. $128
Fundraising $127
Program/Info $64
Underwriting $16

Membership $263

In-kind/Indirect $147

Corporations $148

Auction $23

Foundations $48

Other $83

Private Univ. $10

State/Public University $50

Local Gov't. $32

Other Federal $22

State Govt. $208

1 Estimated
2 Money only to non-station producers
3 Includes $115M in CSGs, $32M in direct programming expenditures
4 Excludes $14M in interstation transfers
Sources: CPB, PBS, BCG Analysis

however, that such influence from time to time occurs, right-wing media groups have offered nothing beyond rhetoric to demonstrate that PBS's or NPR's federal funding makes them more susceptible to such White House spin than network newscasts or CNN (which many on the right also find excessively liberal). If anything, PBS is more likely than most privately owned news organizations to placate the political right—and its corporate and Congressional allies—by spotlighting conservatives. At any rate, all the cable channels, radio talk shows, and Web sites touted by conservatives ought to provide sufficient checks and balances against any marginal propaganda purposes that public television might serve.

With the fear of a propaganda channel largely removed, one of public broadcasting's great statutory barriers can be removed. That is, PBS and NPR exist as entities separate from the CPB because legislators feared that placing control of the broadcasting system and its major programmers in the same body would be too powerful a combination. Particularly in light of recent American telecomunications deregulation (allowing, for example, the merged Time/Warner/Turner to combine production, distribution, and actual cable franchises in the same entity), this fear seems antiquated. As was proposed during the Carter administration, PBS, CPB, and NPR should be merged into a single public telecommunications body, which would eliminate several current overlapping functions.

Moreover, PBS should transform itself over the next decade into a multichannel service. The Markle Foundation has studied the idea of creating a second PBS channel, PBS-2, which would serve as a purely educational supplement to the more popular, quasi-commercial PBS offerings. This is a worthy idea—but why stop at two channels? The multichannel cable future that will theoretically be provided by digitizing the television spectrum could be exploited to serve all of PBS's primary audiences: a Children's Channel, Documentary Channel, African American Programming Channel, Science and Nature Channel, and so on.

WHAT IS TO BE DONE?

If and when the funding for public broadcasting can be made sufficient and renewable, then a series of related reforms can be enacted to bring the service closer to its founding ideals.

Public broadcasting must resist the corporate takeover. The original Carnegie commissioners could hardly have been more clear on this point: the principal reason commercial television failed to deliver its technological promise is because advertising forced the networks to seek maximum audiences. The more public broadcasting relies on the same resources as its commercial cousins, the more it will fall captive to the same narrow vision. Unfortunately, the patterns of commercialism, merchandising, and malling have become so habitual that many public broadcasting officials have ceased to be reliable judges of where the lines between "public" programming and commercial promotion are. Unless it redraws and defends those lines, public broadcasting has doomed itself to being a mildly offbeat niche of the commercial American media market.

The CPB must be liberated from direct presidential control. The architects of public broadcasting anticipated—reasonably enough—that political interference would most likely come from Congress, which controlled the budget. They did not foresee that the CPB appointment process could be perverted into a mechanism of executive containment and control. It is an irreversible accident of history that public broadcasting, in its embryonic stage, had to endure Nixon's destructive wrath, thereby setting the stage for future White House manipulation. But even if Johnson, public broadcasting's presidential progenitor, had chosen to run for reelection in 1968 and served a second term, his control over CPB appointees and the military's influence over the nation's communications and satellite systems make it highly unlikely (as discussed in chapters 1 and 2) that the fledgling public television system would have been allowed to air heated criticism of the Vietnam War.

As with many other commissions and regulatory agencies controlled by presidential appointees, politics has a way of working around any statutory insistence about an agency being nonpartisan. One public television scholar concluded: "The process of board selection has, in fact, lent itself to increased politicization to the point that membership on the CPB board is similar to appointment to a federal judgeship—a plum to be pursued through political channels and awarded on the basis of political considerations."[23]

Of course, the people who run the CPB (or a similar successor agency) have to come from somewhere. If CPB were run simply as a private company, it would be vulnerable to stagnation, as well as to the market pressures public broadcasting was designed to avoid. The best solution, as suggested by the Carter administration's Henry Geller, is to have a merit selection panel, similar to the method used for choosing federal judges. In Geller's scheme, a panel consisting of leaders in education, culture, broadcasting, business, and labor, as well as representatives of women's and minority groups, would submit five names to the President for each CPB opening; the President would then make appointments from that roster.[24] This will not eliminate political influence, but will help mitigate its excesses by opening up the selection process. A second force to mitigate presidential power would be to have two CPB directors come from within public television and radio (they could be producers; station managers; program developers; officials from NPR, PBS, Pacifica; and so forth). These board members could be selected for one six-year term by the other board members, or CPB could create an internal process for selecting them.

Democratize the local boards. Professor Pat Aufderheide, who has studied public broadcasting extensively, notes: "Local stations aren't accountable to the public in any way, they're only accountable to their boards."[25] Board members, in turn, are often accountable only for the bottom line, because many—probably most—directors on local public television station boards are there primarily for fund-raising purposes. Especially at larger stations—the ones currently producing the bulk of the system's programming—the directors are drawn heavily from business executives and/or the independently wealthy. The chasm between what those elites wish to provide and what local communities actually want is so great that some have called for board seats on local stations to be elected positions. "No greater defect of Public Television exists than the utter lack of accountability of the stations to their individual communities of service," said one California public broadcaster in 1978.[26] "PUBLIC television will not exist until full ownership and control of the stations rests directly with the elective control of the local communities."

Electing the board members of local stations might prove cumbersome and may not guarantee anything; one major station that already does have elected positions, San Francisco's KQED, has still not quelled accusations that it fails to meet its audience's needs. Still, electing board members—presumably from a pool of station contributors—is a worthwhile experiment in democratizing local boards. If stable, long-term financing for public broadcasting can be found, then director slots at local stations could be pried away from these financial rainmakers. In their place, boards could be elected or appointed that would put the public back in public television: community activists, artists, journalists and broadcasters, labor leaders, educators, clergy. Of course, the pronounced decentralization of public broadcasting makes it impossible for such democratic transfers to be mandated at 350 different stations across the country. But if viewers and PBS station "members" could be enlisted in a "Take Back Public TV Campaign" at the system's largest stations—New York's WNET, Boston's WGBH, Chicago's WTTW, Los Angeles's KCET—their democratization could have a significant ripple effect.

Of course, the very notion of the local television station may have to evolve into that of a local channel. By transforming itself into a multichannel cable/ satellite service, public television as it exists today could—in communities where cable penetration is 90 percent or higher—afford to greatly pare down the size and number of local stations without a drastic reduction in service. Local "stations" could then concentrate their resources on producing programs tailored to their own communities. (As it is today, some of the locally produced material could be made nationally available on the cable/satellite feed.)

Cut back spending on children's programming. These are perhaps the foulest words that can be uttered in the presence of public broadcasters and their Congressional supporters. The debate over public broadcasting has become so infantilized that *Sesame Street* puppets have been deployed in Congressional committee hearings. As I have noted throughout the book, there is no cow more sacred, and no selling point more effective, in public broadcasting than the quality and popularity of its children's programming.

Yet altogether too much attention and expectation has been invested in the educational qualities of children's television presented on PBS. The 1996 agreement that President Clinton struck with commercial broadcasters to provide three hours of "quality" children's programming should, in theory, provide competition for PBS's aging classics, and may serve to further erode the service's identity (alternately, it could mean that the more successful programs will be snapped up for commercial purposes and leave PBS with second-tier programs). The lure of *Barney* and *Sesame Street* is far too strong to expect that they will ever fade away, and few parents will ever be convinced to cease thinking that because children appear to be learning something from watching such fare, they are therefore learning, thus justifying the programs. As argued at other points during this book, the undeniable success of PBS's children's programming has, in some ways, hindered the development of other areas: huge blocks of the weekly PBS schedule are reserved for children's programming, regardless of how effectively they educate children.

There is a singular perversity to a country where television programs for pre-school children have lavish budgets and multimillion-dollar marketing schemes, while urban schools suffer for lack of desks, classroom space—and sometimes even heat. The nation's educational system would be better served if the money for a season's worth of *Barney*, or 5 percent of the annual budgets of New York's WNET or Los Angeles's KCET, were spent on a two-hour public television documentary showing the appalling conditions that prevail in those cities' public schools. Simply put, children are no longer an underserved audience on public television. This is not to argue that public television should end its programming for children, some of which is excellent and has given public television one of its great successes. But it is past time for national programmers to be more discriminating, to try to gauge the genuine educational value of PBS children's fare instead of striving to find the next show whose merchandising offshoots can be sold to Toys R Us.

Restore public broadcasting's mandate for minority and other underserved audiences. "Public Television," said the original Carnegie report, "is capable of becoming the clearest expression of American diversity, and of excellence within diversity."[27] Public television and, to a lesser extent, public radio can point to proud moments in their history when they have realized this vision of serving the country's various minority audiences (at least in comparison to their commercial counterparts).

Yet while public television in the '90s has been able to find room for every conceivable stripe of conservative, white male opinion-monger—from John McLaughlin to Ben Wattenberg to William F. Buckley, Jr.—it has not generated a successful adult black- or Latino-oriented program in more than a decade. (This is excepting the more than $1 million PBS spent to acquire the rebroadcast rights and fund a sequel to the NBC series *I'll Fly Away*.) Sadly, the strongest commitment PBS today makes to adult minority programming is in cooking programs. Almost any group of Americans that can claim to be underserved by commercial television—women, the elderly, the disabled, rural populations—can make the same claim about public television.

Curiously, as commercial television networks expanded from three in the 1970s to six in the 1990s, the newcomers—Fox, the Warner Brothers (WB) network, and the United Paramount Network—based a reasonable part of their success on generating comedy series—many of dubious quality—for black audiences. Surely between those programs and the continued absence of people of color on public television there can be some effective middle ground. It goes without saying that adding minority voices to the decisionmaking levels of public broadcasting is an essential, but not sufficient, step to diversifying the public dial.

Encourage more independents. One of the most significant changes to the legal underpinnings of public television occurred in 1988. The second Carnegie Commission had recognized that public television was becoming a closed, almost stagnant system, relying too heavily on the same tiny pool of producers and stations.

To open the system up, Congress amended the law to create a $6 million independent production system. One result was the Independent Television Service (ITVS). Although it took several years to get off the ground, during the 1990s ITVS provided some of the most challenging and innovative programming available on public television, including the human rights program *Rights & Wrongs*; the quirky history of television called *Signal to Noise*; a biography of the late black lesbian poet Audre Lorde (which aired as an episode of *P.O.V.*); and *The Gate of Heavenly Peace,* a unique, sweeping documentary made from inside China's Tiananmen Square massacre that was broadcast in the spring of 1996.[28] In a decade when PBS's largest programming projects have aimed for relatively safe examinations of events from deep in America's past (notably the acclaimed Ken Burns series *The Civil War* and *The West*), ITVS has sought out territory where the controversies have global implications. Congress should take the funding of independent producers a step further, and amend public broadcasting legislation to disperse an increasing portion of its funds to new and unaffiliated producers and directors.

Make public broadcasting more accountable. All media that seek a broad audience and address important issues of the day will generate controversy, and consumers who seek redress. On the national level—and in most cases on local levels—public television has almost completely evaded its responsibility to its viewers. There exists no official mechanism through which parties who feel aggrieved or underserved by public television broadcasts may make their voices heard.

The accountability vacuum raises deep doubts about whether public television's commitment to democracy is anything more than lip service. In 1996, for example, public television earned accolades by announcing a nationwide series of debates called the Democracy Project, in which candidates in local House and Senate races participated in simultaneous televised debates, following a nationally broadcast debate between Congressional leaders. Like commercial broadcasters over the years, however, many public television stations wanted to keep out any candidates who were not Democrats or Republicans. This exclusion ran afoul of the Eighth Circuit U.S. Court of Appeals, which ruled that public television stations are a "limited public forum," and that they must not omit "any candidate, legally qualified under state law, from a debate"; the Supreme Court declined to hear an appeal of this ruling. (After being excluded from a 1992 debate, a minor-party candidate had sued the Arkansas Educational Television Commission.)[29]

Since approximately two-thirds of public television stations are state-owned, this ruling, which was handed down just a few weeks before the planned Democracy Project debates, had a broad impact on the PBS debates. Rather than embrace this ruling as an expansion of public television's commitment to wide-spread free speech and the democratic process, however, Ellen Hume, director of PBS's Democracy Project, said it was "definitely having a chilling effect on the planning" of the Congressional debates. "We haven't kept a tally of the number of stations that have dropped out of the program . . . but there is really serious concern across the system, and I suspect some would have to be canceled. I don't see how they can get around the ruling."[30] The strategy of adhering to the law by including minor-party candidates seems never to have occurred to Hume.

Such public arrogance has driven some—notably Accuracy in Media—to seek to redress what they see as PBS bias. Their arsenal has included petitions to the FCC and courts, although perhaps the most efficient, effective, and corrupting weapon is the use of political backchannels. The flaws in such a system are obvious: only those with political clout will be heard, and their "success" (as in the broadcast of AIM's rebuttal to PBS's *Vietnam* series) will serve primarily to irritate those who have not been similarly placated.

To remedy this distance from their audience, public television and radio should create accountability offices—comparable to newspaper "ombudsmen"—to investigate and report on major questions of conflicts of interest, unbalanced reporting, etc. In Canada, Europe, and a handful of places in the U.S., local governments sponsor public "news councils" to publicly air such disagreements in commercial media, designed as an alternative to libel suits.[31] The structure and jurisdiction of such groups could function as a model for similar boards for NPR, PBS, and other public broadcasters. While such offices will never satisfy all critics, audiences stand only to gain by a public airing of the process through which their programs are assembled and chosen for broadcast.

BEYOND THE HALF-LOAF

How likely are these reforms to come about? The availability of resources and the political opinions of Members of Congress have fluctuated widely in recent years, making accurate predictions difficult. In late 1994, the total privatization of public broadcasting seemed a reasonably certain bet. Yet a combination of White House support, top-level lobbying, political compromise, and a well-orchestrated public support campaign "saved" the federal funding of public broadcasting—although for how long and at what cost to programming remains unclear.

As the modern system of public broadcasting enters its fourth decade, even its most obvious allies display a weariness for asking and answering the larger questions. One of the chief obstacles to substantial reform is the public broadcasting community itself; the stations and national leadership have become so accustomed to preserving the status quo—regardless of how ineffective or inadequate the status quo may be—that they have failed to offer the broad and distinctive vision necessary to gain support for genuine change. They have become masters of the half-loaf argument. In the absence of bold and broad-based thinking, the "supporters" of public broadcasting have lost, for the moment, the rhetorical and political ground to those who would starve or co-opt it. Those who advocate "saving" public broadcasting too often neglect to define what it is they seek to save; nor do they acknowledge that with their survival prescriptions come hidden side effects. Eliminating overlapping stations may produce vitally needed short-term savings and apparent efficiencies, but what are the effects on already dwindling community programming? The ubiquity of corporate underwriting makes possible some programming that might not otherwise air, but is it always the most appropriate or necessary programming?

There must be a full, honest, and informed debate about the *mission* of public broadcasting before there can be any meaningful discussion about whether and how it can be saved. That discussion has to begin with a reassertion of fundamentals. Henry Becton of WGBH suggests three: public broadcasting must be universally available, it must be noncommercial, and it must qualify in some way as educational and/or informational.[32] Of those three, the noncommercial status of public broadcasting is certainly the most threatened. It needs a spirited defense. The task of treating audience members as participating citizens instead of mere consumers must be rejuvenated if the true project of public broadcasting—as opposed to a marketing technique that labels itself "public"—is to survive. It may be the case that—just as old Trotskyites argued that it was impossible for a single socialist nation to exist in a capitalist world—it is impossible for a noncommercial system of communication to survive in what is one of the most powerful and aggressively commercial environments the world has ever known: American television and radio. But if we assume from the beginning that such a system is impossible, we ignore public broadcasting's more innovative and progressive historical achievements, and ensure that they will never be repeated.

NOTES

NOTES TO INTRODUCTION

1. Gingrich quoted in Associated Press story, December 7, 1994.

2. This comment was made during an hour-long special episode of *The Charlie Rose Show* that aired on June 3, 1992.

3. Pressler's remark was made on ABC News's *Nightline*, January 3, 1995.

4. *Congressional Record*, January 24, 1995, p. S1414. Pressler later amended his remarks (*CR*, February 16, 1995, p. S2902), noting that the demographic data referred to WETA donors, not its viewers. This was one of several gross exaggerations Pressler made about public broadcasting in the early months of 1995.

5. "GOP win is PBS nightmare," *New York Post*, November 16, 1994, p. 69.

6. "'Defunding' Public Broadcasting: Conservative Goal Gains Audience," *Washington Post*, April 15, 1996, p. A4.

7. "Channel 12 alliance with Limbaugh a little show of broadcast history," *Rocky Mountain News*, September 20, 1995. Limbaugh's syndicator, Multimedia, agreed to provide the series to KBDI for one year without cost. In 1996, Limbaugh ceased producing a television program altogether.

8. Alexander Cockburn, "Beat the Devil," *The Nation*, March 6, 1995, pp. 299–300.

9. Lewis Lapham, "Adieu, Big Bird," *Harper's Magazine*, December 1993, pp. 42–43.

10. Cited in *Frequently Asked Questions About Public Broadcasting* (Washington, D.C.: Corporation for Public Broadcasting, 1995), p. 11.

11. Corporation for Public Broadcasting press release, May 14, 1996.

12. *Frequently Asked Questions About Public Broadcasting*.

13. Raymond Williams, "Impressions of U.S. Television," *The Listener*, June 7, 1973, included in *Raymond Williams on Television: Selected Writings*, ed. Alan O'Connor (New York: Routledge, 1989), pp. 24–9.

14. Robert McChesney, "Public Broadcasting in the Age of Communication Revolution," *Monthly Review*, December 1995, vol. 47, 7, p. 10.

15. Willard D. Rowland, Jr. "Continuing crisis in public broadcasting: A history of disenfranchisement," *Journal of Broadcasting and Electronic Media*, vol. 30, no. 3 (Summer 1986), 251–74.

16. *Frequently Asked Questions About Public Broadcasting*, p. 10.

17. "Nugent's 'Wild' pledge fever no longer contained in Michigan," *Current*, November 28, 1994, p. 5.

18. *Public Television: A Program for Action* (New York: Bantam Books, 1967), p. 98.

19. Willard D. Rowland, Jr., "Public Involvement: The Anatomy of a Myth," in *The Future of Public Broadcasting*, ed. Douglass Cater and M. J. Nyhan (New York: Praeger, 1976), pp. 109–39.

Although some of this essay is an analysis of a specific piece of legislation and is therefore dated, Rowland's acute critique of the lack of public involvement has become even more relevant.

20. The PBS documentary series *Frontline* does have a letter-reading segment, as do National Public Radio's *Morning Edition* and *All Things Considered*.

21. Robert Cirino, "An Alternative American Communications System," *College English*, vol. 38, 8 (1987).

22. Patrick Watson, host of *The 51st State*, quoted in James Day's *The Vanishing Vision: The Inside Story of Public Television* (Berkeley: University of California Press, 1995), p. 206. *The 51st State* aired nightly on WNET-TV in New York in 1972–73. Watson's refusal to bow before America's altar of journalistic "balance" may have come from his Canadian heritage.

23. As discussed in chapter 6, the structure of public radio—more stations, more varied programming, and national shows with portions designed for local breakaways—has allowed for a generally better balance of local and national needs.

24. *Public Television,* p. 92.

25. Lapham, "Adieu, Big Bird," p. 38.

26. "WNET sends new signal; New NBC link, funding ploys part of revamp," *Crain's New York Business*, February 8–14, 1993, p. 3.

27. Ibid.

28. One notable example is Dr. Gloria Anderson, a black woman who in the mid-'70s became one of the fiercest critics of PBS's failure to hire and promote women and people of color, despite the fact that she was appointed by Richard Nixon.

29. Interestingly, Honey Alexander's original advocate was none other than NPR president Frank Mankiewicz—a Democrat—and he was pushing her on the Carter administration. (Alexander's résumé and Mankiewicz's April 7, 1980, letter to White House staffer Rick Neustadt are in the Carter Library, Corporation for Public Broadcasting, Vacancy file #6.) Since no more than a given number of CPB board members may, by law, be from the same political party, Democratic presidents must occasionally appoint Republican board members and vice versa—a handy way of currying favor with key politicians.

30. What's more, Moyers's Iran-contra episodes, titled *High Crimes and Misdemeanors*, were pulled from a scheduled PBS rebroadcast during the Gulf War for fear they "might appear to undermine the President's credibility." (See Howard Kurtz, *Washington Post*, February 19, 1991.)

31. Statement by President Bill Clinton, White House, release from Office of the Press Secretary, February 29, 1996.

32. Remarks by Vice President Al Gopre in Address on Public Broadcasting, American University, Washington, D.C., March 2, 1995.

33. A fine history could be written of the symbiosis between cable television companies and politicians, beginning with the Nixon administration. Herb Schiller's *Information Inequality: The Deepening Social Crisis in America* (New York: Routledge, 1996) and Leo Bogart's *Commercial Culture: The Media System and the Public Interest* (New York: Oxford University Press, 1995) both contain valuable discussions of the move toward commercialization of the public sphere and its consequences.

34. In 1996, PBS did broadcast its own special on domestic violence, hosted by Diane Sawyer and sponsored by Warner Lambert, which wove its slogan, "We help people feel better," and a National Domestic Violence Hotline into the conclusion, implying that both would help alleviate the problem.

35. The determined producers of *Rights & Wrongs* had, at the time of this writing, managed to put the program on many PBS stations for four seasons—though without a dime of support from PBS.

36. Ken Burnes quoted in "When Agencies and Clients Produce the TV Programs," *New York*

Times, July 8, 1991, p. D6.

37. I am grateful to Ellen Cohn, who has covered public broadcasting extensively for *The Village Voice*, for bringing this photo to my attention.

38. In 1995, Kohlberg Kravis & Roberts divested itself of the Nabisco holdings.

39. Peggy Charren quoted in press release from Fairness and Accuracy in Reporting (FAIR), December 4, 1996.

40. While virtually no books on public television were published in the 1980s, many valuable policy books on public television have been published in the last few years: Ralph Engelman's *Public Radio and Television in America: A Political History* (Thousand Oaks, Calif.: Sage, 1996), William Hoynes's *Public Television for Sale: Media, the Market, and the Public Sphere* (Boulder: Westview, 1994), and Marilyn Lashley's *Public Television: Panacea, Pork Barrel, or Public Trust?* (Westport: Greenwood Press, 1992). A book that delves more deeply into PBS programming is James Day's *The Vanishing Vision*. A more tendentious but informative history is Laurence Jarvik's *PBS: Behind the Screen* (Rocklin, Calif.: Prima Publishing, 1996).

41. Interested readers should consult W. Wayne Alford's two-volume *NAEB History* (Washington, D.C.: National Association of Educational Broadcasters, 1966) and Robert Blakely's excellent *To Serve the Public Interest: Educational Broadcasting in the United States* (Syracuse: Syracuse University Press, 1979).

42. Although there have been several books published about public radio in the last few years, they tend to have a specific focus; a broad history has yet to be published. Thomas Looker's *The Sound and the Story* (New York: Houghton Mifflin, 1995) examines the internal staffing of NPR and some of the debate about the makeup of its programming.

43. Intriguingly, the charge that *Sesame Street* teaches children little more than what they could learn from other television programs has been made from critics on both the left and right. See, for example, James Bowman's essay "The Dirty Little Secret of Educational TV," January 1–8, 1996, *Weekly Standard*, as well as Billy Tashman's article, "E-Z Street: 25 Years and Still Counting," *The Village Voice*, November 23, 1993, p. 56.

NOTES TO CHAPTER 1

1. *Public Television: A Program for Action* (New York: Bantam, 1967), p. 1.

2. Ibid. p. 92.

3. The McLuhan connection to American public broadcasting is not merely an affinity. The National Association of Educational Broadcasters frequently used McLuhan as a paid consultant in the mid-1960s.

4. *Public Television*, p. 93.

5. Hyman H. Goldin, "Commercial Television," in *Public Television*, p. 232.

6. Lester Markel, "A Program for Public Television," *New York Times Magazine*, March 12, 1967.

7. Robert Blakely, *To Serve the Public Interest: Educational Broadcasting in the United States* (Syracuse: Syracuse University Press, 1979), p. 172.

8. Watson's remark is noted in *Congressional Quarterly Weekly Report*, September 29, 1967, p. 1952. Watson also introduced a floor amendment to essentially kill the bill; it failed by a surprisingly close vote of 120 to 111.

9. Senate Commerce Committee hearing, 90th Congress., 1st Session (90-S1807-1), hearings on the Public Television Act of 1967, p. 90.

10. Ibid., p. 249.

11. Ibid., p. 456.

12. Fred Friendly, *Due to Circumstances Beyond Our Control* . . . (New York: Vintage, 1968), pp. 294–95.

13. John Fischer, *Harper's Magazine,* cited in *A True Fourth Network:Why and How*, NET pamphlet written by Frederick Jauch, editorial director of the National Education Television and Radio Center public information division, mid-1960s. Fischer was actively involved in National Educational Television throughout the 1960s.

14. Lyndon B. Johnson, 1967, *Public Papers of the Presidents of the United States* (Washington, D.C.: Office of the Federal Registrar, 1968), p. 474.

15. The details of LBJ's media holdings are discussed in Robert A. Caro's *Lyndon Johnson: Means of Ascent* (New York: Alfred A. Knopf, 1990), pp. 82–113.

16. Ibid., p. 115.

17. Douglass Cater, telephone interview with the author, December 9, 1994.

18. Johnson's undersecretary of HEW, Wilbur Cohen, also had a hand in getting the public broadcasting legislation through the House. The last and largest grant ever given under the 1962 ETV Facilities Act went to WWVU in Morgantown, West Virginia. Seven days later, the House Interstate and Foreign Commerce Committee began its hearings on the public broadcasting bill; its chairman, Harley Staggers, represented the Morgantown district. (See John E. Burke, "The Public Broadcasting Act of 1967, Part III: Congressional Action and Final Passage," *Educational Broadcasting Review* vol. 6, no. 4 [June 1972], p. 256.)

19. Interview between James Robertson and Hartford Gunn, April 1981, "Public Television's roots" Oral History Project, 1979–82 (Wisconsin SHS.)

20. Burke, "The Public Broadcasting Act of 1967," p. 260.

21. *Public Television*, p. 41.

22. Ibid., p. 69.

23. Interview between James Robinson and Hyman Goldin, "Public Television's Roots" Oral History Project, 1979–82 (Wisconsin SHS.)

24. Herbert Marcuse, *Negations*, trans. Jeremy J. Shapiro (Boston: Beacon Press, 1968), p. 224.

25. Weidenbaum speech, cited in Seymour Melman, *Pentagon Capitalism: The Political Economy of War* (New York: McGraw Hill, 1970), p. 13.

26. Cited in Herbert I. Schiller, *Mass Communications and American Empire* (New York: Augustus M. Kelley, 1969), pp. 66–67.

27. *Office of Telecommunications Policy (The White House Role in Domestic Communications)* (New York: The Network Project, 1973), p. 10.

28. Ibid.

29. Elliot Richardson, *Reflections of a Radical Moderate* (New York: Pantheon, 1996), p. 7.

30. The connection between Sputnik and the taxpayer financing of educational television is discussed in chapter 4 of W. Wayne Alford's *NAEB History, Volume 2: 1954 to 1965* (Washington, D.C.: National Association of Educational Broadcasters, 1966.)

31. Ibid. p. 53.

32. National Educational Television Annual Report, 1968 (NPBA).

33. *New York Times*, July 14, 1968; cited in Schiller, Mass Communication and American Empire.

34. Erik Barnouw, *Tube of Plenty:The Evolution of American Television*, 2nd rev. ed. (New York: Oxford University Press, 1990), p. 399.

35. *Ford Foundation Activities in Noncommercial Broadcasting 1951–1976* (New York: Ford Foundation, 1980), p. 1.

36. Fred Friendly, interview with the author, December 1994.

37. Friendly's version of these years is related in his book *Due to Circumstances Beyond Our Control*. . . .The Hughes Aircraft connection is intriguing, since as recently as 1995, the

Corporation for Public Broadcasting gave more than $140,000 to Hughes for "system support."

38. Cited in a White House summary of FCC filing, dated August 15, 1969 (NPM).

39. Hartford Gunn interview with James Robertson, "Public Television's Roots," p. 55.

40. Senate Commerce Committee hearing, April 1967, p. 385.

41. Douglass Carter, interview with the author, December 1994.

42. Johnson, 1967, *Public Papers of the Presidents of the United States*, p. 766.

43. As an indication of how sensitive satellite information is, it is not unusual for 20–25 years to pass before certain executive branch documents on satellite technology are declassified.

44. *Final Report of the President's Task Force on Communications Policy* (Washington, D.C.: U.S. Government Printing Office, 1968), chapter V.

45. Johnson, 1967, *Public Papers of the Presidents* of the United Stades, p. 346.

46. Memo from Ken Cole to President Nixon, May 20, 1969 (NPM).

47. "Rostow says FCC inquiry on CATV caused delays," *Electronic News*, March 17, 1969, p. 51.

48. *Final Report of the President's Task Force on Communications Policy*, Appendix D, p. 4.

49. Ibid. Appendix D, p. 3.

50. Cornelius Ryan, *The Longest Day* (New York: Touchstone, 1994), pp. 48–49.

NOTES TO CHAPTER 2

1. Some argue that Carnegie commissioners made a great error with their coinage. In his excellent history, *To Serve the Public Interest: Educational Broadcasting in the United States* (Syracuse: Syracuse University Press, 1979), Robert Blakely vehemently insists that the term "educational broadcasting" should have been retained.

2. Marilyn Lashley, *Public Television: Panacea, Pork Barrel, or Public Trust?* (Westport: Greenwood Press, 1992), page 19.

3. Marilyn A. Lashner, "The Role of Foundations in Public Broadcasting, Part I: Developments and Trends," *Journal of Broadcasting*, vol. 20, no. 4 (Fall 1976), p. 533. Not surprisingly, as James Day points out in *The Vanishing Vision: The Inside Story of Public Television* (Berkeley: University of California Press, 1995), most of the money behind Houston's KUHT was from an oil tycoon, Hugh Roy Cullen.

4. The details of Ford's life are drawn from David L. Lewis, *The Public Image of Henry Ford: An American Folk Hero and His Company*, (Detroit: Wayne State University Press), 1976.

5. Dwight MacDonald, *The Ford Foundation* (New York: Reynal Press, 1956), p. 26.

6. Lashner, "The Role of Foundations," p. 532.

7. Cited in *Ford Foundation Activities in Noncommercial Broadcasting 1951–1976* (New York: Ford Foundation, 1980).

8. McDonald, *The Ford Foundation*, p. 56.

9. C. Scott Fletcher interview with James Robertson, January 1981, "Public Television's Roots" Oral History Project, 1979–1982 (SHS).

10. Fred Friendly, *Due to Circumstances Beyond Our Control . . .* (New York: Vintage, 1968), p. 307.

11. National Education Television annual report, 1967 (NPBA).

12. This representative *Omnibus* episode is available for viewing at the Museum of Television and Radio, New York City.

13. MacDonald, *The Ford Foundation,* pp. 91–92.

14. *Ford Foundation Activities,* p. 10.

15. Unfortunately, no single comprehensive work discusses the variety of NET programming; my abbreviated history here owes much to chapter 5 of James Day's *The Vanishing Vision*, and to the enormous stockpile of NET material at the State Historical Society in Wisconsin.

16. Robert Hudson, a senior vicepresident of NET, said in 1971: "[The Carnegie Commission's] prime mission was to find a way for financing ETV stations, and almost always its choices were to find politically acceptable ways of channeling Federal funds to them. . . . NET and its board never had a chance of qualifying as such an institution." (Hudson is cited in S.G. Frederickson's unpublished master's thesis, *John F. White: One Man's Contribution to Educational Television in the United States*, University of North Dakota, p. 66).

17. From WQED 1958 annual report, contained in John White papers, NPBA.

18. In one of the few general assessments of public television's effectiveness in serving black communities and audiences, Jannette L. Dates concluded that public television "has consistently failed to address the concerns of African American groups" ("Public Television," in *Split Image: African Americans in the Mass Media*, ed. Jannette L. Dates and William Barlow (Washington, D.C.: Howard University Press, 1990), p. 303. Dates, however, does not analyze the NET period.

19. Day, *The Vanishing Vision,* pp. 86–87.

20. Day, ibid., puts the origin of *Black Journal* in late 1967; the entry at the Museum of Television and Radio says 1968.

21. A description of this battle is in Thomas Lindley Ehrich,"Our troubled stations—1. Boston: the uneasy years," *Columbia Journalism Review*, July / August 1972, p. 28.

22. "Farrakhan, The Minister," *Soul!* October 29, 1972, T:11132 at Museum of Television and Radio.

23. Erik Barnouw, *Tube of Plenty: The Evolution of American Television,* 2nd. rev. ed. (New York: Oxford University Press, 1990), p. 394.

24. White sent transcripts to the Members of Congress, and told them it was going to be aired. According to S.G. Frederickson's research on White, two members apologized, and the rest made no further contact.

25. Robert Lewis Shayon, "ETV at Its Best: An Evening of WHYY, Philadelphia," *Saturday Review of Literature*, February 10, 1968, p. 41.

26. Frederickson, *John F. White*, pp. 52–53. See also "NET Aide Warns of Interference— Alleges State Support Makes TV Afraid of Controversy," *New York Times*, June 11, 1966.

27. Richard Elman, "Educational TV: The Timid Crusaders," *The Nation*, March 1, 1965, pp. 217–21. Ralph Engelman's *Public Radio and Television in America: A Political History (Thousand Oaks, Calif.: Sage, 1996)* explores in more detail NET's establishment constraints.

28. Interview with Avram Westin, former president, PBL, New York, N.Y., October 27, 1994.

29. Public Broadcast Laboratory "Preliminary Fact Sheet," in Avram Westin papers, State Historical Society, Madison, Wisc. (hereafter referred to as AW papers).

30. Interview with Westin.

31. Douglass Cater, interview with the author, December 9, 1994. Chalmers Marquis, an educational television veteran who was a public broadcasting lobbyist for decades, has maintained otherwise. In Jim Robertson's *Televisionaries* oral history (Charlotte Harbor, Fla.: Tabbey House Books, 1993), Marquis claimed that Cater had received an advance script of the PBL debut and that "they were displeased in the White House to see how the president and the government were being castigated on behalf of civil rights." Marquis adds that the signing ceremony for the legislation was moved from Denver to the White House, essentially as a way for LBJ reassert symbolic control over the medium.

32. Public Broadcasting Laboratory, debut episode, November 5, 1967 (MTR).

33. Stephen E. Ambrose, *Nixon: The Triumph of a Politician, 1962–72* (New York: Simon and Schuster, 1989), p. 265.

34. Minutes of PBL editorial policy board meeting, October 25, 1967, AW papers.

35. *PBL* debut, November 1967 (available for viewing in the Museum of Television and

Radio). The notion of giving cameras to working-class Americans for them to document their lives retains its ability to shock. In 1996, the PBS series *P.O.V.* aired a film called *AKA Don Bonus*, in which a teenaged Cambodian refugee filmed his everyday life in a dangerous California town, to the shock of many newspaper critics.

36. "An Experiment That Aims to Rock Status Quo," *New York Times*, November 6, 1967, p. 94.

37. *Congressional Quarterly*, November 10, 1967, p. 2263.

38. Minutes, PBL editorial policy meeting, September 13, 1967, AW papers.

39. Interview with Westin.

40. Ibid.

41. A copy of the PBL board's evaluations is in the AW papers.

42. This unsigned memo is in the AW papers.

43. "NET Moves In," *Newsweek*, July 1, 1968, p. 79.

44. Senate report by Abe Ribicoff to Chairman John McLellan, permanent Subcommittee on Investigations of the Committee on Government Operations, May 1968.

45. George Gent, "Producer Ousted in a P.B.L. Dispute," *New York Times*, January 11, 1969.

46. See, for example, Day, *The Vanishing Vision,* pp. 111–12.

47. See, for example, ibid. p. 113.

48. Abel testified before the Judiciary Committee's Subcommittee on Constitutional Rights, February 17, 1972.

49. *The Great American Dream Machine*, debut episode, January 6, 1971 (MTR).

50. Miles Kirkpatrick quoted in United Press International story, February 29, 1972.

51. Bob Williams, "On the Air," *New York Post*, April 14, 1967.

52. *New York Times*, June 1, 1966, p. 95.

53. Avram Westin, *Newswatch: How TV Decides the News* (New York: Simon and Schuster, 1982), p. 251. See also Frank J. Prial, "The Platformate Flap: Some Claim Shell's Ads Aren't All They Seem," by *Wall Stret Journal*, January 18, 1968, p. 1. Having searched through a reasonable portion of NET records, I have been unable to find any supporting documents for Westin's recollection that Shell withdrew its support.

54. *New York Times*, October 31, 1967, p. 91.

55. Malcolm Carter, "Policing Public Television," *More* magazine, vol. 1, no. 3, 1971, p. 12. This episode is also discussed in Les Brown's *Televi$ion: The Business Behind the Box* (New York: Harcourt Brace Jovanovich, 1971), pp. 336–38.

56. Marshall Efron, in a Museum of Broadcasting seminar on *The Great American Dream Machine*, recorded February 16, 1988, T88:0354, MTR.

57. *Variety*, April 5, 1967. Not all of educational television's antitobacco ideas panned out, however. When Lewis Freeman, vicepresident of programming at New York's WNDT, was dismissed in late 1966, it was, according to some accounts, because his plan for a televised "smoker's clinic" angered tobacco representatives on the station's board. (See *Newsday* columnist Barbara Delatiner, April 4, 1967).

58. John F. White, president's speech to NET affiliates, New York City, April 22, 1968 (copy of speech in White files, NPBA).

59. Brown, *Televi$ion,* pp. 319–20.

60. Minutes of the 1960 meeting of affiliates of NETRC, May 24, 1960, Chicago (NPBA).

NOTES TO CHAPTER 3

1. H. R. Haldeman letter to Rogers Morton, March 26, 1969 (NPM).

2. Joseph C. Spears, *Presidents and the Press: The Nixon Legacy* (Cambridge: MIT Press, 1984), p. 150. Although Colson denied in a television interview that he had made these threats,

Stanton testified in a sworn statement that he had taken notes during this conversation.

3. At least not judging by available historical records: as detailed in the Appendix, huge portions of the Nixon-driven attack on public broadcasting have never been released to the public.

4. Whitehead to Dwight Chapin, May 6, 1969, Rogers collection.

5. John Heidenry, *Theirs Was the Kingdom: Lila and DeWitt Wallace and the Story of the Reader's Digest* (New York: W. W. Norton, 1993), p. 347.

6. Memo from Peter M. Flanigan to President's file, October 27, 1969, Rogers collection.

7. Memo from Flanigan to President, June 18, 1971, Rogers collection.

8. See memo from Jonathan Rose, July 19, 1969. Flanigan repeated this suggestion in a 1971 memo to the President.

9. Whitehead memo to Flanigan, October 30, 1969, Rogers collection.

10. Memo from Colson to Larry Higby, November 10, 1971, reproduced in *From the President: Richard Nixon's Secret Files*, ed. Bruce Oudes (New York: Harper & Row, 1989), pp. 333–34.

11. Stephen Ambrose, *Nixon: The Triumph of a Politician, 1962–72* (New York: Simon and Schuster, 1989), p. 232.

12. William Safire, *Before the Fall: An Inside View of the Pre-Watergate White House* (New York: Doubleday, 1975), p. 343.

13. Douglass Cater, "The politics of public broadcasting," *Columbia Journalism Review*, July/August 1972, p. 12.

14. *One Week of Educational Television* (Blooomington, Indiana: National Instructional Television Center, 1970).

15. Columbia University *Survey of Broadcast Journalism*, 1970–71, p. 13.

16. Memo from Bill Duke to Peter Flanigan, November 26, 1969, Rogers collection.

17. Steve Millard, "The Story of Public Broadcasting," *Broadcasting*, November 8, 1971, p. 33.

18. *Soul!* broadcast, "Ain't Supposed to Die of Natural Causes," 1971 (available for viewing at MTR).

19. Geoffrey Cowan, "Public TV: Going Private?" *Village Voice*, March 19, 1970, p. 13.

20. In *Tube of Plenty: The Evolution of American Television, 2nd. rev. ed.* (New York: Oxford University Press, 1990), Erik Barnouw lists *Who Invited US?* as one of the documentaries that brought on the wrath of the Nixon White House. There is no documentary evidence to support this assertion, and the fact that the film was not shown on WETA makes it even less likely.

21. Letter from PBS president John Macy to Nixon, January 26, 1970 (NPM).

22. See Whitehead memo to John Price, March 16, 1970 (NPM). The specific White House file on this conference appears to be missing from the National Archives (see Appendix). In addition, some of the memoranda located in the 1979 Carnegie FOIA request about this conference have still not been released to the public.

23. A complete list of *Firing Line* guests from 1966–1988 was published in Buckley's book *On the Firing Line: The Public Lives of Our Public Figures* (New York: Random House, 1989).

24. "Realities: Galbraith vs. Buckley," November 23, 1970, available for viewing at MTR.

25. Karayn, in a speech before the annual meeting of SECA, San Antonio, Texas, March 22, 1972 (SHS).

26. White House press office special report, January 1972, *Conservatives & 1972*, Box FG103 (NPM).

27. Memo Flanigan to Whitehead, August 26, 1970, Box FG103 (NPM).

28. Attorney James Finney, cited in *Banks and the Poor* (New York: National Educational Television, 1970), prod. by Morton Silverstein, 58 min., color, available for viewing at MTR.

29. See, for example, Marilyn Lashley, *Public Television: Panacea, Pork Barrel, or Public Trust?*

(Westport: Greenwood Press, 1992), p. 50.

30. Malcolm Carter, "Policing Public Television," *More* magazine, vol. 7, no. 3, 1971. Former FCC commissioner Nicholas Johnson stated that Philadelphia's WHYY, one of the largest stations in the PBS system, refused to air *Banks and the Poor* because its chairman was also the president of a bank featured in the documentary (Johnson, speech to Harvard Law School, February 11, 1972), RM papers.

31. Jan Nugent Pearce and Lawrence Laurent, "TV Show on Banks Arouses Protest," *Washington Post*, November 9, 1970.

32. Résumé of Michael Gammino, in NPACT papers (SHS).

33. Memo from Flanigan to Cole, November, 9, 1970, Rogers collection. Cole's response, which conceded that every once in a while the system produced some "very sour" programs, encouraged Flanigan to watch *Sesame Street*, Julia Child, and other mass-appeal shows, indicating that to some degree Cole had gone native.

34. James Day quoted in *Public Television: A Question of Survival*, by Fred Powledge (New York: American Civil Liberties Union Report, 1972), pp. 28 ff.

35. In his groundbreaking book *Nixon and the Politics of Public Broadcasting* (New York: Garland Publishing, 1985), David Stone notes: "NPACT's creation represented CPB, PBS and the Ford Foundation's single most decisive and substantive step away from the programming predominance of NET . . . . Public television leaders Hartford Gunn, John Macy and Fred Friendly saw the creation of a national public affairs production center. . .as a way of distancing the system from past, as well as future controversies." (p. 81).

36. Memo from Huntsman to Flanigan, September 23, 1971, Rogers collection.

37. Stone, *Nixon and the Politics of Broadcasting,* p. 88.

38. Memo from Huntsman to Flanigan, September 23, 1971, Rogers collection.

39. Memo from Alvin Snyder to Peter Flanigan, November 22, 1971, in Rogers collection.

40. Memo from Clay Whitehead to H. R. Haldeman, November 24, 1971, cited in *Nixon Administration Public Broadcasting Papers—A Summary 1969–1974* Commerce Department), pp. 48–49.

41. "Public TV Pays High for Buckley, Moyers," *Washington Daily News*, November 29, 1971.

42. "Public TV Probe Looms," *Washington Daily News*, December 1, 1971.

43. The producer of this infamous segment was the radical documentary filmmaker Saul Landau.

44. Letter cited in Carter, "Policing Public Television," p. 12.

45. Ibid.

46. Alvin Perlmutter, "The Museum of Broadcasting Series: *The Great American Dream Machine*," seminar recorded February 16, 1988, T88:0354, MTR.

47. Throughout this section I am relying in part on a 24-page unsigned document, "Historical Summary of the Development of PBS Functions," dated May 9, 1973, found in the Rogers collection.

48. Remarks of Clay Whitehead, director, Office of Telecommunications Policy, 47th Annual Convention, National Association of Educational Broadcasters, Miami, Florida, October 20, 1971, Rogers Collection.

49. *The Nixon Administration Public Broadcasting Papers,* p. 65. The congressman was Clarence Brown.

50. Details of the Allen film are taken from Jack Kuney, "The Closing Down of Woody Allen," *Television Quarterly*, vol. 19, no. 4 (Winter 1983), pp. 9–16.

51. Ibid. p. 15.

52. "Something Funny About PBS Swap of Pat for Woody," *Variety*, February 23, 1972.

NOTES TO CHAPTER 4

1. National Public Radio, January 12, 1972. Writing in *Variety*, Leonard Traube said of Whitehead's remark: "Since the birth of the Republic there can hardly have been more than a handful of statements made by a White House aide that matched in narrowness and cynicism the one credited to Clay T. Whitehead in [this] declaration." *Variety*, February 23, 1972.

2. Letter from Flanigan to Springer, in FG103 (NPM). The FG103 file was opened to the public in December 1995.

3. Personal and confidential memo from Helen M. Dubino, executive assistant to William Springer, to Peter Flanigan, January 5, 1972, Rogers collection.

4. Speech of Hartford N. Gunn, Jr., president, Public Broadcasting Service, before the Western Educational Society for Telecommunications, San Francisco, March 1, 1972 (NPBA).

5. Memo for the record, Clay Whitehead, June 26, 1972, Rogers collection.

6. Ibid.

7. David Stone, *Nixon and the Politics of Public Broadcasting* (New York: Garland Publishing, 1985), p. 196.

8. Note in the news summaries of the Nixon Presidential Materials Project, 7/1/72, cited in Stephen E. Ambrose, *Nixon: The Triumph of a Politician 1962–1972* (New York: Simon & Schuster, 1989), p. 572.

9. James Day, *The Vanishing Vision: The Inside Story of Public Television* (Berkeley: University of California Press, 1995), p. 229.

10. Robert Avery and Robert Pepper, "The Evolution of the CPB-PBS Relationship 1970–1973," *Public Telecommunications Review*, September/October 1976, p. 15.

11. The legend of Bohemian Grove features public nudity and all-day revelry.

12. Letter from Moore to Flanigan, August 1, 1972, Rogers collection.

13. The phrase "tough appointees" or "tough and on our team" appears at least a half-dozen times in various memoranda concerning CPB.

14. Ehrlichman to Whitehead, April 4, 1970, cited in *Nixon Administration Public Broadcasting Papers—A Summary 1969–1974* (Commerce Department), p. 16.

15. Gloria L. Anderson, interview with the author, Atlanta, February 1996.

16. Memorandum, Whitehead to Flemming, April 19, 1970 (NPM).

17. Day, *The Vanishing Vision*, p. 229.

18. "'Tampering' Cited in Public-TV Role," *New York Times*, April 24, 1973, p. 1.

19. Interview with Loomis, cited in Stone, *Nixon and the Politics of Public Broadcasting*, p. 192.

20. Cited in internal CPB memoranda, MacNeil papers, Box 17 (SHS).

21. Copy of telegram in SHS.

22. Memo from David Wimer to Al Haig, June 8, 1974, Ford Library.

23. Letter, January 3, 1996, from Laurel Lambert, KCET director of advertising and promotion, to the author.

24. In 1986, while serving on the PBS board, Banowsky was also a board member of the Los Angeles–based Thrifty Corporation. According to government investigators, Banowsky tipped off his friends and family members to a pending takeover of the company; their stock trading netted them nearly half a million in illegal profit. While Banowsky did not formally admit guilt in his settlement with the Securities and Exchange Commission, the SEC described his action as "fraud" and forced Banowsky to pay more than $750,000 in fines and penalties.

25. Letter from Lehrer to Mrs. Randy Engel, October 16, 1972, Robert McNeil papers,

State Historical Society, Madison, Wisc. (hereafter referred to as RM papers).

26. Letter from Golden to Lehrer, November 17, 1972, RM papers.

27. Letter from Lehrer to Golden, November 20, 1972, RM papers.

28. This section of the Public Broadcasting Act is 47 USCA 396(g) (1) (D).

29. Letter from Lehrer to David Stewart, CPB, December 26, 1972, RM papers.

30. Bruce Jay Friedman, interview with the author, November 27, 1996.

31. "*Steambath* Still Has Magic After Ten Years," *Los Angeles Times*, August 21, 1982.

32. Donald Taverner quoted in John Carmody, "On TV 'Immorality,' " *Washington Post*, May 31, 1973.

33. The CPB minutes are quoted in Stone, *Nixon and the Politics of Public Broadcasting*, p. 283.

34. Letter from James Killian, March 9, 1979, on file with the preparatory materials for the second Carnegie Commission, Columbia University.

35. This is the title of Day's chapter 13, *The Vanishing Vision*.

36. Ralph Rogers quoted in Laurence Jarvik's *PBS: Behind the Screen* (Rocklin, Calif.: Prima Publishing, 1996), p. 29.

37. Letter (handwritten) from George Bush to Ralph Rogers, July 18, 1972, in the Rogers collection (NPBA).

38. A detailed account of these negotiations can be found in Day's chapter 13, "The Man Who Saved Public Television," *The Vanishing Vision,* especially pp. 238–45.

39. *A Public Trust* (New York: Bantam Books, 1979), p. 47.

40. Gladys Engel Lang and Kvet Lang, *The Battle for Public Opinion: The President, The Press, and the Polls During Watergate* (New York: Columbia University Press, 1983), p. 62.

41. Stone, *Nixon and the Politics of Public Broadcasting*, p. 290.

42. Lang and Lang, *The Battle for Public Opinion*, p. 63.

43. This evaluation comes from an evaluation of the summer 1973 PBS season for PBS station managers, RM papers, Box 14 (SHS).

44. This judgment is based on reading dozens of letters in the RM papers, Box 14, SHS.

45. Lang and Lang, *The Battle for Public Opinion*, p. 86.

46. Karayn interview in Stone, *Nixon and the Politics of Public Broadcasting*, p. 293.

47. Erik Barnouw, *Tube of Plenty: The Evolution of Public Television, 2nd. rev. ed.* (New York: Oxford University Press, 1990), p. 455.

48. This discussion is in Alan Brinkley's *The End of Reform: New Deal Liberalism in Recession and War* (New York: Alfred A. Knopf, 1995), especially pp. 19–20.

49. CPB annual report, 1974.

50. Jannette L. Dates, "Public Television," in *Split Image: African Americans in the Mass Media* ed. Jannette L. Dates and William Barlow (Washington, D.C.: Howard University Press, 1990), p. 315.

51. This difficulty in calculating the amount of federal support is discussed in the second Carnegie report, *A Public Trust*, pp. 125–26.

NOTES TO CHAPTER 5

1. As recently as 1993, SECA received a $100,000 television programming grant and $93,000 in "system support" from the Corporation for Public Broadcasting.

2. Cooke's candid opinions are in the retrospective catalogue *Mobil and Masterpiece Theatre: 15 Years of Excellence* (New York: Museum of Broadcasting, 1986).

3. Nielsen data cited in *A Public Trust* (New York: Bantam Books, 1979), p. 40.

4. See Billy Tashman in *The Village Voice*, November 23, 1993, pp. 55–56, and James

Bowman in *Weekly Standard*, January 1–8, 1996.

5. Memo from Cole to Peter Flanigan, November 21, 1970, Rogers collection.

6. Al Gore, "Address on Public Broadcasting," presented at Georgetown University, March 2, 1995.

7. Author interview, Gloria Anderson, February 1996, Atlanta, Georgia.

8. Letter from Killian to President Ford, August 27, 1974, Ford Library (hereafter F).

9. Memo from Terry O'Donnell to Max Friedersdorf, September 19, 1974, Ford library.

10. Memo from Tod R. Hullin to Terry O'Donnell, October 31, 1974, Ford Library.

11. Memo from James Cannon to James Cavanaugh (n.d.), Ford Library.

12. Marilyn Lashley, *Public Television: Panacea, Pork Barrel, or Public Trust* (New York: Green-wood Press, 1992), p. 55. Lashley's book—which applies a sociological approach to public broadcasting—assigns numbers to sources who she has interviewed and granted anonymity. Skepticism toward her reporting on the Ford administration is especially warranted because she identifies General Al Haig as Ford's chief of staff, a post he held for only a few weeks.

13. Memo for the President, September 5, 1974, from David J. Wimer through General Alexander Haig. This paragraph was lifted, word for word, from a Nixon White House memo, dated March 20, 1974, from Jerry Jones to Haig.

14. Ibid. p. 6.

15. The famous conservative publishing heir Clare Booth Luce also withdrew herself from the CPB running, because she wanted to remain on the President's Foreign Intelligence Advisory Board. As of late 1972, the board already had a neoconservative publisher: Irving Kristol, the publisher of *The Public Interest* and arguably America's most prominent neoconservative, had been appointed by Nixon in late 1972.

16. Ford note to Doug Bennett (n.d., but likely from June 1975) (F).

17. Résumé of Charles W. Roll, Jr., on file in Box FG-103, (F).

18. Letter from Charles Roll to President Ford, Box FG-103, (F).

19. "The Case for Insulation," prepared by the Public Broadcasting Service, May 1975.

20. Memo from Shepard to William Timmons, September 13, 1974, (F).

21. Report 94-2451, part 2. *Public Broadcasting Financing Act of 1975,* Remarks of Mr. Flood, from the Appropriations Committee, July 22, 1975.

22. Patrick Buchanan, "The electronic pork barrel," *Chicago Tribune*, January 15, 1975, p. A14.

23. Public Broadcasting Act, sec. 396.

24. Quoted in James Day, *The Vanishing Vision: The Inside Story of Public Television* (Berkeley: University of California Press, 1995), p. 206.

25. The speaker is Senator Orrin Hatch, *Congressional Record*, S12803, July 26, 1977.

26. "FCC wants to know who should ride herd on PBS obectivity," *Broadcasting*, January 29, 1973, p. 60.

27. *Accuracy in Media v. FCC*, 521 F.2d 288, 292–296 D.C. Circuit. The court's decision is dated October 16, 1975.

28. From Congressional testimony by Accuracy in Media chairman Reed Irvine (submitted 6/15/77, S261–90, pp. 79–81).

29. Hatch, *Congressional Records*.

30. Stanhope Gould, "Coors Brews the News," *Columbia Journalism Review*, March/April 1975.

31. A comprehensive view of the Coors family's support of conservative and fringe-right organizations can be found in Russ Bellant, *The Coors Connection: How Coors Family Philanthropy Undermines Democratic Pluralism* (Boston: South End Press, 1991).

32. Joseph Coors, interview, *Rocky Mountain News*, August 25, 1974.

33. Gould, "Coors Brews the News."

34. This figure was cited passim in the Coors confirmation hearings before the Senate

Commerce Committee, 94th Congress, 1st Session, September 9–11, 1975 (S261-19).

35. The film was produced by Chicago's PBS affiliate, WTTW.

36. Joseph Coors to Henry Loomis, January 10, 1975, in Public Broadcasting—Coors nomination file (F).

37. Letter from Joseph Coors to Henry Loomis, July 24, 1975, cited in U.S. Congress, Senate, Committee on Commerce, hearings on nomination of Joseph Coors, 94th Cong., 1st sess., 1975, p. 213.

38. Letter from Henry Loomis to Joseph Coors, August 29, 1975, ibid. p. 216.

39. Coors testimony, ibid., p. 46.

40. Letter from John Moss to Senator Pastore, May 23, 1975, (F).

41. Lyndon B. Johnson, 1967, *Public Papers of the Presidents of the United States* (Washington, DC: Office of the Federal Registrar), p. 766.

42. "Public Radio Needs a Satellite Interconnection System," speech given by Lee C. Frischknecht, April 26, 1977.

43. Quoted in "Satellite Technology Demonstration," pamphlet published by the Federation of Rocky Mountain States, Denver, 1973.

44. The ATS-6 was manufactured by Fairchild Industries, a large Maryland-based NASA contractor.

45. Marilynne R. Rudick, "Innovative Uses of Telecoms: A Summary of Experiments, Demonstrations and Applications," July 1978 (filed with papers for second Carnegie Commission, SHS).

46. Satellite Technology Demonstration project 1975 annual report, p. 3, in Duane G. Straub Papers (NPBA).

47. Ibid.

48. Lawrence Grossman, interview with the author, April 1996, New York City.

49. Ibid.

50. CPB statement in FCC docket #19816, May 12, 1972.

51. Ibid.

52. From CPB annual report, 1974.

53. Annual report of the Corporation for Public Broadcasting, 1975, p. 29.

54. *Report of the Task Force on Women in Public Broadcasting* (Washington, D.C.: Corporation for Public Broadcasting, 1975), p. 8. See also Muriel G. Cantor, "Women and public broadcasting," *Journal of Communication,* vol. 27 (1977), pp. 14–19.

55. "Record Increase Shown in Public Television Viewing by Racial Minorities, Low-Income Households," PBS press release, March 8, 1977.

56. House Subcommittee on Communications, April 8, 1975, p. 84.

57. Tony Brown quoted in *Jet*, February 22, 1973, p. 10.

58. Tony Brown, testimony, Senate Commerce Committee hearing, August 6, 1974.

59. House Subcommittee on Communications hearing, April 8, 1975.

60. *Alabama Educational Television Commission*, FCC decision 74–1385, adopted December 17, 1974, released January 8, 1975.

61. Ibid.

62. Ibid.

63. "Alabama Group Regains Control of Public TV Stations," Associated Press, January 14, 1980.

64. Tony Brown letter quoted in "The Documentary That Was too Frank for Television," *New York Times*, June 8, 1975, section II, page 1.

65. Ibid.

66. Gloria Anderson, interview with the author, February 8, 1996, Atlanta, Georgia.

67. Ibid.

NOTES TO CHAPTER 6

1. Douglass Caters interview with the author, December 1994. Others have argued that, thanks to lobbying from those involved in educational radio, a role for radio was included in earlier drafts of the legislation. (See the interview with Jerry Sandler, Burt Harrison papers, NPBA.)

2. Prior to 1967, for example, radio stations could not participate in the production facilities program run by the Department of Health, Education, and Welfare.

3. Don Quayle, "National Programming for Public Radio," January 1973, Frischknecht papers (NPBA).

4. A copy of the NPR mission statement can be found in the Frischknecht papers (NPBA); it is dated April 2, 1971.

5. A fuller discussion of Siemering's background and radio philosophy can be found in Ralph Engelman's *Public Radio and Television in America: A Political History* (Thousand Oakes, Calif.: Sage, 1996) pp. 89–91.

6. The premiere *ATC* broadcast can be heard at the Museum of Television and Radio, New York City.

7. *All Things Considered* case study, prepared for second Carnegie Commission, box 13, folder 1 (SHS).

8. Bruce Porter, "Has Success Spoiled NPR? Becoming Part of the Establishment Can Have Its Drawbacks," *Columbia Journalism Review*, Sept. / Oct. 1990, p. 27.

9. In his exhaustive dissertation on the early years of NPR, Michael McCauley points out that by limiting funds for the CPB, the Nixon administration helped perpetuate the "culture of poverty" that has always plagued NPR. He also notes that several top NPR officials saw the handwriting on the wall when Nixon officials attacked PBS, and tried to adjust NPR accordingly. (Letter to the author, March 1997).

10. *A Public Trust* (New York: Bantam Books, 1979), p. 50.

11. Thomas Looker, *The Sound and the Story* (New York: Houghton Mifflin, 1995), p. 109.

12. Porter, "Has Success Spoiled NPR?" p. 28.

13. Both the Frischknecht memo (April 19, 1976) and Zelnick's fiery response to it (May 3, 1976) are in the Frischknecht papers, series 1, Box 3, folder 3-1 (NPBA).

14. "National Public Radio Network Downplays News," *New York Times*, May 10, 1976.

15. Memo (n.d.) from Jack Mitchell, Susan Stamberg, Bob Zelnick to Lee Frischknecht re: proposed reorganization. Copy in Frischknecht papers, series 1, box 3, folder 3-1 (NPBA).

16. Memo from Jack Mitchell to Pres Holmes, April 28, 1976, "Re: Sanctions Against Staff Members," Frischknecht papers, Box 3 (NPBA).

17. Tony Barrett, program director of KERA, made this claim, cited in "NPR News and Public Affairs Reorganization: Brings Resignations, Morale Drop," *Access*, no. 36, p. 15.

18. Cited in a memo from Frischknecht to authorized NPR stations, October 7, 1976, Frischknecht papers (NPBA).

19. Letter from Ken Curtis, Democratic National Committee, June 17, 1977. Written on DNC letterhead, the letter reads: "Don MacNeil of CA is being interviewed as a candidate for president of National Public Radio, on June 25. I believe you and Barry Jagoda will have some input on this subject. For your information, Don formerly served as Chancellor of the University of Maine and in that capacity he distinguished himself as someone who would be well-suited to this type of admnistrative role." Carter Library, Jordan files, Box 43, NPR folder.

20. *CPB Report*, February 20, 1978.

21. *Congressional Quarterly*, January 14, 1978, p. 70.

22. Larry Josephson quoted in Brooke Gladstone, "Public Radio Turns to Ratings," *Current*, March 30, 1981, p. 4.

23. Ibid.

24. "Who Listens to NPR Member Stations," research study dated September 1, 1981 (Washington, D.C.: National Public Radio), p. 2.

25. Looker, *The Sound and the Story*, pp. 126 ff. NPR, of course, already had some reporters with print experience prior to this period, including Bob Zelnick and Nina Totenberg.

26. Details about the NPR financial crunch come from "NPR's Deficit at $6.5 million; Auditors question its ability to survive," *The Public Broadcasting Report*, June 17, 1983, vol 5. no. 11.

27. Mary Collins, *National Public Radio: The Cast of Characters* (Washington, D.C.: Seven Locks Press, 1993), p. 65.

28. Reactions to the NPR fiscal crisis are cited in *Public Broadcasting Report*, June 17, 1983, vol. S, no. 11.

29. Collins, *National Public Radio*, p. 73. There were differing estimates of NPR's defect. Michael McCauley, who has studied NPR extensively, asserts that Mankiewicz believed that CPB board member Sharon Percy Rockefeller wanted him out, which, along with other factors, accelerated his departure. (Letter to the author, March 1997.)

30. Collins, *National Public Radio* p. 74.

31. Ibid.

32. Looker, *The Sound and the Story*, "Has Success Spoiled NPR?" p. 133.

33. Porter, op cit, p. 32.

34. This topic is discussed in a February 3, 1997, *New York Times* media column entitled "Does National Public Radio feel pressure when foundation donors specify topics?" p. D7.

35. My discussion of Pacifica's history is indebted to Clare Spark, "Pacifica Radio and the Politics of Culture," in *American Media and Mass Culture: Left Perspectives*, ed. Dan Lazere (Berkeley: University of California Press, 1987), pp. 577–s90.

36. Joe Domanick, "Left for Dead: How KPFK Missed the Radio Revolution," *Los Angeles Weekly*, October 4, 1996, p. 22.

37. Jannette L. Dates and William Barlow, eds., *Split Image: African Americans in the Mass Media* (Washington, D.C.: Howard University Press, 1990), p. 235.

38. Michael C. Keith, *Signals in the Air: Native Broadcasting in America* (Westport Conn.: Praeger, 1995), p. 10.

39. *Los Angeles Times*, September 7, 1990, page F2.

40. See, for example, Hefley's testimony before the Committee on Appropriations (Subcommittee on Labor, Health and Human Services, and Education), January 19, 1995.

41. See, for example, comments made by Congressman Bill Richardson of New Mexico, on July 12, 1994 (140 *Congressional Record*, E 1431).

42. Spark, "Pacifica Radio."

43. Sara Diamond, *Facing the Wrath: Confronting the Right in Dangerous Times* (Monroe, Maine: Common Courage Press, 1996), p. 9.

44. Jan Levine Thal, "Notes from a ne'er-do-well," quoted in e-mail to the author from WORT director Tom Waters, December 16, 1995.

45. Letter from Take Back KPFA to Pacifica Radio chair Jack O'Dell, May 1, 1996.

46. Porter, "Has Success Spoiled NPR?" p 28.

47. "On the Line" transcript, WNYC-AM, May 31, 1994.

48. FAIR advertisement, *New York Times*, June 7, 1994.

49. Fallows resigned his advisory position in mid-1996 after he became editor-in-chief of

U.S. News & World Report. Intriguingly, appointments to this Asian-Pacific Trade Commission became the subject of controversy in late 1996 when it was disclosed that Charles Trie received a position on the commission shortly after making a large (and improper) contribution to the Clinton legal defense fund. Fallows insisted that he never saw Trie at any commission meetings.

50. Porter, "Has Success Spoiled NPR?" p. 29.

51. *Washington Post*, "NPR Sued for Bias", p E 7, November 21, 1995.

52. Author telephone interview with Kathy Scott, February 3, 1997.

53. Blackmun's statement is in his opinion from *Callins v. Collins*, February 22, 1994.

54. Bruce Drake quoted in *Public Broadcasting Report*, May 20, 1994.

55. Author interview, Mumia Abu-Jamal, Huntingdon, Pennsylvania, July 1994.

56. *Congressional Record,* vol. 140, S 5773, May 17, 1994.

57. John Dinges comment on WNYC-AM's *On the Media*, July 1994; *On the Media*, hosted by former *New York Times* reporter Alex Jones, later became a nationally distributed NPR program.

58. *All Things Considered*, March 26, 1996.

59. American Public Radio became Public Radio International, and the Boston-based Monitor Radio, affiliated with the *Christian Science Monitor*, also made significant inroads into NPR territory until mid-1997, when it ceased operations due to financial difficulties.

60. Much of this section is derived from the original, unpublished reporting of *Village Voice* writer Thomas Goetz, who generously allowed it to be used here.

61. The interviews in this section were conducted by *Village Voice* writer Thomas Goetz in 1994 and 1995.

NOTES TO CHAPTER 7

1. Barry Chase quoted in "Sponsors Call the Shots on Public TV," *Variety,* November 13, 1985, p. 93.

2. Stephanie Fitch, "Moscow Gold," *The Nation*, May 1, 1995.

3. The section on the business woes of McDonald's is taken from Maxwell Boas and Steve Chain, *Big Mac: The Unauthorized Story of McDonald's* (New York: Dutton, 1976).

4. Ibid. p. 104.

5. Ibid. p. 201.

6. Asked to confirm or refute this information, McDonald's corporate communications office said that it does not provide information on its corporate gifts.

7. WQED annual report, 1958, in John White files (NPBA).

8. "Status Report of Public Broadcasting: 1977," National Center for Educational Statistics.

9. Figures from Margot Cozell and Roland Fenz of PBS, cited in David Ermann, "The Operative Goals of Corporate Philanthropy: Contributions to the Public Broadcasting Service, 1972–1976," *Social Problems*, 25, pp. 504–14.

10. House Commerce Committee hearing, April 9, 1975.

11. Ermann, "The Operative Goals," p. 507.

12. John Witherspoon and Roselle Kovitz, *The History of Public Broadcasting* (Washington, D.C.: Current, 1987), p. 54.

13. Herbert Schmertz, *Good-bye to the Low Profile: The Art of Creative Confrontation* (Boston: Little, Brown and Company, 1986), p. 222.

14. Testimony of Herbert Schmertz before Carnegie Commission, February 21, 1978, cited in *A Public Trust* (New York: Bantam Books, 1979), p. 108.

15. Schmertz, *Good-bye to the Law Profile*, p. 209.

16. Ibid. p. 210.

17. Walter W. Powell and Rebecca Jo Friedkin, "Politics and Programs: Organizational Factors in Public Television Decision Making," in *Nonprofit Enterprise in the Arts: Studies in Mission and Constraint* (New York: Oxford University Press, 1986). p. 267.

18. "Funding Patterns of the 1977 PBS National Program Schedule, original broadcast hours," memo from Michael Ambrosino to PBS station managers, program managers, and development officers, June 1, 1978.

19. Spina quoted in *Fortune*, April 22, 1991, p. 17.

20. Richard Nixon letter to Rawleigh Warner, Jr., chairman of board Mobil Oil Corporation, December 9, 1970 (NPM).

21. Daniel Yergin, *The Prize: The Epic Quest for Oil, Money and Power* (New York: Simon and Schuster, 1991), p. 656.

22. Morton Mintz and Jerry Cohen, *Power Inc.: Public and Private Rules and How to Make Them Accountable* (New York: Viking, 1976), pp 140–41.

23. Schmertz, *Good-bye to the Low Profile*, pp. 219–20.

24. See Michael Schudson's book *Advertising, the Uneasy Persuasion: Its Dubious Impact on American Society* (New York: Basic Books, 1984).

25. Timothy Brennan, "Masterpiece Theatre and the Uses of Tradition," in *American Media and Mass Culture: Left Perspectives* (Berkeley: University of California Press, 1987), p. 375.

26. Michael Mooney, *The Ministry of Culture* (New York: Wyndham Books, 1980), p. 133.

27. "Pervasive Albion," in Michael Arlen's collection *The View from Highway 1* (New York: Farrar Straus Giroux, 1976), p. 190.

28. In an interview with the author, Grossman recalled making this remark in the late '70s; he also mentions it in a review of James Day's *The Vanishing Vision: The Inside Story of Public Television* (Berkeley: University of California Press, 1995) published in *The Washington Monthly*, January 1996.

29. See David Bianculli, "From BBC: The English channel," *New York Daily News*, March 27, 1997, p. 113.

30. Brennan, "Masterpiece Theatre."

31. Pierre Bourdieu, *Distinction: A Social Critique of the Judgement of Taste*, trans. Richard Nice (Cambridge, Mass.: Harvard University Press, 1984), pp. 56–57.

32. Mark Mooney, *The Ministry of Culture: Connections Among Art, Money, and Politics* (New York: Wyndham Books, 1980), p. 119.

33. Lawrence Grossman, *The Electronic Republic* (New York: Viking, 1995), p. 52.

34. The contents of this letter were reported at the time. As of 1996, most Carter administration files pertaining to relations with Saudi Arabia remain unavailable to the public.

35. Grossman, *The Electronic Republic*, p. 53.

36. Mobil advertisement, "A New Fairy Tale," 1980, reproduced in Schmertz, *Good-bye to the low Profile*, p. 171.

37. Lawrence Grossman, interview with the author, New York City, April 2, 1996.

38. From *Muir v. Alabama* (82-1185), quoted in *New York Times*, March 8, 1983.

39. Spina, in interview with Laurence Jarvik, cited in Jarvik, "PBS and the Politics of Quality: Mobil's *Masterpiece Theatre*," *Historical Journal of Film, Radio and Television*, vol. 12, no. 3, 1992, p. 255.

40. This observation was made by Jeannie Bunton and S. Young Lee, both of the CPB, in an interview with the author, August 1996.

41. See Robin Epstein, "PBS: Labor's Love Lost," *City Limits*, June/July 1997, p. 6, and James Ledbetter, "PBS Strikes Labor," *The Nation*, June 30, 1997. Bizarrely, PBS officials insisted that producers of its programs were not subject to the same strict conflict-of-interest standard as underwriters, even though producers have greater control over program content.

42. Quoted in "WNET Tactics Emulate Commerical TV," *Crains New York Business*, November 18, 1991.

43. "KQED Lets Sponsors Deceive Viewers," *San Francisco Bay Guardian*, October 2, 1996, and "Rotting on the vine," *San Francisco Bay Guardian*, December 4, 1996.

44. Powell and Friedkin, "Politics and Programs," p. 251.

45. This information comes from staff at the *NewsHour*. Robert McNeil's papers also indicate that on at least one occasion, he gave a speech to Exxon executives; that speech will not become publicly available until the year 2000 (SHS).

46. William Hoynes, *Public Television for Sale: Media, the Market, & the Public Sphere* (Boulder: Westview, 1994), p. 81.

47. These figures, provided by Common Cause, are cited in "Dwayne's World," *Mother Jones*, July 1995.

48. ADM chairman Dwayne Andreas is a close friend of Brinkley's, and once brokered a deal for Brinkley to purchase a Florida condominium at a healthy discount.

49. The figure comes from Alexander Cockburn's "Beat the Devil," *The Nation*, November 13, 1995, p. 564.

50. Mark Whitacre quoted in "My Life as a Corporate Mole for the FBI," *Fortune*, September 4, 1995, p.55. Whitacre was himself later indicted for his role in the ADM scandal.

51. J. Max Robins, "Do the Networks Take It Easy on Their Favorite Store?," *Variety*, January 15–21, 1996, p. 10.

52. "I told the *Variety* reporter there had never been an occasion when a NewsHour editorial decision had been influenced by our underwriting—and there never will be. I say the same to you now because that is the truth." Letter from Lehrer to the author, January 26, 1996. Lehrer's letter did not address the specific ADM stories I had presented to him.

53. Ferguson develops this view in his book *Golden Rule: The Investment Theory of Political Parties and the Logic of Money-Driven Political Systems* (Chicago: University of Chicago Press, 1995), as well as in a *Mother Jones* article, "Bill's Big Backers," from November/December 1996.

54. Peter Dykstra, "Polluters' PBS Penance," *Extra!* May/June 1990, vol. 3, no. 5, p. 4. Dykstra at the time was a communications officer for Greenpeace.

55. See Joshua Hammer's article "Nigeria Crude," *Harper's Monthly*, June 1996, pp. 58–70.

56. This September 1996 report was issued by the Environmental Working Group and the United States Public Interest Research Group.

57. "Sponsors Call the Shots on Public TV."

NOTES TO CHAPTER 8

1. Neil Hickey, "Who's in Charge Here?" (second of three parts), *TV Guide*, July 30–Aug. 5, 1977, p. 20.

2. "'Watchdog Unit' of Corporation for Public Broadcasting Dissolved," *New York Times*, September 10, 1977.

3. Quotes from *A Formula for Change*, report of the Task Force on Minorities in Public Broadcasting, and from a letter from Global Village's John Reilly to Frank Lloyd, September 6, 1977 (copy in Carter Library, [hereafter C], Neustadt files, public broadcasting folder 2 8/24/77–3/8/79).

4. President Carter interviewed in *TV International*, February 1977.

5. Cronkite on "Ask President Carter," CBS Radio, March 5, 1977.

6. Anne Edwards—Press Advance file, box 2, "Black Perspective on the News—PBS, The

President, Map Room, 4/5/78" (C).

7. A Roper survey done in 1976 for NPR found that although public radio and public TV audiences and the general population contained more Democrats than Republicans, the composition of public radio and TV audiences is slightly more Republican and slightly less Democrat than the population as a whole. General population: (47.1 percent Democrats, 22.3 percent Republicans, public television audience: 44.2 percent Democrats, 23.9 percent Republicans, public radio audience: 45.2 percent Democrats, 24.6 percent Republicans. Obviously, after Ronald Reagan brought a new lustre to the GOP, these numbers changed significantly.

8. Statement of the President, October 6, 1977.

9. Published in August 1976 by the Washington, D.C.-based Citizens Communication Center. A copy can be found in Frank Lloyd's papers at the Carter Library.

10. Ralph Engelman's discussion of this bill is in *Public Radio and Television in America: A Political History* (Thousand Oaks, Calif.: Sage, 1996), pp. 181–83.

11. Unpublished study by the Office for Telecommunications Policy, cited in Dix memo to Frank Lloyd, Neustadt file, box 62, folder "Public Broadcasting—General, 7/6/77–10/29/78" (C).

12. Memo from Stuart Eizenstat, Barry Jagoda, and Bo Cutt to President re: public broadcasting 8/29/77, WH Office of counsel to the president (McKenna), box 137, folder "Office of Telecommunications Policy—Public Broadcasting, 2/15/79" (C).

13. "Horowitz on PBS: Live from the White House," *Washington Post*, February 11, 1978. Horowitz did evidently receive a large sum from the international syndication rights to the performance.

14. Ibid.

15. "The East Room Was Barely Big Enough," Paul Hume, *Washington Post*, February 27, 1978, p. B1.

16. The telegram was sent February 6 or 7, 1978.

17. S. 15444, *Congressional Record*, September 19, 1978.

18. Memo dated September 21, 1978, "Talking Points for Meeting with Senator Goldwater," Rafshoon files, box 58, folder Public Telecommunications Financing Act S. 2883, Carter Library.

19. Author interview with Lawrence Grossman, New York City, April 2, 1996. See also Senate hearings S181-32.3.

20. Memorandum to the President from Frank Moore and Hamilton Jordan, March 26, 1977 (C).

21. Ibid.

22. Memorandum from Rick Neustadt to Stu Eizenstat, Barry Jagoda, Si Lazarus, and Steve Simmons, November 3, 1977. Eizenstat box 263, folder O/A 6243 (C).

23. This exchange took place in a White House press conference on November 10, 1977.

24. *Broadcasting* magazine, November 14, 1977.

25. Jagoda and Neustadt to Jordan, Neustadt Box 23, "CPB vacancies" folder (C).

26. Memo from Neustadt to Jim Gammill (dir. of personnel), January 30, 1978, CPB vacancies (5), 1/24/78–2/28/78 folder (C).

27. Frederick Breitenfeld, executive director of the Maryland Center for Public Broadcasting, quoted in *Congressional Quarterly*, January 14, 1978, p 69.

28. *A Public Trust* (New York: Bantom Books, 1979), p. 11. One of Carnegie II's most intriguing legacies is the Freedom of Information Act request its researchers filed for Nixon administration documents related to public broadcasting. The request created a legal dilemma for the Carter administration, which wanted to reveal the depth of Nixon's wrongdoing, but did not wish to create a precedent for release of its own deliberations. As I discuss in the Appendix,

despite the release of some 1,000 pages of material, much of the documents gathered for that FOIA request are still hidden from public view, more than 20 years after Nixon left office.

29. Ibid. p. 107.

30. Ibid. pp. 281–82.

31. States News Service dispatch, October 26, 1984.

32. *Quality Time? The Report of the Twentieth Century Fund Task Force on Public Television* (New York:Century Fund, 1993), p. 95.

33. Penn James, quoted in "The Politics of Public Television," *Commentary*, December 1991, p. 30.

34. In addition to a six-figure salary, WQED provided Kaiser and other executives with leased brand-new Mercedes sedans (see "WQED: Big Money for Tin-Cup TV Station," *Pittsburgh Post-Gazette*, September 22, 1978, p. A1). An internal CPB audit of the station found that it had improperly reported income from an associated monthly magazine, which caused the station's federal grant to be reduced.

35. Kenneth Towery was a partner in the firm of Blythe, Nelson, Newton & Towery, while William Hanley worked in the notoriously hardball GOP firm Black, Manafort, Stone & Kelly.

36. Letter from Brookhiser to White House associate counsel D. Edward Wilson, Jr., August 2, 1982, Wilson collection, Brookhiser file folder #1 (RR).

37. Rivera was quoted in "Sonia Landau, At the Controls," *Washington Post*, December 12, 1984.

38. There has long been overlap between the personnel of USIA and public broadcasting. James Killian, chair of the original Carnegie Commission, had worked there, as had Nixon nominee Henry Loomis; one of Jimmy Carter's nominees, Geoffrey Cowan, would go on to head the propaganda agency in the Clinton administration.

39. Quoted in *Time*, February 8, 1982.

40. Richard Brookhiser, author interview, New York City, June 13, 1996.

41. Ibid.

42. Landau said in her farewell speech to the CPB board that "these were not our finest hours," cited in "Politicization charged at Corporation for Public Broadcasting," *Christian Science Monitor*, November 20, 1986, p. 49.

43. The trip was made in early August 1985; the relevant memoranda can be found in the White House Central file FG001–02, Personal Representative of the President, Reagan Library. As of 1996, the actual letters of accreditation were unavailable to the public under the "national security classified information" restriction.

44. Many of the documents needed to prove or disprove this theory had not yet been made public as this book went to press; however, internal White House correspondence makes it clear that Landau regularly met with Reagan administration officials, including Pat Buchanan, to discuss CPB issues.

45. Cited in "Producing More Food Does Not Feed the Hungry," United Press International, June 7, 1985.

46. Martin Lee and Norman Solomon, *Unreliable Sources* (New York: Lyle Stuart, 1990), p. 87.

47. Ibid. pp. 90–91; see also *Los Angeles Times*, June 9, 1989.

48. "The Africans: An Insider's Non-Western View," *Los Angeles Times*, October 6, 1986, part 6, page 1.

49. Ibid.

50. Ibid.

51. *Congressional Record*, 132 Cong Rec E 3740, October 17, 1986.

52. Rockefeller quoted in "Politicization charged at Corporation for Public Broadcasting," p. 49.

53. Christensen quoted in "PBS to Review Programming Policies," United Press Inter-

national, October 24, 1986.

54. The minutes from the May 15, 1984, CPB meeting are cited in James Day, *The Vanishing Vision: The Inside Story of Public Television* (Berkeley: University of California Press, 1995), p. 294.

55. This incident is recounted in "Sonia Landau: The Uneasy Chair of CPB," *Washington Journalism Review*, January 1986, p. 42.

NOTES TO CHAPTER 9

1. Peter Stoler, *The War Against the Press* (New York: Dodd Mead, 1986), p. 134.

2. Anthony Lewis, "If the Press Were Tame," *New York Times*, June 27, 1985, p. A23.

3. "Rebuttal to 'A Television History,' " *Washington Journalism Review*, June 1985.

4. Arguably, one concession made to the left is that not long after the Fairness and Accuracy in Reporting (FAIR) study accusing it of overwhelming establishment bias, *The MacNeil/Lehrer NewsHour* began using Erwin Knoll, editor of *The Progressive*, as one of its regular regional commentators in the early '90s. When Knoll died in 1994, he was not replaced with any person identifiable as being from the left.

5. *Regardie's* magazine, cited in Eric Alterman, *Sound and Fury: Punditocracy in America* (New York: HarperCollins, 1992), p. 116.

6. Doug Ireland, "Press Clips," *The Village Voice*, May 15, 1990, p. 8.

7. Jeff Cohen and Josh Daniel, "The Right-Wing Agenda: Buying Media Clout," FAIR study, 1992.

8. To be fair, a certain amount of this two-pronged strategy occurs on the other side: the John D. and Catherine T. McArthur Foundation funds both PBS programming and FAIR, which has done studies about PBS right-wing bias.

9. S. Robert Lichter, Daniel Amundson, and Linda A. Lichter, *Balance and Diversity in PBS Documentaries* (Center for Media and Public Affairs, March 1992). This study has several methodological pitfalls, notably that documentaries make up only a small portion of most public television programming (generally under 10 percent), and that the study makes no effort to sort out documentaries that aired systemwide or on a majority of stations versus those that ran only on WETA. An enlightening counter study is *Public Television "Prime Time": Public Affairs Programming, Political Diversity, and the Conservative Critique of Public Television* by David Croteau, William Hoynes, and Kevin Carragee (unpublished, 1993).

10. Lichter, Amundson, and Lichter, *Balance and Diversity*, p. 159.

11. Ed Hyman, speaking on *Adam Smith's Money World*, February 6, 1992.

12. Interview between Larry Belsky and David Horowitz, July 14, 1993, broadcast on KPFK.

13. "PBS Finally to Air 'Building Bombs,' " *Los Angeles Times*, August 10, 1993, p. F12.

14. Filmmaker Robert Richter claims that PBS official Sandy Heberer told him this; subsequently other PBS officials disavowed the comment, but the film never aired on PBS.

15. *Public Television: A Program for Action* (New york: Bantam, 1967), p. 92.

16. Letter (n.d., 1994), from Coaltion vs. PBS Censorship to Jennifer Lawson.

17. Letter from Jennifer Lawson to to Paul Rosenberg, September 28, 1994.

18. *Public Television: A Program for Action*, p. 97.

19. Interview with the author, 1995; this producer prefers to remain anonymous.

20. Letter from Laurel Lambert, KCET director of advertising and promotion, to the author, January 3, 1996.

21. The mid-1995 reduction of the LUD—a cost-cutting move—caused dozens of stations to move to a completely national schedule. Some stations have been allowed to retain the discount because they are the only stations in their markets that carry certain children's pro-

grams. (Source: Stu Kantor, PBS spokesman.)

22. From promotional material provided by WCEU-TV, Daytona Beach, Florida.

23. Sandra Session-Roberston, WCEU-TV director of public relations, interview with the author, February 1995.

24. Ibid.

25. Quoted in "57 Channels (and *Nova's* On)," by Thomas Goetz, *Village Voice*, February 21, 1995.

26. "Report on Survey of Acceptance and Rejection Patterns of Network Programs by Educational Radio and Television Stations," November 3, 1969, published by National Association of Educational Broadcasters, Washington, D.C., p. 39.

27. Ibid., p. 40.

28. David Davis quoted in *Broadcasting*, August 19, 1991. A few stations did eventually air *Stop the Church* during this time, with a Los Angeles–based panel discussion afterward.

29. *Congressional Record*, S 8140, June 12, 1992.

30. Letter from Donald Wildmon to members of Congress, cited in *A Turn to the Right* (Washington, D.C.: People for the American Way, 1995), p. 27.

31. This material is recounted in *Artistic Freedom Under Attack* (Washington, D.C.: People for the American Way, 1995), p. 50.

32. "Flap Erupts over PBS Refusal to Fund 'More Tales of the City,'" *Boston Globe*, April 13, 1994, p. 76.

33. Another gay-themed program that disrupted the PBS world was a 1992 adaptation of *The Lost Language of Cranes*; a week before it was to air on the PBS series *Great Performances*, Texaco pulled its funding.

34. "Public TV: That Delicate Balance," *New York Times*, October 25, 1987, section 2, page 1.

35. Walter W. Powell and Rebecca Jo Friedkin, "Politics and Programs: Organizational Factors in Public Television Decision Making," in *Nonprofit Enterprise in the Arts: Studies in Mission and Constraint* (New York: Oxford University Press, 1986), p. 259.

36. Interview with the author, December 1994.

37. "Refunds for Fans of 'Floyd,'" *New York Times*, December 7, 1986, section 11NJ, p. 11.

38. Lawson cited in James Day, *The Vanishing Vision: The Inside Story of Public Television* (Berkeley: University of California Press, 1995), p. 308.

39. Jennifer Lawson, telephone interview with the author, April 1992.

40. Study done by *Forbes MediaCritic*, Summer 1995, vol. 2, no. 4, p. 68. The period represented was September 2, 1994, to March 10, 1995. It is worth questioning whether *U.S. News & World Report*'s ubiquity on public television is related to the fact that it is owned by developer/publisher Mort Zuckerman. Zuckerman sits on the board of WNET, the system's largest station, and in 1996 served as a guest host on *The Charlie Rose Show*, where he interviewed a reporter from *U.S. News & World Report*.

41. Ibid.

42. "New Quiz Show out of Schedule Come January," *Current*, November 14, 1994, p. 11.

43. These included Christopher Ruddy's work in the now-defunct *Guardian* of Long Island, and the right-wing *Jewish Press*. Important work on exposing inaccuracies in *The Liberators* was also done by Jeffrey Goldberg, both in the New York–based weekly *Forward*, and in his article "The Exaggerators: Black Soldiers and Buchenwald," *New Republic*, February 8, 1993, pp. 13–14. WBAI, New York's Pacifica station, also cast doubts on the documentary's accuracy.

44. The second half of chapter 6 in Laurence Jarvik's *PBS: Behind the Screen* (Rocklin, Calif.: Prima Publishing, 1996) contains a thorough and concise summary of the *Liberators* flap.

NOTES TO CHAPTER 10

1. Testimony of L. Brent Bozell III, January 19, 1995, before the Subcommittee on Labor, HHS, and Education Appropriations of the House Appropriations Committee (104th Congress, 1st session, H181–13), p. 949. Bozell's racy reading was more than twice as long as the portion excerpted here.

2. Gingrich, interviewed on C-SPAN, December 30, 1994.

3. *Nightline*, January 3, 1995.

4. Pressler's comment was made on the PBS program *Technopolitics* in November 1994.

5. *The MacNeil/Lehrer NewsHour*, March 15, 1994.

6. William F. Buckley, Jr., syndicated column, February 15, 1995. It is conceivable that Buckley himself would have been forced to answer this questionnaire. Although *Firing Line* had not received any direct CPB grants in years, the program's backer, the Southern Educational Communications Association, reported in 1992 a $300,000 CPB grant for three two-hour special *Firing Line* debates.

7. "The $92,000 Question: CPB's Exhaustive Reply to Pressler's Query," *Washington Post*, February 14, 1995, p. B2.

8. Laurence Jarvik, "Fiscal Questions About Public Broadcasting," *COMINT*, pp. 69–70. The conservatives critique is slightly schizophrenic: since they are theoretically in favor of free enterprise, it seems odd for them to attack people for making money in public broadcasting. As for the refusal of people in public broadcasting to disclose their salaries, no private company is required to disclose its salaries simply because it contracts to provide a service with a federal or semiprivate agency, whether it be the Pentagon or the Corporation for Public Broadcasting. When CPB answered Pressler's questions about employees, none were shown to be paid more than $100,000 a year, which, in American broadcasting, is extraordinarily low.

9. "Public Broadcasting's Private Panic," *Washington Post*, December 12, 1995, p. B1. The incident prompted some debate about what role, if any, the Clinton White House played in quashing the CPB investigation.

10. *Quality Time? The Report of the Twentieth Century Fund Task Force on Public Television* (New York: Twentieth Century Fund, 1993), pp. 138–39.

11. *Congressional Record*, S 1412, January 24, 1995. In his more seasoned comments, Pressler was very careful to mention the salutary roles played by South Dakota Public Radio, and declared himself "particularly interested in reforms that enhance the capabilities and creativity of small city and rural broadcasters."

12. Cited in "GOP's Targeting of Public Television's Subsidy Creates Fuzzy Image of What's Behind the Scenes," *Wall Street Journal*, February 22, 1995.

13. *Washington Times*, February 9, 1995.

14. Robert Novak, "The Newt Connection," syndicated column, February 13, 1995.

15. *Washington Times*.

16. Ervin Duggan cited in "All the Right Moves," *Extra!* March/April 1995, p. 19.

17. "Gingrich Tapes Pitch for Public Television," Associated Press, March 4, 1995.

18. "PBS Announces Successful Pledge Drive," PBS press release, March 29, 1995.

19. "Kellner Suggests PBS Partnership," *MediaWeek*, January 16, 1995, p. 3.

20. Kent Gibbons, "PBS Uncertainty Lures Interest from Telco, Cable," *Multichannel News*, January 30, 1995.

21. During the 1996 legislative session, the Fields bill never made it out of subcommittee. Its Senate counterpart, handled by South Dakota's Larry Pressler, was never formally introduced; Pressler lost his 1996 reelection bid in part, according to some analysts, because his

1995 attacks on public broadcasting were considered extreme.

22. David Croteau, William Hoynes, and Kevin Carragee, *Public Television "Prime Time": Public Affairs Programming, Political Diversity, and the Conservative Critique of Public Television* (unpublished, 1993).

23. Thomas Goetz, *The Buzz on B is,* Jan. 28, 1997, p. 45.

24. Hundt made this comment in a March 27, 1996 hearing, of the House Commerce Committee, Subcommittee on Telecommunications and Finance, 104th Congress, H271-48.1.

25. Gita Bajaj, interview with the author, May 1996.

26. Joel Bleifuss gives a full and politically contextual account of this sale in "Public Television on the Block," *In These Times*, July 8, 1996, pp. 12–13.

28. Bruce Christensen quoted in Pat Aufderheide, "A Funny Thing Is Happening to TV's Public Forum," *Columbia Journalism Review*, November 1991, p. 60.

29. Remarks by Vice President Al Gore in address on public broadcasting, American University, Washington, D.C., March 2, 1995.

30. "NPR Game for Commercial TV Try," Reuters wire story, February 28, 1997.

31. *Public Television: A Program for Action* (New York: Bantam, 1967), pp. 232–33.

32. Duggan, speech to the National Press Club, January 17, 1995.

33. Eric McNulty, author interview, January 1995.

34. *Inside Media*, March 1, 1995.

35. Cited in financial data provided by KCET.

36. Chuck Furman, author telephone interview, January 1995.

37. *Advertising Age*, June 26, 1995, p. S-8.

38. "MCI and PBS announce venture to offer on-line, Internet and CD-ROM new media services," PBS/MCI press release, March 23, 1995.

39. Lawrence Grossman, author interview, April 2, 1996, New York City.

40. " 'This Old House' goes commercial," *Advertising Age*, January 22, 1996, p. 1.

41. "KQED Crunch," *San Francisco Examiner*, March 3, 1996, p. A1.

42. *Public Broadcasting Report*, July 12, 1996.

43. All these products were available in 1994 through a New York–based company called Baseball Licensing International, Inc.; by 1996, the company no longer had a directory listing in New York.

44. Schecter made these remarks during a panel discussion at the Media and Democracy Congress in San Francisco, March 1996.

45. *Strategies for Public Television in a Multichannel Environment* (Washington, D.C.: Corporation for Public Broadcasting, 1991), pp. 14–16.

46. Pat Aufderheide, author interview, Washington, D.C., July 1991.

47. Robert Lipsyte, author interview, June 1991.

48. *Strategies for Public Television*, p. 5.

49. "WNET tactics emulate commercial TV," *Crain's New York Business*, November 18, 1991, p. 9.

50. "Common Sense for the Future," CPB Financial Study (Washington, D.C. 1995), p. 7.

51. "Van Gordon Sauter: Back in TV (in a Small Way) and Still Making People Mad," *New York Times*, March 18, 1996, p. D7.

52. "Perceptions of Commercial Activities in Public Broadcasting," *CPB Research Notes*, no. 84, February 1996.

53. Clarke's comment was made at a hearing before the Subcommittee on Telecommunications and Finance, September 1995.

NOTES TO CHAPTER 11

1. "Living with television: the violence profile," *Journal of Communication*, vol. 26 (1976) pp 173–99.

2. Douglas Kellner, *Television and the Crisis of Democracy* (Boulder: Westview Press, 1990), p. 173.

3. This is the premise of Postman's *Amusing Ourselves to Death* (New York: Viking, 1986).

4. Robert W. McChesney, "Public Broadcasting in the Age of Communication Revolution," *Monthly Review*, December 1995, p. 15.

5. The current reigning wisdom about the future is that digital television will offer consumers the ability to use their computers and televisions on the same device at essentially the same time. As Joel Brinkley wrote in 1997, "With digital television, viewers will be able to download an infinite range of movies, music, video games, or anything else. They can page through interactive home-shopping catalogs . . . then press a few buttons to order the product. Viewers will be able to take interactive college courses at home, search electronic Yellow Pages, summon menus from local restaurants and then make a reservation or place an order to go." From *Defining Vision: The Battle for the Future of Television* (New York: Harcourt Brace, 1997), p. xi.

6. The broadcast of editorial meetings proved a bit of an embarrassment for PBS. In October 1972, NPACT carried an editorial meeting of the *Atlanta Constitution* as that paper deliberated over its presidential endorsement. A few days later, the paper broke with its 70-year-tradition of endorsing Democrats and endorsed Nixon's reelection. A week later, however, it was revealed that James M. Cox, Jr., owner of the paper and seven others in the Cox chain, had sent a directive on September 21 "expressing his personal conviction that the president deserved reelection." The paper's editor was aware of this memo, but PBS officials were not until after the broadcast. (See Nancy L. Ross, "Paper politics," *Washington Post*, November 3, 1972.)

7. See Lewis Lapham's recollections of his dicussions with PBS programming chiefs in "Adieu, Big Bird," *Harper's Magazine,* December 1993.

8. Beginning in the early '90s, New York City's Time Warner cable system began an all–New York news channel called New York 1, which, in its better moments, has shown that a local cable station can supplant many roles of a truly public television station. (The Time Warner system in Rochester, New York, has a similar service, and in early 1997, Time Warner announced it was launching an all-news channel in Orlando, Florida.) In addition to nightly public affairs discussion programs, New York 1 covers breaking news and telecasts neighborhood meetings, press conferences, local arts award ceremonies, parades, etc. Although the station is widely applauded among New Yorkers, it has yet to be widely imitated on other cable systems.

9. See "Pulling the Plug on Capitol Hill," *Washington Post*, February 13, 1997, p. C1.

10. Moyers quoted in *Washington Post,* January 6, 1995, p. C6.

11. See part IV of Ralph Engelman's book, *Public Radio and Television in America: A Political History* (Thousand Oaks, Calif.: Sage, 1996), especially chapter 12, "The Struggle over the Future of Community TV."

12. Ibid. p. 264.

13. Vidal, "The End of History," *The Nation*, September 30, 1996, pp. 11–18.

14. Hundt quoted in "FCC Approves 2d Channel for High-Definition Television," *New York Times*, April 4, 1997, p. D1. Hundt had actually made this remark in mid-1996.

15. *Community-Service Broadcasting of Mid-America, Inc et al v. FCC and USA*, U.S. Court of Appeals decision 76-1081, decided September 15, 1977.

16. This figure includes funding for Voice of America/Worldnet ($238 million), Radio Free Europe and Radio Liberty ($230 million), Radio and TV Marti to Cuba ($25 million), and Radio Free Asia ($10 million). These figures were provided to the author by the United States Information Agency, which oversees all of the above.

17. This is, for example, one of the principal recommendations made by William Hoynes in *Public Television for Sale: Media, the Market, and the Public Sphere* (Boulder: Westview Press, 1994).

18. Lawrence Grossman, interview with the author, 1992.

19. These figures, culled from the Television Bureau of Advertising and the networks, were cited in *U.S. News & World Report*, January 30, 1995.

20. These proposals are summarized in the opening argument of C. Edwin Baker's *Advertising and a Democratic Press* (Princeton: Princeton University Press, 1994).

21. Veteran PBS producer Alvin Perlmutter estimated in 1994 that "just 1 percent of the estimated gross annual revenues of commercial TV stations would yield $260 million, almost matching the $285 million that public broadcasting now gets from Washington." See "The One Percent Solution," *New York Times*, December 29, 1994, p. A21.

22. The chart was easily and justly ridiculed by conservative critics during 1995 Congressional hearings.

23. Joseph D. Hughes, "Heat Shield or Crucible," *Public Telecommunications Review*, November–December 1977.

24. Geller's plan was sketched out in a memo to the President; the memo is undated, though it probably was written in early 1979. (A copy is in Neustadt Box 61, Carter Library.) The historical record indicates that the idea was tabled by top Carter aide Bert Lance.

25. Pat Aufderheide, interview with the author, Washington, D.C., August 1991.

26. Larry Hall of the California Public Broadcasting Forum, testimony before second Carnegie Commission, San Francisco hearing, April 13, 1978.

27. *Public Television: A Program for Action* (New York: Bantam, 1967), p. 18.

28. The ITVS-sponsored China documentary, shown as an extended episode of *Frontline*, spilled over into a debate on *The Charlie Rose Show* (June 4, 1996), thus providing public television with an in-depth debate about an international event of major historical importance that was impossible for network TV.

29. The suit is *Forbes v. Arkansas Educational Television Commission*.

30. Hume quoted in *Broadcasting & Cable*, September 23, 1996, p. 18.

31. See, for example, "Rare Breed: Media Watchdog with Some Bite," *Wall Street Journal*, November 20, 1996, p. B1.

32. Becton made these remarks on the NPR program *On the Media* in March 1996.

APPENDIX

Although the Nixon White House's attempts to subvert and control public television are now more than a quarter-century old, the full documentary record of those actions remains hidden from public view. That is not for lack of probing. On November 9, 1978, the Carnegie Commission on the Future of Public Broadcasting filed a Freedom of Information Act (FOIA) request for "all records within the custody of the National Telecommunications and Information Administration (NTIA) dealing with public broadcasting from 1967 to the present." (The NTIA, a division of the Commerce Department, was the successor agency to Clay Whitehead's Office of Telecommunications Policy [OTP], the nerve center of the administration's maneuvers regarding public broadcasting.) Shortly thereafter, similar FOIA requests were filed by the Ford Foundation, *The New York Times*, *Broadcasting*, and other publications.

Henry Geller, a Commerce assistant secretary in the Carter administration, coordinated the response to the FOIA request, assisted by Gregg Skall and Robert Sachs. By January 1979, he had accumulated more than 10,000 pages of material relevant to the request. A Justice Department attorney who reviewed the material declared that many of the documents appeared to be exempt from FOIA disclosure under 5 U.S.C. Sec. 552 (b) (5), which allows agencies to withold interagency or intraagency memoranda that reflect deliberative or policymaking processes. Geller argued, however, that because of compelling public interest—expressed by Carnegie, the press, and many on Capitol Hill—in knowing the complete record of executive interference with public broadcasting, *all* the material should be released (including a smaller amount of material from the Ford and Carter administrations).

Geller's view—although consistent with a May 1977 directive from Carter's attorney general encouraging FOIA cooperation "even if the documents technically fall within the exemptions in the Act"—did not prevail. On February 23, 1979, the administration released approximately 1,000 pages to the Carnegie Commission. (The Carnegie Commission was a temporary entity; the released documents are currently stored as part of the Ralph Rogers papers in the National Public Broadcasting Archive in College Park, Maryland. The Commerce Department published a useful summary of the material called *The Nixon Administration Public Broadcasting Papers—A Summary 1969–1974.*)

The whereabouts of the other 9,000-plus pages remains a mystery. It would be reasonable to assume that much—even most—of the material would be part of the Corporation for Public Broadcasting file (classified as FG-103) in the White House Central File at the Nixon Presidential Archive in College Park. FG-103 was not processed for public review until December 1995. I reviewed all of FG-103 on the day it became available. Although there was some previously unavailable material in the file, it did not contain anything approaching the 9,000 pages Geller said he had located. In fact, FG-103—which is the official historical record of the Nixon-era CPB—did not even contain copies of many of the documents released in 1979.

This is a very disturbing omission, one of several I encountered at the Nixon Presidential Materials Project. A file designated MC3-2, which should be the complete record of a 1970 White House conference on food, nutrition, and health—carried in its entirety on public television—was not in the appropriate box and thus could not be located. At times, when sifting through material dealing with the administration's obsessive secrecy and documented cover-ups, it can be difficult to keep one's paranoia in check: Cover-up or librarian's error?

In the Carter Library, there is a memorandum dated February 15, 1979, from Geller to Stuart Eizenstat and Robert Lipshutz, which contains a one-sentence summary of each of the documents Geller's staff located (this memorandum is filed under White House Office of Counsel to the President, Box 137, Office of Telecommunications Police—Public Broadcasting, 2/15/79 I, and is referred to hereafter as the "Geller memorandum"). It includes descriptions of material not released to Carnegie, though it does not indicate where those materials currently are. Telephone interviews in 1995 with Geller and his former assistants Skall and Sachs did not yield any clues; they recalled having the unreleased documents in their offices, but could not speak to their present location.

Part of the difficulty stems from the fact that the bureaucratic legacy of federal telecommunications policy overlaps substantially with the military and its attendant systems of classification. Even though the day-to-day activities of the OTP concerned primarily mundane issues—formulating federal cable policy or tracking down potential appointments to the Corporation for Public Broadcasting—its duties had the overlay of military secrecy, due to the continued military importance of telecommunications. A Nixon executive order issued March 8, 1972, expanded this substantial military-communications tie by making OTP one of the few civilian agencies with the authority to classify documents as "top secret."

The dominant barrier to complete disclosure, however, is not military classification but the privacy claims of former administration officials, especially Nixon himself. It should be noted that Nixon officials are by no means unique in stalling the production of what are—in my view—public documents. On a memo-for-memo basis, I found a greater proportion of withheld documents in the Carter Library than in the Nixon Presidential Materials Archive.

What follows is a list of known material from the Nixon administration that has never been made public; the list is surely incomplete. Some of the material is probably trivial; some, however, seems of true historic interest. It is conceivable that copies of some of these documents exist somewhere. The fact, however, that none can be readily located in what should be the relevant official historical file is an indication of the absurd limitations on primary research of material that should have become public long ago. One cannot help but see this as an epistemological warning: if these records are not available on a topic as relatively tepid as public broadcasting, the knowledge gaps for subjects that truly vexed the administration—Vietnam, Watergate, the Justice Department's aborted antitrust inquiry into ITT—are likely to be much wider.

A "G" following a document means that it is listed in the Geller memorandum; "NPM" indicates that a record of the document—though not the actual document—is available in the Nixon Presidential Materials archive.

Letter, [CPB public affairs director] William Duke to Whitehead, re: "public relations benefits for Administration in public broadcasting and telecommunications." January 31, 1969, 2 pp. (G)

Whitehead, "Note to file: re 'people who have worked on PTV.'" February 24, 1969, 1 page. (G)

Note to file: re "conversation between Whitehead and Arthur Albert of Public Broadcasting Lab." March 10, 1969. 1 page. (G)

Memo from Robert Ellsworth, Assistant to President, to H. R. Haldeman, D. P. Moynihan, L. A. DuBridge, H. G. Klein, and Robert Mayo inviting them to meeting with John Macy, CPB. March 13, 1969. 1 page. (G)

Notes on arrangement for WH screening of 2 PBL films. March 25, 1969. 4 pp. (G)

Memo from Rosel Hyde [of the FCC] to Whitehead re FCC policy regarding presentation of sponsored material or educational broadcasting. 3 pp. May 19, 1969. (G)

Memo to Whitehead from Bill Duke re Pubic [sic] Broadcasting's Relevancy in Helping Solve Domestic Problems. July 14, 1969. 8 pp. (G)

Letter: John Macy to Peter Flanigan transmitting memo on how public broadcasting could be used to solve domestic problems, w/ attachment. July 17, 1969. 9 pp. (G)

Memo to Whitehead from Duke re types of participants at proposed telecommunications conference. July 17, 1969. 4 pp. (G)

Memo to the Staff Secretary from Peter Flanigan re Clark Molenhoff's proposal for legislation to require the networks to make complete transcripts of every show touching on government or politics, w/ attachments. November 22, 1969. 6 pp. (G)

Letter: Flanigan to Macy re Corporations Report on the experiment in the use of TV in connection w/ the Conference on Food, Nutrition, and Health. February 24, 1970. 11 pp. (G)

Letter to Paul Bartlett, *Variety* magazine, from Whitehead re article on communications. February 25, 1970. 3 pp. (G)

Letter to FCC Commissioner Nicholas Johnson from Whitehead in response to Johnson letter of 2/11 to Nixon re public broadcasting, w/ attachments. February 26, 1970. 6 pp. (G)

Memo to Whitehead from Henry Loomis re *Variety* magazine article, w/ attachment. March 2, 1970. 5 pp. (G)

Notes re CPB Board appointments. March 3, 1970. 7 pp. (G)

Whitehead phone log re conversation w/ Duke about nutrition film. March 13, 1970. 1 page. (G)

Memo: William M. Lyons to Whitehead re "Current Problems in Broadcasting—Public Broadcasting." June 8, 1970. 5 pp. (G)

Letter: Whitehead to Macy re Richard Gould. September 9, 1970. 1 page. (G)

Letter: Macy to Whitehead re Richard Gould. September 14, 1970. 1 page. (G)

Misc. notes re CPB Board appointments w/ attachment. November 23, 1970. 27 pp. (G)

Memo: Whitehead to Flanigan re "Advocates" program on guaranteed minimum income. December 8, 1970. 11 pp. (G)

Memo: Bruce Owen to Whitehead re "Fourth Network." March 24, 1971. 8 pp. (G)

Memo: Scalia to George Crawford (Flanigan's Ofc) re Macy letter of 5/12, w/ attachments. May 25, 1971. 10 pp. (G)

Memo: Whitehead to Scalia w/ handwritten notes (on 6/3 mtg [?]). June 4, 1971. 2 pp. (G)

Notes re Zelma George appointment to CPB Bd. June 18, 1971. 2 pp. (G)

Memo: Alvin Snyder to Colson, Flanigan, Scalia, Whitehead re *NY Times* article on PTV, attached. July 12, 1971. 4 pp. (G)

Ehrlichman to Flanigan, Re: "Corp. for Public Broadcasting." October 6, 1971. (NPM)

Memo: Flanigan to Ehrlichman re letter from Wrede Petersmeyer. October 7, 1971. 9 pp. (G)

Misc notes re CPB invitation to suggest names for NPACT Bd. October 26, 1971. 5 pp. (G)

Flanigan to Haldeman, re: "Corp. for Public Broadcasting." November 26, 1971. (NPM)

Memo: Whitehead to Flanigan re salary issue. December 1, 1971. 6 pp. (G)

Memo: Whitehead to Fred Malek re "Great American Dream Machine" Sequence on the American Communist Party. December 2, 1971. 2 pp. (G)

List of Ford Foundation grants in the field of noncommercial broadcasting. December 22, 1971. 1 page. (G)

Memo: Ehrlichman to Whitehead re FTC. January 14, 1972. 3 pp. (G)

Flanigan to Fred Malek, Re: "CBP [sic]." January 28, 1972. (NPM)

Memo: Scalia to Whitehead re CPB Bd appts. February 22, 1972. 2 pp. (G)

Memo: Whitehead to Malek re CPB Bd appts. February 28, 1972. 3 pp. (G)

Letter: Whitehead to Cong. Torbert MacDonald re Whitehead mtgs w/ public broadcasting representatives. March 2, 1972. 6 pp. (G)

Draft reply for Colson to Cong. Brown's letter of 3/28 re public broadcasting and CPB appts. April 18, 1972. 12 pp. (G)

Flanigan to Richard Nixon, re: "Progress Report on Public Broadcasting." May 1, 1972. (NPM)

Memo: Whitehead to Peter A. Michel re network antitrust suits. June 5, 1972. 3 pp. (G)

Memo: Bruce (Owen) to Whitehead re "Fourth Network." June 29, 1972. 1 page. (G)

Letter: Whitehead to Cong. Bill Springer re Accuracy in Media complaint concerning NPACT program on Vietnam. June 29, 1972. 9 pp. (G)

List of people Whitehead and Brian (Lamb) called re CPB veto. June 30, 1972. 1 page. (G)

Memo: Bruce Owen to Whitehead & Scalia re "Picking up the pieces." June 30, 1972. 4 pp. (G)

Letter: Tod R. Hullin, Asst to Ehrlichman, to Jim Barrett, NPR, re NPR. July 20, 1972. 2 pp. (G)

Memo: Whitehead to Flanigan transmitting Memorandum for the President re "Tax Exempt Foundation Support of Challenges to Broadcast License Renewals," w/attachments. September 5, 1972. 6 pp. (G)

Memorandum for the President from Whitehead re "Tax Exempt Foundation Support of Challenges to Broadcast License Renewals." September 8, 1972. 2 pp. (G)

Flanigan to Richard Nixon, re: "Corporation for Public Broadcasting." September 18, 1972. (NPM)

Confidential memorandum to the President from Flanigan re: Tax exempt foundations/broadcast license renewal. September 19, 1972. (NPM)

Memo: Whitehead to Herb Klein re Orange County PTV station. October 26, 1972. 4 pp. (G)

Letter: Neal Freeman to Loomis re WNET program on abortion. December 18, 1972. 3 pp. (G)

ARCHIVAL RESEARCH

The following are the major research facilities used for this book. In notes, I have used capital-letter abbreviations for the archives and individual collections to indicate where the materials are located.

Carter Library, Atlanta, Georgia. February 1996. (C)

Columbia University Rare Books and Manuscripts Library. Many of the preliminary materials for the second Carnegie Commission report are housed here. (CU)

Gerald R. Ford Library, Ann Arbor, Michigan. September 1995. (F)

Museum of Television and Radio, New York, N.Y. Frequent visits, 1994–96. (MTR)

National Public Broadcasting Archive. College Park, Maryland. Frequent visits, 1995–96. The Ralph Rogers papers at the NPBA contain the Nixon-era documents released under the Freedom of Information Act, and are referred to throughout my citations as the "Rogers collection." Other valuable collections here include John White's papers and Lee Frischknecht's papers. (NPBA)

Nixon Presidential Materials Archive. College Park, Maryland. December 1995. (NPM)

Ronald Reagan Library. Via correspondence. Note: as of mid-1997, many of the Reagan White House papers relevant to public broadcasting had not yet been processed. (RR)

State Historical Society, Madison, Wisconsin. May 1995 and September 1996. The State Historical Society houses many collections related to public broadcasting, including many of the research papers produced for the second Carnegie Commission, the personal files of Robert MacNeil (RM), and voluminous records from National Educational Television. In addition, the SHS holds the Avram Westin papers, cited throughout chapter 2. (SHS)

SELECTED BOOKS, ARTICLES,
AND MANUSCRIPTS

Alford, W. Wayne. *NAEB History, Volume 2: 1954 to 1965*. Washington, D.C.: National Association of Educational Broadcasters, 1966.

Ambrose, Stephen E. *Nixon* (vol. II: *The Triumph of a Politician, 1962–72*). New York: Simon & Schuster, 1989.

Arlen, Michael. "Pervasive Albion." In *The View from Highway 1*. New York: Farrar Straus Giroux, 1976.

Avery, Robert K., and Robert M. Pepper. *The Politics of Interconnection: A History of Public Television at the National Level*. Washington, D.C.: National Association of Educational Broadcasters, 1979. (Also appeared in J/F and S/O 1976 issues of *Public Telecommunications Review*.)

Baker, C. Edwin. *Advertising and a Democratic Press*. Princeton: Princeton University Press, 1994.

Barnes, Fred. 1986. "All Things Distorted: The Trouble with NPR." *The New Republic*, October 27, 1986, pp. 17–19.

Barnouw, Erik. *Tube of Plenty: The Evolution of American Television*, 2nd. rev. ed. New York: Oxford University Press, 1990.

Bellant, Russ. *The Coors Connection: How Coors Family Philanthropy Undermines Democratic Pluralism*. Boston: South End Press, 1991.

Blakely, Robert J. *To Serve the Public Interest: Educational Broadcasting in the United States*. Syracuse: Syracuse University Press, 1979.

Bleifuss, Joel. "Public Television on the Block." *In These Times*, July 8, 1996, pp. 12–13.

Boas, Maxwell, and Steve Chain. *Big Mac: The Unauthorized Story of McDonald's*. New York : Dutton, 1976.

Brennan, Timothy. "Masterpiece Theatre and the Uses of Tradition." In *American Media and Mass Culture: Left Perspectives*, ed. Donald Lazere. Berkeley: University of California Press, 1987. Originally published in *Social Text*, no. 12 (Fall 1985).

Brown, Les. *Televi$ion: The Business Behind the Box*. New York: Harcourt Brace Jovanovich, 1971.

Burke, John. "The Public Broadcasting Act of 1967, Part III: Congressional Action and Final Passage." *Educational Broadcasting Review*, vol. 6, no. 4 (June 1972), pp. 251–266.

Cantor, Isabel, and Caroline Isber. *Report of the Task Force on Women in Public Broadcasting*. Washington, D.C.: Corporation for Public Broadcasting, 1975.

Cater, Douglass. "The Politics of Public Television." *Columbia Journalism Review* (July/August 1972), pp. 8–15.

Collins, Mary. *National Public Radio: The Cast of Characters*. Washington, D.C.: Seven Locks Press, 1993.

Croteau, David, William Hoynes, and Kevin Carragee. *Public Television "Prime Time": Public Affairs Programming, Political Diversity, and the Conservative Critique of Public Television* (unpublished, 1993).

Dates, Jannette L., and William Barlow, eds. *Split Image: African Americans in the Mass Media*. Washington, D.C.: Howard University Press, 1990.

Day, James. *The Vanishing Vision: The Inside Story of Public Television*. Berkeley: University of California Press, 1995.

Engelman, Ralph. *Public Radio and Television in America*. Thousand Oaks, Calif.: Sage Publications, 1996.

Ermann, M. David. "The Operative Goals of Corporate Philanthropy: Contributions to the Public Broadcasting Service, 1972–1976." *Social Problems* 25, pp. 504–14.

Frank, Ronald E., and Marshall G. Greenberg. *Audiences for Public Television*. Beverly Hills, Calif.: Sage Publications, 1982.

Frederickson, S. G. *John F. White: One Man's Contribution to Educational Television in the United States*. Unpublished master's thesis, University of North Dakota, 1972. (A complete copy is in the White files at NPBA.)

Friendly, Fred W. *Due to Circumstances Beyond Our Control . . .* New York: Vintage Books, 1968.

Gould, Stanhope. "Coors Brews the News." *Columbia Journalism Review* (March/April 1975) pp. 17–29.

Heidenry, John. *Theirs Was the Kingdom: Lila and DeWitt Wallace and the Story of the Reader's Digest*. New York: W. W. Norton, 1993.

Hoynes, William. *Public Television for Sale: Media, the Market, & the Public Sphere*. Boulder: Westview Press, 1994.

Jarvik, Laurence. *PBS: Behind the Screen*. Rocklin, Calif.: Prima Publishing, 1996.

Keith, Michael C. *Signals in the Air: Native Broadcasting in America*. Westport, Conn.: Praeger Publishers, 1995.

Kellner, Douglas. *Television and the Crisis of Democracy*. Boulder: Westview Press, 1990.

Kuney, Jack. "The Closing Down of Woody Allen." *Television Quarterly*, vol. 19, no. 4 (Winter 1983), pp. 9–16.

Lapham, Lewis H. "Adieu, Big Bird: On the Terminal Irrelevance of Public Television." *Harper's Magazine* (December 1993), pp. 35–43.

Lashley, Marilyn. *Public Television: Panacea, Pork Barrel, or Public Trust?* Westport, Conn.: Greenwood Press, 1992.

Lashner, Marilyn A. "The Role of Foundations in Public Broadcasting Part I: Development and Trends." *Journal of Broadcasting*, vol. 20, no. 4 (Fall), pp. 529–47. "Part II: The Ford Foundation." *Journal of Broadcasting*, vol. 21, no. 2 (Spring), pp. 235–54.

Lee, Martin, and Norman Solomon. *Unreliable Sources*. New York: Lyle Stuart, 1990.

Looker, Thomas. *The Sound and the Story*. (New York: Houghton Miffling, 1995.

MacDonald, Dwight. *The Ford Foundation*. New York: Reynal Press, 1956.

McChesney, Robert W. *Telecommunications, Mass Media, & Democracy: The Battle for the Control of U.S. Broadcasting, 1928–1935*. New York: Oxford University Press, 1993.

Mintz, Morton, and Jerry Cohen. *Power, Inc.: Public and Private Rulers and How to Make Them Accountable*. New York: Viking, 1976.

Mooney, Mark. *The Ministry of Culture: Connections Among Art, Money, and Politics*. New York: Wyndham Books, 1980.

Pepper, Robert M. *The Formation of the Public Broadcasting Service*. New York: Arno Press, 1979.

Porter, Bruce. "Has Success Spoiled NPR? Becoming Part of the Establishment Can Have Its Drawbacks." *Columbia Journalism Review* (Sept./Oct. 1990), pp. 26–32.

Powell, Walter W,. and Rebecca Jo Friedkin. "Politics and Programs: Organizational Factors in Public Television Decision Making." In *Nonprofit Enterprise in the Arts: Studies in Mission and*

Constraint. New York: Oxford University Press, 1986.

Powledge, Fred. *Public Television: A Question of Survival*. New York: American Civil Liberties Union, February 1972.

Public Television: A Program for Action. Report of the Carnegie Commission on Educational Television. New York: Bantam, 1967.

A Public Trust: The Report of the Carnegie Commission on the Future of Public Broadcasting. New York: Bantam Books, 1979.

Quality Time? The Report of the Twentieth Century Fund Task Force on Public Television. New York: Twentieth Century Fund, 1993.

Robertson, Jim. *Televisionaries*. Charlotte Harbor, Fla: Tabbey House Books, 1993.

Rowland, Willard D., Jr. "Continuing crisis in public broadcasting: A history of disenfranchisement." *Journal of Broadcasting and Electronic Media*, vol. 30 no. 3 (Summer), pp. 251–74.

Schiller, Herbert I. *Mass Communications and American Empire*. New York: Augustus M. Kelley, 1969.

———. *The Mind Managers*. Boston: Beacon Press, 1973.

Schmertz, Herb (with William Novak). *Good-bye to the Low Profile: The Art of Creative Confrontation*. Boston: Little, Brown and Company, 1986.

Spark, Clare. "Pacifica Radio and the Politics of Culture." In *American Media and Mass Culture: Left Perspectives*. Berkeley: University of California Press, 1987.

Spears, Joseph C. *Presidents and the Press: The Nixon Legacy*. Cambridge, Mass.: MIT Press, 1984.

Stoler, Peter. *The War Against the Press*. New York: Dodd Mead, 1986.

Stone, David M. *Nixon and The Politics of Public Broadcasting*. New York: Garland Publishing, 1985.

Tashman, Billy. "E-Z Street: 25 Years and Still Counting." *The Village Voice*, November 23, 1993, pp. 55–56.

Westin, Avram. *Newswatch: How TV Decides the News*. New York: Simon and Schuster, 1982.

Witherspoon, John, and Roselle Kovitz. *The History of Public Broadcasting*. Washington, D.C.: Current, 1987. Zuckerman, Laurence. "Has Success Spoiled NPR?" *Mother Jones*, June/July 1987, pp. 32–39, 44–45.

INDEX